W9-CGQ-356

The Social Bond

IV

THE SOCIAL BOND

An Investigation into the Bases of Law-abidingness

WERNER STARK

Volume IV

Safeguards of the Social Bond
Ethos and Religion

New York
FORDHAM UNIVERSITY PRESS
1983

© Copyright 1983 by FORDHAM UNIVERSITY PRESS
All rights reserved
LC 76–4712
ISBN 0–8232–1083–9 (*clothbound*)
ISBN 0–8232–1084–7 (*paperback*)

Printed in the United States of America

Contents

Contents

Preface

As every sociologist knows, and as every layman can easily see for himself, social life is dominated by two contradictory tendencies: one stream of life leads upward toward ever more social peace and social harmony, toward unity, and another downward toward progressively looser forms of social integration and, finally, toward endemic conflict. With the publication of the present volume I have brought to a close my analysis of the former—the positive and constructive—forces. It remains for me to give an account of the negative trends, and I consider it as my personal duty to elaborate it. Without it, the study of the social bond which I have undertaken would not be comprehensive and complete.

The content of this Volume IV is closely connected with the contents of Volumes II and III. In Volume II I showed how each entrant into society acquires the habitual modes of action expected of him by his neighbors; differently expressed: I discussed the internalization of norms and values. Here I am concerned with the mental modes, the thoughts and feelings, which go with those internalized norms and values and form a whole with them. In Volume III I investigated the order-creating influences known as custom and the law and came to the conclusion that, strong as they are, they are yet not strong enough to underpin a truly pacified, moderately harmonious social life. Here I explain how ethos and religion supplement them and provide the safeguards which they are not able to provide. As for the relation between Volume I and Volume IV, they are antithetic. Volume I shows up the modest beginnings of social integration, the mere possibility of it given along with, and contained in, man's animal nature; Volume IV on the other hand throws light on the imaginable acme of social development, the vision, ever pursued and never realized, of a flawless and all-embracing community.

Speaking of religion, I must say a word about the apparent, but in reality non-existent, link between the third and fourth chapters in this book and my former treatise *The Sociology of Religion* (5 vols. [London & New York, 1966–1972]). There is no identity, no repetition; there are, in fact, two different if contiguous investigations. In the earlier work, my subject was the social forms of religious life; I presented an analysis of a largely independent phenomenon *within* inclusive society. In the present treatise I endeavor to elucidate the operation of those religious conceptions and convictions which form an aspect *of* inclusive society; I am speaking, not of religion as such, and even less of its organizational forms, the churches and sects, but of the social *function* of religion, its role in the system of social ordering, of social control.

W. Stark

Salzburg, May 1983

Mental Modes of Social Control

ETHOS AND ETHICS

112. So great is the prestige enjoyed, in the last 300 or 400 years, by the natural sciences and the technological disciplines connected with them that they are widely regarded as the best, if not indeed the only, models which the social sciences must emulate and imitate. The history of sociology would have been very different from what it has in fact been if this conviction had not been so firmly established in many minds. Some have based themselves on biology and tried to show that society is an organism of a kind; others have taken their cue from physics and interpreted society, and especially the social economy, as an equilibrium system. But a brief critical examination can prove, and prove conclusively, that physiology and mechanics are spurious rather than appropriate models for the social sciences—models which they should eschew rather than follow. The facts which the natural sciences endeavor to study are what they are, and must be taken for what they are: the terms "better" and "worse" or "good" and "bad" cannot be meaningfully applied to them. But a society may be different from what it is: it may be imagined more strongly integrated and coherent (and in this tangible sense better) or less so, and this basic fact will unavoidably affect the methods and the modes by and in which it is studied. Even if the social analyst is strictly factual and hence scientific, even if he excludes from his thought any possible wish that society be more firmly ordered or, alternatively, that the individuals be more largely free, the very nature of his material will force on him a mentality which is in many ways unlike that of the student of physical and biotic phenomena.

The extreme adulators of the natural sciences have gone so far as to ban the very word "morality" from the dictionary of the social branches of learning. Morals, they assert, are concerned with what ought to be rather than with that which is; and moral considerations can therefore claim no place in a true science because a true science must stick to the data and not venture one step beyond them. This attitude is wrongheaded because it is blind to the most basic fact of social reality: that man is not born social and has to be socialized through education, or, more technically expressed, through the internalization of norms and values. It was precisely the physical sciences in their radical, delusion-free pursuit of absolute truth, which have brought home to us this perhaps unwelcome, but certainly inescapable, insight. I have discussed this matter in the first two volumes of the present work, and have shown there not only that socialization is needed if a society is to exist for any length of time, but also the way in which it is brought about in the case of each individual human being. One thing has become very clear in the course of my exposition: the process of socialization appears, when the truth is told, as a process of moralization. It is moralization up to a certain point. Upon the measure to which it is achieved depends the quality of the social life concerned and, above all, the smoothness (or otherwise) of the interaction—differently expressed: of the cooperation—which represents the very core of any and every kind of social co-existence.

The point of which I have just spoken, the measure of basic moralization to which I have referred, is manifestly of critical importance for the sociologist. There is a morality which inheres in the very folkways or customs which constitute a concrete society and the implementation of which keeps it going. Those who copy the exact sciences will say: within the social order under consideration, the members in fact respect each other's property. Those who claim the freedom to develop a more humanistic discipline may prefer to say: within the social order under consideration, the moral principles "Thou shalt not steal" and "Thou shalt not covet thy neighbor's goods" are successfully inculcated. But the two formulations are identical in content, and obviously so. In this book I propose to call the factually observable, successfully inculcated principles of human conduct the *ethos* of the society concerned. It is the mental side, as it were, of the characteristic and dominant modes or style of human behavior. In my third volume I demonstrated how these generally accepted, harmonizing principles informing the dealing of men with each other arose and gained their specific character. Here, in the fourth volume, I shall try to do the same for the generally accepted, harmonizing principles informing the mental life of the consociated men. I shall place, alongside my study of the folkways, an account of the thoughtways which invariably accompany and match them.

The ethos of a society shows what the society-building collective forces have achieved; but it also shows, and that *uno actu*, what they have not, or not yet, achieved. There is always, to quote a popular proverb, room for improvement. Now, a proper science of society—and this is what we all wish sociology to be—cannot discuss what might come to be or what is desirable; else it would lose the solid ground under its feet and turn utopian. Sociology is not ethics. But *ethics*, as it has, over the centuries, developed as a branch of philosophy, has an entirely realistic, analytical aspect as well as a speculative and wishful one. Successive cultivators of that field have had to ask themselves what given elements of human nature (to use for once this unsatisfactory term) might in the future become the bases of more highly ethical modes of action, what given and concretely observable endowments of man may prove to be usable for that purpose or capable of development in that direction. A study of what the leading moral philosophers have had to say on this topic will not take us beyond the proper limits of the science of sociology. On the contrary! It is needed to round off the picture of social reality which it is the chief task of the sociologist to elaborate.

STATIC AND DYNAMIC RELIGION

113. But the analysis presented in my earlier volumes needs completion in yet another direction. I have pointed out that the rules which guarantee the normal functioning of a society—the minimization of friction and conflict, and the maximization of peaceableness and cooperation—are backed by pressures, and I have adduced two of them: the informal pressure brought to bear by all on all (in Jeremy Bentham's terminology: the moral sanction) and the formalized pressure exerted by specialized agencies of society, like the police, on lawbreakers (the sanction which Bentham called legal). There is, however, yet a third kind of pressure, and it is very powerful in most cultures; our own, deeply influenced as it is by the revolutionary movement known (somewhat inappropriately) as the Enlightenment, has sensibly diminished its efficacy, but by no means nullified it. I am speaking of the religious sanction. A man may forbear to go beyond the limits set by society, first, because he is anxious not to arouse the ill will of his neighbors, and then we see informal, simply moral pressure at work; or, secondly, he may remain within the bounds of ordinance because he is afraid of judge and jailer, of fine or imprisonment, and then it is formal, legal pressure which has become active; but, thirdly, he may also decide not to offend and not to break the law because he believes that there is an all-seeing, all-knowing Deity who may condemn him, after death, to condign punishment, either temporal, in purgatory, or eternal, in hell. This is the religious sanction to which Jeremy Bentham refers. In discussing it, I have no need whatever to enter into the debate between theists and atheists; whether or not the belief in a personal God be justified or not, the religious sanction—that third and in many ways crowning type of social pressure—will be equally efficacious if only the belief itself is objectively present within a culture and subjectively anchored in the human beings whom it shapes.

In spite of the many theologies and churches which exist, religion *per se* is widely regarded as a unitary phenomenon, but Henri Bergson has opened our eyes to the fact that it is two things rather than one. In *Les Deux Sources de la morale et de la religion*, he distinguishes static and dynamic religiosity. They are, in many historical religions, in a manner linked or even merged, but they are essentially contrasting and, in the final analysis, irreconcilable. Static religion is, as the name indicates, conservative. It sanctifies the state. It solidifies the existing forms and institutions of social life. It is, therefore, close to legalism. The Eternal Judge it preaches is a complement to the temporal judge and makes up for the weaknesses from which the latter, as a human being, unavoidably suffers. Dynamic religion is of a very different nature. It is, in a deeply spiritual sense, progressive. It is revolutionary. It does not sanctify the state or solidify the existing forms and institutions of social life. On the contrary. It calls the believers to rise above them and to build a community which has no need of law enforcement simply because it has no need of laws. It would substitute love for legality. Even if it is clear that the grand aim of dynamic religion cannot be realized among creatures who are, while their earthly existence lasts, tied to a self-preferring body, this highest form of religiosity has not been without its practical importance in the history of the human race. For it has added, to the system of social pressures, a great social aspiration, and, no matter how many or how few have made it their own, it has introduced a leaven which has always worked and is working still and has given a better taste to the bread of life.

It should be obvious without wasting many words that the distinction between static and dynamic religion lies parallel to the distinction between ethos and ethics. Both static religion and societal ethos are part and parcel of ongoing social life, immersed in the patterns of our workaday world, while ethics and dynamic religion tend to lead beyond them into a purer realm where the tone of existence would be set, not by self-preference and narrow interest, but by brotherliness and widening sympathy. The difference between ethos and ethics, on the one hand, and static and dynamic religion, on the other, is merely a difference in level. Both constitute mental modes of social control and should therefore be considered together, as they will be within the covers of this book; and both should also be seen in their close relationship with the physical modes of social control analyzed in the previous volumes with which they form, in life, an indivisible whole.

1

The Development of a Societal Ethos

114. For most people, the process by which the societal ethos established around them is introduced into their minds, into their deepest selves, begins very simply with the listening to fairy tales.

Fairy tales are folk tales. They are akin to folkways. They arise in the same manner, evolve, change, and decay in a similar fashion, and fulfill a parallel function in the economy of socialization and continuing social intercourse.

Before developing a detailed analysis, it is necessary to remove a basic misconception which is no less foolish for being rather widespread: the idea that fairy tales are told and retold merely in order to amuse the child. Certainly, many grownups have only that purpose in mind when they entertain a little one with the story of Cinderella or Little Red Riding Hood. But in so doing, they fulfill a deeper social necessity as well as a lighter familial task: we have before us an instance of the phenomenon known as the "heterogony of purposes," that important concept of social philosophy, which has revealed that men, when they pursue a personal and possibly humdrum aim, often contribute—unbeknown to themselves—to the basic social need of integrating society and keeping that integration safe and sound.

Even experts in the field have at times fallen into the error which we have to combat. Thus J. G. Hahn writes on the first page of the first volume of his work *Griechische und albanische Märchen* (Leipzig, 1864): fairy tales are "light, ill-ordered concoctions of the playful imagination. Anyone can produce something of this kind, provided he has a certain talent." Two things strike the critical reader on encountering this statement which one need not hesitate to call utterly foolish: first, its flat rationalism and, secondly, its implied individualism. One is totally unrealistic if one assumes that thought contents cannot be of vital importance for social life if they lack in formal logic: as if social order itself were permeated anywhere by consistency! And one is also totally unrealistic— one is missing the truly decisive point—if one fails to recognize that the classic fairy tales, those which have gripped children since time immemorial and still keep them spellbound, are invariably the products, not of a personal genius for fabulation, but of the collective unconscious, growths from the deep roots of the collective life.

Two external facts, one geographic, the other historical, go to show that fairy tales serve a much more serious purpose than merely to bring a little amusement into the nursery: their spread over the surface of the earth is as wide as that of the human race itself, and their history is as long as that of human culture. Surely, we may conclude, be it at this point only in a preliminary way, that a universal phenomenon owes its universality to a universal need.

To speak of the former aspect first: not surprisingly, two contrasting theories have done battle in this field, as in so many others, one monogenetic and diffusionist, the other polygenetic and convergionist. The monogenetic–diffusionist approach suggested that the various fairy tales arose at one specific place and then traveled from there to other areas. Theodor Benfey, for instance, maintained that the cradle of this kind of folk poetry stood in India, and that its inspiration came in the final analysis from Buddhism or Buddhist literature. But Benfey's great strength—to wit, his deep knowledge of the Indo-Germanic origins of the modern languages—was also his greatest weakness. Fairy tales, similar in content to the Indo-European ones, developed in many other countries as well, and developed there from undeniably local roots. An even better expert than Theodor Benfey, Jacob Grimm, had, long before the appearance of Benfey's *Pantschatantra* in the year 1859, strongly pressed the opposite polygenetic–convergionist conviction. "Abandon the delusionary opinion," he had pleaded in 1846, "that fairy tales developed on some particularly propitious spot and traveled from there, by some ways or paths which we may be able to trace, into the distance" (Introduction to the German translation, by Felix Liebrecht, of Giambattista Basile's *Pentamerone* I ix). And in the famous collection called *Deutsche Kinder- und Hausmärchen*, prepared by the same Jacob Grimm in collaboration with his brother Wilhelm, we read, in a passage which reflects the views of both these classic researchers:

> There are circumstances which are so simple and so natural that they exist everywhere, just as there are ideas which appear as of themselves. In the same way, the most diverse countries could give birth to the same or at least very similar fairy tales. We may compare them to the words which even totally unrelated languages have gained through the imitation of natural sounds and which are (in them all) either only slightly different from one another or even totally identical [cited by Antti Aarne, "Ursprung der Märchen," in *Wege der Märchenforschung*, ed. Felix Karlinger (Darmstadt, 1973), pp. 46, 47].

It may be confidently asserted that this polygenetic–convergionist position of the Grimms has won the contest on a broad front and that the Benfey theory has remained a minority opinion (see the remarks of Karl Reuschel in ibid., pp. 88, 11–13). There has, of course, been diffusion; fairy tales do travel from culture to culture. But why do they travel? Because they contain a common human, all-human element. This alone makes it possible for them to jump across linguistic and cultural barriers.

The parallel fact—namely, that the main themes of the fairy tales are as omnipresent in history as they are in the contemporary world—hardly stands in need of extensive illustration; it is generally known and admitted. The legends of the Argonauts, of Perseus and Andromeda, of Cupid and Psyche, were old even in the far-off days of classical Greece. They show the same basic preoccupations as later folk stories: in the tale of Phrixos and Helle in the Argonauts the hatred of a stepmother for her stepchildren, for instance, or in the story of Cupid and Psyche the jealousy, the ill will, which sisters may feel for a more favored sibling. Fairy tales are permeated, so to speak, with historicity; they bear the marks of their distant origin openly on their face. "In contrast to the modern story writer's striving after originality of plot and treatment," writes Stith Thompson in *The Folktale* (New York, 1951; pp. 4, 5), "the teller of a folktale is proud of his ability to hand on that which he has received. He usually desires to impress his readers or hearers with the fact that he is bringing them something that has the stamp of good authority, that the tale was heard from some great story-teller or from some aged person who remembered it from old days." Of course, this is truer of pre-modern cultures than of present circumstances; today fairy tales are read rather than orally related. But this has made little difference. Even "the great written collections . . . copy and recopy. . . . However well or poorly such a story may be written down, it always attempts to preserve a tradition, an old tale with the authority of antiquity to give it interest and importance."

In view of these facts, one of the most prestigious students of mythology and its neighboring fields, Mircea Eliade, has expressed the conviction that fairy tales are not tied to an assignable stretch of history or relative to a limited culture, but much rather "express a-historical and archetypal attitudes of the soul." This formulation immediately reminds one of Carl Gustav Jung and his depth psychology to which we owe so many invaluable insights—for instance, in connection with the attempt to grasp the power which the Christian sacraments have always had over the masses of believers (see Werner Stark, *The Sociology of Religion*, 5 vols. [London & New York, 1966–1972], IV 245; V 112ff.). Eliade, however, remains on a more descriptive level. He asserts that there is a great similarity between fairy tales and initiation rites, and this suggestion is entirely sound. We must make it unhesitatingly our own. Listening to fairy tales is in fact a kind of initiation and as such part and parcel of early and basic socialization.

Eliade's analysis has so much to give us that we can hardly do better than to hand on one of his most essential passages (see "Wissenschaft und Märchen," in *Wege der Märchenforschung*, ed. Karlinger, pp. 318, 319):

One might go so far as to say that the fairy tale repeats the exemplary scheme of the rite of initiation [openly observable in many so-called primitive societies] on a different level and with the aid of new means of expression. It transfers initiation to the level of imagination. Only to an impoverished consciousness, and above all to the consciousness of modern man, can the fairy tale appear as a means of entertainment and as a flight from reality. In the depths of the unconscious, the rites of initiation incorporated in the fairy tales retain their importance; there they effect, as in times past, changes and transformations. While modern man imagines that he is merely amusing himself or escaping from reality when he reads a fairy tale, he unconsciously undergoes the influence which initiation, in the guise of the story, exerts on him. It is justifiable to assume that the wonder tales became, even very early on, lighter imitations of the myths and rituals to which we have referred, and that they had the function of re-actualizing, on the level of dream and fantasy, the tests connected with [the original] initiation. This interpretation will surprise only those who see in initiation exclusively a pattern connected with tradition-bound societies.

But today we are coming gradually to realize that what is called initiation is a basic situation inseparable from human existence as such, and that every human life consists of a series of testings, of deaths and resurrections, whatever the terms employed by modern linguistic usage to describe these (originally religious) experiences.

Eliade's theorizing is certainly bold, but it is nonetheless realistic. His fundamental thesis can easily be sustained. In order to develop it in a strictly empirical manner, let us ask what the living reality is into which the child is initiated—or, more simply expressed: introduced—when his father and mother acquaint him with a traditional fairy tale. It is, in the first place, the contrast between good and evil—moral good and moral evil, to be exact.

To the grownup this distinction is so familiar that he may well misunderstand and underestimate what it means. The recognition of which we are speaking works a proper revolution in the rudimentary mind of the developing infant; it engineers a proper jump ahead. To the small child, good and evil are exclusively physical. Good is the milk which flows from the mother's breasts; good is the warmth which comes from the pillows which line the cradle; bad is the need to wait for nursing; bad too is the wind which rages in the intestines. Connected with this is the fact that, on the threshold of the infant's humanization, good or evil are merely feelings, not concepts. This may at first be only a concern of epistemology and not of sociology, but the sociologist's interest is definitely involved. For feelings are always concrete, and that means restricted to one specific experience, while concepts are abstract and therefore transferable to other phenomena and contexts. The child who learns that it is bad to appropriate pieces of candy also learns that it is bad to steal cookies or apples. The human ability to generalize is in this way one of the helpmates of socialization and hence one of the mainstays of sociality.

The internalization of the concepts of moral good and moral evil is greatly aided by the tendency toward exaggeration which is inherent in the style of traditional storytelling. In real life good and evil are mostly mixed; both are traits of the personalities whom we meet and even of those whom we see represented on the stage. Where the stage presents characters painted in black and white, as in some morality plays of the past—the angelic maiden and her devilish seducer, for instance—we are in fact face to face with folk-tale material and not with psychological explorations. Little Red Riding Hood is all goodness; the Big Bad Wolf is all wickedness. Cinderella and Snow White are blameless and pure; the jealous sisters of the one and the envious stepmother of the other are abysmally hateful. We have here a simple, but effective, didactic device which even a rationalized and sophisticated system of education is constrained sometimes to use. The great exaggerations which we invariably encounter in folk and fairy tales should not be thought to make them entirely unrealistic. They do not drive the child in the direction of a delusion-bound worldview. The child knows well enough that fact and fancy mix in the inherited and tradited tales of wonder, but he also realizes that the traits presented in them in glaring colors are in fact present in the workaday world, if in somewhat muted hues. Perhaps we are not overly bold when we assert that the child intuitively grasps that figures like Little Red Riding Hood and the Big Bad Wolf are *symbolic* of good and evil rather than realistic examples of them. But it is through symbols that we all learn what we need in and for life.

One way of summing up the gist of the foregoing paragraph is to say that fairy tales help children to *visualize* moral good and evil, i.e., to see them with the mind's eye, and thus to know them as directly and as clearly as what one knows with and through the eyes of the body. "The human race requires to be instructed in parables," writes Joan Rockwell in her book *Fact in Fiction: The Use of Literature in the Systematic Study of Society* (London, 1974; p. 27), and in another context (pp. 25, 76) she asks: "Why should . . . norms . . . not be clearly and simply stated in abstract terms; why should they appear dressed up as symbolic persons in symbolic situations?" "There seems to be no logical reason for this," she answers, "but empirically there does seem to be a human tendency to deal with any idea whatsoever, no matter how abstract, in terms of human personification, envisioned human action, or human sense impression. . . . People find it easier to see an example than an abstraction, and so the fictional person is created to be the standard of behaviour. . . . Personification is the process by which norms and values are made visible. . . ." All this is said with an eye more on the adult than on the youngster, but what is true of the former is still truer of the latter, as the writer whom we are quoting has clearly understood. "To a greater extent than is generally realised," she says (p. 23), "the lessons of socialisation—how should the baby behave? what should he believe?—are taught by presenting a series of fictional actions and their consequences. . . . Whole codes of conduct are impressed on the child by simple exemplary tales, songs, and proverbs, in which people, or animals functioning symbolically as people for the time, teach a lesson through a statement of desirable or undesirable conduct."

Because fairy tales are spontaneously grown from a collective root and not artificially conceived by individual persons, they show a great deal of complexity and even of self-contradiction, but that makes them even more acceptable to half-developed minds and even more valuable as educational devices. A good illustration is the story of the princess Turandot whose basic theme figures in many traditional folk literatures and has entered into the highest reaches of sophisticated art in Giacomo Puccini's opera of that name. (Shakespeare's *The Taming of the Shrew* should not be forgotten at this point either.) Turandot does not wish to marry; she puts off her successive suitors by asking them to resolve some well-nigh insoluble riddles until one day a prince appears who looks through her stratagems and thus gets the better of her. A feature of this tale is, of course, Turandot's haughtiness and pride: nobody is good enough for her, and this theme is present even in some of the most popular versions (see Lutz Röhrich, *Märchen und Wirklichkeit* [Wiesbaden, 1974], p. 234). But this is certainly not the detail which makes the story most meaningful for the young, in this case especially for those in their early teens. As far as boys are concerned, Turandot symbolizes the riddle of femininity. He who penetrates the mystery of the other sex has reached maturity. It is easy for a young man to identify with Prince Calaf for he achieves what every male youngster wishes to achieve, and knows that he has to achieve. The appeal to girls is different, but certainly no less powerful. The awakening of sexuality is puzzling; it is connected with vague but in many instances intense fears. This fear is in itself complex: there is the fear of the unknown; there is, more concretely, the fear of the pain involved in defloration; there is, on the more social side, the fear of subordination to another person and of the duties of the marital status. There is even an element of revolt against fate: the virgin may be a virago, a woman who would rather be a man. Freud's concept of penis envy clearly enters into this tissue of feelings as well and makes it more complicated still. And there is, finally, the reassuring and soothing suggestion that one day a partner will appear before whom all the established defenses will collapse as the walls of Jericho did before Joshua, the son of Nun.

Not all the strands in this multicolored web are of interest to the sociologist. He is concerned mainly with two of them, and they are not only different, but sharply contrasting. On the one hand, fairy tales help to build up a personal and collective ethos; on the other, they also aid the individual in dealing with his personal difficulties—in Freudian language, in abreacting the tensions which beset him. The latter property helps the traditional material to enter into the personality and its psyche, and thereby to carry the mores of society into the inner self. If a somewhat *risqué* comparison be permitted, fairy tales are like a pill: chocolate-coated and therefore readily accepted by the unsuspecting young, but containing a center which is far less pleasant and which might well be rejected if it were not so cleverly hidden away.

Some of the most distinctive features of folk tales are better understood if they are approached from the individualistic and psychological side, and not from the collective and sociological angle. Often specters and demons play a great part. Whence these imaginings? It seems certain that they are projections, externalizations, of part of the self. Even the devil, as he occurs in many a traditional story, is essentially a mirroring of the antisocial tendencies which the child knows he is carrying within himself as soon as societal norms begin to be pressed on him. We may, in this matter, accept the guidance of a great novelist who was also a very great psychologist: Fëdor Dostoevski. In *The Brothers Karamazov*, Ivan, in a hallucinatory experience, confronts the devil and struggles with this dread appearance. He fights him off and sobers himself up by saying: "You are a symbolization of myself, or rather of one aspect of myself. You are an incarnation of my own most stupid and most disgusting thoughts and feelings. . . . You are myself but with a different face!" (4.11.9). It need not, however, be a personification of one's sense of sin which is encountered in a spectral or demonic figure. It may be one's fears; it may be one's suppressed wishes; it may be anything which is contained in one's unconscious. Particularly revealing are the fairy tales which relate how a man fashions a doll in order to play with it and then finds to his horror that, like Pygmalion, it develops a life of its own and ultimately destroys him. What is this but a visionary presentation of the fear that one's lower self may gain the upper hand and lead one into disaster? Another frequently elaborated theme is the marriage between a boy and a girl, a human, on the one hand, and an animal or a sprite, on the other (a classic example being Dvořák's enchanting opera *Rusalka*). Every marriage is, in the nature of things, a union between two physically distinct creatures, and the difference between male and female is simply being exaggerated and hypostatized, in these stories, into the contrast between a human, on the one hand, and a water nymph or a frog or a toad, on the other. Here, too, a suppressed fear is at work: the fear that the common life of the partners may be ruined by all-too-deep dissimilarities in nature and outlook, by mutual misunderstanding—an apprehension very natural in those who are moving into the age of marriageability. (On all this, see Lutz Röhrich, *Sage und Märchen* [Freiburg, Basel, & Vienna, 1976], esp. pp. 15, 37–39.) It is characteristic, and a very clear hint to the analyst, that demons, specters, sprites, and talking animals usually appear as isolated figures and are seen or experienced by solitary individuals. These encounters are asocial simply because they are self-confrontations of a split personality.

Personal problems which make themselves felt, in a parallel fashion, in many individuals, exert in this way a strong influence on the collective imagination which has created, and ever re-creates, the most important fairy tales. But the need of society to anchor its ethos in the minds of its new members—social interest—is not slow to assert itself. We see its power very clearly in the tendency to re-interpret archaic lore—more concretely expressed: to make moral tales out of nature myths. One well-known nursery story is called "Snow White and the Seven Dwarfs." Why seven? Why not five or nine or any other number? Because there are seven planets which circle around the sun. Originally, so we may assume, Snow White was a symbol of the sun, but later the primal myth was, so to speak, transposed into another key, the social key. The Sleeping Beauty awakened from her slumbers by Prince Charming recalls, as of itself, the Germanic saga of Brunhild and Siegfried, of whom the former is obviously in the final analysis a symbol of nature held captive by snow and ice, and the latter of spring, and more particularly the spring sun, which brings the forests and fields back to life. There is no moral element in the older version; there certainly is in the later. The Big Bad Wolf in Little Red Riding Hood is a personification of the night, the fearsome dark, while his victim is a personification of the day, the beloved light. The night as such, as a purely physical phenomenon, cannot be considered, in any culture, as morally reprehensible, but the ravenous wolf can, because greed is his characteristic vice (see Heinrich Günter, *Psychologie der Legende* [Freiburg, 1949], pp. 54, 55, 69, 70). Two further traditional tales (numbered 62 and 33 in the classic collection of the brothers Grimm, known under the title *Kinder- und Hausmärchen*) are interesting in this connection, "The Queen of the Bees" and "The Three Languages." In "The Queen of the Bees" the *dramatis personae* are ants, ducks, and bees; in "The Three Languages," dogs, frogs, and birds. Even in these two cases it is possible to recognize a basic naturalistic layer, later overlaid by moral conceptions: ants and dogs represent the earth; ducks and frogs, the water; and bees and birds, the third element, the air.

All this is surely interesting, but we have not yet laid our finger on the truly salient point. We did not say enough when we pointed out that, in the tissue of

most fairy tales, there run, side by side, an individualistic and a social or socializing strand. There is in fact not only the co-existence of these two tendencies,
but a clash between them. While, seen from one side, the stories traditionally
told to young children appear as moralizing influences, they show, when viewed
from the other side, a far less pleasant face. They reflect human disagreements
and conflicts, indeed, often downright hatred, and very frequently even hatred
of those whom, by common consent, one ought to love. This duality, this inner
dividedness, of the fairy-tale material may strike the logician as a tremendous
weakness; the sociologist, on the other hand, should consider it a great strength.
One and the same tale will be able, just because it is internally broken, just because it is both socially constructive and humanly estranging, to satisfy contrasting and shifting moods. One day the teller of the story will elaborate more
on the one aspect and the listener more carefully listen to it, another day a different detail will be singled out for preferential treatment; and the placing of
the emphasis need by no means be the same with the listener as with the teller.

In the nature of things it is unavoidable that there should be tensions, wax-
ing and waning in intensity, between parents and children and also between
siblings. To speak of sibling rivalry first: it is represented by at least three dramatic incidents related in the Bible—Cain and Abel, Jacob and Esau, and
Joseph and his brothers. In Greek mythology, the story of Eros and Psyche
carries the same content, for Psyche has two jealous sisters who want to ruin
her, and even the goddess Venus does not wish her well. From Psyche to Cinderella there is only the smallest of steps. She too is humiliated and trodden
under foot by her elder sisters; and she too is the more virtuous as well as the
more beautiful one and gains the upper hand in the end. The fact that the very
same story is part of age-old Chinese folklore shows that we are confronted
with a universal theme. The variants are legion. Sometimes a wicked female
substitutes herself for her beautiful and virtuous sister and deceives her bridegroom by means fair or foul (mostly by foul means, such as sorcery); sometimes "a brother and sister have been promised to a water spirit or some other
kind of monster," and "after they enter the services of the monster, the sister
marries him and plots against her brother" (Thompson, *The Folktale*, pp. 117,
113). Occasionally we encounter two kindred versions of the same tale, one
of which pillories the unkindness of man to man in general, and the other the
yet more distressing enmity between brother and brother. Thus one story relates how a lusty youngster leaves his home and wanders out into the world. On
his journey, he meets two others who join him, and then the adventure begins.

> The three companions come to a house in the woods. They take turns in keep-
> ing house while the others are abroad. One after the other they are attacked
> by a monster who comes from an opening in the earth. On the third day the
> hero keeps house and chases the monster through the hole to his abode in the
> lower world. His two companions let him down after the monster by means
> of a long rope, and they [promise to] await his return while he has adventures
> in the lower world. There he finds a marvelous sword and conquers several
> monsters and rescues three maidens. He returns to the rope and has his com-
> panions raise the girls to the upper world. They take the girls off with them and
> leave him to his fate below.

This pattern also occurs in a version in which the three are, not strangers, but brothers. The differences are negligible because they are due, not to any dissimilarity in the psychological root, but merely to the surface play of the imagination.

> A monster comes in the night and steals from the king's orchard. One after the other, the king's sons guard the orchard and watch for the monster. The youngest son pursues the thief and follows him into the lower world. The elder brothers wait for the hero, expecting to pull him up on a rope. The treacherous abandonment, the theft of the girls, and the conclusion of the story are exactly like the final stages in the other variant [ibid., p. 33].

The whole adventure, needless to say, has a happy ending. The abandoned hero manages to escape from his underground place of confinement and arrives in time to claim and secure his due reward. Insofar as he is a paragon, insofar as virtue is triumphant and vice exposed and punished, these stories have a socializing tendency. They propagate the idea that in social life everything works out, in spite of appearances to the contrary, as it ought. But this message will be largely lost on the very young. In order to receive it, a mind must already be socialized to some extent. Before it is—and we saw in the second volume that the process of socialization takes its time—the child will see only one thing: the victory of the person whom he favors and with whom he identifies.

It is an old experience that fairy tales of this kind also appeal to only children even though they have no competitors in their homes. They still believe, when they are in an appropriate mood, that life is unkind to them and that others are better off. But in their case, stories centering on the friction between parents and offspring or mothers and children will awaken more interest and yield more satisfaction. Traditional tales of this type are about as widespread as those considered before, and, needless to say, they have as much meaning for boys and girls who have also to contend with siblings and to abreact their tensions with them. If the story of "The Singing Bone" (no. 28 in the Grimm collection), which deals with fratricide, is to be met with in many places, that of Hansel and Gretel (ibid., no. 15) is still more universally known. The woodcutters drive their children out; they expose them to darkness, hunger, and cold. It is the mother who has hatched out that terrible plan; the father who (mildly) opposes it is overruled. This tale is somewhat unusual because it is—at least in some of its variants—the mother, the real mother, who abandons her own flesh and blood. The standard figure is, of course, not the real mother, but the loveless, hateful stepmother. But the small child is not likely to make a sharp distinction between the stepmother and the real one. When he is in a pet, that is, when he feels that he is being treated as if he were a stepchild, the two otherwise so different figures will flow into one. Often two persons in a fairy story are experienced as symbolizations of a father or mother, and this fits in with the child's ambiguous feelings about a parent, or both of them. Papa and mama may have at the same time an angelic and a demonic face, as they have two sides in real life: they are at the same time the youngster's protectors and his disciplinarians; they do things which he will welcome and others which he rejects. He can hate the nasty giant and the ugly witch who stand for the father's and mother's negative, nocturnal side, without the definite feeling that he acts wrongly, for giants and witches are inhabitants of fairyland, that is, of a never-never land— which does not mean that they do not play a very real role in the child's imaginative life.

Contending with one's siblings, especially insofar as they are competitors, and dealing with one's parents, especially insofar as they are educators, are to the developing child a trial and a test. But every trial and every test generate in those who are subject to them a desire of success, of ultimate triumph, and this desire is satisfied, in and by the typical fairy tale, by means of identification with the hero, by means of vicarious participation. In the preface to his book *Märchen und Wirklichkeit*, Lutz Röhrich asserts, and rightly, that "the most general scheme which lies at the bottom of the popular fairy tale is this: difficulties and their conquest, struggle and victory, task and its completion, expectation and fulfillment," a list of associated dualities to which he adds, on another page (p. 14), bewitchment and release from it. It is largely because it offers this pattern of trial and triumph that the fairy tale has an appeal so strong and so permanent that society could make it a carrier of moral conceptions, an instrument of social education, and an abiding element in the system of mental control.

The collective imagination of the human race has been particularly fertile in elaborating tests of maturity for the young seeking admission to full social life, and the search for appropriate forms has taken two contrasting, if also comparable, directions. There is (as we have hinted already), on the one hand, the development of initiation *rituals* before or during which trials have to be undergone, and there is, on the other, the provision of *fairy tales* in and through which trials of a similar nature are lived through in imagination. As the reader can see, we are returning here to Mircea Eliade's great intuition which we have made our own. Initiation ritual and initiation story have a tendency to go over into each other. Thus Stith Thompson writes about a part of the primitive world particularly noted for its initiation ceremonies: "Over practically the whole continent a considerable portion of the tales of the North American Indians are concerned with the exploits of heroes who overcome seemingly invincible adversaries. Frequently, as in familiar European tales, the hero is deliberately sent out with the idea of having him killed, though sometimes the principal motive seems to be merely to subject him to a series of very difficult tests" (*The Folktale*, p. 329). The heroes of the fairy tales which have been received into the canon of the so-called civilized nations are said to encounter the same or similar situations and to rise above the same dread experiences as their counterparts among the Indians. There are journeys to hell and heaven; there are death and resurrection, and more of this kind: the fundamental patterns are the same. When Emanuel Schikaneder wrote the book for *The Magic Flute*, he based the opera, in the second act of which the audience follows Tamino and Pamina through their successive ordeals to their eventual initiation into the sacred mysteries of Isis and Osiris, on the selfsame time-hallowed model, and the music of Wolfgang Amadeus Mozart then raised it to almost unearthly heights of sublimity and grace.

The tests are indeed of the most varied kinds: trials of patience, of obedience, of skill, of strength, of valor, of cleverness, and of wit (see Röhrich, *Sage und Märchen*, p. 18). Just very occasionally they concern self-control and are thus openly and definitely connected with the socialization process. As we demonstrated in Volume III of this work, society is above all anxious to discipline the two great natural drives inherent in the human body: greed and sex. They are now and then the center of a fairy story. Thus in "The She-Raven" (the Grimms's no. 93) the hero is asked to deny himself by refusing the food and drink offered to him. In "Jack and His Bargains" (see K. M. Briggs, *A Dictionary of British Folk Tales* I [Bloomington, Ind., 1970], p. 315), the hero is nearly at the end of his tribulations. Jack knows that the princess will be his. He is admitted to her chamber and to her bed, yet he does not touch her for three nights. Only then is the marriage ceremony performed and the common life (which, we are told, produced many children) begun. The salient point of this curious story is, of course, that Jack had first to prove his manhood: he had to prove it, not by performing the sex act, which is easy, but by withstanding the sexual instinct, which is difficult. A true man is only he who is master of and not slave to his body.

There are, as we can see, fairy tales which preach self-restriction, but the bulk of them are not so much repressive as emancipatory. The very fact that most of them begin with the hero's leaving his home and going out into the unknown world is symbolic of the child's (expected or real) leaving of the nursery, or even of the family, and joining adult society—an adventure which may well inspire apprehension and fear in the inexperienced youngster. The main message of the fairy tale is: Don't be afraid! Everything will turn out right in the end! No wonder that children love their stories. Indeed, they need them if they are to develop what we all need: enough courage to endure life. Perhaps there is no small boy or girl who does not fear, deep down in his unconscious, that he may one day be abandoned and exposed to starvation. The story of Hansel and Gretel will then enthrall him, and he will be greatly reassured by its end: how the wicked witch is burnt to cinders and they are enabled to return home with pearls and precious stones in their pockets. The happy ending is the hallmark of the fairy tale as a literary category. We shall see that it is the trait which distinguishes it most sharply from the saga.

Some well-meaning but ill-advised educators have pleaded that the traditional fairy tale should be abandoned, for the talk of giants and sorceresses, they suggest, may awaken fears in the infant. This is a superficial, indeed, a foolish, attitude. The fears are there anyway. They stem simply from the fact that the child is small and weak and without experience. What the fairy tales do is, first of all, to put a face on the fear: the fear is at first diffuse and therefore all the more threatening; it is then concentrated, personified, in a demonic figure and thereby already somewhat reduced. But not only is it reduced, it is conquered, it is overcome, when the story is told to its end. The giant turns out to be less frightening than it appeared: he cannot gobble up the child after all. The sorceress is weak in spite of her spells: her magical power is less potent than the counter-magic which is invariably in friendly hands. Very revealing is the way in which the devil is depicted. He is either described as stupid and therefore easily duped, or depicted as clever, but then he is a friend rather than an enemy, a helper rather than a fiend.

As we can see, the typical fairy tale has two *foci*: on the one hand, the hard trial; on the other, the happy ending. In the traditional stories, both aspects are present, and in the process of stereotyping which has taken place over the centuries, they have achieved a satisfying balance. Indeed, they get stereotyped precisely because there is a deep-rooted wish to elaborate and to preserve both, and the balance between them as well. It is true that in "The Ugly Duckling" the transformation into a beautiful swan—the happiest of happy endings —is achieved without effort, without tribulation, simply by the natural process of growing up. But this story has not sprung from the collective unconscious; it is an artifact; it has flowed from the pen of Hans Christian Andersen. Andersen was a clever writer and even a good child psychologist; but he could not match the wisdom of the folk; one mind, however brilliant, never can.

In spite of the initial sorrows of the ugly duckling, Andersen presents a pleasant rather than a distressing picture of the background, but another author who has had an equally powerful appeal to the young depicts a world of ugliness and aggression, and he was taken to task for it. Yet he knew how to ward off the attack. "Robert Louis Stevenson," Joan Rockwell reports (*Fact in Fiction*, p. 32), "defended himself against Henry James's criticism of the brutalizing effect of the killings in *Treasure Island* by claiming that this literary violence was natural to children: 'Was there ever a child which did not imbrue its little hands in gore—except Master James, of course?' " he sarcastically retorted. Little though we may like it, the superior realism, the deeper psychological insight, lie with Stevenson. It is true that he addresses the teenager rather than the school-entrant, but this makes surprisingly little difference. Even the small child likes to hear of cruelty for, let us not forget it, he is as yet not fully socialized. So prominent is the account of cruel actions retailed, and often detailed, in the traditional material that Immanuel Kant expressed a definite disgust with the whole literary category. "The fairy tales of the crazy French [*des französischen Aberwitzes*] are the most abominable caricatures [*Fratzen*] which have ever been thought up" (*Werke*, Gesammelte Schriften, ed. Königlich Preussische Akademie der Wissenschaften, 22 vols. [Berlin, 1902–1938], II 215). The great philosopher was somewhat unfair to the French when he made this statement for there is a good deal more cruelty in the classic German collection by the brothers Grimm than in the classic French collection of Charles Perrault. But he was not only unfair; he was also blind to the facts. And the salient fact is that cruelty does not appall the young; on the contrary, it appeals to them. Kant was a rationalist, and rationalism has ever had a delusionary idea of human beings. They are not exclusively reason, let alone pure reason. They are creatures of flesh and blood with many an inborn trait, including a tendency toward violence; and this trait, this violence, is even stronger in boys and girls than in men and women, for the socializing and moralizing influences of culture have not yet had time to work. Not only Charles

Perrault, but also Jacob and Wilhelm Grimm toned down some of the stories, yet they found that they could not totally expurgate their material without utterly falsifying it. The hard fact of the matter is that cruelty is of the essence of the fairy tale.

It is not difficult to provide documentation in support of this last statement; or rather, if there is any difficulty, it is the one called, by the French, *embarras de choix*. The material is overwhelming. Lutz Röhrich, two of whose books we have already quoted, has investigated this topic very conscientiously, and we can hardly do better than to translate from his paper ("Die Grausamkeit im deutschen Märchen," *Rheinisches Jahrbuch für Volkskunde* [1955], 176ff.; repr. in *Märchen und Wirklichkeit*, pp. 123ff.) the passage in which he sums up what he has found in the *Kinder- und Hausmärchen* of the brothers Grimm (see "Die Grausamkeit," 177):

> Children, especially orphans, are tortured, for the fun of it, by their foster parents (stories no. 21, 24, 130, 185, 186), driven out and disowned (15, 201), and even murdered (13, 53). A faithful friend can be brought back to life only through the blood of two innocent infants, who have to be killed for the purpose (6). At the birth of a baby girl, a father threatens to kill his twelve sons (9). Children are caught by a witch and fattened up in order to be eaten later on (15). A boy is bestially slaughtered by his mother and served as a meal to his father (47). Another father mercilessly deprives his daughter of both her hands because she refuses to do as he says (31). Hundreds of young girls are delivered to an evil dragon so that he can feed on them (60). We find instances of revolting cannibalism (15, 47) and human sacrifices (6, 60). There is fratricide (28 and 60) and the murder of spouses (16, 126). A mother who has just given birth is being choked in the bath (11). People are blinded (107, 121), cruelly dismembered (47), or buried alive (16). Rejected suitors are executed without compunction, and their heads exhibited on the castle wall (191). A sadist murders in a disgusting manner a large number of girls whom he has enticed into his house; [he perpetrates crimes] in a blood chamber by chopping up their bodies and throwing the bleeding limbs into a bowl (46).

Lest it be thought that these abominations occur only in one area (one hesitates to write: in one culture), let us quickly add that they are found everywhere. Attacks of fathers on the lives of their sons, for instance, are related in Finnish and Estonian folk tales (Röhrich, *Märchen und Wirklichkeit*, p. 278n61). The variant of the Turandot story current among the Transsylvanian gypsies is in fact still more nauseating than that related by the brothers Grimm (in their number 191). The princess has the young men who cannot solve her riddles castrated and proudly shows her visitors a tower decorated all over with the severed parts (see Röhrich, *Märchen und Wirklichkeit*, p. 142).

We take no pleasure in enlarging on this horrible subject, but for the sake of realism and completeness it should be pointed out that Röhrich's list, and the Grimm collection on which it is based, understate rather than overstate the amount of cruelty contained in the traditional tales. Even our beloved tale of Little Red Riding Hood exists in far more off-putting variants. In one, for instance, Little Red Riding Hood is forced to fry the thickened blood of her grandmother in butter; she is expected to eat her grandmother's teeth, as if they were beans or rice; the bones lie under the bed as if they were firewood, and the intestines are used to tie up the door (ibid., p. 126)!

The question may, of course, be asked why these distressing aspects of folk tradition should be brought up at all in a book which deals with the development of a societal ethos, but there is a very good reason for it. The purple passages make the stories exciting and are one explanation why they are liked by the children. Within living memory a semi-professional storyteller plied his trade in the southern Black Forest and was interviewed by a researcher who reports: "It is precisely what is gruesome, uncanny, and horrible, that which in editions destined for children is so often smoothed over or omitted, that the children are most anxious to hear, as Grandfather Schwarz assures us. He says that he must go in particularly great detail into such scenes and is not allowed to slur over anything. . . . He himself, he says, could retain the fearful stories best in his memory" (ibid., p. 155). We may revert here to our earlier simile and say that the blood-curdling passages are part of the chocolate coating which induces the young to swallow the fairy tales as a whole, including the bitter kernel, the educational and socializing moral, which they contain.

But in spite of all that has been said, we should not lightheartedly characterize the young as sadistic. This would be just as wrong as regarding them as angelic, a mistake which today is far more often made. What to some extent excuses, or at least explains, their pleasure in listening to cruel tales is—strange though it may sound—their egocentricity, the psychological feature which we so carefully discussed in the second volume. They know only one kind of pain, and that is pain in their own bodies. If there is any other person in the world whose pain they can see and sympathize with, it is the hero with whom they identify. All others are so strange, so psychologically remote from them, that their suffering is nothing to them; they do not even realize that it hurts. This may be difficult for an adult layman to believe, but a human being before the successful conclusion of the socialization process is simply very different from a human being who has gone through and emerged from it. Lutz Röhrich understood this very well, and we may quote him once again with approval and agreement. This is what he writes:

> Moral judgments [pronounced in fairy tales] do not have the character of objectivity. Everything is seen from the point of view of the hero and, in accordance with this, cruelty is considered as cruelty only if the hero has to endure it, not if he inflicts it. The fairy tale does not label the immoral actions of the hero as immoral, and this is connected with the sympathy of the teller of the tale and the hearer for the hero, i.e., their narrow psychological relationship. . . . The hero may even murder his own children without a moral shadow falling on him, [as in the story no. 6 of the Grimm collection].

"This egocentric attitude of the fairy tale," Röhrich continues on the next page, "does not fully enter the consciousness of the story teller and his listener. . . . The brutal crimes which are being committed and suffered in fairy tales do not become concretized and present to the mind." Hence, there is no gloating over human suffering, nothing which could justifiably be described as sadism. "The severing of the fingers (no. 25) or the hacking off of [part of] the heel (97) takes place without any shedding of blood and without apparent pain. . . . There is no talk of pain either when first one and then the other eye of the poor tailor is gouged out (107). All that is noted is that he does not see any more" (ibid., pp. 151, 152). In yet another context of his most revealing book (ibid., p. 229), Röhrich draws attention to the egocentric, and hence asocial, or even antisocial, character of this whole literary category. "The union of two lovers is as a rule seen only from one side and is of interest only so long as it is not yet brought about; once the two come together, the fairy tale stops. It is also a striking fact that the fairy tale knows almost exclusively merely individual problems (like birth, maturity, marriage, and death), but no group problems (as for example, national ones or such as concern a . . . village community)."

The individualistic character of the typical fairy tale, though very real, must not be exaggerated. Even the element of cruelty has its social implications and indeed a certain positive influence on socialization. For the worst forms of harshness appear regularly in connection with the punishment of some crime—with poetic justice, if the term be allowed in this context. The victims, it is often suggested or at least implied, get only what they have asked for. We modern people, and we grownups, do not think so; to us the punishments inflicted appear unnecessarily harsh or even grotesquely exaggerated, but children feel differently, and so did earlier times, if the legal historians are to be believed. "It is a striking fact that the death penalty is almost the only punishment known to the fairy tales," writes Röhrich.

> Besides execution, there occur above all terrible mutilations, in part as torturing antecedents of execution itself. In [the Grimms's no.] 76, the king orders the wicked cook to be torn into four pieces (similarly in 111). . . . The murderer of his brother in [story no.] 28 is sewn into a sack and drowned alive; in [no.] 9 the evil stepmother is put into a cask filled with boiling oil and, in addition, paradoxically, also with poisonous snakes. . . . The false bride in [no.] 89 [who has wickedly ousted the real one] is stripped of her clothes and put into a cask which is studded with sharp nails on the inside; two white horses are harnessed to it which drag her through the streets [ibid., p. 143].

"Even smaller misdemeanors, such as, for example, mere curiosity (46), envy (21, 101, 142), haughtiness (24), impatience, indifference, or simple laziness, greed, hardness, and other kinds of unsocial conduct are cruelly avenged in the fairy tales. . . . In the story of Snow White (53) . . . the nasty stepmother has to step into red-hot iron slippers and dance in them until she falls dead to the ground" (ibid., pp. 146, 147). Some will plead that such horrible punishments are bound to have a brutalizing rather than a socializing effect, but we must not forget that—given the basic psychology of the child discussed above and in greater detail in Volume II—punishments will only be grasped as punishments, will only be understood, if they are wildly exaggerated. If there were only talk of fines or reprimands, the words would pass over the youngsters' heads without making any impression whatsoever.

If we try to understand the psychological and moral (or antimoral) effects of the accounts of exemplary punishments contained in fairy tales, we shall be led to the conclusion that we have, analytically, to distinguish three points. The first is that such accounts complete and support the happy endings of the stories. The triumph of the hero is only entire if his adversaries are annihilated. The child's mental images are not painted in pastel colors; they are in black and white, and the white is only really white when the black is really black. The brothers Grimm refused to expurgate their stories (though they muted some of the harsher tones); Charles Perrault, on the other hand, tended to omit what he thought was too offensive. For instance, the Grimms end the tale of Cinderella (their no. 21) by relating that the wicked stepsisters have their eyes picked out, while Perrault omits this traditional end-bit. But the collection of the Grimms has had a far stronger appeal, and therefore been a far more effective vehicle of moral conceptions, than the collection of Perrault.

A second function of these—to the adult distressing—elements of the traditional lore is to satisfy the child's craving for vengeance. We all have to agree that such a desire should not exist; but we should also realize, especially if we are scholars bound to the truth even where it is unpleasant, that it does exist. If wickedness were not punished with a hard hand, the child would come away with the conviction that the powers which rule the world do not care very greatly whether a person acts kindly or otherwise, and this would be a poor preparation for social life. Even grownups feel similarly. If, by some mischance, a murderer is freed by the courts, the next of kin to the victim feel, as all observers confirm, revolted and outraged, and their attachment to society is bound to be weakened.

A third aspect relates to justice. Even if, in the fairy tales, the punishment does not fit the crime, it is due retribution. Only the guilty are attained; the innocent are always vindicated. The desire for justice is psychologically so closely connected with the desire for vengeance (even if, ethically considered, they appear as contrasts, and indeed sharp ones) that where the latter is present, even the former may get a foothold. Differently expressed: there may be a shift, in the growing personality, from a craving for vengeance to a wish to see justice done, and it is precisely one of the chief tasks of social and moral education to bring it about. Because, in the fairy tales, misdeeds are invariably followed (if *pede claudo*) by correction, there develops, in the child, a conviction that there is, at the bottom of reality, all appearances to the contrary notwithstanding, a law which leads to the triumph of the good and the discomfiture of the wicked, and this impression, once established, is a bridge over which a good deal of the societal ethos may enter into individual minds. We would beg leave to quote once more from Röhrich's excellent analysis (ibid., p. 235):

> It is not blind chance which rules. Behind all that is happening there stands the latent belief in a destiny which grants success to him who is worthy of it and sends failure to him who is not. . . . The chosen hero attains his end while his adversaries go astray. . . . If, for instance, a wicked person tries to repeat the happy adventure of a good person, he either incurs punishment or has to face destruction [see, for example, *Kinder- und Hausmärchen*, nos. 13, 24, 87, 107].

The belief in a latent law which sees to it that everybody is treated according to his merits or his faults is greatly strengthened by stories which suggest that it is unfailing in its operation. Under the chapter heading "Truth Comes to Light," Stith Thompson writes as follows (*The Folktale*, p. 136):

> If the rewards and punishments given by our mysterious strangers are filled with magic and miracles, even more marvelous are the ways of divine justice in uncovering hidden crime. Even an idea usually so foreign to the peoples of western Europe as reincarnation is used to reveal a murder in the story of "The Singing Bone" which not only appears as a popular folktale but is sung as a ballad throughout northern and western Europe and the United States. The details of these stories show considerable variation. Usually in the prose form we have the murder of one brother by another, whereas in the ballad we are dealing with two sisters. In any case, the murdered person is either buried or left in the water where he has been drowned. Sometimes a harp is made from various parts of the body, or a flute from a bone, or some other instrument from a tree which has grown over the murdered person's grave. The musical instrument is played in public and sings out the accusation of the murder.

This story is known in England as "Binnorie" (see Joseph Jacobs, *English Fairy Tales* [London, 1890], no. 9) and corresponds to the Grimms's no. 28. A similar tale is called "The Rose Tree" in England (Jacobs' no. 3) and "The Juniper Tree" in Germany (the Grimms's no. 47). Sometimes punishment comes in another way, but the point is that it does come. "There are . . . a large number of stories about the unquiet grave," writes Thompson (*The Folktale*, p. 257), "all telling of some reason why the dead person is unable to rest in peace. It may be because of a great sin—murder, suicide, adultery, or even, in medieval tales, the taking of usury."

In some pieces (and we may surmise that they have come down to us in a particularly archaic form) we find the same thought pattern as in the Old Testament: the *lex talionis*—an eye for an eye, a tooth for a tooth. The witch who plans to roast Hansel is herself thrown into the oven destined for him and burned to cinders. The wayfarer who deprives his traveling companion of both his eyes is in the end blinded himself (Grimm collection, nos. 15 and 107). But occasionally we find a far less mechanical—modern man would say: a far truer—conception of justice, as André Jolles explains (*Einfache Formen* [Tübingen, 1972], pp. 239, 240):

> In "Puss in Boots" we behold the poor son of a miller; he appears by the side of his brothers, both of whom have inherited valuable objects: the one, the mill; and the other, the donkey. He himself has received only a valueless thing: the cat. In and by itself, this fact or this situation is not immoral, yet they awaken in us both the feeling of injustice and the feeling that this injustice must be remedied. In the course of the tale, we get the satisfaction we desire: precisely that valueless thing, the cat, becomes the instrument of a change for the better. In the end the happiness of the less generously treated boy surpasses that of his brothers by the same margin as that by which it was, to begin with, inferior. This is certainly no ethic in the philosophical sense of the word; we are not told who or what is virtuous, who or what is not. We cannot say that the miller who has provided for his two older sons better than for the younger is wicked, and the two older brothers are, in this story, not depicted as morally inferior to the third. All the tale teaches is that if our sense of justice has been upset, a series of events, a happening of a special kind, must restore it.

Here a rather fine conception of equity is at work, and that proves that some at least of the fairy tales carry and communicate an ethos which has left the crudity of the *lex talionis* far behind.

This brings us at long last to the socializing and moralizing kernel of the fairy stories. We shall pass over rather quickly an intermediate form (intermediate between the individual and the social aspects in the sense of the scheme here developed): the warning tale.

One example is the story of the "Three Little Pigs." Two of them are so impatient to start amusing themselves that they scrimp their work and build themselves only feeble shelters, one of straw and the other of wood. These are a poor protection from the ravenous wolf: he breaks in and eats them up. The third pig erects a solid structure of stone and postpones the period of play in order to be safe, and he *is* safe. The wolf can do him no harm. The message is: for your own sake, put first things first. Another example is Little Red Riding Hood (Grimms's no. 26). Little Red Riding Hood is told by her mother that she must not leave the path which leads through the woods, but she does not listen. Looking, in her playful way, for flowers, she gets deeper and deeper into the thicket and that gives the Big Bad Wolf the chance to reach the grandmother's house before her and to gobble her up. The obvious message of the story is: Obey! But the obedience aims here at the protection of the child, i.e., an individual, and therefore has little, if any, general social implication. What is inculcated is caution, not kindness. An older theory derived the cannibalism none too rarely encountered in this literature from a supposed earlier, prehistoric ritual (and possibly real) anthropophagy. Such artificial constructions are not necessary to explain the phenomenon. If the child is really to be impressed, the consequences of his disobedience must be painted in garish colors, and what could give him a more salutary fright than the prospect of meeting a wolf or a witch and being devoured?

Though, as we pointed out, the norms contained in warning tales are essentially self-protective and not social commands, we should not be blind to the socializing effect which may yet issue from them. Norms are norms, whatever their content. If self-protective norms are internalized, others may come to be internalized too. There is such a thing as the learning of learning. The child who learns obedience to rules which are in his favor will be more easily led to learn obedience to rules which are for the benefit of others.

But let us now turn to the main contribution which the telling of, and the listening to, fairy tales makes to the socialization of an incoming generation. Besides the many stories which speak of jealous siblings or wicked stepmothers, there are others which extol the love of brothers and sisters for each other. Folk traditions are self-contradictory and unavoidably so, simply because the life which they reflect and subserve is also self-contradictory. To go for a moment beyond the limits of nursery stories: Greek lore knows both sibling rivalry and sibling devotion. In Aeschylus' *The Seven Against Thebes*, the brothers Eteocles and Polyneices bitterly hate each other, and are slain by each other's hands. But their sister Antigone, the heroine of Sophocles' tragedy, is faithful to the very end. In "Hansel and Gretel" the woodcutters' children are one heart and one soul. They escape destruction mainly because they stand by each other. The Grimm collection contains three further faithful-sister stories (nos. 9, 25, and 49). Even more interesting is a faithful-stepsister story which we may allow Stith Thompson to relate:

> As in a number of folk stories, the father takes a second wife against the advice of his child. In this story the stepmother is very cruel to his little boy. Her own daughter, little Mary Ann, however, is fond of the boy and helps him all she can. One day while the father is away the stepmother closes the lid of a chest on the boy and kills him. She cooks him and serves him to his father, who eats him unknowingly. Little Mary Ann gathers up the bones from under the table where the father has thrown them and buries them under the juniper tree. The next day a bird comes forth from the grave. The bird goes to various places and sings a song about the murder. He receives presents, which he takes back to the juniper tree. He drops a ring for his sister, slippers for his father, and, at last, a millstone on the stepmother. At her death the bird becomes a boy again.

This is the tale, already referred to, called "The Juniper Tree" and numbered 47 in the *Kinder- und Hausmärchen* of the brothers Grimm.

Not surprisingly, faithfulness of husband and wife to each other is also often extolled. A frequent pattern is that some magic deprives a man of his memory so that he forgets his first and real wife and is induced to wed another. But the ruse invariably fails in the end. The true spouse is recognized and reinstated in her rights. In the Grimms's tale no. 38, "The Marriage of the She-Fox," a widowed vixen rejects all her suitors until she finds one who resembles her departed spouse. (The story is not, however, without ambiguities.)

Most moving, of course, are the tales which speak of the love between mother and child. It is shown to be so great that it defies and overcomes even the barriers erected by death. The murdered mother returns to her child (the Grimms's stories 11 and 13) and the dead child to its mother (109). In the latter instance, the child pleads with the mother to end her weeping. "All these are not simply sagas of revenants," writes Lutz Röhrich in *Sage und Märchen* (p. 13).

> They are tales which speak of the close and vital relationships of the living to the dead and the dead to the living; they undertake to show that death does not divide mother and child, husband and wife, bride and groom. They are at the same time tales which relate how grief may be overcome and how sorrow can be borne in the proper manner, but they also teach that sadness has its true measure and its own limits. . . . Popular poetry treats love as a timeless phenomenon. Love endures even after death.

The last three paragraphs have clearly shown that there are specific human relationships which the fairy tales surround with a halo, which they glamourize and sanctify, and thereby also undergird and strengthen. But there are, in addition, impressive, indeed moving, stories which glorify love in general and whose tendency it is to spread a willingness to bond, a spirit of mutual devotion, through the whole of society. They are usually of the boy-meets-girl type, and nothing would be more natural at this time and age than to see them in the light of romantic attachment, if not in the light of sexuality. But this would be a great mistake. Without denying that there are implications and aspects of this type, the real aim of these tales is to show the greatness, the sublimity, of compassion. Perhaps this will become quite clear when we look at one or two examples. "La Belle et la bête"—classically formulated by Gabrielle-Suzanne Barbot de Villeneuve and by Marie Leprince de Beaumont—is as good an illustration as any of a tradition which is not only old but widespread and profound. Prescinded from all embellishments and with the plot reduced to its barest bones, the story runs as follows. A man has three daughters, the youngest being (as is usual in fairy tales) the most beautiful and the most charming. He has to travel abroad and falls one day into the power of a monstrous creature—the "beast" of the title. That beast threatens to kill him but relents and lets him go, under the condition that he send one of his daughters to take his place. Returned home, he finds that only the youngest—*la belle*—is prepared to join the monster in his castle. There she is very well received, but the beast asks her over and over again to marry him, a proposal which, not surprisingly, she steadfastly declines, though with the greatest kindness. One day the beast gives her leave to return home for a week, provided she then will rejoin him. Once in her father's house, she is put under pressure by her two sisters and prevailed to break her promise, and so she remains in fact beyond the eighth day. But then she dreams of her loathsome suitor: he is in deep distress; he cannot live without her graceful presence. She is profoundly moved and returns to the beast forthwith. She realizes that she too loves him, and she agrees to the marriage. Immediately a miracle happens: the monster disappears and in his place there stands a handsome prince. So they could live happily ever after.

We said: she loves him, not she is in love with him. We contrast the two terms because the latter has romantic and sexual implications, whereas the former is of a more general, more generically human, meaning. We might also say: a more Christian meaning, though then we should in all probability be guilty of an anachronism. There are two reasons why a one-sidedly sexual interpretation of the tale appears inappropriate. The first is that it is after all a fairy story, addressed to children and not to the nubile. A seventeen- or eighteen-year-old would hardly take to the idea that you should amorously associate with a monster or (as in the Grimms's version called "The Three Feathers," no. 63) with a toad. The second reason why we should not consider such stories (and there are many versions) as primarily romantic and sexual is the fact that they also occur in civilizations which have not, like ours since the days of chivalry, romanticized the relation between the two sexes. Stith Thompson reproduces in his survey a North American Indian variant (*The Folktale*, p. 337; see also p. 98). He writes:

> Particularly popular over the whole Plains and Plateau areas is the story usually known as Dirty-Boy. The outline of the story is simple. A supernatural being assumes a humble disguise. There is to be an open contest with the prize to be marriage to the chief's daughter. The loathly boy . . . wins the contest. . . . The chief is not willing to give his daughter at the end of the first contest, but does so after [a] second. The chief sends his three daughters and commands

them to marry Dirty-Boy. Only the youngest goes on to him and cares for him. At the end of three days he transforms himself and his surroundings and magically beautifies his wife.

The very geographical area in which this version was collected proves that we can hardly assume Christian influences to have been at work. And yet, the core of "La Belle et la bête" is a sentiment which is closely akin to, if not indeed identical with, the attitude which Christianity has ever tried to develop in the human heart. Lutz Röhrich is certainly correct when he writes, not with an eye on the animal bridegroom or animal bride stories, but in a generalizing vein (*Sage und Märchen*, pp. 19, 20):

> The liberation of the good out of the clutches of the wicked and the necessity of redeeming love are the most frequently found conceptions of the wonder tales and at the same time the basic ideas of the advanced religions. There is liberation from poverty, from humiliation, from disgusting ugliness, from an animalic exterior, redemption through love and marriage. . . . The decisive point is that this supremely important and in the final analysis religious concept of redemption dominates popular poetry. Redemption relates to a fundamental need in man; it means liberation in the widest sense of the word.

Perhaps we are not becoming unduly rhetorical here when we say that not only man needs redemption but also the fairy tale which he has evolved: redemption from the cruel streak which inheres in his animal nature and has, as we have seen, entered, on a broad front, into the tradition of folk poetry. However disgusting the semi-sadistic incidents are with which we meet, however purple the passages in which they are presented, they lose their importance, they dwindle to almost nothing, if we see them alongside "La Belle et la bête" and its message of mercy. Taken as a whole, the fairy tale is a prime vehicle of moral conceptions, one of the truly great building stones of societal ethos.

A kindred trait is often, not to say always, overlooked: the exaltation of inner over merely outer nobility. Often the groom is a prince; the bride, a village girl. How is it that they can come together? Because we are here in a world of make-believe, it will be said, and this is, of course, true, but it is not the entire explanation. The distance between the prince and the beggar-maid is regularly shown to be far smaller than it appears, and it is by no means obvious on which side the superiority rests. In Madame Leprince de Beaumont's version of "La Belle et la bête," the monster is in fact a bewitched prince, while his beloved is merely a merchant's daughter. But who is the nobler of the two? Surely she whose heart beats with compassion, whose virtues are more precious than the most sparkingly bejewelled crown.

Besides developing the general quality of compassion, the traditional fairy tales extol and thereby propagate specific virtues. We can do no more than give a few stray illustrations. Promises must be kept. The princess in "The Twelve Brothers" could save herself from certain death if only she would open her mouth and defend herself against the accusations of her wicked mother-in-law. But she has promised to keep silent for seven years, a condition for the rescue of her twelve brothers, and she will not be untrue to her word and to them. Patience and long-suffering must be shown. One princess is forced to herd the geese, another to sweep the floor, but they carry their hard fates with dignity. Besides faithfulness and patience, gratitude is invariably lauded. In several stories—for instance, "The White Serpent"—hero or heroine is kind to some animals, and these animals then repay the kindness a hundredfold (Grimm collection, nos. 9, 65, 89, 17).

In the nature of things, every virtue has its parallel vice, as every positive value has its negative counterpart, and though nothing could be less systematic than the moral tradition incorporated in the wild-grown fairy-tale material, we find most of the chief vices described and condemned. Animals are divided into good ones and bad ones. Some of them are said to have refused to do their part when a necessary common task, such as the building of a road or the digging of a well, was performed, and they are then excluded from the benefits of the thing created by joint labor. "Thus laziness on this occasion explains why the snake may not use the road . . . or why certain animals may not drink from a river or spring" (Thompson, *The Folktale*, p. 242). Dishonesty and theft are pilloried and depicted as fraught with dire consequences for the perpetrator, as for instance in the following story: "A sea captain steals the [magic] salt mill [from the hero] and takes it aboard ship where he commands it to grind salt. He is unable to stop the mill, which keeps on grinding even after the ship sinks under the weight of the salt. This is the reason why the sea is salt" (ibid., p. 73). This is clearly a version of the well-known story of "The Sorcerer's Apprentice" made famous by Goethe and Dukas. It damns not only thievishness but carelessness and presumption as well. Another unprepossessing trait of many people is also frequently discussed: miserliness. A hardhearted peasant woman who refuses to give shelter to a person without a roof over his head is severely punished. Her property and she herself are washed away by the waves (Waltraud Woeller, "Der soziale Gehalt und die soziale Funktion des deutschen Volksmärchens," *Wissenschaftliche Zeitschrift der Humboldt-Universität zu Berlin* [1961], 440). Miserliness brings us close to unkindness in general. This too is invariably avenged. A legend which was perhaps, at its inception, the work of some poet and not a proper folk tale, but which entered the body of folk poetry and circulated far and wide as a folk tale (Thompson, *The Folktale*, p. 150), relates how St. Peter's mother was sent to hell for her uncharitableness, and how the saint received permission to pull her out of the flames on a stalk and thus to bring her up to heaven. Yet when other unfortunates caught hold of her feet and tried in this way to enter blessedness together with her, she kicked them off, and this cruel and selfish act sealed her own fate. She fell instantly back into the inferno, there to burn forevermore.

As we might expect, lack of gratitude is a frequent target of the moralizing tendency inherent in most fairy tales. One of the shortest stories in the Grimm collection (no. 145) is called "The Ungrateful Son." A husband and his wife sit down to enjoy their meal, a roast chicken. When the man sees his old father approaching, he hides the chicken and sends him off without anything to eat. But what does he see when he wishes to place the bird once again onto the table? It has turned into a loathsome toad! This toad he must now entertain day in, day out, and he soon realizes that he cannot free himself; he knows that if he would refuse, it would jump into his face and gnaw his flesh. A characteristic local folk tale from Lorraine relates how a snake lives in a cowshed and is daily fed by the kindly milkmaid. Her brutal employer discovers this and sends her packing. But the snake also leaves, and then disaster comes to the property while good luck attends the milkmaid and "God's blessing rested visibly upon her house" (Röhrich, *Märchen und Wirklichkeit*, p. 73).

If we now survey the fairy-tale tradition as a whole, we are, as sociologists, led to a somewhat surprising conclusion: far from being mere fantasy, far from being mere wish fulfillment, the fairy tale has a rather realistic kernel. This basic fact has struck even the literary historian Lutz Röhrich whom we have quoted just now and several times before. He places his finger on the salient point when he writes (ibid., p. 13): "The fairy story starts in most cases from a situation of moral disorder and re-establishes the disturbed order after removing the conflicts." On another page (ibid., p. 233) he tells us what he means when he talks of disorder and conflict, or moral disturbance, and also of the "inherent realism" of the folk story:

> Children are abandoned; the bridegroom is separated from his true bride; a girl is in the power of a fiend. The struggle against dragons, giants, man-eaters, sorcerers, and witches is also a life-and-death struggle. The tasks and tests laid on him must always appear to the hero, to start with, as unfulfillable. . . . Loss of parents, poverty, hunger, and want are invariably treated as sources of very serious suffering. The breaking of prohibitions lands the hero in extremely critical situations in which his life is at stake.

Will it be said that this is not realism? Of course, it is not realism in the literal sense of the word, but it is most assuredly substantial realism. Indeed, we are confronted with a double dose of realism. There is, first of all, the psychological realism of the tales. Dragons do not exist, but there certainly are vague fears which gain a face, so to speak, when they are concretized in, and symbolized by, this fabulous beast; giants do not exist, but there are threatening grownups whose power, and whose secret and suspect intentions, may well alarm and oppress. But greater still than this psychological realism of the fairy tales is their sociological realism. Surely, there is nothing more real in the social world than the ever-threatening fact of conflict. This fact, this threat, is the deepest root of the romancing which we behold in the fairy tales. The final solutions may be and are imaginary, but the set problems themselves, the problems which provide the plots, are, even if they appear exaggerated—a mere poetic license—reflections of social life itself, of the difficulties and dangers, the pains and curses, of a sociality which is woefully imperfect.

Perhaps we may go even further. On analysis, there appears yet a third characteristic which proves that, at a profound level, the fairy tale is, in spite of its fantastic detail, essentially close to the facts and needs of life. Besides its psychological and its sociological realism there is a realistic streak which might be called ethical. G. K. Chesterton, not a scholar in the technical sense of the word, but a man of deep intuitions, presents in his book *Orthodoxy* (New

York & London, 1909) a chapter entitled "The Ethics of Elfland." In it, he investigates the question of how close the morality wrapped up in the fairy tales comes to Christian conceptions, and decides that there are several points of contact. "There is the lesson of 'Cinderella,' which is the same as that of the Magnificat—*exaltavit humiles.* . . . There is the chivalrous lesson of 'Jack the Giant Killer.' . . . There is the great lesson of 'Beauty and the Beast'; that a thing must be loved *before* it is loveable" (pp. 88, 89). We can learn much from such incidental remarks. But we can learn most from the following passage (p. 99):

> according to elfin ethics all virtue is in an "if." The note of the fairy utterance always is "You may live in a palace of gold and sapphire, *if* you do not say the word 'cow' "; or "You may live happily with the King's daughter, *if* you do not show her an onion." The vision always hangs upon a veto. All the dizzy and colossal things conceded depend upon one small thing withheld. All the wild and whirling things that are let loose depend upon one thing that is forbidden.

If we try to unwrap the serious and essential meaning from these flippant, indeed frivolous, words, we encounter the conviction which is the very basis of all pacified and civilized social life: the recognition that the most indispensable precondition of both individual and collective safety, development, and well-being is the acceptance of those limitations which are technically known as folkways, mores, or social control. This vital insight has to be conveyed to the young and anchored in their minds, their hearts, and their wills, and that is precisely what the folk tales do—not alone, of course (we are as yet only at the beginning of our investigation), but in a basic and incomparably efficient manner. The mechanism through which it achieves its purpose is, as we have hinted once or twice before, rather simple. A child in the grip of fear or in the throes of envy will find reassurance and relief if he listens to a fairy tale, for this demonstrates in an impressive manner that dangers can be overcome and that injustices will in the end be remedied. But when the story is taken in and digested, the moral message which it carries is also internalized. It remains in the personality as an invaluable deposit, an understructure, on which a wider ethos may be built.

Psychologists are in the habit of using in this context a certain phrase which, when rightly understood, helps to elucidate the process. They say that the child "works the material through." Lying in his bed after the nightly story has been told, he will daydream for a while about and around it, identifying all the while with the hero and reliving his trials and his triumphs. In this way he will also participate in the hero's tests, in his valor, in his patience, but also in his uprightness, his self-discipline and self-conquests, his love for men and beasts, his exemplary goodness. The ethos contained in the fairy tale will thus come to him from inside as much as from outside; it will, to say the least, not appear to him as an alien element, an imposition. It is this all-important circumstance which gets the norms and values which the collectivity has laid into the stories past the child's defenses. He is increasingly prepared to feel and to act as he should, not because the agents of social control demand it, but because his alter egos in the beloved fairy tales do so. We are exaggerating a little, but not very much, if we say that we have before us a process of self-instruction.

We can express this insight a little differently and say that the fairy tale is, not didactic, but suggestive. It does not preach. Preaching would at best bore the child and might even alienate, annoy, and offend him. Unfortunately the rationalist mind (essentially a naïve and oversimplifying one) is blind to the facts which our analysis has revealed. In France, the position held in Germany by the *Kinder- und Hausmärchen* of the brothers Grimm was for a long time occupied by the collection edited, in 1697, by Charles Perrault which we have already, in passing, referred to. But Jacob and Wilhelm Grimm were representatives of romanticism, while Charles Perrault was a disciple of rationalism, and this made a great difference. The very title of the French collection is revealing: *Histoires ou contes du temps passé avec des moralités.* By spelling out the moral implications of the tales, by formulating propositions which might satisfy a professor of ethics, Perrault no doubt believed that he was increasing the educational effectiveness of the stories, but he was very much mistaken. This is one of the many cases in which theoretical cleverness turns out, in practice, to be sheer folly. All Perrault succeeded in doing was to change the character of the tradition. Lest it be thought that this is an unduly harsh statement, let us quickly add an illustration. Perrault's "Little Red Riding Hood" ends tragically. The wolf remains unpunished; the girl, unresurrected. It is easy to guess why Perrault steered his account toward this conclusion. There are two reasons which we can see. One is to get rid of the miracle. In the Grimm version it is, of course, an event beyond the limits of credibility which restores her to life. This is the negative reason: a concession is made to rationality. The other, positive, reason is to make the tale more useful: a concession is made to utilitarianism. Perrault presents a warning tale. Many fairy stories are, of course, at the same time warning tales, but this didactic intention is as a rule only a by-product and remains well hidden. Where it becomes the main content of the whole, where it sticks out, so to speak, the attitude of the listener will be totally altered. He will be little interested in the message, indeed, in all probability quite deaf to it. In any case, a warning tale is individualistic; the welfare of the child is at its center—which means that the interest of society, the task of socialization, is only secondary, if it is attended to at all.

But Perrault took only the first step. Others after him went much further. The dragons, for instance, disappear, and highwaymen take their place. Those who initiated such changes certainly meant well, as Charles Perrault also did: was it not better to remain in the observable world instead of stimulating, or overstimulating, the child's imagination? But what the child, psychologically speaking, needs is an appropriate symbolization of his fears, and a concrete, observable human person cannot act as such an appropriate symbol. To mention only one reason why he cannot: the child's fears are multiform and indefinable; they are certainly not fears of criminal assault. But even if they were—and we repeat that they are not—a robber would not do as a representation, for he commits only one crime; he is not even a suitable personification of criminality as such, criminality as a diffuse threat, let alone of apprehensions without clear shape and without recognizable number. To banish the fear of criminality, a simple reference to the police would do; but the fear of the evil lurking in life and hiding behind its surface cannot be conquered in this easy manner.

Grownups, of course, have largely overcome this fear—to a large extent because fairy tales have helped them—and if they are rationalists, they find it difficult to understand what goes on in the infant psyche. Some, in their blindness, have even concluded that fairy tales create this fear instead of soothing it—an idea which in the final analysis is irrational because it is unrealistic. Undue rationality destroys the sympathy needed to comprehend the welter of sentiments generated in a child when he wakes up to the hard facts of human coexistence. So some who see themselves as children's friends have set about depriving the traditional fear-inspiring figures of their fearfulness. Walt Disney's certainly charming movie "The Reluctant Dragon" is a good example. His dragon is a thoroughly good-hearted, jolly old fellow—nothing to be afraid of. Such a story may be a means of amusement, but it will assuredly not act as an instrument of catharsis; the clouds overhead will not be blown away.

One further cause of the impoverishment of the folk-tale tradition has still to be mentioned: its literary fixation. As long as the tradition was oral, it was flexible; as soon as it was reduced to writing, it lost a good deal of that flexibility. The teller of a tale, unlike the reader of it, can introduce variations. He can elaborate on the aspects which fascinate the particular child or children before him and downplay the others, and in the case of close contact, the little listeners themselves will be able to steer the stream of the account—an invaluable help to the effectiveness, sociological as well as psychological, of the stories. Even if we were to assume that the bookish versions emerging in the nineteenth century were in line with the best variants handed down—an assumption not entirely unrealistic, for many editors, like Jacob and Wilhelm Grimm, had too much veneration for the past to change very much—even if we were to assume that the optimal forms elaborated, over the centuries, by the process of collective cooperation were in fact preserved for the future, this would only mean that the *outlines* were entirely satisfactory from the point of view of child psychology and the needs of socialization; it would not mean that it would not be desirable to have that flexibility as to *detail* which oral transmission can offer and literary fixation has to deny.

To what extent is the socializing fairy tale still alive at the end of the twentieth century? The question is easier to pose than to answer, for there is conflicting evidence. Even a far-flung empirical (questionnaire-using) investigation would not tell us all, for it would not be sufficient to know how often parents or educators tell fairy tales; we should need to know as well the content and character of each of these fairy tales. We have, on the one hand, a rather widespread attitude to the effect that fairy tales are old-wives' tales and should be gotten rid of, like popular superstitions, for instance; we have, on the other, the hard fact that radio, television, and the movies continue to cultivate the old tradition in however bowdlerized a form, that storybooks of the traditional kind are frequently reissued and widely bought, and that even commercial advertising generally presupposes some knowledge of at least the most beloved tales and figures. Indeed, even oral transmission has not come to a complete stop. The task of this book, however, is not statistical, but analytic, and our analysis has shown, to say the least, that the folk tale, that sister of the folkway, was, and still is, a most important aid in the elaboration and perpetuation of a societal ethos.

Rationalism has, however, not only tried to oust the fairy story from the nursery; it has also endeavored to provide a substitute: the fable. We must discuss it in due detail. But before we do so, we must cast a brief glance at a phenomenon at one time closely allied to the fairy tale, though now largely bereft of importance: the saga. The next section is devoted to it.

THE SAGA

115. In the classic literature on folk poetry, little difference is made between fairy tale and saga. Wilhelm Grimm, for instance, offers us no clearly defined dividing line between the two. This is partly due to the general dislike of the romantics for the pigeonhole: life, they felt, is too multiform, but also too floating in its forms, to allow of universal definitions. But there is a second reason as well, and it is more important. Both fairy tale and saga go back to some primeval stock of ideas the content of which we cannot fully comprehend. We see it merely in and behind the folklore of later times. We know enough of it, however, to realize that this lost philosophy of early man was largely mythical, indeed, that it was largely a mythologizing of the forces of nature. Awakening culture needs an element of this kind. Without going so far as Henri Bergson and speaking of a myth-making function, it is true that man, since he is endowed with a mind, has a desire to understand the universe in the midst of which he has his being, and this desire is satisfied by a certain kind of poetizing, the poetizing which we call mythology. This mythology split in the course of time into two separate halves. We might well, with Bergson, speak here of a divergent evolution. One half moved in the direction of the classic fairy tale; the other, in the direction of the historical saga. Thus the myth of the winter, and the winter's night, which swallows up the friendly season and the sun became, on the one hand, the fairy tale of "The Sleeping Beauty" awakened from her slumber by Prince Charming, the symbol of spring, and, on the other, the saga of Brunhild and Siegfried, the meaning of which is in the final analysis, in spite of all the dissimilar detail, quite the same.

It is this similarity, due to the common origin, which makes it difficult to separate saga and fairy tale in a completely convincing manner. Yet if it is true that there has been divergent evolution, it must be possible to indicate broad contrasts, and they will do in lieu of discriminating definitions. One such contrast emerges very clearly when we compare two versions of the same story, originally quite obviously part and parcel of some unitary primal lore. Both in the German fairy tale known as "The Juniper Tree" (no. 47 in the Grimm collection) and in the Greek saga of the House of Atreus, a father unknowingly eats his own offspring's flesh, but the consequences of this gruesome canni-balistic meal are very different in the two cases. In the fairy tale all ends hap-pily: the devoured boy is magically brought back to life. In the saga all ends un-happily. The dreadful sin works an hereditary curse which involves the luckless families of the two protagonists, Atreus and Thyestes. Atreus was the father (or possibly grandfather) of Agamemnon, who was murdered by his wife, Cly-temnestra, who had taken Aegisthes, the son of Thyestes, for her paramour. Not enough of this, the son of Agamemnon and Clytemnestra, Orestes, avenges his sire by killing his mother—a deed of hatred in which he is aided and abetted by his sister Electra. These are merely the bare bones of the story. If it could be told in all its detail, it would reveal itself as still more dreadful than our few sentences would indicate.

The fairy story told by the brothers Grimm ends with the statement that father, daughter, and resurrected son were "in a very happy mood" and sat down to a joyful meal. This ending brings out the first contrast which we wish to demonstrate. The fairy tale is optimistic; the saga, pessimistic—surely a de-cisive difference. We shall go into the ultimate reason for this dissimilarity in a moment. It will reveal to us the specific contribution which the saga makes, or rather made, to the development of a societal ethos. Here let us, as a prelimi-nary, consider the more superficial reasons for the divergence of the two evolu-tions. The fairy story is addressed to the young; the saga, to the adult popula-tion. The child needs reassurance about the dangers of life, a dose of optimism, so to speak, and he receives it. The adult knows too much about reality to be soothed by appeals to his imagination. He would rather hear a tale which squares with his life experience. This difference in the audience explains a num-ber of further differences. The hero of the fairy tale is leaving home and wander-ing off—a symbolization of the child's emergence from the nursery and entry into the adult world. In the course of his travels he meets the supernatural, dragon or witch or whatever else it may be. In the saga the supernatural breaks into the workaday scene, the domestic sphere of the protagonist, creating havoc there, as ill fortune so often does in ordinary life. The miraculous is not sought; it comes unbidden and is unwelcome. With this feature goes a certain tendency, observable in the saga material, to be specific about the place and time of the events. Sagas are often localized; fairy tales, rarely, if ever. The point is im-portant, for it shows up a drift, within the line of evolution which we are analyz-ing, toward a certain relative—however narrowly limited—realism.

This drift toward realism is met by another and, in a sense, opposed tend-ency: namely, the tendency to mythologize historical personalities. Early thought humanized divinities, but it also divinized humans. Thus the Ostro-gothic king Theodoric (d. 526) became Dietrich of Bern of the Nibelungen saga, and Attila, the leader of the Huns (d. 453), the Etzel of the same saga complex. This link with history, however attenuated it may become, imparts a modicum of factualness to the saga material.

But the use of historical names or the reference to concrete times and places contributes very little to the realism of the saga. There is enough of unbridled imagination left to counterbalance such feeble elements of factualness. What does make the saga relatively realistic, and thereby in sharp contrast to the fairy tale, is the deep knowledge that human wishing and even willing are woefully powerless in the world of hard facts. The autocentric child still entertains the happy delusion that he is the king as well as the center of the universe and that therefore his desires are paramount. The allocentric adult has learned the bitter lesson that the world we live in is a world of resistances—absolute in the case of the forces of nature, but also hard to defeat in the case of collective powers or the volitions, the self-preferences, of one's fellow-men. The optimism of the fairy tale stems from the dream that our wishes are fulfillable; the pessimism of the saga, from the realization that they are not.

Yet even this factor is not the core of the saga's relative realism; even the painful insight that our strivings all too often come to nothing is not the ultimate root of the factualness of the saga. The innermost core of the sagas, the most painful insight on which they rest, is the concept of *guilt*, and it is by discussing, by exposing, and by denouncing guilt that they contribute so mightily to the evolution of the societal ethos. The two arch-enemies of social integration—lust and greed—meet us at this point once again. The tragedy of the House of Atreus is a tragedy due to the sin of lust, to the sin forbidden in the Sixth Commandment of Mount Sinai; the tragedy of the Nibelungen, a tragedy due to the sin of greed, the sin forbidden in the Seventh Commandment of the Old Testament. "Thou shalt not commit adultery"—but Thyestes seduces the wife of his brother Atreus, with the result that a deep hatred arises in the latter's heart which in turn induces him to avenge himself in the dreadful manner which we have described—by offering to Thyestes the flesh of his own children as a meat dish. "Thou shalt not steal," or, as the Tenth Commandment even more strongly expresses it: "Thou shalt not covet they neighbor's house . . . nor any thing that is his"—but Wotan so much craves the Rhine gold that he is prepared to commit any crime in order to secure it. The Rhine of this saga is not the river in Germany's west, but the water around the whole world as imagined by the ancients; the gold is not the precious metal, but the reflection of the sun on the surface of the sea (see Stark, *Sociology of Religion*, v 60). What Wotan desires, then, is in effect universal dominion, the ownership of all the earth. But a curse is connected with the "ring": the wages of sin are, even for the archaic consciousness, death. Wotan's sinfulness sets in train a series of evils involving some innocent figures as well as the guilty ones and leads in the end to the "twilight of the gods," their destruction, for even they must pay the price of their misdeeds.

The fate of the sinners in the two sagas reminds us of the fall of Adam and Eve recorded in the third chapter of the Book of Genesis. In all three cases, a moral prohibition is wantonly set aside, and disaster follows. That disaster follows upon the wanton setting aside of a moral prohibition is the great message of the sagas to the human race. Even their formal structure shows that the concept of guilt is at the very heart of the saga tales. Whereas, in the fairy tales, everything leads up to the happy ending—in other words, whereas in the fairy tales the climax lies at the end of the exposition—in the saga the climax lies in the middle and is the center of the story. Indeed, the second part—the description of the evils which ensue when the moral order is broken—carries as a rule more weight than the first part which merely prepares the peripeteia. But the fateful misdeed around which the detail of the sagas is arranged is the center, not only of the sagas themselves, i.e., of the saga stories, but also of the image of man, the philosophical anthropology which they contain. To the sagas, man is essentially a creature who is apt to become guilty. And in other respects, too, man is seen as beset by difficulties and dangers of which not the least is the darkness within his own self. The hero of the fairy tales is, to use a popular phrase, ten feet tall; the chief figure of the sagas is reduced to human proportions. We can hardly speak of heroes in discussing the sagas; their protagonists are often afraid when they meet the unexpected, the demonic, or the numinous. "It seems in fact one of the innermost and most essential differences between the two literary modes," an outstanding expert has written,

> that the one represents the heroic and enterprising; the other, the human and pain-laden experience of the world and the beyond. We are confronted not only with different degrees of vitality, but with basically dissimilar statements concerning the relations of men and fate, life and world, reality and the transcendent. . . . The popular saga is bound to end tragically because, knowing the predominance of the demonic element in and around man, it is unable to bring events to a successful conclusion. . . . The fairy tale leads to the conquest of evil; in the saga, on the other hand, the effort regularly miscarries. It miscarries because he who is entrusted with the deed of liberation is not a hero: he is full of fear, he runs away, he yells with pain, he is not equal to his sufferings, etc. He is like one of us, a creature all too human and imperfect, and therefore no match at all for the overpowering demonic and mythical forces [Kurt Ranke, "Betrachtungen zum Wesen und zur Funktion des Märchens," in *Wege der Märchenforschung*, ed. Karlinger, pp. 339, 336, 337].

The terror of the unknown which pursues man contributes little, if anything, to the development of a societal ethos, but the consciousness of human fallibility which, in the sagas, is connected with it, certainly does. Perhaps we may, in this context, speak of a loss of innocence. The child to whom the fairy tale is addressed knows little, if anything, about the everlasting contest between good and evil. The adult has already eaten of the tree of this knowledge. He has discovered his own inherent self-regard, his desire to ride roughshod over his fellow-men, and the saga reminds him of the sinfulness which lurks within him, which may lead him into temptation and guilt, and finally into disaster and destruction.

The pattern which we have discovered in the tragedy of the House of Atreus and also in the Nibelungen complex—the pattern of the fall from grace—pervades most of the saga literature. Without thinking specifically of our two examples, Lutz Röhrich could therefore write in a general vein in *Märchen und Wirklichkeit* (p. 26): "The orientation of the saga is decidedly much more ethical than that of the fairy tale; crime and punishment are the essential conceptions of its strict ethic." And in his other important book, *Sage und Märchen* (pp. 48, 49, 87, 80), he gives us copious illustrations, culling them from the collection entitled *Deutsche Sagen* edited by the brothers Grimm (see also p. 61

concerning Arnold Bühli's Swiss collection, *Mythologische Landeskunde von Graubünden* (2 vols. [Aargau, 1958, 1966]). He writes:

> The sagas relating to revenants are almost always connected with definite motives of guilt and transgression; such sagas exemplifying immoral human conduct represent, roughly speaking, beside the demonological saga, one half of our whole material. The collection of the Grimms provides a multitude of interesting instances demonstrating the rigorous morality of the sagas and their belief in inescapable retribution. A murderer is overtaken by vengeance (no. 131), and the bold burglar perishes (no. 129). Incredibly hard is the punishment which, in number 231, falls on a juvenile sinner against the Fourth Commandment: not at once obeying the word of his father, he is magically condemned to remain forever standing on his feet, and he wastes away. Punishment for incest (no. 358) dwells cheek by jowl with punishment for perjury (nos. 101 et seq.). . . . Most frequent are sagas connected with curses (nos. 229 et seq.) and above all stories about the desecration of bread (nos. 234 et seq.). . . . A numerous interconnected group of tales could be described as "legal sagas"; but even in them the law is seen more from its negative side, the side of its transgression or undue manipulation.

One recurring theme is, not surprisingly, the shifting of border stones, and kindred transgressions in field and forest are also recorded, together with the severe consequences which they entail. One detail which demonstrates the difference between fairy tale and saga with particular clarity is the treatment of dead mothers revisiting the earth. In the fairy tales it is loving mothers who come back to care for their children; in the sagas it is child-murderesses who must, in expiation, forever wash diapers by the brook. Summing up his far-flung observations, Röhrich writes in conclusion: "To the dominant conceptions of the saga in general belongs an unbending idea of justice: each crime against community and fellow-man must be atoned for, be it even after death."

If it is uncertain to what extent the fairy tale has survived into the twentieth century, it cannot be doubted that the saga has lost much of its ground and much of its grip. Two reasons can be adduced for this involution, one major and one minor. The minor reason is the prevailingly aristocratic character of the traditional stories. Atreus is king of Argos; Gunnar or Gunther is king of the Nibelungs; the protagonists of both saga complexes are in contact with gods, goddesses, and godlings. All this is not sympathetic to the modern democratic mind. Yet another factor is far more decisive. The classic sagas are based on a collectivistic concept of guilt. The sin of one is the sin of a whole family, an entire descent group. A quotation from Aeschylus' *Agamemnon* shows this very clearly:

> . . . whensoe'er the sire
> Breathed forth rebellious fire . . .
> His children's children read the reckoning plain,
> at last, in tears and pain

(*The House of Atreus*, trans. E. D. A. Morshead [London, 1881], p. 19). Such an ethic is not as acceptable to modern as it was to ancient man. The change-over from community to association (in the sense of Ferdinand Tönnies' terminology) has deprived it of all appeal. But, with the basic morality, the tales in which it was wrapped up necessarily had to lose credit.

Still, we must not exaggerate. The subject of crime and punishment can never lose interest. Its actuality is as great today as it has ever been. The message of the sagas was, to say the least, as clearly understandable and as clearly understood in the nineteenth century, when individualism reached its climax, as it was in the days of the Greek poets and Germanic bards. This enabled Richard Wagner to present, in the years between 1869 and 1876, his powerful tetralogy, *The Ring of the Nibelung*, and to be successful immediately. True, much of this success was due to the sublime music which underlies and underlines the stage production, but the text must surely also have counted for something. Odd, not to say ridiculous, when considered from a rational and rationalistic point of view, it assumes at once a character of grandeur if it is seen as a moral tale. Surely, nobody can remain entirely unimpressed when he is told, in so dramatic a manner, that even the Sky-God Wotan condemns himself to death and perdition when he oversteps the limits of law-abidingness, when his greed involves him in crime.

There is no generation, therefore, which does not need the message of the sagas and which is not the better for it. Nor has this voice become totally muted. There has been a change of form rather than an end to the saga tradition. The space vacated by epos and drama has been occupied more recently by the novel. John Galsworthy's *Forsyte Saga*, for instance, is by no means misnamed. Even here we have the sorry tale of a family's decay, and characteristically the climactic part is called "The Man of Property." It is Soames Forsyte's guilt to be unable to love: his possessiveness is too great to allow of a free unfolding of his more tender feelings, indeed, of his more human sympathies. Such sagas are to be found in all modern literatures: there is Zola's *Rougon-Macquart* series; there is Thomas Mann's *Buddenbrooks*; there is Gorki's *The Artamonov Business*. These are only a few titles; many more could be mentioned. In the evolution of a societal ethos, the contribution made by the saga may not be equal to that made by the fairy tale, but it would be wrong to underestimate the role which it has played.

THE FABLE

116. *The Concise Oxford Dictionary* defines the fable as a short story conveying a moral principle, and especially one which uses animals as characters. This simple description is apt to suggest—at least to an unsophisticated observer—that there is little difference between fable, on the one hand, and fairy tale and saga, on the other. The fable is a story conveying a moral principle. So, we have seen, is the fairy tale; so, too, the saga. The fable uses animals as characters; so does the fairy tale and, at times, though less frequently, also the saga. Of course, at a second look, dissimilarities do appear. The moral principle contained in fairy tale and saga is merely implied. It is wrapped up in clouds; in the fable, it stands out and is clear, indeed, unambiguous. The animal characters in the fairy tale cooperate with humans; the realms of creation are mixed. In the fable the animal characters interact with each other; the animals form a society of their own, though human traits are attributed to them. The horses and bears and bees and toads of the fairy tale are mysterious creatures; they know secrets; they work miracles. In the fable they are merely exemplifications of psychic properties—the wolf of greed, the fox of cunning, the lamb of innocence—and there is nothing esoteric about them. Still, these differences have been regarded by many as inessential. It was, once again, the great romantics, who were prepared to include fairy tale and fable in the same category: Herder and the brothers Grimm. And they saw, or rather fancied they saw, a deeper reason why the two types of popular poetry should not be contrasted; both, they believed, had grown from the same mother soil, the collective unconscious. Wilhelm Grimm used the terms fairy tale, saga, and fable as synonyms and expressly asserted that the fable, like the other two variants, had come "out of the mouth of the people." Jacob Grimm is said to have been more careful in his formulations, but even he was not inclined to make sharp distinctions. Still, he discovered one trait which might have led him on to deeper insights if only he had followed his intuition further. The fable, he recognized, often conveys, not a moral doctrine, but a rule of prudence (see Klaus Doderer, *Fabeln* [Zurich, 1970], pp. 187, 247, 248, 254). Thus he had an inkling at least of the wide ditch which, in point of fact, divides the two forms.

This inability to distinguish *distinguenda* has persisted. Reinhard Dithmar, for instance, in his book *Die Fabel* (Paderborn, 1971) asserts that it would be mere hairsplitting—an entirely "artificial" effort—to make a distinction between fable and parable, e.g., the fables of Aesop and the parables of the Gospel. Both are instances of allegorical poetizing. "In spite of many attempts at separation," he writes (p. 98; see also pp. 93, 96, 97), "there is no difference between fable and parable which could be considered as a matter of principle or as generally applicable." This, however, is even more erroneous than the position occupied by Wilhelm and Jacob Grimm, for the typical fable presents a sharply profiled, logically univocal piece of advice; whereas the parables of the Gospel, though by no means unclear, carry a much more complex meaning, and have rightly been compared to an inexhaustible well. It is possible—nay, necessary—to meditate about the Logia of Jesus, but the great authors of fables would have been very unhappy if they had been told that their preaching was not as plain as a pikestaff.

Dithmar based his view on an older study of considerable authority, especially among Protestant theologians, Adolf Jülicher's *Die Gleichnisreden Jesu* (Tübingen, 1910; repr. Darmstadt, 1963), and from this text we can learn a good deal. "The fable owes its origin not to the poet, but to the orator," Jülicher wrote (pp. 98, 99) and Dithmar repeats (*Die Fabel*, pp. 193; see also pp. 120, 121, 122). "The oldest fables were neither sung nor written, but spoken; they were invented on the spur of the moment and in order to serve the needs of the moment—not in order to convey a rule of wisdom or an ethical proposition, but in order to master a difficult situation in which the speaker found himself, and to make sure of the acceptance of his opinion and his judgment." Dithmar provides a very good illustration of this thesis. It is taken from the twelfth chapter of the Second Book of Kings. The prophet Nathan is called upon to reproach King David for his adultery with Bathsheba and his *de facto* murder of her husband, Uriah. The task was difficult, the situation awkward, but Nathan helped himself by telling the guilty potentate a parable:

> There were two men in one city, the one rich and the other poor. The rich man had exceeding many sheep and oxen. But the poor man had nothing at all but one little ewe lamb. . . . And when a certain stranger was come to the rich man, he spared to take of his own sheep and oxen to make a feast for that stranger . . . but took the poor man's ewe, and dressed it for the man that was come to him. And David's anger being exceedingly kindled against that man, he said to Nathan: As the Lord liveth, the man that hath done this is a child of death. . . . And Nathan said to David: Thou art that man.

It is, of course, quite impossible to prove historically and inductively that the fable as a literary category arose in this way, as a rhetorician's artifice rather than as an outgrowth of the collective unconscious, but a good deal speaks in favor of the Jülicher thesis. The educator often finds himself in the position of Nathan the Prophet, not because he is afraid of the child, but because it is not easy to open the child's ear and mind to the admonition which he has to administer. A story is sure to go down better than a sermon. The young mind simply is not yet equipped to receive abstract propositions; it needs to be taught by example and allegory. It is, surely, the essence of the fable to *expose* a truth (or a piece of wisdom) by presenting it *disguised*, and this is a trick, a stratagem, a counsel of cleverness, which points to an origin in rationality and not to a root in irrationality like that of popular romancing. Approaching the problem from an entirely different angle, Stith Thompson, with his unmatched knowledge of all the relevant material, makes a remark which also goes to show that the fable must not be carelessly bracketed with saga and fairy tale. This is what he writes (*The Folktale*, p. 218): "Of the five or six hundred fables belonging to the two literary traditions of India and of Greece, fewer than fifty seem to have been recorded from oral story-tellers, and most of these are of relatively rare occurrence. Even when stories of this kind are actually taken up from unlettered persons, one must be very careful in assuming that they have had any considerable history as oral tales."

It seems, then, that, in contradistinction to fairy tale and saga, the fable is made, not grown, the product of individual intelligence, not of the collective unconscious—in Sumner's terminology, that it is, not crescive, but enacted. It has, in most cases, sprung from individual educative effort, not from the anonymous forces of society. Yet the influence of these forces was certainly not nil; indeed, it must not be underestimated. As the *mot juste* and the well-turned phrase gain currency and enter the canon of the language, so the witty and pithy fable takes wings and spreads far and wide. Differently expressed: there forms a definite fable tradition in which the best, in the sense of the most effective, fables are preserved and handed on. Thus "from ancient down to modern times, many motifs have been reformulated again and again, for instance the well-known fable of wolf and lamb by Aesop, Phaedrus, Boner, Steinhöwel,

Luther, Waldis, Alberus, Hans Sachs, La Fontaine, Lessing, James Thurber, Helmut Arntzen, and many others besides" (Dithmar, *Die Fabel*, p. 121). What happens is that the simile first used in a concrete situation (called, by Dithmar, ibid., p. 123, its "seat in life"), becomes independent of it and drifts away, to gain, in the course of time, general or even universal currency. To that extent, then, the collective forces count for something even in the history of the fable; to that extent, there is a parallel between fable, on the one hand, and saga and fairy tale, on the other. But an essential difference remains. Saga and fairy tale are told and retold by ordinary people, often utterly unsophisticated, utterly simple. The fables are formulated and reformulated by men—like the twelve paraded in our quotation from Reinhard Dithmar—who are anything but unsophisticated, who are sharp-edged intellectuals with a flair for point and wit. And this fact makes all the difference. "The good fable," one of the best analysts of this literary mode has written (Doderer, *Fabeln*, p. 52), "has never been a naïve form of art. Its stylistic leanness and its tendency toward abstraction are, from the very moment of inception, given by the fundamental character of the whole category."

Even where fable and fairy tale come very close to each other, the contrast remains. Both paint in black and white, but the motives behind this technique are not the same. The fairy tale wishes to intensify an *experience*; the fable strives to achieve a better effect, to serve a didactic *purpose* more efficiently. If this looks like hairsplitting, a brief consideration will prove that it is not. A purpose is consciously pursued; it springs from reasoning on the part of the speaker and aims at the reasoning faculty on the side of the listener. "The fable is . . . a linguistic form of critical thought," asserts Dithmar (*Die Fabel*, p. 187), and he is right. "It is turned toward the intellect. It asks to be discussed; it challenges criticism and wishes to sharpen the critical acumen. For this reason it cannot be read or listened to unreflectingly." Fairy tale and saga therefore belong to an entirely different realm. "The fable is totally useless as a vehicle for the transmission of emotions," writes Doderer (*Fabeln*, p. 238), stressing more strongly the negative aspect and thereby once again hitting the nail on the head. But the evocation and satisfaction of emotions are the ultimate effect (the ultimate purpose, if the word may be used here) of the telling of, and the listening to, a typical fairy tale.

The rationalistic character of the fable can easily be proved in two ways—negatively and positively. We do *not* find the fable where rationality has not developed on a large scale. Speaking of Central and Southern Africa, Stith Thompson shows that many foreign fairy tales have penetrated into the area, but "the Aesop tradition seems to be almost entirely lacking": "When we consider all of the borrowings which have thus far been reported [from Africa], we find a total of 119 of the 718 types listed in the Aarne–Thompson catalogue" (*The Folktale*, pp. 285, 286). This is characteristic. But far more convincing is the positive fact that we *do* find the fable, and find it flourishing in the most vigorous manner, where rationality has become the hallmark of an age. The classic times of rationalism are also the classic times of fable-writing. There are two historical climaxes to the development of this literary mode: the sixteenth century (the century of Luther and Calvin) and the eighteenth century—more precisely the time between 1730 and 1790 (the age of Voltaire). The 130 years in between, the High Baroque, produced little, if anything, in this line, and the Romantic Movement, if possible, even less. Among the Reformers we must mention in particular, in this context, Philipp Melanchthon, who in 1526 published a treatise *De utilitate fabularum*. The pedagogical point of view is paramount. To remain, for the moment, in Germany: the country produced, between 1730 and 1760, a flood of fable books; Breitinger, Bodmer (known as admirers of William Shakespeare), Triller, Stoppe, Hagedorn, Gleim, Gellert, Lichtwer, Pfeffel, and Lessing (the great protagonist of toleration) are the most important names. In England, it was also the mentality usually described as the Enlightenment which fostered the appearance and spread of fable collections. Samuel Richardson and John Gay are the most brilliant authors who entered this field. The latter published a first series of *Fables* in 1727, and a second in 1738; the former followed in 1740 with his *Aesop's Fables*. Both collections achieved very wide circulation.

The name of Aesop reminds us that the fable is not an exclusively modern phenomenon, even if the Enlightenment marks its historical acme. Indeed, many of the fables retold in the eighteenth century were first told in antiquity. The very title of Richardson's book shows this, though he indicated even on the title page that he was publishing Aesop's fables "with instructive morals and reflections" of his own. The question which arises at this point is this: Does the fact that fables were already current 2,500 years ago not, after all, speak for a birth of this whole literary category out of the collective unconscious, and not out of the conscious educational effort on the part of individual educators? One argument seems to point in this direction. It has been suggested by Martin Luther (see Dithmar, *Die Fabel*, p. 36) and more recently by the scholar August Hausrath (*Aesopische Fabeln* [Munich, 1940], p. 114) that a man of this name never existed and that Aesop was, like Homer, an "imaginative universal," a personal name fictitiously appended to impersonal or superpersonal forces—an "incarnation of the poetizing popular spirit of Greece." The suggestion of Luther and Hausrath is probably correct. Assertions like those of Herodotus—namely, that Aesop was the slave of a man called Iadmon and that he was murdered in the year 560 B.C.—deserve no credence whatsoever. The parallel between Homer and Aesop seems correct; both (if they existed at all) were at most editors of some traditional material, not the creators of it. But this fact does not force us to come to the same conclusions regarding Aesop as we did, at the beginning of our third volume, with regard to Homer. The traditional material put in order by Homer or some other editor was in the first place popular poetry, shaped by the cooperation of innumerable bards; the traditional material collected by Aesop was the product of pedagogic effort, evidence of the existence of an educational technique, and hence, in its inception, individualistic and rational. The salient contrast thus remains.

Since we know nothing for certain about Aesop, the following two or three sentences must necessarily be considered as speculative. We saw in Volume III that the alleged blindness of Homer places him, with some probability, in a certain professional category: that of the wandering bards who went from place to place to tell their stories of heroes long since dead. The assertion that Aesop was a slave (as was Phaedrus who brought Aesop's stories to Rome in the first century A.D.) also tells us something about him. Slaves were, not surprisingly, inclined to the political left, and this establishes a definite similarity with the writers of the eighteenth century, the century of gathering revolutionary forces —not indeed a similarity with Samuel Richardson, but certainly with men like John Gay and Gotthold Ephraim Lessing in Germany. This kinship in personal–political outlook is matched by a comparability in socio-economic background. The cities developing along the Ionian coast gave birth to a vigorous bourgeoisie, just as the developing national economies of early modern times did, and the bourgeoisie have been the chief carriers of fable stories; fairy tales, on the other hand, have always been treasured and transmitted mainly by the lowest classes, especially the peasantry, but also by such types as soldiers, sailors, day-laborers, shepherds, hawkers, etc. (On this point, see Woeller, "Der soziale Gehalt und die soziale Funktion des deutschen Volksmärchens," 405, 406.) In short, rationalism is rationalism, wherever it appears. Plato, who wished to banish Homer from his ideal republic, was prepared to allot Aesop an honored place. In the same way, the pedagogues of the eighteenth century desired to drive the fairy tale from the nursery and replace it with the fable: hence, the amazing proliferation of the fable literature at the time.

But let us turn, or rather return, to the analysis of the fable as a possible contributor to the development of a societal ethos. Our task is relatively easy, for fable writers, being rationalists, have an inherent tendency to theorize about their craft. We shall, for simplicity's sake, base our remarks more particularly on one of them, Lessing, and that for two reasons: he is outstandingly self-analytical and self-critical, and he comes relatively late in the day so that his *Abhandlungen über die Fabel*, published in 1759, can be regarded as a kind of summing-up, a survey of much work done and theorizing gone through.

We characterized the fable above as essentially an artifact—as "enacted" and not "crescive"—and this characterization is amply confirmed in Lessing's treatise. He defines Aesop's fable as "a poetical invention which pursues a certain purpose," and says of himself: "the one thing I [always] bear in mind is the fable's utility" (*Werke* V, ed. Franz Bornmüller [Leipzig & Vienna, n.d.], pp. 51, 104). Even the *Abhandlungen* are not a purely theoretical treatise, but a textbook intending to teach the correct way to write a proper fable. The main advice he gives to those who wish to enter the field is to be as brief as they possibly can. "Brevity is the soul of the fable." "The story of the fable must be . . . concentrated; it must be as far as possible without embellishments and figures of speech and be satisfied with one thing: clarity." "It must not be difficult at all to recognize the instruction contained in the fable; much rather must it be difficult, if I may so express it, not to recognize it" (ibid., pp. 53, 99, 65). The final task of all fabulation is, of course, moral education. A fable could be called "an illustration of applied ethics." "Whoever conceives the idea of putting anything but a moral proposition into a fable mishandles the matter" (ibid., pp. 53, 76). The great educational trick is to reduce a general ethical truth to the compass of a single case. (We might think here of Nathan's one poor man who is robbed of his ewe-lamb by a rich one: the single case inculcates the quite general ethical demand that the strong must not oppress the weak.) By this artifice the moral doctrine is made visible, as it were (*der anschauenden Erkenntnis fähig*) (ibid., p. 66)—visible like an event, perhaps even visible like a thing. And, being visible, it will then be able to enter into the individual's mind like any other kind of knowledge or object of observation, like a picture which we see and the memory of which we retain.

Up to this point, Lessing remains, as the reader can see, strictly within the framework of factualness, but now he appears to make a large concession to the craving of the young for fiction. The concrete case, with the help of which the moral maxim to be propagated is to be made visible and impressive, must be depicted as a real happening, even though it was thought up by the fabulist. The author of the fable must "raise his piece of poetical invention from the level of [mere] possibility to the level of actuality" (ibid., p. 78; see also p. 74). As Lessing also expresses it (ibid., p. 79): it is necessary to ascribe, to the specific instance used, the character of reality. This appears to bring the fable closer to the fairy tale, but the appearance is somewhat deceptive. For Lessing does not in fact wish to pander to the imagination. Even the fictitious element which he admits and indeed recommends is merely meant as a clever trick, as part and parcel of a strategy. Perhaps this will become quite clear if we use for illustration once again Nathan's attack on David. If Nathan had started his harangue with the words "You have entertained illicit relations with Uriah's wife and in effect killed Uriah. This is as if a rich man were to rob a poor man of his only ewe-lamb . . . ," the impression made on the sinning king would have been nil. His defenses would have gone up at once. But Nathan is not so inept. He leads David, to use a homely phrase, down the garden path. He arouses his ire against the "rich man," induces him to condemn that culprit, and only then comes out with the words "*Thou* art that man"—words which must crush the malefactor, who has in fact spoken his own judgment. The fabulist, Lessing suggests, must always proceed in this fashion. The fable may in truth be no more than a parable, but it must be dressed up as "something which has really happened" (ibid., p. 78). Only in this way can the story told receive the power and the punch which it needs in the pursuit of its grand purpose, the purpose of moral education.

But there is yet another element of fictitiousness, and the reader may well have wondered why it has not yet been brought up. It certainly strikes the eye as no other feature of this literary type does and seems to demand immediate attention; we have, however, postponed its discussion because we wanted to advance from the secondary to the truly essential aspects of the whole phenomenon. The fable in the narrower sense of the word uses *animals* as characters. It confronts, not the rich man and the poor man, as Nathan's address to David does, but wolf and lamb. Why? The question is analytically of supreme importance; the answer, very revealing. Lessing gives in effect two answers, but the one is rather flat. The wolf is known to be cruel, the lamb is known to be weak, he says. If we spoke instead of Nero and Britannicus, we should not be so generally and so readily understood. The point may be conceded, but, as we have just said, it is not particularly essential.

Essential for our understanding is Lessing's second reply. The good author, he urges, uses animals rather than men as protagonists in his story because their doings, and especially their sufferings, leave us comparatively cool. Our judgments are not clouded by aroused emotions, and therefore instruction has no obstacles to contend with. This whole attitude is very characteristic of rationalism and reveals to us the intimate character of fable writing and the weakness and strength of the fable as an ethos-developing device. A somewhat longer quotation is in order here. "The heroic and dramatic poets make the stirring up of the passions their prime end," Lessing writes (ibid., pp. 71, 87).

> The fabulist, on the other hand, has nothing to do with our passions and is concerned only with the gathering of knowledge on our part. . . . Nothing darkens our intellect more than the passions. Therefore the fabulist must avoid the activation of the passions as much as he possibly can. But how can he avoid this—the stimulation of the sentiment of pity, for instance—better than by making the [possible] objects of it less perfect than we are and by putting into the place of humans animals or still more inconsiderable creatures? . . . We feel pity for the lamb; but this sympathy is so weak that it does not sensibly interfere with the vivid apprehension of the moral maxim to be presented.

The radical difference between fairy tale and fable is now clearly in focus. The fairy tale induces the listener to identify with the hero of the tale, the poor boy who is maltreated by his wicked step-mother, for instance. The fable, on the other hand, wishes to prevent, or at least to weaken, such identification, identification with the innocent lamb attacked by the cruel wolf, for instance. But how then can the message of the story reach the listener's innermost self? Doderer (*Fabeln*, p. 80) is quite right: the figures of the fable are merely marionettes. Their cavorting may amuse, but it will hardly move. It is, of course, true that the fable author also aims at his audience, indeed, that he, too, wishes to bring about a sort of identification (intellectual identification). The listener or reader is invited to ask himself: Am I so stupidly innocent, so blindly trusting, as the lamb? Am I so disgustingly greedy, so unspeakably brutal, as the wolf? But the mental mechanism by which the fairy tale achieves its effect is entirely missing. Psychologically the two are as different as night and day. The fable addresses the conscious mind of the child, the fairy-tale the unconscious, and who, in this post-Freudian and post-Jungian age, will venture to say that the former approach can ever be as fruitful as the latter? Besides, the greatest strength of the fable as a didactic device—its clarity—is also its worst weakness. It leaves nothing for the listening child to muse about and to work through. Driven to its logical conclusion, the presentation of an ethical maxim as recommended by Lessing is no different from the presentation of a mathematical proposition. Both may be said to convey a truth, but the recognition that twice two is four can hardly be expected to have an influence on human conduct. Rationalism has its inherent limitations. Here they become painfully obvious. The fairy tale cannot be replaced by the fable. Those who believed that it could were sadly mistaken.

We must not exaggerate, however. The fable is, after all, *meant* to develop a personal ethos and thereby to raise the moral tone in the whole of society, and we should neither be unjust to the good intentions of the writers nor light-heartedly underestimate the beneficial influence of their writings. If the fable is not capable of laying first foundations for a personal and societal ethos, it may yet be able to confirm and support and even to refine the fundamental ethical conceptions once they exist. When both the moral attitude and the reasoning faculty have reached a certain level of maturity, an appeal to a young person's intellect and, through it, to his or her basic human sentiments may well be possible, indeed, effective. Some of the traditional fables evince a strong moral tendency. Thus, one or two of Aesop's pieces "have popularized the tales of those who make immoderate requests: the camel who asks for horns and as a punishment is given short ears, and the bees who pray for a sting but are punished by having their first sting fatal to themselves" (Thompson, *The Folktale*, p. 242). A good modern example of similar bearing is a fable told by the great preacher Abraham a Santa Clara (who died in the year 1709). It confronts two insects, one admirable for its deep sociality, the other despicable because of its crude selfishness—the silkworm and the spider.

> A spider noticed how intent the silkworm was on his work and how he incessantly produced silk. "Dear me," she said, "what a strange fellow you are, striving day and night to produce silk which other people use for their clothing while you, you poor fool, get nothing for your food except a miserable mulberry leaf! You plague yourself merely for the sake of others! I," the spider continued, "am in this respect much more intelligent; for although I also spin, I reap the benefit myself. I make nothing but threads or nets in which I catch gnats for myself. I should be a great fool if I were to tire myself out for the sake of others." The silkworm replied: "You are known as a poisonous beast and have no love whatever for your neighbor. Don't you realize that oxen plow for others, sheep grow wool for others, trees bear fruit for others? He is a wicked person who lives only for himself and does not, at the same time, serve his fellow-men!" [For the original text, see Doderer, *Fabeln*, pp. 138, 139.]

Formally, this story is certainly a proper fable, but its spirit is hardly typical of the species. It was written in the seventeenth century, which, unlike the sixteenth and the eighteenth, had no "genius" for this *métier*, as would have been said at the time. The seventeenth century was the age of the Counter Reformation, of renewed and re-advancing Catholicism, and Catholicism carried with it an ethos which was radically community-centered. Abraham a Santa Clara preached that communitarian ethos, but the great fable-writers of the Reformation and the Enlightenment entertained very different ideas. It is to them that we have to turn if we wish to see the tendency prevailing among the fabulists.

A fable frequently told and retold since ancient times is that of the lion and the mouse. A lion catches a mouse and intends to kill it. The mouse asks to be spared and pleads that, small as it is, it may yet be of use to the lion. The lion merely laughs at this idea, but lets the little fellow go. Then he has the misfortune to be caught in a net and is in dire straits. But he regains his liberty. The grateful mouse gnawed through the strings and so enabled him to get away.

The moral is clear: the powerful should not despise the powerless, or rather apparently powerless, for these may yet be of service *to them*. The argument is that the strong should be kind to the weak, not because this is right, but only because their own interests recommend such an attitude. Moral conduct appears as the reflection of a self-regarding life policy and no more. This, if it is ethos at all, is a low kind of ethos, calculating or utilitarian ethics—*Erfolgsethik* (ethics of success), as Max Weber calls it. It is not *Gesinnungsethik* (ethics of principle) which demands that good deeds be done for their own sake, simply because they are good, and that no ulterior purpose enter into human action. The characteristic ethos of most fables is calculating, utilitarian, and self-regarding. In the final analysis, they convey counsels of prudence and not moral imperatives.

Like Abraham a Santa Clara, Martin Luther was a churchman, but he stood on the other side of the fence. His religiosity was not cheerful like that of the Discalced Augustinian monk from Vienna, but somber and stern, and it was not strongly social but individualistic. While he had not yet reached the position to be taken up shortly afterward by Calvin, who thought of humanity in terms of "total corruption," his anthropology was only slightly less negative. His *Etliche Fabeln aus Aesop* (written in 1530 and published in 1557) have a preface in which he explains why he considers fables as salutary influences. "Truth is the most unwelcome thing on earth," he writes (for the text, see Dithmar, *Die Fabel*, p. 124).

> For that reason wise and highly placed men have composed fables and make one animal speak with another, as if they wanted to say: well, nobody wants to hear or suffer the truth and yet we cannot do without it; so we are forced to adorn it and dress it up in merry deceptive colors and pleasant fabulous tales. Because people do not agree to accept the truth out of the mouths of men, [it has to be presented] through the mouths of animals and beasts in order to be listened to after all.

What happens in the fables is that one animal tells another the unadorned truth, for instance, one wolf another wolf. But human beings too are wolves—two-legged wolves—and therefore it is right and meet that they should be exposed to fables. After all, *tua res agitur*: O man, it is *you* who is spoken of! Luther's comrade-in-arms, Erasmus Alberus, whose *Book of Virtue and Wisdom* (*Buch von der Tugend und Weisheit*) came out in 1550, expressed himself in very similar terms. So did Johann Jacob Breitinger nearly two centuries later, in 1740, when he launched his work *Critische Dichtkunst* (see Dithmar, *Die Fabel*, pp. 124, 125, 45, 46).

Virtue and wisdom may well be related, but if the term wisdom is interpreted as cleverness, as know-how, the two may be or become irreconcilable. Virtue is almost synonymous with selflessness, while cleverness naturally counsels self-defense and self-preference (the reason why Henri Bergson, in his ethical texts, developed an anti-intellectualist stance). A philosophy of the utilitarian, or *Erfolgsethik*, type may well cover up the conflict between virtue and cleverness, social and selfish conduct—cover it up to some extent, but the two will remain an either/or. On which side does the classic fable stand? Obviously on the side of cleverness. What it teaches is, not self-sacrifice, but self-assertion. Even Luther, stern moralist though he is, drifts in this direction. Where he praises Aesop (see Dithmar, *Die Fabel*, p. 34), he says that in Aesop's book of fables "one finds, in the guise of simple stories, the most exalted doctrine, warning, and instruction on how one should conduct oneself, as a householder, in one's dealings with and against the government and the citizens, so that one might live sagely and peacefully among the wicked people of this bad and false world." The individualistic point of view is obviously paramount. We do not find the parable of the silkworm and the spider among Martin Luther's tales!

The character and the drift of Martin Luther's fables can easily be gathered from one sample; the others are in spirit much like it. We have chosen, for our purpose, the story of the dog and the sheep (text in Doderer, *Fabeln*, p. 291).

> A dog sued a sheep before a court of law for [the return of] some bread which, he asserted, he had lent him. The sheep denied this [false] allegation. The dog thereupon called witnesses, and these had to be admitted. The first witness was the wolf who said, I know that the dog lent the sheep some bread. The eagle said, I was present on the occasion. The vulture said to the sheep, how can you so insolently deny the allegation? And so the sheep lost the case. He had, at great loss and at an unpropitious moment, to sell his wool in order to be able to pay for the bread which he did not owe. Moral: beware of your bad neighbors or submit in patience if you wish to dwell among men. For nobody is pleased if somebody else prospers; that is the way of the world.

With the best will imaginable, it is impossible to see in a fable of this kind a positive contribution to the development of a personal and/or societal ethos. Instead of strengthening that basic mutual confidence which is the only enduring basis for pacified human relationships, it sows suspicion and distrust, if not indeed the seeds of antagonism. What it fosters is, not a moral attitude, but downright cynicism.

Even in the eighteenth century, many fables are set in the same key, for instance, those of G. K. Pfeffel (*Poetische Versuche*; Basel, 1789). Indeed, the spirit which we illustrated in Luther's story of the dog and the sheep seems to be characteristic of the entire literary category. We see this if we go for a moment beyond the limits of our own cultural tradition. The *Panchatantra* is an ancient Indian collection, and it tells stories like the following. The owls and the crows are, to begin with, enemies. Then they patch up their quarrels and pretend to be friends. But the old hostility continues to smolder under the cinders, as the owls discover to their cost, when it is too late. The moral of the tale is this: "Never trust those with whom you have clashed in the past, even if they have made friends with you. See how the dwellings of the owls are on fire and are being devoured by the flames fanned by the crows!" (Dithmar, *Die Fabel*, pp. 22, 23). Thus, there is an old tradition whose moral bearing is, to say the least, in doubt. One well-informed modern observer, Klaus Doderer, goes much further and asserts that the fable is not ethical at all. "The fable conveys, when the truth is told, no moral doctrine; it merely gives advice on how to survive in an amoral world," he writes. "The fox within man is to be awakened. . . .

Humility, sympathy, religiousness, and piety are rarely presented as desirable qualities—much rather slyness, cunning, cleverness, and intelligence" (*Fabeln*, pp. 112, 113, 115). Later on in the volume (ibid., p. 243), the same judgment is formulated in even stronger terms: "The didactic fables do not illustrate a normative practical morality, much rather the opposite. They prove, in the examples which they offer, the one-sidedness, indeed, the imperfection, the stupidity, the pigheadedness, even the hopelessness, of the human condition and of human ways of thought." Doderer also quotes another careful analyst, Karl August Ott ("Lessing und La Fontaine: Von dem Gebrauche der Tiere in der Fabel," *Germanisch-romanische Monatsschrift* [1959], 235–66), who comes to the conclusion, as he does, that the fable contains a kind of "negative ethic."

But such criticisms go a little too far. There are fable books whose spirit is quite impeccable and even elevating. An instance is Ulrich Boner's collection, *Der Edelstein*, a work which dates from the middle of the fourteenth century. Even 300 or 400 years later we still find publications which, to say the least, mix merely prudential maxims with true morality. Jean de La Fontaine's *Fables* (1668–1694) are mainly a highly poetical retelling of the traditional tales, but a warm sympathy for the underdog runs through them and gives them a character of their own, a character of kindliness and warmth. D. W. Triller's *Neue Aesopische Fabeln* came out in 1740, right in the middle of the rationalist century, and though they show some of the basic traits of the Lutheran tradition —the typical Lutheran insistence on submission to the dictates of the stronger, for instance—they also oppose many of man's most deplorable vices, such as vanity, pride, undue curiosity, and the like.

We would, however, go even further. Not only is the fable redeemed through the good use which a few writers make of its patterns; the basic pattern itself harbors considerable strength. The fable—*each* fable—is an invitation to think about a moral problem inherent in interhuman relationships, and though this invitation may be lost on small children who cannot as yet handle abstract propositions, it is not lost on the older and riper of all age groups or, at any rate, need not be. The fable reminds the reader, first of all, of his animality in general. It reminds him further of some beastly qualities which adhere to him though they are irreconcilable with a truly humane conception of man. Is it right for a human being, it asks by implication, to be as stupid as the sheep, as sly as the fox, as greedy as the wolf, as brutal as the lion? But it does more than ask these questions. By personalizing (in the fictitious forms of animality) these immoral qualities, it arouses a disgust of them, with consequences which cannot but be conducive to the development of a personal and societal ethos. Even Doderer is not unaware of this fact though he allows it no influence on his final judgment. "Although it is by no means always the good traits which gain the upper hand," he writes (*Fabeln*, pp. 104, 105), "it is not difficult to recognize where the sympathies and antipathies lie" which the typical fable arouses. "The reader of the fable turns rather quickly against the figure who is shown in an unfavorable light, against the vicious, who, generally speaking, is in a position of power." This, however, is a genuinely moral attitude. The sheep, exploited by the dog and martyrized by the wolf, may be stupid, but it is also innocent. We may be invited, by the fable, not to be so stupid and innocent as the sheep, but we are also induced to side with him against his enemies. The fable does not permit identification with its heroes or anti-heroes, but it influences our habitual judgment; it thereby develops in us not only the tendency to take care of ourselves, but also the wish that decency and kindness prevail in our hard world.

It appears, then, that we must recognize in the fable a negative trait, leading to self-preference, and a positive trait, leading in the opposite direction, toward sociality. Needless to say, it is impossible to judge which influence is, generally speaking, the stronger. Even if we concentrate on one single author, it will often be difficult to make out whether he is on the side of the angels or not. But one cannot avoid the impression that, in the course of time, the sarcastic–negativistic tendency has gained on the moralizing, i.e., positive, tendency. It is customary, in this context, to say that the fable has become more an instrument of social criticism. Social criticism is necessary and salutary. But cynicism is not, and a good deal of modern writing is cynical and inviting to cynicism. James Thurber, for instance, whose two amusing volumes *Fables of Our Time* and *Further Fables of Our Time* came out in 1943 and 1956 respectively, often parodies the traditional stories and leads their moralizing aspects *ad absurdum*. The style and the animus of his humor are perhaps best seen in his version of the story of Little Red Riding Hood. This is how he concludes it:

> When the little girl opened the door of her grandmother's house, she saw that there was somebody in bed with a nightcap and nightgown on. She had approached no nearer than twenty-five feet from the bed when she saw that it was not her grandmother but the wolf, for even in a nightcap a wolf does not look any more like your grandmother than the Metro-Goldwyn lion looks like Calvin Coolidge. So the little girl took an automatic out of her basket and shot the wolf dead [*Fables of Our Time* (London, 1951), p. 5].

This is no more than a harmless joke, but other perversions of tradition are more serious. An old proverb says: "Early to bed and early to rise makes a man healthy, wealthy, and wise." Thurber's fable, called "The Shrike and the Chipmunks" (ibid., pp. 21, 22), ends with the following "moral": "Early to rise and early to bed makes a male healthy and wealthy and dead." There is even a story (entitled "The Courtship of Arthur and Al," p. 55) which expatiates on the unwisdom of overly hard work. Whether or not we share this opinion, in favor of which much may certainly be said, the plea to loaf in order to have "a long life and a wonderful time" is hardly in line with the American ethos, even of post-Calvinist days! In short, Thurber's fables are misnamed; they are in fact anti-fables. The cynical attitude, noticeable as early as the sixteenth century, reaches here, in the twentieth, a high-water mark.

Perhaps we may sum up the content of this section by saying that the fable, as a literary category, is an instrument which may be used both constructively and destructively, both for the furtherance of a self-regarding life policy and for the development of a genuinely social attitude. This is hardly surprising for it is, at least in modern times, in the sixteenth and eighteenth centuries, and even to a great extent in the twentieth century, the expression of individualistic value systems; the fairy tale and saga, on the other hand, are the outgrowths of folk societies, or rather of communities, in which self-furtherance does not stand very high in the established order of values, if it is regarded as legitimate at all, so far as the grownup person is concerned. Our final judgment of the educational value or unvalue of the fable is, as can be seen, two-sided, not to say ambiguous. But it cannot be anything else. The two-sidedness, the ambiguity, inheres in the phenomenon itself. The fable is essentially a tool, and any tool may be used for purposes both pure and poisonous.

THE LEGEND

117. In taking up the study of yet another type of educational tale—the legend —we are in fact returning to the true fostering soil of all folk literature, the collective life and its associated mentality. We noted that, in the saga, we meet with heroes who are obviously historical personalities though they have been somewhat transfigured and transformed. The same is true of the legend. But the parallel is rather superficial; the differences are much more telling. The legend is incomparably closer to reality; its subjects are, in the great majority of cases, persons whose birth and death dates we know and of whose doings we are reasonably well informed. Yet the contrast between the two literary modes is not only one of degree; it is also one of essence. It is but a slight exaggeration to say that a saga is the personification of a myth, while a legend is the "mythologization" of a person. Though we cannot fully understand the origination of a saga, we know enough to realize that there is first a mythologizing attempt to interpret some phenomenon of nature, such as day and night or summer and winter, and their imagined struggle, and then human beings are found who can be drawn into the magic circle and made to act within it, such as Siegfried in the Nibelungen tragedy. The tale sinks, as it were, from heaven to earth. In the case of the legend, the direction is reversed. The starting point is invariably a man or woman of flesh and blood who is then raised to a higher status or even to a higher sphere. The kernel of a typical legend is historical.

But the legend is not merely closer to reality; it is, beyond that, different in basic mood. We have noticed that sagas are somber stories, stories of guilt, stories of sin. Legends, on the other hand, are stories of extraordinary achievement, of exemplary merit and even sanctity and the power connected with them, and therefore stories of salvation. They show up, not the likelihood of men's falling into crime and incurring punishment, but their ability to raise themselves above animality and above selfishness, and to set signposts which others are capable of following. The Wotan of the saga tradition is a god whose greed brings destruction upon him and his own; St. Francis of Assisi was a man whose love has collected a large family whose service to the suffering of all nations has been, and still is, immeasurable.

We must not, however, speak at once of the saints of Christianity, although their legends belong in this section. Their case is complicated through the entry into it of the religious element. We must try, to begin with, to see the formation of a legend in its simplest, so to speak leanest, form. The book *Folklore: From the Working Folk of America*, edited by T. P. Coffin and H. Cohen (Garden City, N.Y., 1974), provides some rather eye-opening material. "American folk and semifolk occupations have developed no culture heroes, that is, no mythological figures whose roles are to create and arrange the world where man resides, to instruct man in his function, or even to serve as one of man's gods," the two scholars write in their introductory survey (pp. xl, xli). But, they continue,

> there are many historical and semihistorical heroes whose personalities and escapades stand as models for subsequent generations. These legendary figures tend to fall into two groups: heroes who are models of physical strength and heroes who are models of moral behavior. The first may be called "prowess heroes" like Tim Murphy, the Revolutionary War scout, or Railroad Bill, the meanest outlaw in Alabama. The latter may be called "ethical heroes."

It is these who interest us at this particular moment.

Sometimes it is not an entire life but one deed of bravery and self-sacrifice which becomes the center of a legend. Thus a cowboy ballad records the heroic end of a cattle hand called Utah Carroll, his exemplary conduct during a stampede. The tale is very moving, and we can hardly do better than to quote (from ibid., pp. 70–72) a few of its many stanzas.

> We were rounding up one morning;
> Our work was nearly done.
> On the right the cattle started
> In a wild and maddened run.
>
> The boss's little daughter
> Was holding on that side,
> Started in to turn the cattle,
> 'Twas here my partner died.
>
> On the saddle of the pony
> Where the boss's daughter sat,
> Utah Carroll that very morning
> Had placed a red blanket,
>
> That the saddle might be easy
> For Lenore, his little friend,
> But the blanket that he placed there
> Brought my partner to his end.
>
> When Lenore rushed in on her pony
> To turn the cattle to the right,
> The red blanket slipped from under her
> Caught in her stirrup tight.
>
> When the cattle saw the blanket
> Nearly trailing on the ground,

They were maddened in an instant
And charged it with a bound.

Now Lenore seen in threatening danger,
Quickly turned her pony's face,
While leaning from her saddle
Tried the blanket to displace.

While leaning from her saddle
Fell in front of that wild tide,
"Lie still, Lenore, I'm coming,"
Were the words my partner cried. . . .

As the horse approached the maiden,
Footsteps sure and steady bound,
Utah Carroll leaned from the saddle,
Lifted Lenore up from the ground,

But such weight upon his cinches
Had ne'er been felt before,
His hind cinch snapped asunder
And he fell beside Lenore.

Utah Carroll picked up the blanket
And he waved it o'er his head,
Started out across the prairie,
Again, "Lie still," he said. . . .

When the herd closed in around him
My young partner had to fall,
Never more to sing to bronco
Or give the cattle call. . . .

When we broke into the circle
On a ne'er forgotten day,
From a dozen wounds and bruises
His young life ebbed away. . . .

In some future morning,
I've heard the cowboys say,
They again will meet with Utah
On the round-up far away.

Austin E. Fife, who has collected this song and others as well, expressed the
opinion that the lay of Utah Carroll enshrines the four moral qualities which
the men of the early West most cherished: loyalty, courage, respect for woman-
hood, and a faith in the life hereafter (ibid., p. 421). This is true, but Lenore
obviously was not yet a woman; she was a child; and that makes the hero's
devotion to her all the more poignant. His grave may be without a headstone,
as the ballad says, but the ballad itself is a finer memorial than the most ex-
pensive headstone could possibly be.

The poets of more sophisticated societies have continued this kind of legend building. Thus Goethe's poem "Johanna Sebus" is preceded by a brief note which reads: "Written in memory of the seventeen-year-old fine and good girl from the village of Brienen, who, on January 13, 1809, perished when the Rhine carried much ice and the dam at Kleverham broke, while she was trying to help others." Societies know very well why they should endeavor to preserve and perpetuate the fame of a Utah Carroll and a Johanna Sebus. There will be future stampedes; there will be future flood catastrophes. There is ever a need for heroism.

Sometimes, probably more often, it is an entire life rather than a single deed which gives birth to a legend. One illustration among many is the story of Johnny Appleseed. This man, who was really called John Chapman, lived from 1774 to 1845. He got his nickname from the fact that he made it his business to spread the cultivation of the apple far and wide through the then United States. But this was by no means his only kind deed. A historical source, Rosella Rice's *Recollections* (ibid., pp. 403–408, 448), calls him a "good old man whose loving heart prompted him to go about doing good." A certain lovable eccentricity fostered the formation of a legend around this colorful personality. According to Rice, "he was such a good, kind, generous man that he thought it wrong to expend money on clothes to be worn just for their fine appearance. ... We have seen Johnny frequently wearing an old coffee sack for a coat, with holes cut in it for his arms." "He was never known to hunt any animal or to give any living thing pain; not even a snake. . . . The Indians all liked and treated him kindly." In addition to spreading the apple, he also tried to spread the dog fennel which, he thought, was a specific against malaria. "The overwhelming desire to do good and benefit and bless others induced him to gather a quantity of the seed which he carried in his pockets and occasionally scattered along his path in his journeys, especially at the wayside, near dwellings." What if he had been mistaken, if this plant turned out to have no medicinal value at all and in fact became a nuisance as a weed when it spread? Kindness lies in the intention, not in the result, and the intention was good, or so at any rate thought those who, in after days, remembered Appleseed with very warm feelings. Rosella Rice's account closes with the words: "A life full of labor and pain and unselfishness, humble unto self-abnegation, his memory glowing in our hearts, while his deeds live anew every springtime in the fragrance of the apple-blossoms he loved so well."

As a young man, John Chapman–Appleseed went through a conversion experience, became a devoted Swedenborgian, and claimed to be able to commune with spirits and angels. This brings us to the saints of Christianity whose legends provide the bulk of this genre's literature. Saints are, in the first place, models to follow, just like Utah Carroll or Johanna Sebus, or Johnny Appleseed, for that matter. André Jolles (*Einfache Formen*, p. 36) calls the saint in this sense "a figure in whom we can see, experience, and recognize something which appears to all as worthy of our best efforts, and who demonstrates at the same time the possibility of its realization. In short, he is in all form an *imita-*

bilis," one to be emulated, "a person in whom goodness has achieved an objective existence." Because of this, he is not merely a model, but also a measure, a yardstick, with the help of which we can judge ourselves:

> We may perform good or bad actions without knowing with any precision how we are to be judged and in which direction we are tending. It is only when virtue has become measurable, tangible, comprehensible, when it stands before us unconditionally and unrestrictedly in the saint, that we have a secure test: the saint makes us conscious of what we have to do . . . and to be when engaged in the path of virtue. He himself is this path, and we can follow him.

Of course, the saint rarely stands before us in the flesh; he stands as a rule before us as an image, and this is mediated by his legend. The legend is thus a strong moral influence. "We are not able to calculate, but we may well assume," writes Heinrich Günter, a student of the matter, "that vital values, ideals, and practical attitudes [of an ethical character] have been brought close to the people by the legends which thereby became an incentive for their realization" (*Psychologie der Legende*, p. 24).

In the foregoing lines the term "virtue" has cropped up several times. Virtue comes from the Latin *virtus*, and *virtus* has two meanings: moral excellence, as in English, but also power or strength as in the Italian *virtù*, and this combination of meanings is significant. Rightly understood, it can help our analysis on. The man of virtue is also a man of power. He can help a brother in need. Legends record many miracles, and, in the eyes of quite a few students, this is the chief hallmark of the whole type. It is asserted that, because such inexplicable happenings are the center of the lives of most saints, the legend is closely related to, if not indeed identical with, the fairy tale. But the apparent similarity is not a real one. In the fairy tale, either the miracle is left entirely unexplained or it is ascribed to magic, magic inherent in either a good or an evil agent—for instance, a witch. The irrationality of the tale is complete. But in the legends, the miracles which happen are neither left unexplained nor ascribed to magic. Magic is replaced by prayer; superstition, by belief. True, the consistent rationalist and atheist will see little difference, but until very recently the human race saw reality as the work of a Creator, a Lawgiver of the Universe, and concluded, not illogically, that He who has given laws to the universe may also on occasion suspend them if He sees fit, and if He is asked by a friend to do so. This, however, is precisely what the saints are: friends of God, and this precisely is what they do: intercede with Him for their fellow-men. The magician works his will by dint of his own inherent power. The saint can do nothing for himself; he is mighty only through prayer.

Skeptics may well, in dealing with the contents of legends, fall back on William James's concept of a "will to believe," and the development of such a will to believe is, as we shall see presently, easy to comprehend. But before discussing it, we must emphasize that any will to believe is matched by an equally live will to preserve and perpetuate the facts. The case of the legends, including the medieval ones, is not, in principle, different from that of Utah Carroll or

Johnny Appleseed. Even the interest in relics is an outgrowth of the desire to secure evidence—evidence which will last. "In the beginning, e.g., still with Gregory of Tours or Gregory the Great and others, the legends of the saints do not leave the historical soil," writes Lutz Röhrich in a comparison of legend and fairy tale (*Märchen und Wirklichkeit*, pp. 36, 37), and he recalls a resolution of the Council of Trent: "In the invocation of the saints, all superstition is to be removed." "The miracles of the legends," he also avers, "are nothing unreal; they are a reality out of the ordinary."

This does not mean, of course, that popular imagination has not entered into the detail of the legends as they are told down through the centuries. It has. It would be strange if it had not, for the saints are beloved, and the beloved is always seen in a blaze of glory: this is as true of non-sexual as of sexual infatuation. But the transformation of a sober life story into a legend has a more important characteristic than imaginative adornment. André Jolles has described very well the difference between an ordinary biography and one of the *vitae sanctorum*, and his words show what is essentially involved.

> Historically speaking, we are wont to conceive the life of a man as a continuum, a movement which runs uninterruptedly from a beginning to an end and within which that which follows is connected with that which precedes. If the *vita* were to see the life of a saint in this way, its purpose would not be achieved. What it has to do is to bring about an activation of virtue; it has to demonstrate how active virtue is being backed up by divine intervention. The unity of a human life is not important for it; important only are the moments in which goodness objectifies itself. The *vita*, the legend, breaks what is historically given into its elements; it fills these elements in its own spirit with the value of imitability and then reconstructs the whole on the basis of that imitability.... It is the chief characteristic of an historical biography that the person concerned remains himself; he may be an example for us, but he cannot totally take us in. But when the presentation of a life is so structured that the historical personality is no longer self-enclosed, when it is so made that we are inclined to immerse ourselves in it, it becomes a legend [*Einfache Formen*, pp. 39, 40].

We can sum up this analysis by saying, somewhat more simply, that a legend is a life story the purpose of which is, not to present the facts, but to invite and induce imitation.

The invitation to follow the example set, and the frequent acceptance of such invitations, also explain why saints fall into patterns, why we can observe the formation of families and the firming up of traditions. Thomas de Vio (better known as Cajetan) is said to have been a near replica of Thomas Aquinas, and Joseph of Cupertino almost a double of Francis of Assisi. St. George was the archetype of a Christian knight, and many other knights who achieved sanctity remind us of him. But there is a second and deeper reason why the chain of saintly and sainted persons does not break off. It lies, not on the side of the saints themselves, but on the side of those who are unlike them—on the side of the ordinary people, on the side of the masses; sterner observers might say: on the side of the sinners. Saints are, as we have seen, protectors; and who does not stand in need of protection? The *Legenda aurea* of Jacobus a Voragine says in its prologue: "We are pilgrims and engaged in a perpetual struggle." Homer had expressed this same sentiment of human helplessness—i.e., the helplessness of unaided man—2,000 years earlier: "No other being is more miserable on earth than man" (*Iliad* 17.446); "all men stand in need of the gods" (*Odyssey* 3.48). It is out of this feeling, out of this psychology, that legends grow. To give but one illustration: the saints are said to stand by the side of the innocently persecuted (see Günter, *Psychologie der Legende*, pp. 147, 162, 163). St. James of Compostela, St. Augustine, St. Francis, and, of course, the Virgin Mary are all asserted to have been liberators of prisoners wrongly kept in jail, and a host of minor saints is credited with the same power (see ibid., pp. 161, 162). Legends, Günter writes (ibid., p. 92; see also p. 3), "wish to help by pointing to the supernal powers who alone are able and ready to aid. . . . Their mission is to show that support is available, and where it comes from." Thus they powerfully strengthen the belief that (at least ultimately) good will prevail; they are sources of optimism and tend to spread it through the whole culture. In this respect they are similar to the fairy tales, even though they aim at the psyche of the adults and not of children. But we should stress another aspect much more: not that they are akin in type (so far as their general effect is concerned) to fairy tales, but rather that they are anti-types to the sagas, which, as we have seen, emphasize the fact of sin; they highlight the possibility of salvation. The hope of salvation, of liberation from evil, is eternal in man, and if there is a will to believe, it has here its psychological root.

While we were speaking of the saint as an *imitabilis* and *imitandus*—one who can be and should be emulated—some of our readers may well have spontaneously thought of that great classic of Christian literature, Thomas a Kempis' *De imitatione Christi*. It will be well to conclude this discussion by pointing out that the saints of the legends are, within the Christian tradition, themselves seen as imitators, and not only as the recommended objects of imitation—as imitators, emulators, of the Saint of Saints, Jesus Christ. The bearing of this fact on the development of a societal ethos will, of course, have to be investigated, but this cannot be done at the present point. The topic will be taken up again in the framework of our consideration of the phenomena of religion (see esp. chap. 4).

There remains only one aspect which we have yet to consider here: the question as to what extent the legend has survived the wave of rationalism which has come over the human race since the eighteenth century and which has tended to reduce all thought processes to the registration and analysis of provable facts. As in so many other areas, so in this, the victory of rationality over the play of the imagination has been no more than partial. Legends— whether so called or given another name—are apt to grow around all persons in the focus of public interest, but often we get anti-legends rather than legends, i.e., stories which raise the wickedness of some figure into the light of con- sciousness and represent it as an example to be eschewed rather than as a model to be followed. Such anti-legends have always existed. The story of Ahasuerus who insulted Christ on His way to Calvary and is condemned to live on and on and to lead an unsteady existence until the Second Coming is a case in point. But the numerical relation of proper and improper legends has significantly changed. While societies were still communities in the sense of Ferdinand Tönnies, the great process of selection which is ever carried on by the collective forces sought by preference to identify the good and to preserve their name and fame, while consigning the not so good to oblivion. Cults developed around figures whose love for, and service of, their fellow-men were widely considered worthy of public recognition, and these cults in turn made it possible for the Church to institute a formalized process of canonization which could be sure, in each case, of a reliable basis in the popular consciousness. The Reformation, with its emphasis on the Fall of Adam and Eve, spread the opinion that no man is a saint and hence worthy of emulation; in consequence it changed the entire situation by hamstringing the selective process in the areas in which it prevailed. This led not only to the decay of legends conceived in the style of the Middle Ages, but also to a stronger development of anti-legends. One example is the wicked career and the sorry end of Don Juan; but other, parallel instances are by no means lacking. A recent illustration of this kind of story is the ballads written around the "meanest outlaw in Alabama," Railroad Bill. Though some positive traits which remind one of Robin Hood are not missing, the anti-hero's evil deeds are pilloried, such as the robbing of his neighbors and the murder of a sheriff:

> Railroad Bill got so bad,
> Took all the money that the po' farmers had.
>
> Railroad Bill was the worst ole coon,
> Killed McMillan by the light o' de moon.

(Coffin & Cohen, *Folklore*, pp. 393, 396). The parallel to the legend is obvious. As kindness gains a sort of objective and abiding existence in the legend, so criminality does in the anti-legend. As the one expresses admiration and invites imitation, so the other voices disgust and inspires revulsion. Even physically the contrast between positive and negative model becomes visible: while the places in which saints lived and worked develop into centers of pilgrimage, the venues of crimes and the sites of gallows are widely avoided.

In the case of the anti-legend as in that of the legend, the art of poetry has taken up the task which is no longer quite so readily fulfilled by popular song-making. One instance is Robert Southey's ballad "The Inchcape Rock" (see *The Poetical Works of Robert Southey* VI [London, 1838], pp. 135ff.). The story it tells is simple, but impressive. In the North Sea, off the Scottish coast, there is a rock very dangerous to shipping because it is submerged at high tide. The Abbot of Aberbrothok has a bell fixed to it, to warn the mariners who sail that way of their peril, but Sir Ralph the Rover, a pirate, out of sheer wickedness, cuts the rope and the bell sinks to the bottom of the sea. Then,

> grown rich with plundered store,
> He steers his course for Scotland's shore.

But he is never to reach his home: his own boat is wrecked on the obstacle now hidden beneath the swirling waters; it goes down with its cargo and all hands.

> They hear no sound, the swell is strong;
> Though the wind has fallen they drift along,
> Till the vessel strikes with a shivering shock—
> "Oh Christ! it is the Inchcape Rock!"

> Sir Ralph the Rover tore his hair;
> He curst himself in his despair;
> The waves rush in on every side,
> The ship is sinking beneath the tide.

> But even in his dying fear
> One dreadful sound could the Rover hear,
> A sound as if with the Inchcape Bell,
> The Devil below was ringing his knell.

SYMBOLISM AND CEREMONY

118. The essential assertions of the last section may be summed up by saying that figures like Utah Carroll or, for that matter, Railroad Bill, are symbols— the one a symbol of kindness and devotion, the other a symbol of wickedness and criminality. They are symbols of a special kind, quite unlike the signs of mathematics which are neutral and value-free; they are more like the terms of everyday language, i.e., value-laden and moralizing, inviting to emulation in the one case and to abhorrence in the other. The creation of such symbols is one of the grand proofs for the creativity of the collective consciousness. But symbolization pervades not only the legends and anti-legends which we have just considered but also social life in all its depth and breadth. We must in this context remind the reader of the commanding figure of George Herbert Mead and of the great school of Symbolic Interactionism which has taken its cue from him. According to Mead, all conscious and intelligent conduct is symbolic. Unlike animal behavior, which is reaction to a stimulus, human action is characterized by the entry, between stimulus and response, of a symbolic element, be it only a thought couched in a word. Talcott Parsons, too, is close to this position. He writes in *The Social System* (London, 1967; pp. 386, 387) as follows: "The response of the mother to the crying of a child comes, apparently very early, to be felt as 'symbolic' of her attitude toward the child, not merely as an instrumental measure of relieving the particular distress which occasioned the crying. . . . In a stabilized interaction system all acts have this symbolic quality to some degree, all serve as expressive symbols." With this widest aspect of symbolism and its social significance we are not now concerned. What interests us at this point are the symbols which support the creation, propagation, and perpetuation of a societal ethos. The figures of the saints are such symbols —their personalities and indeed even their names. But though the ethos-creating and ethos-propagating and -perpetuating symbol is brought to the surface only here, it has in fact accompanied us from the very first page of this volume. In the fairy tale, for instance, the king—and also the prince who is a king in the making—is a symbolic figure in at least three meanings of the term: he is a symbol of the state and society; he is also, as the Freudians have emphasized and perhaps overemphasized, a symbol of the father, of fatherhood, and parental authority in general; and he is, thirdly, and most importantly, a symbol of the self. The child can only imaginatively identify with him because he is, from the very beginning, such a symbol. But prince and king are not simply symbols of the self, the self as it is; they are even more symbols of the mature self and thus set up a model toward which the developing child may strive. Even the child has a vague, unfocused idea of what symbolization means. He knows that fairy tales are not accounts of actual and factual happenings, but he is at the same time reluctant to admit that they are merely make-believe. If he could think in concepts, which he cannot do, he would say that the reality in and behind the fairy tales is indeed the reality of lived existence, but transposed into a symbolic key. We can say this for him without fear that we are misrepresenting his mentality.

In the widest sense of the word, a symbol is an object, or a person, or an action or sequence of actions, which has, in addition to its basic and especially physical properties, a superadded and superimposed cultural meaning. It is what it is and at the same time it shows forth a quality which is of much more general importance. Thus St. Francis was a specimen of the species *Homo sapiens*; he was, furthermore, the son of a merchant of Assisi, called Bernardone, and so on, and so forth. But culture has raised him to a far higher position by making his name a byword for all that is noble. It set him up as a model to be admired and imitated. Symbolization is therefore one of the ways in which society endeavors to shield itself against threats to its inner peace and coherence and, beyond that, to improve its tone; it is, in a word, an ethos-building device.

Some sociologists, especially Alfred Fouillée, have asserted that we may speak of a society in the full sense of the word only where its members bear an idea, a representation, of it in their minds; differently expressed: where one's society, the social system, is not merely a vaguely felt or intuited environment, but a *known* entity, apprehended and understood as a whole. This is, of course, merely a matter of definition, but certainly one which draws our attention to an important point. Even the more radical adherents of nominalism like Max Weber, who regard society as merely a multiplicity of individuals, admit that there has to be a portmanteau word to describe this multiplicity. But such a word will not for long remain a shorthand term. Sentiments of loyalty (or, maybe, of hate) will collect around it, and they will become central elements in the societal ethos. But the social forces will go a good deal beyond simple naming. They will, above all, provide symbols which can be seen: the flag which, in itself, is merely a length of cloth yet has often been called an emblem for the sake of which one must be prepared to die; the heraldic animal, eagle or lion or bear, and so on, and so forth. We need not go more deeply into this matter for it is one of common knowledge. Only one analytical remark is necessary. Objects like a flag or an heraldic animal are only indirectly symbols of society. They are much rather symbols of the state in which the society concerned is organized. In practice, this makes very little difference, as long at any rate as society and the state organizing it remain at one. In theory, the attachment of the loyalty-inducing emblems to the state, not to say the state apparatus, rather than to the stream of integrated life which we call society, is a fact not to be overlooked. The state itself, we may say, is a symbol of society as well as an organ of it—a symbol which, on its part, spawns other symbols of various kinds.

How true the remarks are which we have just made becomes doubly clear as soon as we pass from the consideration of symbolic objects to the consideration of symbolic persons. In the classic monarchy the king is the focus of loyal feelings. In republics which are mostly the outcome of a prevailing rationalism, the concept of the state rather than the head of the government is as a rule the focus of these feelings, but even here the supreme functionary—the president—is not unimportant. Yet, even in a monarchy, loyalty is given, not to a person, but to an institution. Certainly, the man on the throne will also evoke feelings of personal devotion in those who are immediately around him, his bodyguard for instance, especially if he is a personality like St. Louis of France or Henry V of England. But for society at large he is unavoidably a symbol rather than a personality. The matter becomes tangible in the tombs which late medieval and early modern times tended to erect for their rulers, and of which Ernst Kantorowicz has spoken so enlighteningly in his great book *The King's Two Bodies*. These sepulchers show the departed potentate twice: once as a man and then also as a king. On a raised platform, resting on four pillars, he lies, an image of glory, surrounded by all his regalia: crown, scepter, sword, orb, ermine cape, and all the rest; on a lower slab, close to the earth, we behold him nearly naked, wrapped in a winding sheet, an image of misery and decay. It shows the whole tremendous strength of symbolism that the brutal exposure of the caducity, the perishableness, of the kings's earthly status has, through many centuries, done nothing to reduce the loyalty inspired by them, a loyalty from which the society which they represented and, so to speak, incarnated, greatly benefited because it strengthened, however indirectly, its sustaining ethos. "In the ideal type," writes Talcott Parsons (*Social System*, p. 400), "the common value sentiments which constitute the collectivity are projected upon the leader as a symbolic embodiment of these values. In so far as this symbolic complex is well integrated, loyalty to these values, to the collectivity, and to his role become indistinguishable." A rather moving illustration from the twentieth century is Joseph Roth's short story *Die Büste des Kaisers*. It will not do to write it off as a piece of poetical invention or mere fiction. The sentiments displayed are those of a very real historical person—Joseph Roth—and certainly not his alone.

There is no reason why a society should not use both objects and persons as carriers of symbolic meanings, but the choice of persons brings a decisive advantage: persons may be symbolic, not only because of what they *are*, but also because of what they can *do*. The social forces have, over the centuries, developed a number of action sequences or action patterns which enshrine and periodically revive the basic societal ethos and more especially the sentiments which feed and sustain it. We may call them, in line with everyday language, ceremonies, reserving the term ritual for religious performances. The symbolic person is the aptest enactor of symbolic acts.

Three subvarieties should be distinguished here. There are, first, ceremonies which show forth and demonstrate the solidarity of the group. They were at the center of Emile Durkheim's analysis, and the totemic dances of the Australian aborigines were his prime example. If our terminology were to be applied, it might be in doubt whether these feastings should be described as ceremonies or as rituals because they are integrated with a set of metaphysical beliefs, because they have referents of a supernatural character. But it was precisely Durkheim's submission that such semi-religious performances also had the effect of purely secular ceremonies in that they strengthened the cohesion of the tribes. In spite of terminological differences, we should certainly accept Durkheim's essential assertion. But there are also innumerable examples of a purely mundane sort. When the President of the United States delivers a Fourth of July address or when the Queen of England drives in her royal coach to Westminster in order to open the Houses of Parliament, they perform ceremonial acts which are meant to give new vigor to the patriotic sentiments of the citizens or subjects. An even simpler example is a familial Thanksgiving or Christmas dinner when the relatives assemble at the house of the common grandfather or grandmother in order to partake of a common meal. Nothing much seems to happen, and yet something does happen: lapsed or relaxed ties are once again retied and tightened.

The second subvariety has a much more specific content. It is connected with the entrustment of certain social and political functions to selected individuals, and centers on their induction to office. A public servant is "sworn in"—taking this phrase in its widest connotation. The ceremonial may be simple, as in modern democracies, or it may be elaborate, as in the ancient monarchies with their rank growth of symbolisms, but superficially it appears everywhere as a rather straightforward event with a single aim: that of bringing together a man and a task. Yet the eye of the analyst will discover an underlying complexity. The ceremony is, of course, in the first place concerned with the strengthening of social solidarity, and in this respect—to that extent—it differs little from the first subvariety. Only the occasion is different, not the effect. But there are two important implications which must be noted. They arise from the hard fact that human sociality is rather limited, or, as we may more appropriately say in the present context, that it stands at all times in need of strengthening. The incoming officer must be reminded that he is only a servant and should remain one, and become no more, while he is in power. Both presidents and monarchs swear that they will respect the constitution, i.e., the rights of those over whom they are going to rule. Even this is a fairly simple matter and easy to observe. But a last element grows from a more hidden root. If a man is raised to a position of influence and power, his neighbors will envy him, be it only on the subconscious level, and this negative sentiment, too, will strive for expression. Demonstrative acts of humility are therefore often built into these ceremonials. There was a time, and it is not long past, when a newly elected pope had to lie flat on the floor, with the cardinals who had elected him stepping over him. A new Speaker of the House of Commons is, even today, *dragged* to the Chair, demonstrating by his symbolic resistance that he does not wish to rise superior to his fellows, that he is taking on a burden rather than occupying a place of authority. The same phenomenon can also be observed much lower down in the social scale. When a printer's apprentice in the city of Salzburg is promoted to the rank of journeyman, he is ceremoniously "baptized," or rather drenched in cold water, on the old market square, by those whose circle he is about to join, and who, deep down, may well resent the bestowal of their position and privileges on a newcomer, hitherto a mere outsider.

Mentioning these printer's apprentices and their painful *rite de passage* reminds us that the phenomenon which we are now studying—the formation of ethos-strengthening ceremonials—was particularly characteristic of the medieval guilds. The records of these brotherhoods would yield illustrations without number. Unfortunately we must not allow ourselves to be lured into this byway; our space is too restricted to permit excursions of this kind, though they would add a good deal of color to our text.

While the second subvariety of ceremony grown from the basic ethos of society is concerned with the elevation of a person to a higher position, the third is, in diametrical contrast, connected with a person's demotion and discomfiture. As honor is bestowed in an elaborate and impressive manner, a dishonor is inflicted in a way which is apt to hold the criminal up to shame and warn the onlooker not to follow in his footsteps. Sentencing a convicted malfeasant is a more or less dramatic occasion everywhere. In a very important paper entitled "Über die Leistung des Rechts" (reprinted in *Stiftung und Leistung* [Munich–Mittenwald, 1979], pp. 199ff.), Mohammed Rassem has drawn an entirely justified distinction between the law of the lawyers and bureaucrats, on the one hand—technicized and manipulating law, as we may call it—and the basic law of societies, the law which underlies social life, the law which is *one* with social life, on the other. The latter must not only be accepted and applied; it must also be possible to *experience* it. Its validity must be shown forth, demonstrated—we might almost say, in a popular phrase: rubbed in—and this can best be done by clothing the pronouncement of a sentence, especially a punitive one, and most of all a sentence of death, in a ceremonial garb. After comparing this final act of a criminal prosecution to a scene in a tragic stage play, Rassem remarks: "Society is [here] offered a very real and repeated *experience* of the law in a form which is not excessively dramatic and yet thoroughly aesthetic in complexion. The manifestly high degree to which such law is accepted rests on this contact with it" (ibid., p. 206). Some of the time-hallowed symbols of the past spring to mind at once: the breaking of the staff when the doom is pronounced, the hoisting of a black flag on the place of execution after the executioner has done his work, and so on, and so forth. This melancholy historical detail does not concern us. What does concern us is merely the fact that a truly living, mind-informing law will need a living, mind-arresting ceremonial to complete it; it has always in the past received such completion. If recent reforms, inspired by rationalism, have abolished some of these age-old and well-tried forms, this can hardly be more than a sign of general social involution. Did not even the fathers of the American and French Revolutions insist on the majesty of the law, and will not all majesty strive to express itself in appropriate symbols and ceremonials?

Akin to, yet different from, the three subvarieties of ceremonialism reviewed in the last few paragraphs are the symbolic acts which we might call bond-creating ceremonies and which belong more to the private sphere. The celebration of a wedding is quite obviously the prime example of this type, and it would be tempting to discuss some of the traditions which have grown up around it. But we must once again resist. We may do so with not too much regret as personal observation will easily fill in the gap which we must leave. Personal observation will also teach that there are other, if mostly minor, ceremonies of the bond-creating kind in use in ours as in other societies. Even the simple handshake belongs in this category. The kiss, too, was once, and in some cultures still is, the sealing of a friendship rather than a sexual experience. It was Judas Iscariot's crime treacherously to break the bond which he had just asseverated in so solemn a fashion. In Russia particularly the kiss has long preserved this non-sexual interpretation, and the bear-hug with which Communist leaders are wont to greet each other is derived from it. But Russia, the Russia of the Orthodox faith, possessed yet another traditional ceremonial which showed its bond-creating character in almost archetypal clarity. It was customary for young men to wear crosses around their necks, and when they wished to confirm a friendship which had sprung up, they exchanged these crosses. It was, for instance, regarded as a charming gesture if future brothers-in-law would go through this little ceremony. In Dostoevski's great novel *The Idiot* (2.4), Rogozhin and Myshkin exchange crosses, and the bond so created and solemnized does not snap even when Rogozhin commits the crime which drives Myshkin finally out of his mind. Needless to say, a good marriage and even a true friendship do not need a prop of this kind, but it is salutary to remind those who are about to enter into such deep human relationships that they are taking a serious step, and this is precisely the effect of the ceremonies and rituals concerned.

LITERATURE: PRELIMINARY DISTINCTIONS AND OBSERVATIONS

119. In the work which we quoted in the last section, *The Social System*, Talcott Parsons draws a distinction between the performer of a symbolic pattern and the creator of that pattern (see pp. 385, 408ff.), a distinction which lies parallel to that between actor and playwright, and no objection can be raised on grounds of principle against this attempt to separate the two types. But if it is implied that the roles are comparable, and especially that both are, in real life, entrusted to assignable individuals, a serious misconception is introduced. The performers of symbolic patterns are indeed as a rule definite persons, such as the Chief Justice of the Supreme Court who swears in the American President or the Archbishop of Canterbury who crowns England's king or queen.

But the ceremonies which they perform are usually the results of slow growth rather than of conscious contrivance. They derive their solemnity, their impressive character, from the fact that generations have collaborated in their formation, each leaving its impress on the whole, each contributing in its fashion to the finally emerging excellence. If individual artists intervene, they frequently merely arrange, extend or shorten, or possibly further embellish, what they find. Indeed, if individual artists are asked to draft the outlines of new ceremonials, and that sometimes happens in our tradition-destroying century, they may, and more often than not will, allow themselves to be guided by older patterns, and they know full well that this is the safest road to a satisfactory result.

But this does not mean that the individual artist is not of the highest importance for our investigation. We saw this already when we pointed out, in passing, that the archaic, anonymously developed ballad finds its continuation and modern counterpart in such poems as Goethe's "Johanna Sebus" (cf. above p. 52). Nor is it only this literary mode which lies parallel to the folkloric legend and carries the memory of heroic deeds into the future. Sir Walter Scott's admirable novel *The Heart of Midlothian*, regarded by many as his finest achievement, is of the same nature. The heroine, Jeanie Deans, who fights so doggedly for the life of her half-sister Effie, was modeled on a real-life figure by the name of Helen Walker. Joseph Sonnleitner's libretto to Beethoven's sublime opera *Fidelio* is also based on an historical incident. The name of the faithful wife who, disguised as a boy, penetrated into prison in order to comfort and, if possible, rescue her husband, seems to have been forgotten, but it is known that she was a daughter of Touraine. Her deed had already been celebrated by a French playwright, Jean Nicolas Bouilly, in his drama *Léonore ou l'amour conjugale*, and he (Bouilly) claims to have known the brave Leonora personally and to have been a witness to her exploit and its success. He was a high official in the area at the time and asserts that he played the role, ascribed, in Beethoven's opera, to the freedom-bringing Minister of State, Don Fernando. Such products of individual pens have the same effect, as far as the creation and perpetuation of societal ethos are concerned, as the legends and ballads of yesteryear.

However: the individual consciousness and even the individual subconscious are not the same as the collective unconscious. What struggles upward in the one is only now and then similar to what struggles upward in the other. We cannot be surprised to find that the artist will use his talents in order to express his personal interests (using the word interest, not in its economic, but in its psychological, sense). If this is, in principle, true of the artistic personalities of all ages, it is doubly and trebly true of the modern artist, and that for two reasons, the one macrosociological and the other microsociological—less technically expressed: the one rooted in the general character of capitalist culture, the other connected with the specific place allotted to the poet, musician, or painter under that dispensation. Since the Renaissance, aesthetic values have been demoted to a relatively humble position in the prevailing *ordo amoris*. One need only compare the high quantity and quality of Catholic art with the relatively small contribution made by Protestantism, and more particularly Calvinism, in this field, in order to see how true this is (see Stark, *Sociology of Religion*, v 159ff.). Modern society is not prepared to reward the creative artist richly; yet if he is not allowed to get rich, he will not be greatly respected in a world which by preference measures with the monetary yardstick, hypocritical declarations to the contrary notwithstanding. This brings us to the second—the microsociological—reason for the individualistic, often even antisocial, attitudes of the modern artist—antisocial not in any absolute sense, but only in relation to the surrounding capitalist system. We see the matter best if we concentrate for a moment on the history of music; other branches fared no better. We may be shocked when we hear that a genius like Joseph Haydn had to take his meals with the menial servants, but he apparently did not mind. He was considered a craftsman, and a craftsman's skills were duly appreciated. More decisively still: he had security, and security is a precious possession. It was lost as soon as the composers had to expect their livelihood from the operation of an anonymous market—a most uncertain resource, doubly uncertain because the public is as a rule wary of wares to which it is not accustomed. The sad fate of Franz Schubert (no less a genius than Joseph Haydn) is archetypal. He, to all intents and purposes, starved to death (see Werner Stark, *The Sociology of Knowledge* [London, 1958], pp. 25ff.). It is therefore anything but surprising that modern artists drifted into a mood of opposition and negation. Radical movements like *musique concrète* and Dadaism in poetry or Cubism in painting are merely the more extreme manifestations of a nearly general mood.

What we need, first of all, then, in this section, is a typology. But before setting it forth, we must make a preliminary remark. The great bulk of literature, as of art generally, is non-political: it is untouched by the struggles for power which rage around it and largely oblivious of them. But on the outer fringes, so to speak, there appears a committed literature, a committed art, which the French call, in a semi-technical term, *littérature engagée*. The Russian poet Nekrasov may be mentioned as a good illustration here. His main work is entitled *Who Lives Happily in Russia?* (1873–1876), and the title alone—which clearly implies the answer: nobody (certainly not the bulk of the population!) —indicates the drift of his poetry. At the opposite pole of the political spectrum stands Glinka's opera *A Life for the Czar* (1836)—again a work which shows quite openly its nationalistic and loyalistic tendencies. But we need not give a list of names. Conservatism and revolutionary sentiment, ideology and utopia make, as everybody knows, their appearance in some of the texts, and where this element strongly prevails, we are confronted with a phenomenon of a special kind which is of lesser importance for our investigation. Not because we underestimate the historical significance of this kind of artistic pronouncement or its possible cultural and more particularly aesthetic value! Far from it! Nekrasov was a fine poet, and he helped greatly to prepare the downfall of the *ancien régime* in his country. Glinka's music is enchanting, and it gives a live impression of the mystique of czardom even now, after the collapse of czarism. But radically revolutionary and radically conservative poetry etc. appear only at crisis points in social development, and our investigation is concerned with the *perennial* problem of ethicizing human conduct—in other words, with that social control which is a functional imperative in *all* social systems. We leave it therefore to the science of politics to deal with the *littérature engagée* which we may call, without being unjust, a kind of propaganda effort for this program or that.

Political art and social criticism are close neighbors and shade into each other. Faced with plays like Alfred de Vigny's *Chatterton* (1835) or Arthur Miller's *Death of a Salesman* (1949) we may well hesitate before deciding— if we can decide at all—to which of the two categories they belong. But we have to distinguish them nonetheless, and this for several reasons. Political art is, in its clearer manifestations, a call to action, to *purposive* action, whereas social criticism is often more a simple revelation of human weaknesses, a pillorying of human insufficiencies; and even where it bares the darker sides of social institutions, it is not necessarily connected with the demand that these institutions should change. In works like *Le Père Goriot* (1835) and *Le Cousin Pons* (1847), Balzac certainly does not spare contemporary France and especially Paris with their disgusting, grasping bourgeois, but does he not accuse the people who allow themselves to be corrupted rather than the society which corrupts them? And does he hold out any hope that human beings will ever be different, will ever be better? The basic mood may thus be fatalistic; and even where it is not fatalistic, where the desirability of change or changes is hinted at, it is often difficult to say whether the thrust is in the direction of revolution and radical reconstruction, or in the opposite direction, toward conservation. There is, after all, such a thing as reform in order to preserve. The facing-two-ways of one of England's greatest writers is well brought out in a convincing remark of Angus Wilson in *The World of Charles Dickens* (London, 1970; p. 73): "Profound disenchantment with social institutions [and] anxiety about any sort of social upheaval go constantly together in his career." Furthermore, social criticism appears not only at crisis points in socio-political development; it is apt to appear in all societies, even relatively well integrated and internally pacified ones, simply because all human conditions are in the final analysis unsatisfactory if they are measured against an imagined ideal. In themselves, these are perhaps minor considerations, but the point last made can lead us on to a more crucial observation and insight. The decisive reason why we should distinguish social criticism from politicized art and include it in our analysis is that, directly or indirectly, it draws attention to the semi-socialized condition of man and thereby to the need of social control, the need to ethicize human actions and attitudes; politicized art is all too often connected with philosophies which are inimical to the development of a societal ethos, either because they deny, at least by implication, the possibility of raising human conduct to a higher level (conservatism), or, on the other side of the fence, because they suggest that man is by nature social and even good and spoiled only by adverse social institutions, a stance which is delusionary and may lead to social experiments which are ultimately sure to miscarry because they must come up against the hard fact of man's self-preferring physical constitution. As against these two variants of political art, both of which are, if in different ways, negative in tendency, social criticism is comparatively positive in its effects. It is surely true, as the proverb says, that self-knowledge is the first step toward improvement!

Very different from the writings which in various ways accuse, judge, and condemn contemporary societies are the books which appear to pander to the primal instincts. We see their character best if we concentrate for a moment on the more popular level. Crime stories appeal to a large public because there are many people who enjoy reading about bloodshed and mayhem. Love stories appeal to an equally large public because there are many people who enjoy reading about sexual adventures, especially if the heroes and heroines defy the social norms which would block their paths. There is a whole gamut of such publications beginning at the one pole with near-pornography and ending at the other with refined novelettes and novels. This type of literature is not, of course, ethos-building, but, curiously enough, we must not rashly describe it as destructive either. Quite apart from the fact that social control usually wins in the end—the criminal is exposed and arrested, the wayward lovers become a normally married couple—the enjoyment of the readers rests on their identification with the main protagonists, with criminal and detective in the one case, with star-crossed lovers or an adulterous pair in the other. But identification leads to what the psychologists call vicarious satisfaction. The reader not only shares in the exploits of the *dramatis personae*, he also relives their eventual exultation, and a feeling of contentment will often be the end result of his reading. Some of the energy of his primal drives will therefore be dissipated and the yoke of social discipline momentarily lightened. To remain within psychological jargon: writings of this kind are "abreactive" and therefore "cathartic." By "abreaction" is meant an indirect, and therefore innocuous, satisfaction of appetites like the craving for excitement or for sexual play; by "catharsis," a cleaning. This type of literature is therefore—as indicated—not necessarily destructive of the societal ethos; indeed, it may even, in favorable cases, strengthen it. It is an outlet of a sort, a safety valve. Still, there are many who claim that crime and love stories may become models of actual behavior and then the consequences may be serious. There may be not only identification with the heroes and heroines but imitation of them, and then criminality and misconduct may come to be the end effect. The question is one of the highest practical importance, and we must deal with it. We certainly shall, but this is not the appropriate context. Society permits the publication of books which present and sometimes even glorify cruelty and license perhaps out of a semi-conscious conviction that, in the final analysis, they do more good than harm. Since our projected fifth volume will be concerned with "contained lawlessness," this whole matter will be duly considered there. Here a passing reference must suffice.

The central subject of this section is a third category of literature which we have to place side by side with social criticism and cathartic writing. It might be called ethos-building, and we have already given it this epithet once or twice before. Joan Rockwell has it in mind when she writes as follows in her book *Fact in Fiction* (pp. 4, 6):

> Fiction is not only a representation of social reality, but also a necessary functional part of social control. . . . It plays a large part in the socialisation of infants, in the expression of official norms such as law and religion, in the conduct of politics, and in general gives symbols and modes of life to the population, particularly in those less easily defined but basic areas such as norms, values, and personal and interpersonal behaviour. . . . Fiction . . . is . . . a normative force in society.

In another context, the educational importance of reading is still more strongly emphasized (p. 81):

> Fiction not only legitimises emotions and aspiration, it also, . . . particularly since the appearance of the novel with its devotion to the minutiae of personal relationships, gives models and patterns of acceptable and unacceptable behaviour. I have certainly noticed that those who never read, or never have read, fiction, tend to be obtuse and insensitive in personal relationships. It does really seem as if the consumption of fiction is a part of the necessary education of modern people in fine points of human relationships: so many examples are given of how people are, how they may be expected to react, and what the harvest is likely to be.

It should not be thought, however,—and Rockwell acknowledges this (see p. 58)—that the influence of literature is restricted to those who regularly read. "Most important," she avers, "it is a simple fact that great art, the greatest literature ever known, can be absorbed and internalised by whole populations. Two examples, Greece and Iceland, are sufficient to prove that the highest form of literature is not the exclusive province of a few specially sensitised individuals, but that Vico was right when he called the poets the teachers of the people; to teach them they must reach them, and they can." The two examples, classical Greece and heroic Iceland, are well chosen (see pp. 5, 55, 56, 30; see also p. 82n2), but others nearer our own time might also have been mentioned. Those whom the Germans like to call their classics, notably Goethe and Schiller, also represented and propagated an ethos which penetrated entire classes—above all, the bourgeoisie—and these poets too may therefore justifiably be called educators of their people. Their historical importance is not diminished by the fact that their teachings were, in the twentieth century, countermanded and overwhelmed by racist doctrines which then held the field for a little while.

Joan Rockwell speaks of fiction in general, but what she says applies in the first place, not to say exclusively, to our third category: ethos-building art. Yet it must be emphasized—though the matter should be obvious to anyone who knows the first thing about the social sciences—that the typological distinctions which we have drawn are merely theoretical and logical. In real life, all three basic attitudes—social criticism, abreaction of primal tendencies, and ethos building—are often united in one work; they are then juxtaposed and sometimes even interpenetrate. As an example, we may, for a moment, take up the second part of John Galsworthy's *Forsyte Saga*, three novels with two linking pieces or interludes, published under the common title *A Modern Comedy*. Galsworthy shows, in one or two incidental remarks, that he is well aware of the abreactive, cathartic element in literature. "Curious how the injured party [the betrayed husband, for instance] was always the one in disgrace," Soames Forsyte muses (New York, 1930; p. 695). "People admired immorality, however much they said they didn't. . . . Was it due to some thing still wild in human nature . . . ?" The question, we should say, is merely a rhetorical one; it is obvious that it demands a positive answer. In another context (ibid., p. 426), the same Soames meditates about his own childhood experiences and comes to a conclusion which is very close to the result of the analysis offered above. He remembers a visit to the circus and forms the opinion that " 'circuses' had their use. They kept the people quiet. Violence by proxy, for instance, was obviously a political principle of some value. It was difficult to gape at the shedding of blood and shed it at the same time; the more people stood in rows to see other beings hurt, the less trouble would they take to hurt others." But Galsworthy is not only theorizing about abreaction and catharsis; he himself is providing an opportunity to abreact and to go through a cathartic experience. For his work reports, in great detail, of two adulteries: that of Irene inflicted on Soames in the first part, and that of Soames's daughter Fleur inflicted on her husband Michael in the second. In addition, or rather in preparation of the grand climax, there is the love story between Soames's daughter Fleur and Irene's son Jon, opposed by their respective parents, and yet brought to final fulfillment at the very end of the whole *Saga*.

Galsworthy apprehended that the title which he gave to his great series of novels might arouse misgivings on the part of the more critical readers and therefore went out of his way in an effort to justify it. "The word Saga," he writes in his short preface, "might be objected to on the ground that it connotes the heroic and that there is little of heroism in these pages. But," he explains, "it is used with a suitable irony." Even these few words reveal the social criticism which the story contains. The bloated capitalists whose enjoyments it describes and whose tribulations it exposes are not admirable like King Arthur and the Knights of the Round Table. The name of the first novel in the series (really a kind of subtitle) gives a sharp point to this social criticism: it is called "The Man of Property." The central figure, Soames, is so filled with the mercantile and monetary spirit of his class that no warm human sentiments can take shape in his innermost self. His marriage is bound to miscarry for he cannot attach himself to a human being, and induce a human being to attach himself or herself to him, as he can and does attach himself to his capital assets. It is true that this emotionally crippled man inspires not only aversion but also some sympathy. This is a significant element which will play some part in our later analyses. But it does not really take the edge off Galsworthy's social criticism. "One has noticed that readers, as they wade on through the salt waters of the *Saga*," he writes in the selfsame preface, "are inclined more and more to pity Soames, and to think in doing so they are in revolt against the mood of his creator. Far from it! He too pities Soames, the tragedy of whose life is the very simple, uncontrollable tragedy of being unlovable. . . ." Perhaps this makes the whole social criticism still more poignant and pungent. Even those who benefit from the institutions of a profit-centered society, who gain the prizes offered by a "possessive world," end up as its victims! If there is anyone in the world whom the aging Soames can be said to love, it is his daughter Fleur. But his relation to her was and remained nearly as unsatisfactory as that to his first wife, who had broken away from him. Looking, at the very end of *A Modern Comedy* (p. 790), back at the whole interplay between father and daughter, Galsworthy says: "He had longed for her affection, and she had not shown him enough. . . . Something in him had repelled feeling, dried up its manifestation." A civilization—that we are clearly given to understand—which produces creatures like Soames Forsyte is a source of many human tragedies. The word "comedy" used in the title of the second part is no less sarcastic than the word "saga" used in the first.

Yet it would be wrong to interpret Galsworthy's novels as merely anti-capitalistic; only a very narrow-minded Marxist could do that. For Galsworthy's attack is directed against a spiritual strain in Victorian England as much as or more than against the socio-economic constitution on which the money-mindedness of the day rested. We must see *The Forsyte Saga* and *A Modern Comedy* alongside such great novels as *Howard's End* and *A Passage to India* by E. M. Forster (see Stark, *Sociology of Religion*, v 183ff.). Soames Forsyte is a typical example of what Forster calls an "undeveloped heart"; his cry, too, would be the cry of Forster's heroes and heroines: "Only connect!"— a wish, a longing, denied to men of his upbringing. The sociologist who has read his Max Weber will be quick to see that Galsworthy's picture of Victorian society confirms, in its own fashion, Weber's thesis of the close kinship, the historical interrelation, between capitalism and Calvinism.

So far, then, Galsworthy's work is evidence of negative feelings toward his surrounding society or at least toward the generation about to pass away. But there is just as strong evidence of positive feelings, of admiration for some inherited and still extant features of English culture. After Fleur has betrayed her husband, Michael Mont, after she has committed adultery with Jon Forsyte, Mont has it in his power to crush her, but he forbears. A deep-rooted chivalrousness stays his hand.

> For her [i.e., for Fleur], Michael felt nothing but compassion. . . . Whatever had been between these two—and he felt it had been all—it was over, and she "down and out." He must stand by her and keep his mouth shut. . . . The bird had been shot with both barrels, and still lived; no one with any sporting instinct could hurt it further. Nothing for it but to pick her up and mend the wings as best he could. Something strong in Michael, so strong he hadn't known of its existence, had rallied to his aid. Sportsmanship—chivalry? No. It was nameless; it was . . . a feeling that there was something beyond self to be considered, even when self was bruised and cast down [*A Modern Comedy*, p. 797].

The sociologist and the historian will not find it difficult to identify the ultimate source of Michael Mont's ("the tenth baronet's") ethos: it is the ethos of a pre-capitalist and pre-Calvinist upper class, an ethos in its inception aristocratic, but one which has penetrated English society to its very bottom layer and thus has become universally binding. The cry "You must never hit a man who is down and out" is heard, and respected, even in the worst, most disreputable drinking dens. Societies are complex, as we can see; so are the works of art which they produce; and this is the point which we wish at present to make. However much Galsworthy deplores and disrecommends the mentality of Soames Forsyte, he invites us to admire the attitude of Michael Mont, and in this way he strengthens, at least in one detail, the societal ethos of his nation.

In the novel's concluding pages, there appears a yet more general ethos-building message. In a way, everything leads up to it. Jon and Fleur get no joy out of their adulterous experience; on the contrary, they emerge from it chastened and depressed and return to their respective spouses. The social institution of matrimony gains the upper hand over the lure of physical passion.

The mixture of elements characteristic of *The Forsyte Saga* and its sequel, *A Modern Comedy*, is observable in many, if not most, works of the literary art, and a good deal of the attractiveness of its productions is due to it. To give complete documentation would mean writing a long learned tome, but for good measure one or two more illustrations may be added here. Henry Fielding's novel *Tom Jones* has been classed as a "bawdy" book, and the hero's amatory exploits certainly occupy a large space in it. Not for nothing was the filmed version such a resounding success! But Tom Jones is a thoroughly nice fellow, and the reader cannot help liking him. Apart from his preoccupation with the ladies, his moral principles are entirely sound and even his one weakness proves to be but temporary. When he succeeds in winning his adored Sophia, he becomes a model husband. An even more interesting instance is a roughly contemporary work, Samuel Richardson's *Pamela*, which bears, significantly, the alternative title *Virtue Rewarded*. Richardson has only one aim: namely, to support the stern sexual morality of his day. He asserts that "Providence never fails to reward honesty and integrity" (2 vols. [New York, 1914], I 461), and refers (ibid., 463) to the "excellency of her [Pamela's] mind, which may make her character worthy of the imitation of her sex; and the editor of these sheets will have his end, if it inspires a laudable emulation in the minds of any worthy persons, who may thereby entitle themselves to the rewards, the praises and the blessings, by which Pamela was so deservedly distinguished." There is in addition a message for young males, especially those in affluent circumstances. Speaking about that Mr. B. whose purpose is to seduce Pamela and whose schemes miscarry because of her fortitude, Richardson writes (ibid., 461): "An edifying lesson may be drawn from [this story] for the use of such as are born to large fortunes." But this aspect—the fact that the hunter is a rich man and indeed his intended victim's employer, and the hunted a poor serving maid—brings a second element into the novel: social criticism. It is only incidental, and one almost has the impression that it is only half-intended, only a trick further to enhance the attractiveness of the picture drawn of the virtuous girl, Pamela. Yet, directly intended or not, social criticism comes to the surface in one or two contexts. Thus Pamela describes to her parents the psychology of her pursuer in the following words (ibid., 220): "His poor dear mother spoiled him at first. Nobody must speak to, or contradict him, as I have heard, when he was a child; and so he has not been used to be controlled, and cannot bear the least thing to cross his violent will. This is one of the blessings attending men of high condition!" A little later, when the pressure on the poor young woman to yield increases, there is an even more impassioned outbreak (see ibid., 234, 235):

> This is a sad letter, my dear father and mother; one may see how poor people are despised by the proud and the rich! yet we were all on a footing originally: and many of those gentry, who brag of their ancient blood, would be glad to have it as wholesome and as *really* untainted as ours!—Surely these proud people never think what a short stage life is; and that, with all their vanity, a time is coming, when they must submit to be on a level with us. The philosopher said true, when he looked upon the skull of a king, and that of a poor man, that he saw no difference between them. Besides, do they not know, that the richest of princes, and the poorest of beggars, are to have one great and tremendous judge, at the last day; who will not distinguish between them according to their circumstances in life; on the contrary, may make their condemnations the greater, as their neglected opportunities were greater! Poor souls! how do I pity their pride!

This passage alone is sufficient to show how unfair Joan Rockwell is when she asserts (*Fact in Fiction*, p. 99) that Richardson "wrote *Pamela* . . . to promote an explicitly bourgeois . . . morality." Quite apart from the fact that the defense of chastity is mandated in many—indeed most—societies, Pamela stands up for a truly universal value. She demands to be treated as a person and not merely as a sex object, a demand which her would-be ravisher ultimately accepts.

Turning now to a closer consideration of the specifically ethos-building literature, we find that it is dominated by certain basic themes of which three appear to be the most persistent. It is truly astounding in how many variations they occur, and how each variant shows a face of its own, a certain originality and freshness! The first of these themes is moral conflict, a fact which will surprise nobody, and certainly not a reader of these pages. Greek mythology presents the matter in its purest, most archetypal form in the legend known as "Hercules at the Crossroads." Hercules, son of Zeus and Alcmene, so the Sophist Prodicus relates, meets with two female figures, the one representing lust or pleasure, the other virtue. The former promises him a life of enjoyments and delights; the latter, one of hardships and only late success. The demigod decides as morality decrees he should: he would rather struggle and endure than sink into sensuality and sloth. The ethos-building character of this tale is manifest. But the discussion of moral conflict is ethos-building even where the hero turns to the wrong side. The main thing is surely that the reader be reminded that there *is* a conflict between the flesh and the spirit (as some would word it), and that *every* man is at all times at the crossroads. The number of novels and plays which treat of this topic is legion. In English literature, Thomas Hardy's *Jude the Obscure* is an excellent example. The hapless Jude Fawley is torn between the sensuous Arabella Donn and the refined Susan Bridehead. In one of the jewels of German literature, in Gottfried Keller's *Der grüne Heinrich*, we find a rather similar set-up, with the giddy Judith paralleling Arabella Donn and the serious-minded Anna, Susan Bridehead. The operatic stage, too, offers numerous illustrations. In Weber's *Freischütz*, Max falls into the clutches of the devilish Kaspar, even though he knows that true salvation lies with his deeply religious bride, Agatha. In Wagner's *Tannhäuser*, the hero feels the seductive power of Venus, but also the greatness of the saintly Elizabeth. In Mascagni's *Cavalleria Rusticana*, Turiddu is attracted by the unprincipled Lola, while decency and honor demand that he should keep faith with the unhappy Santuzza. And so on, and so forth. The subject is ever old and ever new.

Where a man fails to make the choice prescribed by the societal ethos, where he prefers pleasure to virtue or duty, many works of art go on to describe the consequences. Turiddu finds out that the wages of sin are death, for he is killed in a duel by Alfio, Lola's husband, the whole village being on the latter's side. This shows up the second great, indeed commanding, topic of ethos-building literature: the concatenation of crime and punishment. One need not do more than use the last three words in order to be at once reminded of Fëdor Dostoevski's great novel which bears them as its title. Once again, the examples are legion. One of America's most impressive epics, Theodore Dreiser's *An American Tragedy*, also tells of guilt and the price which the culprit ultimately has to pay. To remain for a moment in the United States: William Faulkner's trilogy, *The Hamlet*, *The Town*, and *The Mansion*, too, belongs into this category. The operatic stage provides many instances, but two are particularly impressive: Mozart's *Don Giovanni* and Mussorgsky's *Boris Godunov*. While the Spanish rake is thrust down into hell by the higher powers, the blood-stained czar is destroyed by his own conscience.

A further great theme, but one which has rarely, if ever, been successfully treated, is the portrayal of the truly good, totally guileless, soul. While in Gustave Flaubert's *Trois Contes*, the second (*La Légende de saint Julien l'Hospitalier*) deals with a case of sin and penance, the first (*Un Coeur simple*) presents the image of a selfless woman, the humble servant Félicité, who knows only one aim in life: to make others happy. Jeremias Gotthelf's short story from the Swiss *milieu*, *Das Erdbeeri Mareili*, is somewhat similar. While such tales are often moving, they are ever in danger of becoming maudlin. It is not without deep significance that one of the very greatest novelists of all times, Dostoevski, did not succeed in presenting a really credible picture of a good man. (As for his women, it is well known that they all are and remain shadowy figures.) In *The Brothers Karamazov*, the saintly priest Zossima is removed early on, and the author does not have to explore and describe his character in any depth. His disciple Alyosha also has features of sanctity, but he is a true Karamazov all the same, and that means that he has also a nocturnal, sensual side to his self. Dostoevski's most determined effort to show a pure soul is, of course, Prince Myshkin in *The Idiot*. It is not the fact hinted at in the title that he is an idiot which prevents us from seeing him as an ideally good man; the mental breakdown comes only at the end of the sad tale. It is rather the fact that his physical weakness frees him from the desires of the flesh and that therefore he is, so to speak, only half a man, a man for whom the lure of sexual sinning is no great temptation. He does not have to conquer his animalic ego, and so he is not a moral hero in the full sense of the word (see Nicholas Berdyaev, *Dostoevsky* [London, 1934], pp. 112ff., 95, 119ff.). Other writers have found it no less difficult to elaborate a convincing portrait of a supremely good person. Milly Theale, in Henry James's refined novel *The Wings of the Dove*, is a shining light of selflessness within a society of calculating, hardhearted schemers centered in her "friend" Kate Croy, the girl who tries to exploit her and ultimately destroys her will to live. But, quite apart from the fact that Milly is, like Zossima, not allowed to live long, quite apart from the fact that she is, like Myshkin, beyond the grip of one great temptation, in this case money-grabbing (she is very rich), her character is only sketched—sketched all too lightly. We cannot really *see* her, and all critics are agreed that this is a serious weakness of the book.

A *locus classicus* concerning this whole problem is the introduction to Book 8 of Henry Fielding's *Tom Jones*. An author must remain within the bounds of probability, Fielding argues, and he will often meet with disbelief when he is "painting what is greatly good and amiable." Thus it is advisable to steer clear of this topic. "Knavery and folly will more easily meet with assent." The observation appears to be correct, and it tells us as much about the species *man* as about the subspecies *novelist*. Another important writer shared Fielding's opinion: Thackeray. "Have you ever tried to excite people by describing perfect goodness?" he asks, thinking above all of Amelia in his *Vanity Fair* (see William Makepeace Thackeray, *Memoirs of a Victorian Gentleman*, ed. Margaret Forster [London, 1978], p. 72; see also p. 372).

> It does not work—I notice Dickens in this respect is no better than I—goodness won't get itself pinned down on paper without overtones of sickliness whereas evil, or at least waywardness, makes an imprint straight away. The very qualities we try to define are those that shun definition and we must end with a great many superlatives adding up to nothing much. People won't accept that degree of saintliness without resentment, or a sneer of disbelief, and even when they do they are liable to be bored by a character so blameless.

Perhaps the most ambitious attempt to display purity on the stage is Richard Wagner's "festival play" *Parsifal*. But this takes us into the field of saga and legend and therefore of make-believe. Still, this would not be decisive. Decisive is the fact that Parsifal is conceived as a replica of Jesus Christ. With this oratorio-like work of art, we are no longer in the realm of fiction; we have crossed the borderline into religious conceptions, and their bearing on the societal ethos is a thing apart.

In discussing Richardson's *Pamela* a short while ago, we rejected Joan Rockwell's contention that the novelist wanted no more than to promote an "explicitly bourgeois morality." Thereby hangs a much more general problem which we have to consider. The tradition of historicism is not dead yet, and its basic conviction—namely, that all intellectual life is contained in, and confined to, a limited phase in social development—comes to the surface in Rockwell's remarks. No doubt, a good deal in all novels and stage plays is a reflection of contemporary conditions and preoccupations, but it would be quite wrong to overlook the generically human element which is of supreme importance in our investigation since we are dealing throughout with *man*, and not simply with primitive or feudal or capitalist or post-capitalist humanity. A good opportunity for correcting Rockwell's *outré* stance is offered by her treatment of Sir Walter Scott. "Scott's heroes," she writes (*Fact in Fiction*, p. 120), "were restricted to his own moral universe which, like all other writers, he could not transcend. . . . Scott cannot choose but create heroes in his own image, or the image of his internalised values and norms, derived from nineteenth-century middle-class life." More is untenable in these sentences than the exaggeration contained in the reference to "all other writers" and in such terms as "could not" and "cannot." It was precisely Scott who had deep understanding for societies dead and gone—for the Scottish highland culture which had met its doom in 1745, for instance. We cannot appreciate him at all unless we remember that he was a disciple of the great Scottish social theorists of the late-eighteenth century, men like Adam Ferguson and John Millar. Perhaps even this can be explained along historical lines, but there is still more than that to Sir Walter Scott. One great problem with which he struggles is the position—the predicament—of the man who, in a conflict, has loved ones in both hostile camps and cannot bring himself to break with either. In *Waverley*—to present but one illustration—the young man of that name is torn between his Hanoverian father and his Jacobite uncle and foster-father, and later between loyalty to his native England ruled by George II and sympathy for the cause, adopted by his Scottish friends, of Stuart restoration. It must, of course, be admitted that this romance was inspired by the remembrance and observation of fairly recent historical events, but the dilemma of Edward Waverley is one which is apt to spring up in any and every age. He, too, is a hero at the crossroads. We can clearly see, in contemplating this instance, how justified the adversaries of historicism were when they argued that in the specific we always encounter the universal, and in the historical or local the generically human. It was the generically human, and not the historical or local, which Scott wished to depict. He himself says in the very first chapter of *Waverley* that he intends to deal with

> those passions common to men in all stages of society, and which have alike agitated the human heart, whether it throbbed under the steel corselet of the fifteenth century, the brocaded coat of the eighteenth, or the blue frock and white dimity of the present day. Upon these passions it is no doubt true that the state of manners and laws casts a necessary colouring; but the bearings, to use the language of heraldry, remains the same. . . .

This assertion that "the deep-ruling impulse is the same" in all times and climes should surely have been sufficient to give Joan Rockwell pause.

Of course, Joan Rockwell does not stand alone with her prejudice. Helmut Fend's book *Sozialisation durch Literatur* (Weinheim & Basel, 1979) goes one step further and asserts that the writer's vista is limited, not only by his inclusive society, but, even more narrowly, by his class-affiliation. One wonders whether such authors have ever heard the command: Thou shalt not kill! Is there an age, is there a stratum, is there a group in which it does not apply, and where murder is therefore not an obvious, and obviously moving, topic for literature and art? But we should not wax rhetorical; we have no need to. Our attempt to reduce the influence of historicism to its proper dimensions has copious and convincing material to back it up. A treatise by Horst and Ingrid Daemmrich, with the title *Wiederholte Spiegelungen*, that is, "Repeated Mirrorings" (Bern & Munich, 1978), shows on a broad front how the selfsame themes reappear in successive literatures, in spite of all the transformations and revolutions in the social substructure, simply because they are of perennial concern. One of the oldest of all epics is the *Odyssey*, the tale of the hapless wanderer Odysseus, the victim of wind and waves, who reaches his home only after countless adventures and sufferings. But one of the most successful novels of the twentieth century, too, is called *Ulysses* (using the hero's Latinized name for its title), and between Homer and James Joyce (and beyond) there stretches a long chain of writings which deal with the same motif, Dante's *Divine Comedy* being the most resplendent link. We should not forget, in this context, Bunyan's *The Pilgrim's Progress* either, or, for that matter, Ibsen's *Peer Gynt*. It is true that the sufferer and searcher are painted in very different colors. Two interesting books discuss the variations of this grand theme, W. B. Stanford's *The Ulysses Theme: A Study in the Adaptability of a Traditional Hero* (Oxford, 1954) and Joseph Campbell's *The Hero With A Thousand Faces* (Princeton, 1953). Odysseus may be seen as sad or even despairing, or again as enterprising, confident, and even aggressive. Dante is led, first by human reason which is represented by Virgil, and, on the last stage of his journey, by divine grace mediated by the sanctified Beatrice. Bunyan's Christian, on the other hand, has to undergo trials and tribulations, and it is his inner steadfastness which brings him to "the world which is to come." Nikos Kazantzakis' *Odysseus* (1928) and *Odyssée* (1938) are dominated by yet other philosophical conceptions. But though there *are* variations, there is also *one* theme. Insofar as the surrounding society inclines the writers to one side or the other, the suggestions of the historicist school are justified. Yet all the works concerned center on the basic conviction—we may as well say, the basic fact—that human existence is unavoidably, and hence invariably, a search for some harbor, a last anchor-ground without which the storm-tossed boat must founder and sink.

The figure of Odysseus reminds us of a crucial feature of the fairy tale (whose hero usually leaves his home to wander out into the world) and also of the saga (whose hero invariably experiences the hardships of life and the distressing limitations of the *condition humaine*). But there is yet another great theme derived from the older, more collective forms of poetry which has also entered into modern literature and runs through it: the conviction that *to be* means to undergo test after test, and the knowledge that man in the process has to prove himself strong enough to endure and to conquer. The Daemmrichs consider Alexander Solzhenitsyn's moving book *A Day in the Life of Ivan Denisovich* (1962) and comment on it as follows (*Wiederholte Spiegelungen*, p. 29):

> In the discussion of Ivan's struggle for survival Solzhenitsyn falls back on a thematic constant of Occidental literature. The actors experience existence as a testing. . . . In the solutions of the problem, three preferred forms are to be

discovered: the protagonists fail because of their own insufficiency, they are
overcome by the given circumstances, or they successfully assert their claim to
give shape to their own lives.

Such a *summa summarum* sounds dry, and it certainly gives no idea of the
tremendous variety of the literature whose essence it so tersely encapsulates.
The main point, however, is well taken: there is a universal theme with three
subthemes or variations, and it runs as constantly through the successive variants as the old Hungarian St. Anthony chorale through Brahms's "Variations
on a Theme of Haydn."

The ethos-building tendency of the literary works just reviewed is obvious,
but more obvious still is the positive and often powerful contribution made by
the novels known as educational. A prototype of this kind is Thomas Mann's
four-volume epic called *Joseph und seine Brüder* (1933–1943). It shows its
hero on the way from egocentricity to altruistic service, to devotion to duty
and the welfare of the community. Jacob, a doting father, admires and spoils
his handsome and winsome son until he (Joseph) believes that all around must
love him. But life opens his eyes: he recognizes that his early self-adulation
implied a definite lack of understanding for the needs and desires of others, an
inner coldness and deadness; even self-fulfillment, so he comes to see, depends
on warm human relationships, on the life-giving qualities of the human environment within which one has to fulfill one's destiny. The aging Joseph is
characterized by a deep sympathy and respect for his fellow-men. The work
might be called the study of a metamorphosis. But such a study is also Goethe's
Faust whose hero begins as the reckless seducer of innocent Gretchen and ends
as a high idealist, draining swamps in order to provide new land on which a
free people may live in independence and happiness; such a study is also
Shakespeare's *King Henry IV*, with its sequel *King Henry V*. These royal
dramas record the transformation of a dissolute youth, Falstaff's boon companion, into a king of the highest principles, the glorious victor of Agincourt.

Yet even the educational novel and stage play are not the most impressive
helper of the collective forces in their endeavor to develop and inculcate a
societal ethos. That honor belongs to the works—and they are many—which
deal with a case of ὕβρις, a man's willful rebellion against history, society,
nature, the laws of the universe, or Almighty God. Captain Ahab in Herman
Melville's *Moby Dick* is an illustration; so is the titular hero in Henrik Ibsen's
Brand, and, on a more modest level, James Brodie in A. J. Cronin's *Hatter's
Castle* (1931). On the stage, Shakespeare's *Richard III* represents the type,
and, to some extent at any rate, *Macbeth*, too. The man who unrealistically
thinks that he is strong enough to challenge, defeat, and coerce the powers of
heaven and earth, whose will is so inflated that he sees and sets no limits to
his schemes and ambitions, who imagines that he can ride roughshod over his
fellows and that even God cannot stop him, is bound to come to grief in the
end. Pride goes before a fall—that is the message of many works of art. It is addressed to all men; it is addressed more particularly to the great. Giovanni Boccaccio's *De casibus illustrium virorum* (written ca. 1360, printed in 1475) with
its English pendants, John Lydgate's *Falls of Princes* (first printed in 1494)

and Thomas Sackville's *Mirror of Magistrates* (1559) and *Tragedy of Gorboduc* (1561), imparted to English literature a tendency which it retained for a long time. "A single type of serious story predominated over all others," writes R. G. Moulton in *The Moral System of Shakespeare* (London, 1903; p. 187), and he describes Sackville as "one of the fathers of our modern drama." "Tragedy," he asserts (ibid.), "came into the age of Shakespeare with this special connotation of fallen greatness," and again: "A tragedy is, to Shakespeare's audience and to Shakespeare, a story of a fall."

The failings of the high and mighty are the failings of all men, the only difference being that they have wider opportunities of breaking the moral law because they are aided by power and wealth. Insofar as a public applies the lessons pressed on it in books and plays to humanity in general, insofar as a reader or listener applies them to himself in particular, the societal ethos will be strengthened. But it is possible—indeed, likely—that a negative sentiment will enter in. The upper tens are envied, and their dramatized discomfiture and humiliation may well give pleasure to the lower strata who envy them. In this case the tone of society may be worsened rather than improved. A revolutionary attitude—even a class struggle—can often be justified, for its final outcome may be an invigoration of the social bond; personal ill will toward concrete fellow-humans, never, if the basic social integration is to remain entirely unimpeded. Fire and water cannot be mixed, but as far as the influence of literature on the societal ethos is concerned, we have to recognize that positive and negative, constructive and destructive, tendencies blend and fuse.

LITERATURE: THE DRAMA

120. To the securest possessions of the science of sociology—some would say: to its commonplaces—belongs the distinction between two fundamental forms of social organization, community and association. Community, so we may recall, is a close-knit society; its prototype is the family. The members are tied together by strong emotional bonds; they form an integrated body. In Aristotelian language, the whole is here before the parts, the group before the individuals. The latter receive their lives from the society into which they are born. An associational system, on the other hand, is a loose-textured society; its prototype is the business firm. The members are brought together by coolly calculated prospects of gain and remain together only as long as the profit lasts. In Aristotelian language, the parts are here before the whole, the individuals before the group. The latter comes into existence if and when some persons get together and create by their willing, by the conclusion of a contract, a common institution, a common tool. History has led from a prevalence of the communitarian type to a proliferation of associational formations, though every concrete society has, and must have, both communitarian and associational elements in its makeup.

The importance of this typology, classically developed by Ferdinand Tönnies, for our investigation consists in this: that the effort to build and preserve a societal ethos is different under the two dispensations. First of all, a community, if it is to persist, must put a great deal of energy into the socialization of its members, especially the young ones. It is, if we may so express it, the more ambitious type. Associational societies will be more relaxed because they wish to grant the maximum of independence to the people—the people both as a collectivity and as a multiplicity of individuals. Social control will have a rather negative aim: to see to it that excessive self-regard should not lead to *open* conflict, conflict within the limits of legality being considered as acceptable and even as healthy and desirable. But this is only by the way. The main aspect to which we have to draw attention is that communities and associations cultivate by preference different modalities of literary creation. Because the community centers on the collective—the public—life, it will foster the drama and the stage in general. Because associational society centers on the individual, on private life, it will see in the novel a more attractive alternative. You can read while you are alone; to see a play, you have to repair to the theater. Of course, novels, or preliminary forms of it, will also be written and enjoyed in community-type societies, while the stage has preserved a good deal of its appeal even in our modern culture, which is largely associational. But this takes nothing from the truth of the observations which we have just made.

Classical Hellenic drama, product of a communitarian tradition, showed its moralizing character in an external feature: its inclusion in the ecclesiastical calendar. "Greek tragedy," writes R. G. Moulton (*Moral System of Shakespeare*, p. 186), "was a religious service, commencing with ritual at the altar of Dionysus; the choral odes led the thoughts of the audience in religious meditation. . . . The acted scenes were sacred myths, like the acted sermon of the [medieval] miracle play." Joan Rockwell brings out the same point. "The plays were part of the annual city festivals," she writes (*Fact in Fiction*, pp. 54, 142);

> one play of a trilogy was acted on each of the three days of the festival. . . . Religious ritual contributed to social literature not only a body of myths, but the rituals themselves, from which it is generally agreed that the Greek drama, that most social of social literature, emerged. . . . The rituals embody and unify the whole tribe or clan, and the Athenian drama in a more sophisticated way did the same for the people of the polis.

But Rockwell has another important insight to offer as well. She confirms what we said in the last section about the dual character of literary works:

> The classical drama at once represents, and limits the incidence of, crime. Crimes are described, but never committed; no scene of actual violence may appear on the stage—such matters are obscene (= "off-stage," not to be shown). . . . But at the same time, the emotion of the audience is engaged. . . . They have a surrogate participation in the crime and also in the punishment, identifying now with the criminal, now with the avenging power of society. . . . They see, and, what is more important, they feel, by emotional participation, what is crime and what the punishment must be. . . . Classical Greek tragedy is the drama of crime and punishment. . . .

This lapidary statement is correct, but not to be accepted without closer consideration. In the process of it, a number of important problems will be seen to crop up, and they have to be laid to rest. Here let us, in a preliminary way, support Rockwell's contention, which we share, by an apposite quotation. It is taken from Hugh Lloyd-Jones's translation of the *Agamemnon* of Aeschylus (New York, 1970; p. 100):

> The plunderer is plundered and the slayer slain.
> But it abides, while Zeus abides upon his throne,
> That he who does shall suffer; for it is the law.

On reading these lines, we are at once reminded of the great *lex talionis* which is present in the older parts of the Old Testament: "He that giveth a blemish to any of his neighbours: as he hath done, so shall it be done to him. Breach for breach, eye for eye, tooth for tooth, shall he restore. What blemish he gave, the like shall he be compelled to suffer" (Lv 24:19–20). This kind of justice appears to us crude and even cruel, but it *is* justice of a kind, and by inculcating it, the Greek drama was bound to have a strongly disciplining, society-pacifying and -integrating effect.

Yet, as soon as we enter a little more deeply into the texts, we see that the plunderer is not always plundered and the slayer is not always slain, and herein consists the first difficulty. The criminal deed is often done by one man, while the retribution falls on the head of another. Gyges contracts blood guilt because he deposes and kills Candaules, the king of Lydia. He is the first of the dynasty of the Mermnadae, but it is only the last of this house, Croesus, Gyges' distant offspring, who is punished for the act. The Bible contains similar stories. Noah, unused to wine, gets drunk and lies incapacitated in his tent. His son Cham holds him up to ridicule. When he sobers up and learns what has happened, he exclaims: Cursed be Chanaan! (Gn 9:20ff.). The son is blamed for the objectionable conduct of his father. The principle involved here—the co-responsibility of blood kin, the identity of forebear and offspring—is often expressed in general terms, as if it were a rule of unrestricted validity. In a poem of the seventh century before Christ, "A Prayer to the Muses," the author, presumably Solon, gives it as an article of faith that Zeus infallibly avenges any and every wicked deed. Uncertain are merely the day and hour at which the punishing blow will fall; fall it will. If it comes later rather than earlier, it will attain the culprit's heir and not the culprit himself. This appears to the poet as a principle of divine justice, and he accepts it without demur (see Gustave Glotz, *La Solidarité de la famille dans le droit criminel en Grèce* [Paris, 1904], pp. 577, 578). Within the frame of the Ten Commandments handed by Yahweh to Moses on Mount Sinai (Ex 20:5), the same maxim is solemnly pronounced: "I am the Lord thy God, mighty, jealous, visiting the iniquity of the fathers upon the children, unto the third and fourth generation. . . ." This verse was a scandal to the nineteenth century, but for the anthropologist and sociologist there is hardly a problem. The basic thought of communitarian cultures is collectivistic; the vital and decisive unit is the clan, the descent group, in which the *same* life incarnates itself in superficially different, but ultimately identical, individuals. Gyges is Croesus and Croesus, Gyges; Cham is Chanaan and Chanaan, Cham. According to this mentality, no injustice is involved. On the contrary. According to the ancient Greeks, according to the ancient Jews, justice prevails when Croesus and Cham are overtaken by heaven-sent disaster. Thus, whatever modern man may think and feel about it, the tales contained in the *Histories* of Herodotus (1.7ff.) and in Genesis *were* ethos-building in the societies concerned. We say: *were* ethos-building. We may also say, in permissible generalization: *are* ethos-building in communities. This formulation brings out an important point. The fact that associational societies insist on the principle of individual responsibility while communitarian cultures believe in solidarity, in the sharing of crime and punishment, in original sin, is no argument in favor of historicism. On the contrary, it supports the opposite conception, the typological approach. Even if mankind has in time moved from community with its flanking modes of thought to association with its entirely different ideas and ideologies, the alternative systems are more than historical phases, phases in a developmental sequence. They are ever-possible forms of life, to be systematically and not evolutionally distinguished. Community is not over and done with; it has occurred; it has recurred; in principle, it may occur and recur again.

As can be seen, the observation that, in the old literature, the perpetrator of a misdeed is not always identical with the person who has to pay the penalty for it need not detain us any longer. A second difficulty, however, is more intricate and intriguing. Some literary historians, among them experts of considerable prestige, have asserted that what the Greek tragedians want to demonstrate is, not that sin is always followed by retribution, but rather that man is in the grip of fate, of blind destiny. This assertion was repudiated even before classical Greek drama ever appeared, and that by a voice which cannot possibly be overheard. The *Odyssey* (1.32ff.) puts the following words into the mouth of Zeus which we quote in the English rendering of Alexander Pope (*The Iliad and Odyssey of Homer*, ed. T. A. Buckley [London, n.d.], p. 458):

> Perverse mankind! whose will created free,
> Charge all their woes on absolute decree.
> All to the dooming gods their guilt translate
> And follies are miscalled the crimes of fate.

Such lines must weigh heavy in the scales, and yet it is understandable that the upholders of the theory which urges that we must see classical Greek drama against the background of a deterministic philosophy of life have set them aside. For the material on which they base themselves is, above all, the works of Aeschylus and Sophocles, products of post-Homeric times, and in these, they claim, there is little to support the thesis that the chief subject matter of the Athenian stage-plays is the certain concatenation of crime and punishment. If this were indeed so, the Athenian drama would have tended to weaken the societal ethos of the day, not to strengthen it. Assuming that chance controls the world, not justice, men would have no incentive, or at least one incentive fewer, to obey the laws. Why keep to the straight and narrow path of rectitude if you run no risk by abandoning it? One of the most interesting books in which this matter is discussed is not a scholarly or philosophical treatise, but a novel:

James Hogg's *The Private Memoirs and Confessions of a Justified Sinner* (1824). The author tries to trace the moral decay of a man totally penetrated by the Calvinist doctrine of predestination: his career ends in the devil's carrying off his soul into hell. What is true of the consequences of a deterministic philosophy in A.D. 1800 would be true of a deterministic theory in the year 500 B.C. as well, at least as far as the fundamental tendency is concerned.

The strength of this argument is somewhat weakened by the fact to which we have drawn attention: namely, that the punishment of Croesus and of Chanaan is due, not to a dark and meaningless destiny, but to the clear and meaningful conviction that in a community the sin of one is the sin of all, and the merit of one is the merit of all. But this reference to the collectivistic ethos of early Greek (and Hebrew) society does not allow us to lay the matter *ad acta*. It has to be thoroughly explored.

Perhaps we can best come to grips with the whole problem if we concentrate for a moment on one or two of the *dramatis personae* whose doings and sufferings Aeschylus, Sophocles, and Euripides placed before the people of Athens. Antigone, in the play by Sophocles, disobeys the king, Creon, and thereby commits a crime against the state. Creon has decreed that Antigone's brother, Polyneices, shall remain unburied, his body a prey to dogs and carrion birds. Antigone is appalled by this dishonor inflicted on a dead man and feels —indeed, knows—that it is her duty to bury him who was her next of kin, her blood brother. Condemned to be interred alive, she commits suicide. Is Antigone really guilty, so guilty as to deserve the death sentence? Can the gods as guardians of justice have wished to annihilate her? Later centuries have given negative answers to these last questions, and that with some warmth. Antigone became a heroine to the philosophers of natural right, for did she not appeal to the natural law sanctifying family relationships as against the cold political law, an inferior law, enforced by Creon? She became a heroine even to Christian thinkers, almost a pre-Christian saint like the saints of the Old Covenant, for did she not place the call of piety and love above the commands of vengefulness and cruelty? In Antigone's case, so many have felt, punishment is not preceded and justified by crime.

The case of Orestes is more involved, but the final conclusion drawn by many is similar. His mother, Clytemnestra, and her paramour, Aegisthus, kill his father, Agamemnon, and he, to avenge the deed, exterminates the guilty pair. Thereupon the Furies set upon him and torture him until he finds in the end—after many hardships—purification and release. What right had the Erinyes to drive him almost to distraction? What can possibly justify their relentless pursuit? Modern man will answer: he killed his mother; he deserved what he got. But this argument is weak, if the social setting within which the tragic events take place is taken into account. Aegisthus has usurped the throne. The old and legitimate order in the state has to be restored, and Orestes, as the son of the assassinated lawful ruler, is the person on whom the sacred duty to restore it, falls. As far as Aegisthus is concerned, Orestes is, to the Greeks, not a murderer, but a defender of right. The case of Clytemnestra is different. Though smeared by Agamemnon's blood, she is still Orestes'

mother. Orestes is not unaware of the gravity of matricide. His friend Pylades
has to urge him on, and he does so by reminding him that the god Apollo has
ordered the destruction of Clytemnestra as well as Aegisthus. Who can be
guilty if he does what the higher powers command him to do? Would he not
rather have incurred guilt if he had refused to execute the divine judgment? In
modern times the very word "mother" is considered so sacred and is so steeped
in sentiment that the deed of Orestes must necessarily appear as the crime of
crimes. But the Greeks felt differently. Says Apollo in Aeschylus' *Oresteia* (we
quote here the translation of Gilbert Murray [London, 1928], p. 235, which
offers a more pleasing English version than that of Lloyd-Jones):

> The mother to the child that men call hers
> Is no true life begetter, but a nurse. . . .
> . . . The sower of the seed
> Alone begetteth. Woman comes at need,
> A stranger, to hold safe in trust and love
> That bud. . . .

The mother a stranger to her son? We can hardly grasp such a conception, and
even the Greeks may have seen an exaggeration in this way of putting it. But
they would, all the same, have accepted the basic conviction which rises to the
surface here. A man is in the first place, and in the most sacred sense, a member of his clan, and that membership is mediated by males, and males alone.
The links which tie Orestes to Clytemnestra are little compared to the links
which tie him to Agamemnon and his (Agamemnon's) father (or grandfather),
Atreus.

The upholders of the opinion that the Greek drama, appearances to the
contrary notwithstanding, sets out to teach that justice is invariably done in the
world, have tried to buttress their case by insisting that Antigone and Orestes
are, when all is said and done, in fact guilty. As far as Orestes is concerned, this
is relatively easy, for he has killed his mother. Why did he hesitate, why did he
have to be urged on by Pylades, if he did not know that he was doing wrong?
The case of Antigone is different and more difficult. Yet she resisted established
authority; Creon was after all her king, and the king should be obeyed. Similar
arguments have been put forward by analysts of the Oedipus saga. He slew his
father and married his mother, yet, it is urged, he committed neither parricide
nor incest for he did not know that the stranger he slew—and that in entirely
justifiable self-defense—was his father, and the woman he wed was his mother.
He must be held excused! No, says the opposite party, the fact remains that he
slew a man old enough to be his father and took for a wife a woman old
enough to be his mother, and this precisely was his double crime for which he
was deservedly punished. Such arguments are unconvincing. They are largely
artificial. If such were indeed the contents of the great Greek plays, they would
be poor stuff. In these pages the opinion that the works of Aeschylus and
Sophocles, and even Euripides, are ethos-building—indeed, the thesis that,
in some sense, justice is always done—will certainly be upheld, but, it is hoped,
by better arguments than those just paraded. If we were to condemn Antigone

simply because she set aside a tyrant's unreasonable and inhuman order, we should be judges who ought to be chased from the judgment seat.

What must be avoided at all cost, if the ethos-building bearing of Greek literature is to be understood, is the application of modern hyper-individualistic conceptions. Let us realize, first of all, that Antigone is the sister of Eteocles and Polyneices who are involved in fratricidal war (shades of Cain and Abel, shades of Romulus and Remus!). If they act criminally, and they do, their whole clan is attainted and even accursed. How can Antigone, according to collectivistic ideas, not be involved? Furthermore, all three siblings are children of Oedipus and Jocasta, and even if we hold these two excused because they did not know that their marriage was incestuous, the fact remains that Oedipus was the son of Laius, and Laius laid the foundations of an hereditary curse, i.e., committed an original sin. An oracle tells him that he will perish by his son's hands, and he thereupon orders the destruction of the child. Is it reasonable to obey a dark saying of this kind? Are we allowed to do what is utterly absurd? A representative of the Neo-Kantian school of ethics, Albert Görland, has argued in a very interesting book, *Die Idee des Schicksals in der Geschichte der Tragödie* (Tübingen, 1913), that it was the aim of Aeschylus to expose the immorality of the oracular sayings, and if this is true of Aeschylus, it is true of Sophocles as well. The real killer then is Laius, who, cravenly afraid for his own life, decrees the death of an innocent babe-in-arms, and the disasters which overtake Oedipus, Eteocles, Polyneices, and Antigone, are simply the ultimate consequences of this conduct. The case of Orestes lies parallel. He is the son of Agamemnon, Agamemnon the son or grandson of Atreus, Atreus the grandson of Tantalus, offender of the gods: here we have, in the progenitors, enough guilt to last, according to collectivist conceptions, through many generations and to involve even those whose deeds may, from some points of view, appear excusable.

But our analysis cannot stop even here. We have to dig yet deeper. The modern drama is individualistic and, because it is individualistic, also psychological. If its subject is a crime, it shows how the crime develops out of the character of the perpetrator or out of the conditions within which his life is set. The ancient drama placed the emphasis elsewhere: on the deed done, not on the doer of the deed. We hope we are understood when we say that it was objectivistic and not subjectivistic. "The deed is the deed and nothing else," writes Emil Staiger about the Attic stage in his article "Charakter und Schuld in der Tragödie" (see *Schuld, Verantwortung, Strafe, etc.*, ed. E. R. Frey [Zurich, 1964], pp. 27, 24). "In man, only that is taken note of and acknowledged to exist which is publicly displayed. Whatever is private is inessential." And again, adding a reference to the chorus, which is so important a feature of classical drama:

> In tragedy only that is being discussed which concerns the public, and that means, in this context, the polis. The chorus represents the polis. A tragic destiny is relevant only insofar as it impinges upon the polis. . . . The consequences of the uninterrupted presence of the chorus are important. Because every action and every word are to be submitted to the chorus for its approval,

any interest in a merely internal attitude is excluded. The chorus emphasizes that man counts only insofar as he reveals himself. For this reason we find in Attic tragedy, generally speaking, no monologues, those speeches with the aid of which the hero of the modern theater informs the public . . . about his inner mental life.

What Friedrich Schiller, in his essay "Gedanken über den Gebrauch des Ge-meinen und Niedrigen in der Kunst" ("Thoughts Concerning the Use of What is Low and Mean in Art," *Werke*, ed. Heinrich Kurz [Leipzig, n.d.], pp. 577, 578), says about the drama in general is doubly and trebly true of Athenian drama: "If we are confronted with a serious and terrifying crime, our attention is deflected from its quality and directed toward its distressing consequences. . . . We then do not look backward toward the soul of the perpetrator, but forward . . . toward the effects of his deed."

Let us hear, on this crucial aspect, yet another of the outstanding experts, Kurt von Fritz:

> It is an ancient Greek, and probably pre-Greek, conception that the dreadful nature of an act is tied to the act itself and is independent of the motives of the actor. A man who has accidentally killed his brother or his friend or who was obliged to do so because of a higher duty is no less stained, and no less under the necessity to cleanse himself of the stain, than he who has murdered his brother in anger or out of covetousness. Among the tragedians it was above all Aeschylus who made repeated use of this primitive concept. Orestes is perse-cuted by the Erinyes even though he has acted at the command of a god. The Danaids carry blood guilt even though they have, in desperation, killed their cousins and husbands because of their [insupportable] violence and brutality. It is true that in both cases the perpetrators are finally freed of their guilt by a divinity which bases its judgment on the given motives. Yet it is the curse which clings to the deed itself and is independent of the motives which pro-vides the starting point of the [plays'] action. If we look closely we see that with Sophocles and Euripides [also] the objective dreadfulness of the deed is al-ways clearly distinguished from the subjective guilt, even where both are in fact present, yet never in such a way that the act loses all its terror if only the actor is innocent.

"This feeling," the author ends this remarkable passage, "that an act may be morally shocking even if it cannot be imputed to the actor is in the final analysis very human" (*Antike und moderne Tragödie* [Berlin, 1962], p. 467). We should agree!

Elsewhere in his book (ibid., pp. 15, 16) von Fritz applies this insight to the concrete cases of Antigone and Orestes:

> It is of decisive importance that Antigone herself . . . is not responsible for the situation which becomes so tragic to her. If she had not been placed, from the outside, in a situation in which her brothers had killed each other in a duel and her uncle and king had given the order to throw the body of the one to the dogs because he had fought against his native city, her fate would not have become tragic. The same is even truer of the Orestes of the Aeschylus trilogy and to a certain extent even of the plays of Euripides: he might have ruled as a legiti-mate successor to the throne and a happy king, without passing through any

tragic conflict, if his father had died a natural death and had not been murdered by his [Orestes'] mother. Here we behold an essential . . . contrast between Greek and modern tragedy.

Emil Staiger, in a similar context (see "Charakter und Schuld in der Tragödie," pp. 24, 27), makes an incidental remark which may well strike us as unpleasant and may well be disagreeable to us, but which helps us to understand the Greek attitude to crime as displayed in the great works of dramatic art.

> If we not only wish to understand [classical] tragedy theoretically but try (as it might be expressed) to feel our way into it, we must refer back to those reactions which we, as modern and cultured persons, otherwise suppress or think it our duty to suppress, to that embarrassment, for instance, which comes upon us if we met a man who we know has unknowingly committed a dreadful act. . . . We have the impression: he is stained. There is an invisible mark upon his forehead. . . . What in this situation is darkly at work within us is with Sophocles still strong and clear.

A healthy reminder, this, that, in spite of all the admitted contrasts between ancient and modern culture, community and association, there is yet a bridge between the two because at the basis of both of them there lies a common humanity.

If we now stop to consider what all this means for our analysis, that is, for the build-up of a societal ethos, we are soon led to recognize that the scant attention paid to the psychology of the culprit does not in any way diminish the educational effectiveness of the plays. Perhaps it even increases it! We must look at the whole matter from the point of view of the audience, the Athenian population, the public of the classical dramas. They see crime painted in garish colors—crime itself is the focus, and nothing is allowed to interfere with the impressiveness of the picture. They also see punishment painted in garish colors, and the horror of it leaves a deep impression. Modern man, with his specific psychology, may well feel—indeed, must feel—that an entire dimension is missing, for what is the justification of retribution if there is no justifying sin? But the question which so deeply moves us—do the figures on the stage deserve what is coming to them? does the punishment fit the crime?—was not raised with the same insistence 2,500 years ago. In societies of the community type the individual simply is not so interesting and important as in associational cultures.

Of course, we must be careful here not to overshoot the mark. Though the guilt of the *dramatis personae* is not explored and explained in detail, it would be wrong to assume that it is totally non-existent. Guilt may be of two kinds: it may be a personal sin or it may be a collective sin—an original sin, as those grown up in the Christian tradition would be inclined to say. We have already observed that it is the latter kind of guilt which is in the foreground of collectivist thinking. Antigone, Orestes, and Oedipus may be guilty in the sense that they are the kind of person hereditarily inclined to sinning; the collective sin received from the ancestors may be viewed as a tendency to sin oneself. We are using the terms "inclined" and "tendency" advisedly for nobody is forced to give in to an inclination or to give free rein to a tendency. Might those under a hereditary curse not have resisted the inclination or the tendency which leads to disaster? Are not *all* men prone to evil so that *none* is wholly innocent? In his treatise *The Sociology of Religion* (v 51ff.) the present author has shown that the Greek conception of ὕβρις—the generically human bent toward self-aggrandizement, pride, and all associated forms of egotism—is comparable with, and runs parallel to, the Judaeo-Christian conception of Adam's Fall and its everlasting consequences. It is, to say the least, not certain that Antigone's rebellious attitude is morally superior to the sad, but quiet, submission of her sister, Ismene. Is it not written that the meek are blessed and shall possess the land?

At this point our analysis is likely to run into considerable opposition. We have quoted Kurt von Fritz in support of our argument; now we must face him as an adversary. He pleads that nothing but error can result if we submit to the temptation to see Greek culture through Christian eyes (*Antike und moderne Tragödie*, esp. pp. 20, 51, 466, 468, 469). He severely criticizes Otto Küster's paper "Die Schuld des Königs Oedipus" (*Beiträge zur geistigen Überlieferung* [Godesberg, 1947], pp. 167ff.) because he "operates throughout, now with Old Testament, now with Christian, conceptions." Yet just a few lines later, an argument for possible use by an anti-critic is unwittingly provided. "Küster's interpretation shows a certain affinity to Seneca's opinion of the Oedipus tragedy," Fritz writes (*Antike und moderne Tragödie*, p. 466). But Seneca was a heathen, a man of pre-Christian antiquity. If *he* moves in the direction later taken up by scholars who see a certain kinship between the Judaeo-Christian concept of Original Sin and the Aeschylean and Sophoclean view of man—a thoroughly tragic one—this is a strong indication of the fact that even the ancients saw humanity laboring under a collective guilt, a guilt of which an element is present in every person. Of course, we must be careful. It will not do simply to equate the meaning of ἁμαρτία, said by Aristotle to be the root of the tragic events shown on the stage—a term usually translated as "a tragic flaw"—with "Original Sin." The undertones and overtones are no doubt different. Yet Original Sin has certainly created a tragic flaw on the part of mankind, and it is justifiable, at least to some extent, to invert this statement and to say that the tragic flaw, the ἁμαρτία, of the Greeks is, *mutatis mutandis*, something like the effect of a primordial fall. Von Fritz himself writes (*Antike und moderne Tragödie*, p. 72): "The tragedy of antiquity lays bare . . . the dark underground of human existence." The doctrine of Original Sin is in essence just such a baring of the dark underground of human existence, and therein consists the comparability of the two tragic senses of life.

We can, surely, not do better than to pit von Fritz against von Fritz. This is what he writes (ibid., p. 14):

> The fundamental condition of human existence which is revealed in *Oedipus* consists in this: that it can happen to a man to commit, in ignorance, an action which appears to him as something horrible . . . when he comes to know what he has done; in the *Oresteia*, that a man may drift into a situation in which it becomes his inescapable duty to do something which, when seen by itself, outrages his whole moral sense and will pursue him, as something frightful,

even though it has been his duty; in *Antigone*, that somebody feels obliged, at the insistence of his conscience, to do a deed . . . for which he is not only being punished, but which also fails to meet with an understanding on the part . . . of his friends . . . ; in many other tragedies, but above all in most of the tragedies of Euripides, that a person with the ordinary weaknesses of average human nature which would have allowed him, under normal circumstances, to lead an entirely normal life, may find himself confronted by a situation in which it is far beyond his moral power and his moral insight to act lawfully and correctly, and that he incurs, in the struggle with this situation, sufferings, including even moral sufferings, which are far greater than would correspond to the personal guilt which can be imputed to him.

These words surely mean, and must mean, that man—*every* man—is apt to fail when he is put to the test. The human race does not have the ethos, the ethical stamina, which it would need, and this is precisely the tragic flaw of which Aristotle speaks and which Aeschylus, Sophocles, and even the more individualistic Euripides display on the stage. Even if an Antigone, an Orestes, an Oedipus does not burden himself with a *personal* sin great enough to justify the punishment which will come down on him, he is yet, from the very beginning, also burdened with a *collective* weakness or imperfection which must not be left out of the account. To be *man* is simply to be in some dark, but real, sense *guilty*. This is not believed in the twentieth century, but it was believed in classical Greece. It was also believed in the homeland of Christianity and, until very recent times, in the Christian οἰκουμένη. Thus the moral metaphysic of the Athenians is not entirely different from the moral metaphysic of the Bible. A careful comparison of the two is permissible, and it sheds light on the moral bearings of Greek drama. It taught its audiences what man is: a creature weak, fallible, and inclined to sin.

In case the argument of the last few paragraphs lacks convincingness because it is somewhat abstract, let us put some flesh on its bare bones. The tragic flaw or original sin, call it what you will, is above all also the cause of men's inability to build a truly satisfactory society—more technically expressed: a truly integrated social whole. Because of men's self-preference, their restlessness, their combativeness, and so on, *conflict* becomes an ever-present reality in their midst, and it is conflict which leads Antigone, Orestes, and even Oedipus into the situations in which they become guiltlessly guilty. Antigone is beset by a clash of duties, a conflict of laws. There is the law of the city, on the one hand, and the law of the clan, on the other. The former says: let Polyneices remain unburied; the latter: grant him the burial rights to which a blood brother is entitled. Antigone *must* become guilty for there is no way out. Whichever way she turns, she does wrong. The fault is therefore not hers so much as that of her society which generates predicaments of this kind— the case is typically of a societal, collective nature. With Orestes it is the same thing. A look at a detail will bring out the essential point. Clytemnestra murders her husband, Agamemnon, yet the Erinyes who deal so barbarously with her own slayer, Orestes, take no notice. "Nowhere in Greek mythology," writes William Chase Greene in his great book *Moira* (Cambridge, Mass.,

1948; p. 17), "do the Erinyes pursue Clytemnestra for the murder of her husband, for he was no blood relation of hers." Yet, by the same token, they should not have pursued Orestes either, for, as we have seen (see p. 82 above), no blood relationship exists, according to archaic Greek law, between mother and son; blood relationship is mediated exclusively by males. But not only should the deed of Orestes have been ranked as a minor crime because it destroyed merely a stranger, and that a guilty one, it should have been lauded for it was done in fulfillment of the clansman's most sacred duty, the duty of blood revenge. Clytemnestra had spilled the blood of Orestes' father, and that meant the blood of his clan and his own blood—his body's and his collectivity's blood. How could he *not* have avenged this? We are, as can be seen, confronted by a confusion. The reason for this confusion is the co-existence, in contemporary society, of two laws—even more: two principles—of social integration. According to the one, a mother means relatively little to a son for she is not of the same blood, and a husband means relatively little to a wife, for the very same reason. According to the other, a mother means as much to a son as his father and a husband means as much to a wife as any member of her family of origin. The former is the law of the clan, that primordial society which still lived on in Aeschylean times—lived on because it was deeply rooted in tradition and in sentiment. The latter is the law of the associational society just coming into existence and whose grip was as yet weak because its rationality had only a moderate appeal. Orestes, like Antigone, *had* to do wrong; he had to sin either against the law which saw the descent group as holy, or against the law which pronounced the core family—more precisely: the marriage contract—inviolable. It is his particular misfortune that the two norm systems are as yet equally strong. To which side *should* he have inclined, if the two sides of the scales were in equilibrium? *That* they were in equilibrium is made unmistakably clear in the last part of Aeschylus' trilogy. Orestes is placed before the court of the Areopagus, and half the votes go against him, while the other half are in his favor. It is only the gracious intervention of the city goddess, Pallas Athena, which breaks the deadlock and gains him his final acquittal. The tragedy of Oedipus goes back to a similar self-contradiction. We have seen already that the guilt lay with Oedipus' father, Laius, and that he and his children are involved is a proof of the continuing strength of archaic, communitarian ideas. But Laius, too, is in an insoluble quandary. Either he must let Oedipus live, but then he sets aside the advice of the oracle, a divine voice; or he must remove him, but then he must stifle his parental feelings and act brutally, inexcusably. Again, the former is the command of an older, slowly decaying, but not yet decayed culture; the latter, the command of a new culture, a culture more rational than religious. No matter! A decision is to be made, but it cannot be made without grievous harm. It is: heads I lose, tails you win. Greek tragedy places this profound problematic of social life—all social life known to them, and, to a large extent, all social life known to us, all social life suffering from any kind of inner dividedness—squarely before its audience. It pleads: know yourselves! know your weaknesses! Its influence is thus profoundly ethical. Once again we must quote the old adage which asserts that self-knowledge—here self-knowledge of a collective kind—is the first step toward improvement.

Two supplementary remarks are necessary before we leave the fascinating subject of Greek drama. Even if we assume that a person, Antigone, for instance, acts in a morally impeccable manner, he or she may yet incur guilt if the justified end is pursued by unjustifiable means. Machiavelli is supposed to have taught that the end justifies the means. Greek morality asserted the other way around: that the means may taint the end. According to one of the most deep-rooted convictions of the Hellenic ethos, all exaggeration is deplorable, if not indeed culpable. But Antigone may be said to overact. Joan Rockwell makes the point very well though she is unaware of the deeper importance of her words: "Classical tragedy is essentially devoted to the theme of the heroic individual who, by excess of virtue, becomes a breaker of norms and thus a criminal. Tragedy is by definition the destruction of a person of extraordinary merit through the excess of this which leads to *hubris*" (*Fact in Fiction*, p. 50). And von Fritz, who should also have paid greater attention to this aspect, shows us that the Greeks themselves laid great stress on this failing on Antigone's part. In the Sophoclean play, he points out (*Antike und moderne Tragödie*, p. 239), the chorus (in lines 853ff.) emphasizes "that Antigone has, by her deed, overstepped the limits set in the state for men and, above all, for women, and that she therefore suffered no injustice even if Creon's decree was unjust." This is surely yet another proof that the concatenation of guilt and retribution is the great topic of Greek drama, and the reference to ὕβρις shows that something like a concept of Original Sin is not far away.

There is finally yet another and rather different aspect which must be considered. Even if the Greek dramas had struck their audiences as demonstrating the rule of injustice in the world rather than the ultimate, if tardy, victory of justice—or, to be more careful: to the extent that the Greek dramas led to this impression—they still helped to build the societal ethos. For what happens when we see the good suffer? Powerful emotions are aroused in us: anger certainly, but also sympathy. Antigone, Orestes, and Oedipus are pathetic figures, and pathos, if it is displayed in a truly artistic fashion, is a stimulant of fellow-feeling. If the tragedies had argued that sin is invariably followed by due retribution and that the heaviness of the penalty is in proportion to the culpability of the crime, indeed, if only one step had been taken in the direction of mathematical exactitude, the plays would have failed to move and to impress. The concatenation of cause and effect is, in matters moral, not a mechanical one. To assert that it is, with however many provisos, destroys credibility and makes a work of art either icy cold or unbearably mawkish. Thus even the element of real injustice which remains when all the apparent injustices are shown to be no injustices at all for collectivist, communitarian thought helped to lead society in the direction of a more highly ethicized life.

In sum, then, the Greek stage was, by and large, ethos-building. Our analysis of it was complicated, and unavoidably so, because its material is extremely complex. It could not be otherwise. Hellenic drama arose from, and reflected, the underlying social order, and that was—as every society is—imperfect, to some extent chaotic, and even self-contradictory. Yet this constituted its strength rather than its weakness. It constituted its nearness to life and its reaction to life. When, at the end of antiquity, Seneca demanded that every stage play suggest a clear moral maxim, this indicated a decay rather than a maturation of classical tragedy, even insofar as it may be considered, not only as a work of art, but also as an ennobling influence.

Aeschylus, the most archaic of the great tragedians, was born in 525 B.C.; Euripides, the most modern, died in 406. In the intervening century, Greek, and especially Athenian, society made half a move in the direction of an associational order, and this fact is fairly well reflected in the stage plays. Sophocles (born in 495 B.C.) does not feel quite like Aeschylus. "With Aeschylus the chorus is filled with the most virulent hatred of Clytemnestra and Aegisthus and urges Orestes and Electra on when they still hesitate. Even with Sophocles the chorus does not side with the murderers of Agamemnon. But it does try to quiet Electra down . . ." (von Fritz, *Antike und moderne Tragödie*, pp. 132, 133). This concentration on one person is characteristic, and new. While her two sisters are prepared to live in and with the situation which arose through the murder of Agamemnon and the usurpation of his throne by Aegisthus, Electra is not. She feels greater loyalty to her father and greater hatred for her mother and her paramour; Sophocles, von Fritz informs us, had shifted from the objective to the psychological aspect. Yet Sophocles has still little understanding of romantic love, that characteristic phenomenon of an individualistic culture. In his *Antigone*, Haemon's attachment to the hapless girl is described as a kind of madness, while Euripides treats the relation of Achilles to Iphigenia with sympathy and tenderness. Whereas both Aeschylus and Sophocles justify the act of matricide perpetrated by Orestes, Euripides condemns it; the clan spirit, the spirit of blood vengeance, is no longer alive (ibid., pp. 235, 236, 130, 149; see also pp. 147, 148, 478n65). Speaking of Euripides, Staiger writes as follows: ("Charakter und Schuld in der Tragödie," p. 26):

> The unsettling and exciting implication of his appearance consists in this: that he . . . begins to muse about men's motives and endeavors to explore the inner life. We see this as early as his *Alcestis* where Admetus becomes so ambiguous a figure precisely because we begin to speculate, with the poet, about his springs of action. We see it in particular in his *Hippolytus* where the fully worked out and highly problematical portrait of Phaedra's soul surprises us. Hand in hand with this goes a loss of importance on the part of the chorus, and we can understand why this happens. . . . This means in further consequence a loosening of the relationship to the polis. . . . Private affairs are now being considered, affairs which—to use Greek expressions—concern, not the πολίτης, but the ἰδιώτης, the private individual. The ἰδιώτης is interested in psychology. It is psychology which, in Euripides, in the end destroys Attic tragedy as a literary mode.

In Euripides, then, Greek thought took one step toward the mentality congenial to an associational society, just as the contemporary economy took one step toward a market society. This tendency achieved its full unfolding in philosophers like Protagoras and Diogenes of Sinope, that is, the schools known as the Sophists and the Cynics, but these were never more than a small minority. The principle of association had to wait another 2,000 years before it could attempt to conquer the world. It had to wait for the Renaissance and the Reformation of the West.

Both the Renaissance and the Reformation were inclined toward a deterministic world-view, though in saying this we must confess to using the term "determinism" rather loosely. During the Renaissance astrology developed and gained many adherents; it asserted that the constellation of the stars at the moment of a man's birth fixes his destiny in advance. The Reformation presented a theology of predestination, and though predestination is not quite the same as predetermination, it comes fairly close to it. The appearance of the new—Newtonian—physics strengthened both these trends. No wonder that an element of fatalism appeared in the literature of the day. Theodore Spencer speaks about it in his book *Shakespeare and the Nature of Man* (Cambridge, 1943; p. 62):

> one of the most popular types of narrative was the kind of story which described the downfall of a great man through the caprice of Fortune; various collections of such stories had been popular in the Middle Ages, and a fresh collection, which was to be continually added to for more than twenty years, had been published in 1559 under the title of *A Mirror for Magistrates*. The plots of no fewer than thirty Elizabethan plays are taken from this work, and when the dramatists studied those plots in their source they invariably found them employed to illustrate a general truth: that there is no use in being proud or ambitious, since Fortune's wheel is never still, and that if one day you are seated on a throne, on the next you may be grovelling in misery.

Even Shakespeare drifted at times into this mood. Thus we read in *King Lear* (IV.i.36):

> As flies to wanton boys, are we to the gods;
> They kill us for their sport.

Yet we must not think that this stray remark reflects one of the basic convictions of the great dramatist. On the contrary. It was his decided opinion that the sufferings which come to us stem as a rule from deeds which we ourselves have voluntarily committed, and it is precisely *King Lear* which proves that this is so. As we can see, the interpretation of Shakespeare poses the same problem as that of Aeschylus, but the difference is that the voluntarism of the Englishman is much more easily demonstrated. And this indicates already that his dramas are particularly potent supporters of societal ethos.

In the second scene of *King Lear*'s first act, Edmund has this to say on the topic of free will, and the weight of his words is increased rather than diminished by the fact that he is the villain of the piece, for he ought to know precisely what he is talking about:

> This is the excellent foppery of the world, that, when we are sick in fortune,—often the surfeit of our own behaviour,—we make guilty of our disasters the sun, the moon, and the stars; as if we were villains by necessity, fools by

heavenly compulsion, knaves, thieves, and treachers by spherical predominance, drunkards, liars, and adulterers by an enforced obedience of planetary
influence; and all that we are evil in, by a divine thrusting on: an admirable
evasion of whoremaster man, to lay his goatish disposition to the charge of a
star.

The same idea is expressed in *All's Well That Ends Well* (I.i.235–237), but
turned in a more positive direction:

> Our remedies oft in ourselves do lie,
> Which we ascribe to heaven; the fated sky
> Gives us free scope. . . .

Such quotations are not incidental remarks put into the mouth of this character or that in order to reveal a momentary mood; they belong to the firm
substratum of the Shakespearean world-view. "Shakespeare . . . rejects the idea
of Destiny as a force controlling events," writes R. G. Moulton in *The Moral
System of Shakespeare* (p. 309), a treatise which has lost none of its value
since it was published in 1903. "The supernatural has no power over men except by their own consent" (p. 304). "The influence in Shakespeare of the
supernatural on persons is seen to emphasise and assist, but never to initiate or
alter, a course of action" (p. 306). It is true that oracles and witches make
their appearance in some Shakespearean plays, but they merely foretell the
future course of events; the events themselves are due to natural causes, chief
of which is the conduct of the men involved. Even in *Hamlet*, the ghost merely
confirms the Prince's suspicion that his mother and uncle have committed a
crime; the suspicion itself is there before the apparition. Speaking of the royal
dramas, Moulton remarks (p. 296): "Throughout the ten plays there has been
no hint of malicious destiny mocking strenuous endeavour . . . ; there has been
no unnatural interference with the consequences of acts."

Before continuing with our analysis, we must pause for a moment to consider an incidental problem. We have talked as if William Shakespeare were
the undoubted author of the thirty-six plays contained in the first folio edition
of 1623, and we shall continue to talk this way; but *Henry VIII*, for instance—
or, to speak more correctly, *The Famous History of the Life of King Henry
VIII*—is almost certainly, at least in part, the product of other pens. This is a
serious difficulty for the literary historian; for the sociologist it is none. For the
sociologist is concerned, not with the poet's relation to his works, or even with
the works themselves regarded as artistic achievements, but rather with the influence of such plays on their publics—those prepared to see them on the stage
and willing to receive their message. That message, however, was a thoroughly
salutary one because it invariably helped to further the cause of social integration and harmonious co-existence.

What makes the ethos-building tendency of the plays traditionally ascribed to
Shakespeare so much more obvious than it is in the classical Greek tragedies is
that their author's image of man is consistently dualistic. Man is forever poised
between good and evil, and he has to choose: he is Hercules at the crossroads,

without necessarily possessing Herculean strength. "The web of our life is of a mingled yarn, good and ill together," says one of the French noblemen in *All's Well That Ends Well* (IV.iii.83–87); "our virtues would be proud if our faults whipped them not; and our crimes would despair if they were not cherished by our virtues." The same estimate of man is charmingly expressed in *Romeo and Juliet* (II.iii.23–24, 27–28). Good Friar Laurence returns to his cell with a basket full of herbs and philosophizes as follows about their dual character, applying his observations to human beings as well:

> Within the infant rind of this weak flower
> Poison hath residence and medicine power. . . .
> Two such opposèd foes encamp them still
> In man as well as herbs, grace and rude will.

Of course, the greater clarity (to us!) of Shakespeare as compared to Aeschylus or Sophocles is simply due to his relative nearness, temporal and intellectual, to modern conditions and conceptions. He is, in a sense, an individualist. "It is an essential trait of classical Greek tragedy that the tragic situation comes [to the hero] from outside, even where it is connected with the weaknesses of the hero, as is frequently the case with Euripides," writes Kurt von Fritz (*Antike und moderne Tragödie*, p. 54). "This is entirely different in most of the great tragedies of Shakespeare. Here the tragic situation arises with necessity from the innermost character of the hero, and the external world and its events determine merely the particular outline which it assumes." *Hamlet* seems to constitute an exception, for is not the problem which confronts the Prince of Denmark the same as that which confronts Orestes, the Prince of Argos? In each case, a king has been murdered by his wife and her lover, and, in each case, the son of the murdered king and his criminal wife is called upon to avenge the bloody deed (see ibid., pp. 55, 56, 116). But *Hamlet* is a psychological drama. Its hero (or is he more of an anti-hero?) finds it difficult to act— differently formulated: is beset by an inhibition—and this surely is an aspect of his character as a person, a side to his individual soul. Thus even this particular play is at most the exception which confirms the rule enunciated by von Fritz: that Shakespeare is a typically modern dramatist.

But Shakespeare's individualism in no way militates against his moralism; on the contrary, it makes it all the more apparent and impressive. "The world created by Shakespeare is profoundly ethical," writes Moulton (*Moral System of Shakespeare*, p. 106); "no interest underlying it is greater than the interest of human character." One of the tersest and most penetrating summations of the Shakespearean spirit is the following remark from Theodore Spencer's pen (*Shakespeare and the Nature of Man*, p. 73): "Such is the general plan of all Shakespeare's historical plays, as it was of the [medieval] moralities. . . . An existing order is violated, the consequent conflict and turmoil are portrayed, and order is restored by the destruction of the force or forces that originally violated it." In another context, Spencer puts it even more strongly: "individualism," he says (ibid., p. 212), is made, "in Shakespeare, one of the attributes of villainy." Needless to say, we must see this latter statement in the light of the former. The individualism which is an attribute of villainy is the self-preference which violates the order of the common life.

Shakespeare's thought, then, is based on a belief in free will. In *Othello* (I.iii.323–327, 339–340) Iago reveals the dramatist's conviction:

> 'tis in ourselves that we are thus, or thus. Our bodies are our gardens, to the which our wills are gardeners; so that if we will plant nettles or sow lettuce, set hyssop and weed up thyme, supply it with one gender of herbs or distract it with many, either to have it sterile with idleness or manured with industry, why, the power and corrigible authority of this lies in our wills. If the balance of our lives had not one scale of reason to poise another of sensuality, the blood and baseness of our natures would conduct us to most preposterous conclusions; but we have reason to cool our raging motions, our carnal stings, our unbitted lusts, whereof I take this that you call love [the love of woman] to be a sect or scion. . . . It is merely a lust of the blood and a permission of the will.

The dualism of Shakespeare's philosophy becomes visible, once again, in these last words, as well as the cornerstone of his ethics—the demand that the will put a bridle on the body's lusts. One of the figures whom Shakespeare holds up most mercilessly to contempt is Cressida in *Troilus and Cressida*. She knows no self-control. As Ulysses says of her (IV.v.54–57):

> Fie, fie upon her!
> There's language in her eye, her cheek, her lip,
> Nay, her foot speaks; her wanton spirits look out
> At every point and motive of her body.

With this abominable whorish woman we may contrast Shakespeare's ideal man as depicted in words placed into Hamlet's mouth (*Hamlet*, III.ii.75–78):

> Give me that man
> That is not passion's slave, and I will wear him
> In my heart's core, ay, in my heart of heart. . . .

Nothing is more revealing of Shakespeare's deep morality than a rhetorical question which he puts later in the same play (IV.iv.33–35) and immediately answers:

> What is a man,
> If his chief good and market of his time
> Be but to sleep and feed? a beast, no more.

King Lear echoes the same thought (III.iv.110–111): "unaccommodated man is no more but . . . a poor, bare, forked animal. . . ." His lust-ridden daughters, Goneril and Regan, are consistently described in metaphors taken from the world of beasts. They are called tigers and wolves, vultures and serpents. They deserve to be so called because they refuse to put a bridle on their wicked drives.

A certain objection to our interpretation is imaginable here, and though it would be a very weak one, it deserves to be taken up. Not a man's free will, it might be said, is held responsible for the misdeeds which are being committed by him, but his character. Such a distinction between free will and character would be mere hairsplitting, yet even so fine a commentator as Moulton speaks of character as "one of the forces modifying personal will" (*Moral System of Shakespeare*, p. 244). But he himself closes the gap which he is artificially and needlessly opening up. "A man's character is the momentum of his past," he writes on the selfsame page, and he goes on to refer to the "accumulated tendencies and habits which are passing on from the past to the future of that life," the life of the *dramatis persona* concerned. And later on he states even more clearly: "for the determination of individual character the individual himself is solely responsible" (ibid., p. 294).

A side glance at Shakespeare's humor is in order at this point. According to the Shakespearean definition of the man whose chief good is but to sleep and feed (and, so we may add, to chase women), Falstaff is "a beast, no more." But such is the poet's artistry that he is able to hold the fat knight up to ridicule and contempt without inducing us to hate him. Moulton goes so far as to assert that we may even be induced to love him, yet, as he rightly adds, without being any the less disgusted with his bibulousness and his *turpis amor senilis*:

> We enjoy Falstaff's humiliation, yet have no sense of triumph over the man. . . . All the while we are doing involuntary homage to the strength of moral law in our amused surprise at the colossal invention that can rise superior to it. . . . Falstaff, the supreme humorous creation of Shakespeare, is exhibited as violating every law of righteousness and beauty: we who read love Falstaff, yet in no way lessen our love of law.

Thus even humor contributes to the build-up of a societal ethos. Moral censure is combined with a graceful, if not indeed indulgent, smile.

But to return to the more serious side of the great dramatist. He makes his point often by sharply contrasting good and evil. Thus in *Measure for Measure* purity and passion are pitted against each other; we behold at the same time the fateful tension between the individual and the law, and it is not, even for one fleeting moment, doubtful on which side the author stands. Another impressive comparison is that between Imogen in *Cymbeline* and Cressida in *Troilus and Cressida*. In *Romeo and Juliet*, Friar Laurence and the Apothecary are like white and black: the former pursues the study of plants and herbs only in order to be able to help and heal; the latter, who wickedly sells poison to the hapless youth, has far less admirable motives. Yet the strongest use of this dramatic device is the contrasting of the villainous Richard III with the open, manly, and thoroughly sympathetic Henry V. Richard III characterizes himself, at the very end of *The Third Part of King Henry IV* (V.vi.68, 80–81), as the perfect egoist:

> I, that have neither pity, love, nor fear. . . .
> I have no brother, I am like no brother;
> And this word "love," which greybeards call divine,
> Be resident in men like one another
> And not in me: I am myself alone.

There is only one person whom Richard truly loves: himself. In his great so-
liloquy at the end of the play which shows his downfall, he says: "Richard
loves Richard" and "I love myself" (*The Tragedy of King Richard III*,
V.iii.184, 188). Thus the root of all evil thrives unchecked in him. Evil is
something which Richard consciously embraces. In the first few lines which he
speaks in the drama which bears his name (ibid., I.i.30), he says:

> I am determinèd to prove a villain.

He certainly carries out his design! But what is the consequence? Not the
triumph of evil, but its poetic punishment. If we may once again quote from
Moulton's excellent analysis (*Moral System of Shakespeare*, pp. 41, 42, 45,
46): the history of the War of the Roses

> is presented by Shakespeare as retributive history. In the heart of the drama
> Margaret's curses emphasise the thought that what the various personages of
> this Yorkist story are suffering at one another's hands is retribution upon the
> whole house of York for their earlier cruelty to Lancastrians; Richard's retort
> upon Margaret is a reminder that such cruelty to Lancastrians was itself nemesis
> upon them for still earlier outrages upon Yorkists. Thus history is made to take
> the form of the pendulum swing of retribution between one and the other of
> the sinful factions. Again, a similar spirit is read into the experience of the
> crowd of inferior personages who make the underplot of the play.

Moulton is thinking of Clarence, of Hastings, and of Buckingham. After discussing their fates he remarks: "in each single case there is a sudden recognition
of the forgotten principles of justice, or an appreciation of some bitter irony:
fate seems to move forward with the rhythmic march of nemesis. Thus, apart
even from the case of Richard himself, the plot of the play is an intricate net-
work of retribution in its varied aspects—a pendulum of nemesis, a chain of
retribution, a rhythm of retributive justice." It is as if Shakespeare were trying
to reveal the secret of history—but not only the secret of history, far more: a
metaphysical principle. Moulton speaks in conclusion of "a universe which, in
this . . . drama, is presented as a complex providential order every element of
which is some varied phase of retribution." In a word: *The Tragedy of King
Richard III* presents the ethos-building concatenation of crime and punishment
in its purest, most archetypal form.

How different is Shakespeare's portrait of Henry V, a "king . . . full of grace
and fair regard" (*The Life of King Henry V*, I.i.22)! Henry is no prig; he is
no paragon; his image is not overdrawn, but precisely that makes him all the
more credible. He is an ugly duckling turned into a beautiful swan, but his
conversion, as the Archbishop of Canterbury avers, is complete (I.i.25–30):

> The courses of his youth promised it not.
> The breath no sooner left his father's body
> But that his wildness, mortified in him,
> Seem'd to die too; yea, at that very moment
> Consideration like an angel came,
> And whipp'd the offending Adam out of him,
> Leaving his body as a paradise. . . .

Later in the play (II.ii.32–36), Henry himself conveys in a resounding passage his idea of the good man. He is

> Free from gross passion or of mirth or anger,
> Constant in spirit, not swerving with the blood,
> Garnish'd and deck'd in modest complement,
> Not working with the eye without the ear,
> And yet in purgèd judgement trusting neither. . . .

His own conduct is in line with these principles. Though rudely provoked, he does not rush into the French war with blind fury. He considers calmly whether he may "with right and conscience" accept the challenge which the Dauphin's ambassadors convey. But we say no more. It is necessary to see this grand play in order to appreciate Shakespeare's artistry in shaping the alluring image of a brave king who is also a fine human being.

In the days when he wrote *Hamlet* and *Othello*, Shakespeare came to the conclusion that the bulk of mankind is like Richard III rather than like Henry V. "Hamlet discovers the evil in his mother, Troilus in his mistress, Othello (as he thinks) in his wife, Lear in his daughters, Macbeth in the dusty fulfillment of his ambition—while Timon discovers evil in all mankind." "In *Measure for Measure* we are shown that the baser elements in human nature are the important ones—lust, not reason, motivates mankind" (Spencer, *Shakespeare and the Nature of Man*, pp. 183, 123). Yet the poet knows where the remedy lies:

> There is a law in each well-order'd nation
> To curb those raging appetites that are
> Most disobedient and refractory.

Shakespeare puts these words, asserting the necessity of social control, into the mouth of one of his more sympathetic characters, Hector, in *Troilus and Cressida* (II.ii.180–182).

Shakespeare's last completed play was, in all probability, *The Tempest*, and it is fitting that we should close our study of this genius with a look at the view of man exhibited in it. There is one ideal figure, Miranda, and she must be regarded as "a symbol of humanity at its best" (Spencer, *Shakespeare and the Nature of Man*, p. 196). She is a dream rather than a reality. As for the other figures, low types like Caliban, or higher types like Ferdinand, they "go through some kind of punishment or purgation. The low characters . . . are merely punished, they get befouled and belabored. . . . they are incapable of purgation. But the courtly figures . . . lose their human faculties for a time, to emerge purified as rational beings." "There is a re-birth," writes Spencer (ibid., p. 200), an "awareness of the beauty of normal humanity after it has been purged of evil." This opinion has been considered as proof of a softening of the aging dramatist's attitude to humanity, but this interpretation of the last play or plays is not fully convincing. We would rather see in it a closer approach to the tenets of traditional religion. Caliban is the image of fallen man; Miranda, of a redeemed humanity. There is still the conviction, basic to all Shakespeare's lifework, and basic, too, to the present treatise, that man, as he comes from the hands of nature, has to be remodeled and refined if he is to become a truly social being.

In analyzing the classical Greek tragedians, we came upon the problem of Antigone—the problem posed by the sufferings of the just. We meet with the same problematic here, for Cordelia, in *King Lear*, is a parallel figure. What has she done to deserve her cruel death? It has been asserted that her grievous fault is obvious: she has called the French into the country, a sin against patriotism, a dastardly deed. This is about as convincing, or rather unconvincing, as arguing that Antigone should not have opposed her country's king, even if he did wrong. No, the true interpretation lies elsewhere, and we must be glad that Moulton spells it out for us in all desirable detail and clarity. How is the untoward fate of Cordelia to be explained, he asks, and he answers (*Moral System of Shakespeare*, p. 47): "The plot of the play at this point is dominated, not by nemesis, but by another dramatic motive; it is not satisfying our sense of retribution, but exhibiting the *pathos* that unlocks the sympathy of the spectator, and sheds a beauty over suffering itself. Cordelia has devoted herself to her father: fate mysteriously seconds her devotion, and leaves out nothing, not even her life, to make the sacrifice complete." This is well said. "The moral system of Shakespeare," Moulton also writes (ibid., p. 50), "gives full recognition to accident as well as retribution; the interest of plot at one point is the moral satisfaction of nemesis, where we watch the sinner found out by his sin; it changes at another point to the not less moral sensation of pathos, our sympathy going out to the suffering which is independent of wrong doing." In yet a third passage (ibid., p. 49), Moulton digs even deeper, and we quote his lines which throw light on the case of Desdemona and Othello as well as on that of Lear and Cordelia—indeed, which throw light even on the case of Antigone—without apology, for they are truly revealing and convincing:

> if the connection between character and fate were immutable—if righteousness necessarily and inevitably brought reward, and guilt necessarily and inevitably ended in ruin—then in so mechanical a life men would be forever choosing between prosperity and adversity, while there would be no opportunity for the higher choice between right and wrong. In *Job*, the Council in Heaven recognises that the unbroken prosperity of the patriarch has made it impossible to say whether his life is a life of true piety or of interested policy; it is only when unmerited calamities have overwhelmed him that Job can reveal his higher self with the cry, "Though he slay me, I will trust him." . . . It is the exceptions to the universality of retribution that make the free atmosphere in which alone the highest morality can develop.

With this truly splendid passage we must—reluctantly!—conclude our study of the ethical bearings of English dramatic art, merely recording our complete agreement with Diana Spearman's assertion (*The Novel and Society* [London, 1966], p. 93), that "tragedy has, in English in general, followed Shakespeare in making the intrusion of evil the fulcrum of disaster."

To complete this analysis of the relationship between drama and ethos, it would, of course, be highly desirable to discuss other national literatures as well, above all the French and the German, dramatists like Corneille and Racine or Goethe and Schiller. We have no space to do it in, but we may assert, and assert with conviction, that the end result of a careful examination would be the same as that presented on the foregoing pages. Great drama everywhere is a great help to society in its effort to build an appropriate and vital ethos. Schiller's trilogy *Wallenstein*, for instance, is from beginning to end an illustration of the working of νέμεσις. The titular hero becomes guilty of ὕβρις. He should have used the power given him by his master, the emperor, in the service of his master, but he wishes to be master himself, and that prepares his downfall, and not the stars in which, as an adept of astrology, he believes. In *Maria Stuart*, the Scottish queen comes to understand that her sufferings are the just punishment for her own sinful conduct. Most interesting of Schiller's stage plays, however, is *Die Braut von Messina*, for in it the author sets out to show the force of destiny. In the end, however, it is not the force of destiny which leads to disaster so much as human weakness and wickedness, incarnated in the sinister figure of Don Cesare. The two concluding lines of the drama could not be clearer:

> Our life is not the highest of our goods,
> But guilt the greatest evil of them all.

The case of Pierre Corneille is very easy to discuss because he was not only a great practitioner of the dramatic art but a thoughtful theoretician as well. Two of his essays are important for us: *Discours de l'utilité . . . du poème dramatique* (1660) and *Discours de la tragédie* (of the same year) (see *Oeuvres de Pierre Corneille* I, ed. M. C. Marty-Laveaux [Paris, 1910], pp. 13ff. and 52ff.). He raises the question as to whether the dramatist should aim at the entertainment of the theatergoers rather than at their moral instruction and improvement or vice versa, and ranks the former purpose above the latter. Yet, this said, he immediately points out that it is impossible to please the public without offering them a play which is morally satisfying as well as attractive from an aesthetic point of view. The stage therefore *does* serve a moral purpose, simply because the public wishes it so—a wise remark. Corneille clearly saw, what the sociologist also knows, that a society which ranks the social values very high and which is concerned about the preservation and the strengthening of the social bond, will use even the stage for its advantage, not, of course, by coercion, but rather by the socialization and moralization of the dramatist's deepest self. The theater promotes the social ethos in several ways, but especially in two: it depicts virtue and vice in their true colors and shows how virtue is rewarded and vice in the end rebuked. The public expects —so Corneille repeatedly asserts—that virtue will have its due reward and vice meet with a rebuff, and, he says, the playwright would fail if he were to refuse to fall in with this expectation. He himself certainly did fall in with it. In his *Horace* he paints the terrible consequences of overheated ambition; in his *Polyeucte*, the beauty of piety; and in his *Cinna*, the generosity of Augustus. All three plays are highly ethos-building, the first by discouraging self-regard, the other two by encouraging truly social—indeed, noble—attitudes.

Corneille's younger contemporary Jean Racine appears, from the point of view of our investigation, of a similar mind. His plays, too, circle around the two problems of sinfulness and self-conquest. In *Phèdre* he presents to us a woman dragged down and ruined by an uncontrolled illicit passion; in *Iphigénie*, a girl who has mastered her self-centeredness and risen as high as any human being can hope to rise: like Shakespeare's Miranda, she is a symbol of what man might be and should be.

What is so admirable about Corneille and Racine is their ability to serve, *uno actu*, both the finest ethical and the most exalted aesthetical values. The Greek ἀγαθόν and the Greek καλόν—righteousness and beauty—are reconciled in their works, simply because they understood that, at the deepest level, the two are identical: ethical conduct, especially when it assumes heroic dimensions, is the most beautiful thing there is. But even in their own day a different opinion made itself heard. André Dacier, in his treatise *La Poétique d'Aristôte* (1692), thought that the dramatist must make himself the propagator of ethical conceptions and relegate aesthetical considerations to second place. Justice—the unfailing connection between crime and punishment—should be his first, if not indeed his only, concern. As we can see, French drama, not to say European drama, modern drama, turns in the same direction as ancient: Dacier is a distant disciple of Seneca. If this didactic conception of the dramatic art (which was an effect of the spread of rationalism and runs parallel to the desire to replace the fairy tale with the fable) had gained the upper hand, not only would that art have sunk to a lower level, but its ethos-building power would have been weakened, too—perhaps even extinguished. For who wishes to be preached at all the time?

Needless to say, it was not allowed to gain the upper hand. In the year 1784, the young Friedrich Schiller gave a lecture at Mannheim which was later published under the title "Die Schaubühne als eine moralische Anstalt betrachtet" ("The Stage Considered as a Moral Institution," *Werke*, ed. Kurz, pp. 84ff.). In it, he strongly—indeed, passionately—asserted that dramatic art has an ethical mission. Here is an example of his flamboyant style: "When justice allows herself to be blinded by gold and is silent because she is in the pay of vice, when those in power in their wickedness sneer at her impotence, and fear of the mighty paralyzes the arms of authority, the stage takes hold of sword and scales and brings corruption before its awesome tribunal" (ibid., p. 87). The question, however, is: How can the stage discourage vice and encourage virtue? By preaching? Schiller did not think so. In a somewhat later essay, "Über den Grund des Vergnügens an tragischen Gegenständen" ("Why We Take Pleasure in Tragic Subjects"; ibid., pp. 177ff.), he protests against any attempt to reduce the drama to mere moralization. Though he does not express it exactly in this way, we may sum up the gist of his argument by saying that the more a poet endeavors to moralize, the less he will in fact be moralizing, i.e., the smaller the success of his moral appeal will be. He will gain influence only if he pleases. But *how* can he hope to please? What *will* please people? The reply to these queries is revealing and crucial: the defeat of the "interests of sensuality" will please, he answers, "the experience of the victorious power of the moral law" (ibid., pp. 184, 183). Thus there is no conflict between ethical and aesthetic values;

the more the latter are cherished, the better the former will be served. The theory, as can be seen, is roughly identical to Corneille's. Yet Schiller's formulation has more depth than the Frenchman's. Whereas Corneille suggests that the playwright fulfills a whim or a wish of the public when he gives an ethical content to his productions, Schiller knows and avers that, in doing so, he satisfies a wish and, indeed, a *need* of *all* men, a need of society at large. In this insight he left a splendid legacy to us later students of the social bearings of great literature. What he maintains is the truth. Revolutionary and cathartic plays are in a different category, but the drama whose tone and whose tendency spring in the final analysis from the collective unconscious is a repository of society's vital values and therefore a powerful helpmate to the other integrative and peace-promoting forces.

LITERATURE: THE NOVEL

121. At the time when Schiller wrote the two essays which we have just discussed, at the time also when he gave to the world his powerful plays, the stage had already, for about a century, lost the commanding position which it had occupied earlier on within the field of literature and yielded pride of place to a new art form, the novel. The novel is not just formally or technically unlike the drama; it is, sociologically speaking, an altogether different phenomenon. As we have hinted already, the drama is part and parcel of public, the novel of private, life. The drama is at home in the culture of community, whereas the novel is a spontaneous product of associational society. The fact that antiquity did not know the novel as an art form is highly characteristic.

The very term "novel" is derived from the Italian *novella*, and this linguistic derivation gives us a first clue as to the time and place of its origin. On hearing the word *novella*, we immediately think of Giovanni Boccaccio, who lived in Florence and died in the year 1375. Florence at the end of the fourteenth century was a city of highly developed trade, a proto-capitalist city, and though the writing of the *Decamerone* had something to do with the raging of the plague, the spirit of its tales also reflects something of the *joie de vivre* of a society which has risen superior to both the poverty and the puritanism of the Middle Ages. Boccaccio's environment, we may say, was a bourgeois environment, and even the fully evolved novel of the future was destined to be and to remain closely linked with the class known as the bourgeoisie. We possess two sociological studies of the novel, both of which have already been mentioned in these pages: Diana Spearman's *The Novel and Society* and Joan Rockwell's *Fact in Fiction*. Many important disagreements divide these two authors since Rockwell is a Marxist and Spearman decidedly is not, but on the point on which we are touching at this moment they are agreed. "The novel is still held to be the emanation of the middle classes," writes Spearman (*Novel and Society*, p. 20), and Rockwell expresses herself as follows: "The novel is *par excellence* the product of bourgeois society" (*Fact in Fiction*, p. 121). Spearman justifies her judgment by a reference to the period during which the novel evolved and gained its first classical form: "It is generally accepted that the society of eighteenth century England . . . produced or moulded the eighteenth century novel" (*Novel and Society*, p. 71), but it was eighteenth-century England, the economically most highly developed country at the time, which had advanced furthest in the formation of a typically bourgeois world-view. Rockwell also justifies her judgment, but in a much more interesting way. She picks out a significant detail: the importance of the love interest in the modern novel, which is a trait appertaining to, and exclusively characteristic of, a bourgeois culture. "Passionate and romantic love certainly appeared in literature before the novel," she writes (*Fact in Fiction*, pp. 94–96).

> Greek pastoral romances are full of it, troubadourial poetry and "heroic romance" is infested with it. . . . In *Njal's Saga* there are two love-matches. . . . But in all these cases, love is treated as a catastrophe, a disaster. . . . It remains for the novel to present love as the normal preliminary to marriage. . . . This is really a radical break with the social system which had obtained for hundreds of years, in which marriages were arranged between families and the young persons involved were simply the representatives of each side. . . . To demand that the disposition of property, the future of the family, the construction of the basic unit of society, should depend on an exclusive sexual and social attraction which transcends in importance all other considerations, is really to make an extraordinary claim. This claim is only possible on the basis of the supreme importance of the individual which is implicit in the Protestant ethic and bourgeois norms. . . . The supreme importance of the idea of the individual as the judge and centre of everything is basic to bourgeois morality.

Rockwell's analysis is not acceptable without some modifications. The origin of romantic love, as the modern novel understands it, goes back much further, into truly archaic times (see Werner Stark, "Peasant Society and the Origins of Romantic Love," *The Sociological Review*, 9 [December 1953], 83ff.). Yet this does not entirely invalidate her argument. Its main assertion stands: the novel is individualistic, and individualism is the hallmark of bourgeois culture.

So far, so good. But the further disquisitions of our two authors demand more critical examination. Both take a rather negative view of the novel, and the question is if, or to what extent, such a negative view is justifiable. Spearman suggests first of all that the novel is not only just individualistic, but often excessively so: "It does not look at first sight as if story-telling which depends on language could have any . . . solitary aspects. There is, however, a clear connection with it and day-dreaming, which is also a self-rewarding activity, and one which is essentially solitary" (*Novel and Society*, p. 299). This statement is still justifiable. There is, to say the least, a tendency toward super-individualism, not to say solipsism, in the novel: witness the "stream-of-consciousness" novels of such authors as Virginia Woolf, of which Spearman might have made a good deal. But her criticism of the novel goes much deeper. She sees in the entire literary mode a definite tendency toward degeneration, a weight which pulls it down.

> When the story, perhaps originally merely a day-dream, becomes a commodity which can be exchanged for some kind of reward, these influences may begin

to mould the form and modify the content. . . . Fantasy, as indicated by Scott [in *Waverley*] and elaborated by Freud [especially in *Introductory Lectures on Psycho-Analysis*], is largely concerned with the more fundamental biological activities. Even when it becomes written fiction, it frequently treats of what was described in the sixteenth century as "open manslaughter and bold bawdry" and is lamented today as "sex and violence."

The reason for this sinking in moral tone is easy to identify; and in identifying it, Spearman moves very close to Marxism without apparently noticing it: "The novel . . . was from the first written for a market" (ibid., pp. 231, 230, 136), "but on a market the masses have the whiphand. Publishers aiming, under capitalist conditions, at maximum sales, must cater to their taste, and that is low." This is certainly true, but does it apply on a broad front? Does it apply to the novel as such? Does it not apply exclusively to trash?

We must attempt to answer this question, but before doing so we should take note of Rockwell's strictures. Her argument is more macrosociological: she blames the weaknesses she detects, not on the nature of capitalist publishing, but on the fundamental constitution of capitalism as a whole. This is what she writes (*Fact in Fiction*, pp. 90, 91, 85, 86, 93, 92):

> The novel's prescriptive territory is that part of human activity which is devoted to getting established and settled in life. Novelists who have daringly varied the prescription by taking up the story after marriage usually soon reveal themselves to be doing nothing more original than arranging a settling with a different partner. In any case, the story is substantially that of attraction–pursuit–success, and concomitant upward mobility, either symbolic or real. I would like to offer the hypothesis that the novel adopts this particular set of patterns . . . because the themes of individual success, individual choice of marriage partner, pursuit of money and social mobility, correspond to the ideal norms of bourgeois society. . . . Kipling, in his anonymous "Epitaph" (in the Saturday Review) of the old-fashioned three-volume novel, which he likens to a three-decker ship, sums up the typical ending:
>
> > All's well, all's well aboard her, there's dancing on her decks.
> > I left the lovers loving, and the parents signing checks. . . .
>
> The requirement of *success* in the novel—the hero or heroine must move upwards in society and in wealth—corresponds . . . with the moral imperatives of the Protestant ethic: Work! Venture! Succeed! . . . Success, not virtue, is the attraction. So much so that virtue itself is rewarded with success.

The last sentence in this quotation is by far the most important in the context of this book. It controverts, if only to some extent, the position which Joan Rockwell has taken up. For is it merely a demand of the bourgeois novel, of the bourgeois class, that virtue be rewarded with success? Is this not a demand of all truly socialized men and of all societies concerned with their coherence and survival as an integrated whole? Even if we must, up to a point, agree with both Rockwell and Spearman, we have to suggest that they both overshoot the mark.

The truth is that both authors think far too little of the greatest novelists of modern times—of Tolstoy and Dostoevski, of Stendhal and Hugo, of Scott and Mann. *They* should have been at the center of the analysis, not so much be-

cause of their artistic excellence as because of their influence, which exceeded
that of all others in width and breadth. If the analysis had in fact been concentrated on them, and those comparable to them, an entirely different picture
would have resulted. It would have been seen that they stand for a more than
temporarily valid and class-bound ethos, that they are in fact the continuators
and heirs of the great dramatists who had gone before them. A work devoted
to the study of the process in and by which the societal ethos is founded and
built up must not only pay close attention to them; it must also allot to them
the place which they deserve.

In Diana Spearman's book there are one or two stray passages which alone
are sufficient to show that the thesis of the exclusive modernity of the novel must
not be overdone. It is shown that some of the classical novels are similar in
content to traditional fairy tales.

> Pamela is a variation of Cinderella, and Clarissa of the story of the persecuted
> maiden. . . . Tom Jones, from one point of view a realistic novel of eighteenth
> century life, from another is a variant of the story of the lost or hidden heir;
> perhaps also of the common phantasy of childhood, that the child is in reality
> born of people more splendid than his parents. It has also something of the
> ultimate European day-dream, the dream that everyone's story will end happily.

The observation is certainly correct, but it is superficial. The link of the modern
novel, meaning thereby not trash, but works of substance, is much closer, and
lies at a deeper, perhaps, indeed, at the deepest, level. The great modern novel
is as ethos-building as the drama of earlier, and the folk tale of archaic, times.

We have seen before that literature in general helps in three ways to raise
men above their natural self-regard and to socialize them: first, by bringing
home to them the existence and the inevitability of conflict and choice between
alternatives; secondly, by showing up the contrast between good and evil; and,
thirdly, more specifically, by revealing, and insisting on, the tendency of crime
to recoil on the perpetrator's head, to end in poetic justice, in condign punishment. In all these respects the modern novel is entirely like drama and folktale.
A few—alas! far too few!—examples will show that this is indeed so.

First, then, to the existence of conflict and the need to choose. In Dostoevski's
The Idiot, Prince Myshkin is confronted with two women who are for him
femmes fatales: Nastasia and Aglaia. Nastasia has been a rich man's mistress;
she is a "fallen woman." Myshkin loves her, but this love is based on pity, on
sympathy in the sense of fellow-suffering; it is a sentiment which has much of
the Christian ἀγάπη in it. Aglaia is the daughter of a rich family and on the look-
out for a suitable husband. She is interested in Myshkin, in spite of his oddity
and sickliness. Myshkin loves her too, but this love is quite different from the
one he feels for Nastasia. It is inspired by physical attraction, by ἔρως. It is
Myshkin's saintliness and at the same time his folly that he cannot get rid of
the idea that he should marry Nastasia Filippovna and thus re-introduce her
into society and heal her wounds. But this is not the only poignant, self-
lacerating quandary which is presented to us in this grand work of art. Nastasia
Filippovna, too, is torn between irreconcilable tendencies; she too has to fight
out a conflict between her higher and her lower nature. Out of love for Myshkin

she wishes to set him free, to manoeuver him into a marriage with Aglaia Ivanovna. It is for this reason that she goes off with Rogozhin, a person whom she does not even like. But the intended sacrifice is too much for her; she cannot, in the end, give Myshkin up. Both these conflicts are in their nature insoluble. The book had to end tragically, and it does.

In the Anglo-Saxon world, the name of the Swiss Conrad Ferdinand Meyer is not overly well known, but it ought to be, for he was one of Europe's finest, most delicate, novelists. No fewer than five of his novels deal with the conflict between the need to submit to a given and determined situation and the duty to rise superior to it and to assert one's freedom. Most moving perhaps is *Die Versuchung des Pescara* of 1887. The very title gives away the content. Pescara is tempted—tempted to stretch out his hand for political power. But he resists and desists. He will not do what he knows to be wrong.

While *The Idiot* describes an involved situation which holds no seeds of happiness for anybody, Tolstoy's *Anna Karenina* contrasts good and evil, darkness and light. It paints no crude black-and-white picture; there is no open moralization. We have in this justly famous book a good illustration of the Corneille–Schiller thesis that morality is better served by not expressly moralizing. The adulterous Anna Karenina is no despicable woman. She is more sinned against than sinning for she was married off, far too young, to the ice-cold Karenin whom she cannot possibly love. And when she experiences true love for Vronsky she shows one great moral quality: she refuses to be hypocritical, to hide her attachment, though she finds it in the end impossible to live with the situation which she has created. The two men in this triangle, Karenin and Vronsky, are not despicable either. Karenin always acts correctly; there is little he can be reproached with; Vronsky is a true gentleman. Yet—and this is the message of the tale—adultery is adultery and must lead to dire consequences. To the threesome Anna–Karenin–Vronsky, Tolstoy contrasts twosome Levin–Kitty, two innocent, upright, well-intentioned people, who, after some childish difficulties, settle down happily to a life of harmony and usefulness to others. In spite of all complexity, the gist of the book, its moral, is simple: Anna Karenina in despair throws herself under a moving train, while Kitty cradles her infant son, a woman adorned by both youthfulness and motherhood.

Perhaps the most central theme of the modern novel is the concatenation of sin and retribution. Not only did Dostoevski write *Crime and Punishment*, but this subject also dominates two other of his greatest books, *The Possessed* and *The Brothers Karamazov*. In both works, the problematic involved is presented in the most glaring colors and driven forward to an almost unbearably intense climax. Nikolai Stavrogin is evil incarnate. Others for him are no more than playthings; he tortures them in order to experiment, to manipulate, and to procure for himself the pleasures of nervous titillation. But his touch is deadly; in one way or another he kills all those around him. In the end he himself is burnt out and commits—has to commit—suicide. The whole logic of his life leads to this consummation. *The Brothers Karamazov* tells the story of a judicial error. Not Dmitri Karamazov is guilty of his father's death, but his half-brother Smerdiakov. Yet Dmitri comes to the conclusion that innocent suffering, like his own, is not meaningless. All men are in a mysterious, but real, manner guilty, and all must share in the suffering which the sinfulness of humanity entails. *The Brothers Karamazov* is the answer, as it were, to *The Possessed*. While moral nihilism, like that of Nikolai Stavrogin, stands at one end of the gamut of human action, the willingness to assume the burden of collective sin, to which Dmitri Karamazov fights his way, stands at the other. He becomes— like his brother Alyoshka before him—a disciple of the monk Zossima, who, earlier in the book, has so impressively preached that the human race is *one* in guilt and redeeming love. It is not, as many have thought (see Karl Hermanns, *Das Experiment der Freiheit* [Bonn, 1957], pp. 88, 175), in *The Idiot* that Dostoevski speaks most clearly in the accents of Christianity, but in the closing pages of *The Brothers Karamazov*. While, on a secular level, punishment is the due and inevitable consequence of crime, in a higher view love, like that displayed on Mount Calvary, is the antidote to both crime and punishment.

It is perhaps permissible to doubt if other national literatures have anything to offer which can compare with this highest peak of the art of novel-writing, but they too contain much which can help to develop ethical conceptions by demonstrating that evil will breed greater evil, and that with moral inevitability. Let us now take one or two illustrations from French culture. In Stendhal's *Le Rouge et le noir*, the hero, Julien Sorel, is a young man of low social origin but high natural gifts and, not surprisingly, he is plagued—indeed, obsessed— by a painful inferiority complex. His *beau idéal* is Napoléon Bonaparte, the man who rose from the ranks to the position of supreme war lord, commander of invincible armies and terror of the world. But Sorel knows that in his day the black soutane of the priest is more highly respected than the red coat of the soldier, and so he decides on an ecclesiastical career, even though he has not the necessary moral qualities. Clever as he is, he takes his superiors in. He is recommended to a M. de Rênal as tutor for his children. In the family, he is highly regarded, but he has nothing but contempt for the "good society" of the small Burgundian town of Verrières to which fate has brought him. Mme de Rênal develops motherly feelings toward him, but he soon conceives the idea that he would humiliate the local respectability if he were to seduce her. He succeeds; a scandal results; Julien Sorel has to disappear. In spite of his misbehavior, he boldly enters the seminary at Besançon. There he once again deceives his superiors. The rector induces the influential Marquis de la Môle to appoint him his private secretary. He is now well placed, but the devil in him still urges him on. De la Môle's daughter Mathilde takes no notice of him; he is beneath her notice. He decides to conquer her as he had Mme de Rênal. Cleverly he realizes that wooing her would not lead to the desired consummation, that the surest road to the fulfillment of his schemes is to treat her haughtily. This the proud Mathilde cannot abide. She falls into his arms. De la Môle agrees to a marriage and promises to set them up as befits their high social standing. But the first sin now comes home to roost. Mme de Rênal informs M. de la Môle of Sorel's earlier conduct. She exposes his villainy. In passionate anger he rushes back to Verrières where he finds his discarded mistress at prayer in church. She, unlike him, repents. He fires two shots at her, hitting, but luckily not killing, her. He is arrested, and though Mme de Rênal forgives him and Mathilde de la Môle endeavors to free him, he is condemned to death and executed. The price is paid. Today the punishment no doubt appears excessive, but what we have to understand is that Sorel is executed, not for the two shots fired in the church of Verrières, but for a life dominated by vanity, arrogance, and overwhelming ambition. His selfishness was too great to allow his peaceful integration into society.

Another splendid example is Victor Hugo's masterpiece, *Les Misérables*. The plot is too complex to allow of a terse summary, but the gist of the story is as follows. Jean Valjean is a former galley slave, but, under the influence of the kindly Bishop of Digne, known to the people, because of his charity, as Bienvenu, he reforms. He works hard and is highly successful. But the police inspector Javert knows of his past. He is determined to ruin him, in spite of his impeccable life, in spite of his devoted work for the poor and distressed. During the street fighting in June 1832, Valjean and Javert meet face to face. Valjean could easily kill his tormentor, but he does not. He has become too good a man to avenge himself. Javert is overwhelmed. He realizes that his conception of the law as unbending is deeply inhuman and immoral and sets an end to his life by throwing himself into the Seine. Valjean, however, dies a happy man.

Turning now to Great Britain, we meet of course with the grand figure of Sir Walter Scott. One of his chief admirers, Harriet Martineau, in an essay entitled "Achievements of the Genius of Scott" (see *Miscellanies* [Boston, 1836], pp. 27ff.), has praised him by saying that "he has taught us the power of fiction as an agent of morals and philosophy" (p. 52). In another passage (p. 28), she is even more emphatic:

> There is little reason to question that Scott has done more for the morals of society, taking the expression in its largest sense, than all the divines, and other express moral teachers, of a century past. When we consider that all moral sciences are best taught by exemplification, and that these exemplifications produce tenfold effect when exhibited unprofessionally, it appears that dramatists and novelists of a high order have usually the advantage, as moralists, over those whose office it is to present morals in an abstract form. . . . When we, moreover, consider the extent of Scott's practical influence, and multiply this extent by its force, there will be little need of argument to prove that the whole living phalanx of clergy, orthodox and dissenting, of moral philosophers, of all moral teachers, except statesmen and authors of a high order, must yield the sceptre of moral sway to Scott.

Yet, if the subject which interests us most at this point—the concatenation of human conduct with its consequences, reward and punishment—is considered, it seems as if Sir Walter had treated it in a somewhat unorthodox, not to say antimoral, manner. In his great romance, *Ivanhoe*, it is not Rebecca, all along presented in glowing colors, who is allowed to marry Wilfred, but Rowena. Rebecca has to fight down her love and leave the country. Scott was criticized for this unhappy ending even in his own day, but he knew how to defend himself (see Martineau, *Miscellanies*, pp. 50, 51): "The character of the fair Jewess," he wrote,

found so much favor in the eyes of some fair readers, that the writer was cen-
sured, because when arranging the fates of the characters of the drama, he had
not assigned the hand of Wilfred to Rebecca, rather than the less interesting
Rowena. But, not to mention that the prejudices of the age rendered such an
union almost impossible, the author may, in passing, observe, that he thinks a
character of a highly virtuous and lofty stamp, is degraded rather than exalted
by an attempt to reward virtue with temporal prosperity. Such is not the
recompense which Providence has deemed worthy of suffering merit. . . . A
glance on the great picture of life will show, that the duties of self-denial, and
the sacrifice of passion to principle, are seldom thus remunerated; and that the
internal consciousness of their high-minded discharge of duty, produces on
their own reflections a more adequate recompense, in the form of that peace
which the world cannot give or take away.

Thus it is by no means an ethically objectionable ending to which Scott leads
in *Ivanhoe*. He, too, thought that men reap what they sow, and that the novelist
must teach this truth. What distinguishes him from others is merely the definition of reward. True reward, he felt, does not, and cannot, consist in riches;
it does, and should, consist in an ennoblement, an inner refinement, of the
personality.

If some have doubted—mistakenly, it would appear—that Scott sees a
principle of justice operative in the world, no such doubt can possibly be
aroused by the novels of George Eliot. In every one of her works, nemesis
overtakes the culprit. Thus Hetty Sorrel in *Adam Bede* and Gwedolen Harleth
in *Daniel Deronda* pay heavily for their moral weaknesses, as do the brothers
Godfrey and Duncan Cass in *Silas Marner*. But Silas Marner, who befriends
and protects a luckless child, is richly rewarded for his good deeds. What is so
impressive in the writings of George Eliot is the firmness with which she presents her moral convictions. Disciple of Auguste Comte that she was, she comes
close to suggesting that there is an inescapable natural law of retribution comparable to the absolute laws ordering the physical world (see Werner Stark,
"The Sociology of Silas Marner," in *Research in Sociology of Knowledge,
Sciences and Art* II, edd. R. A. Jones and Henrika Kuklick [Greenwich, Conn.,
1979], pp. 189ff., esp. p. 205). This conviction may not square with ordinary
experience, but this fact takes nothing from the great power and the ethicizing
effect of George Eliot's tales. On the contrary.

As far as twentieth-century England is concerned, we have already spoken
of Galsworthy's *Forsyte Saga*. A German masterpiece, Thomas Mann's *Die
Buddenbrooks*, runs curiously parallel to it. The typologist will not easily over-
look the kinship of the two stories! Thomas Buddenbrook is not unlike Soames
Forsyte. Both are dominated by capitalist considerations and conceptions and
unable to understand the artistic temperament. But both marry artistic women:
Forsyte, the pianist Irene Heron; Buddenbrook, the violinist Gerda Arnoldsen.
The consequences are what they must be. Deep sorrow comes to both Soames
Forsyte and Thomas Buddenbrook when their wives turn away from them. But
Die Buddenbrooks ends even more tragically than the *Forsyte Saga*. The whole
family decays. Mann does not point an accusing finger, but his entire text sug-
gests that these rich people have loaded themselves with grievous guilt. This is

more easily recognizable in the subplots than in the main plot. A half-uncle, Gotthold, is treated shabbily; a brother, Christian, is driven into rebellion because he is confronted with the conviction that a Buddenbrook who does not like trade, who is so low a type as to be interested in the stage, must be a miscreant; a sister, Tony, is forced into a mercantile marriage which ends in divorce, and then induced to make a second unfortunate match only in order to wipe away the stain which lies on her and her family. No doubt: *Die Buddenbrooks* is a book which demonstrates the slow, but sure, working of nemesis, the power of poetic justice in the world.

In studying the drama, we encountered the pathetic figures of Antigone and Cordelia; the novel is not without corresponding features—a proof that the novel, like the drama, develops not only the sense of rectitude, but also the sentiment of compassion. Jean Valjean appeals to our sympathy as long as he is unjustly persecuted; our heart aches for Daria Shatova whose humble devotion to Nikolai Stavrogin is totally disregarded and spurned by the soulless nihilist. There is no need to present a long series of names; whoever has read a good novel knows what we are talking about. But it is worth noticing that there is a novel, not perhaps as great as the works of Hugo and Dostoevski, yet a book of considerable power, which deals expressly with this matter: Thomas Hardy's *Tess of the d'Urbervilles*. A spirit of atheism, of neo-heathenism, blows through its pages: there is no justice in the world. Tess, Hardy tells us, possesses nothing except a consciousness of her own worth; everything else has been denied her "by an unsympathetic First Cause" (New York, 1919; p. 174). She guiltlessly loses her innocence—a catastrophe in the Victorian world. There is not technically a rape, but her ravisher takes advantage of her total physical and mental exhaustion after an overly long day. She is "a girl of simple life, not yet one-and-twenty, who had been caught during her days of immaturity like a bird in a springe." She has not deserved the hard fate which is in store for her. "Where," Hardy asks (p. 80),

> where was Tess's guardian angel? where was the Providence of her simple faith? Perhaps, like that other god of whom the ironical Tishbite spoke, he was talking, or he was pursuing, or he was in a journey, or peradventure he was sleeping and was not to be awaked. Why it was that upon this beautiful feminine tissue, sensitive as a gossamer, and practically blank as snow as yet, there should have been traced such a coarse pattern as it was doomed to receive; why so often the coarse appropriates the finer thus, many thousand years of analytical philosophy have failed to explain to our sense of order. One may, indeed, admit the possibility of a retribution lurking in the catastrophe. Doubtless some of Tess D'Urberville's mailed ancestors rollicking home from a fray had dealt the same wrong even more ruthlessly upon peasant girls of their time. But though to visit the sins of the fathers upon the children may be a morality good enough for divinities, it is scorned by average human nature; and it therefore does not mend the matter.

It certainly does not diminish our sense of outrage when we learn that the unfortunate girl, after a whole string of misfortunes, falls into the hangman's hands. Though Hardy's tale may well shake any facile belief that an unfailing principle of justice is operative in the lap of reality, it is yet ethos-building in effect, because it teaches us to feel for and with those who are humiliated and crushed by the iniquities which infest our sin-ridden societies.

122. In his investigation *Real and Imagined Worlds: The Novel and Social Science* (Cambridge, Mass., & London, 1977; p. 26) Morroe Berger has drawn attention to the similarity sometimes discoverable between books on good behavior and novels, even great ones. "The relation between the conduct book and the novel [is] illustrated by the novelistic aspects of Eliza Haywood's conduct book, *The Tea-Table* (1725), as well as by the guidance offered in a proper novel of nearly a century later, Jane Austen's *Pride and Prejudice*," he writes (p. 26). "In *Pride and Prejudice*, Austen frequently includes advice on domestic affairs reminiscent of the conduct books of a much earlier time." In these words we behold, once again, an observation which is entirely correct, but which touches only on a secondary or tertiary feature. Berger greatly exaggerates when, later in his book (p. 48), he gives it as his opinion, following Paul Hunter's analysis in *The Reluctant Pilgrim*, that Daniel Defoe's *Robinson Crusoe* "is a guide or conduct book, seeking to persuade readers to moral and virtuous behavior, a form that was one of the foundations of the novel." Conduct books are didactic; novels are not. Novels are artistic; conduct books are not. If a novel were to carry too much instruction, it would cease to fascinate or even to interest. A manuscript venturing too far in this direction would probably never get anywhere near the printing press.

There is, however, room for books which offer models or patterns of conduct for imitation, and they have a function to fulfill in the economy of education, though we should not typologically confuse them with novels, even if they are dressed up as such, as are some of the works which we shall have to survey. A book like *Pride and Prejudice* may give a hint here and there, but the perfection of this species is reached only when we are confronted with a paragon, that is, a *comprehensive* model of excellence. One of the most attractive treatises of this kind is called *Il Cortegiano* and came from the pen of the Italian humanist Baldassare Castiglione, who published it in the year 1528. Castiglione states in passing that "Homer described two excellent men as patterns of human life—the one in deeds (which was Achilles), the other in sufferings and endurance (which was Ulysses)" (see *The Book of the Courtier*, trans. E. L. Opdycke [New York, 1903], p. 284), but it goes without saying that it was not Castiglione's intention to offer something like the *Iliad* or the *Odyssey*.

The greatness of *Il Cortegiano* is brought home to us if we remember that it came out but fifteen years after Niccolò Machiavelli's *Il Principe, The Prince*. It is certainly true that the moral strictures so often directed against the Florentine are as a rule exaggerated and in part undeserved. Machiavelli, too, had his human ideal, as can be seen in and from his main work, the *Discourses on the First Decade of Livy*: the upright Roman of republican days was for him the model personality. But in a world fallen as low as Italy in his own time, he thought, people had no choice but *vulpinari cum vulpibus*—to howl with the wolves, as we say in English. Castiglione did not share this pessimism, this skepticism, this cynicism. Man, as he comes from his mother's womb, is indeed a creature without culture, but culture can be instilled in him. Education will do the job, and the presentation of a paragon will help. Whereas Machiavelli saw man as permanently in thrall to his lower nature, Castiglione preached that he could, should, and normally would unfold his higher endowments and become social, neighborly, good, and religious.

Castiglione's sociological theory is surprisingly modern. We are using the term "sociological theory" deliberately, for it is entirely justified. It is not an anachronism. On reading *The Courtier*, we are repeatedly reminded of Sumner's *Folkways*. The basic conceptions displayed in the book are also the basic conceptions at the bottom of the present treatise. Particularly clear is the following passage taken from "The Fourth Book of the Courtier," i.e., the final chapter.

> I think that the moral virtues are not in us by nature wholly, for nothing can ever become used to that which is naturally contrary to it; as we see in the case of a stone, which although it were thrown upwards ten thousand times would never become used to move thither of itself; hence if virtue were natural to us as weight is to the stone, we should never become used to vice. Nor, on the other hand, are the vices natural in this sense, for we should never be able to be virtuous. . . . The law presumes that the virtues can be learned, which is very true; for we are born capable of receiving them and the vices also, and hence custom creates in us the habit of both the one and the other, so that we first practise virtue and vice, and then are virtuous or vicious [*The Book of the Courtier*, trans. Opdycke, p. 253].

Everything, then, depends on education. We are forever at the crossroads, one path leading to sociality and morality, the other to selfishness and even bestiality:

> In our soul there are three modes of perceiving, that is, by sense, by reason, and by intellect: from sense springs appetite, which we have in common with the brutes; from reason springs choice, which is peculiar to man; from the intellect, by which man is able to commune with the angels, springs will. . . . Being by nature rational and placed as a mean between these two extremes, man can at pleasure (by descending to sense or mounting to intellect) turn his desires now in the one direction, and now in the other [ibid., pp. 288, 289].

We are always in peril, for "there is some grain of folly in each of us, which being quickened can multiply almost infinitely" (ibid., p. 15). But there is at all times the opposite posibility as well—a turn toward upward mobility in the moral sense of the word, a turn toward nobility.

The use of the term "intellect" in this context is intriguing, and it would be tempting to look at its philosophical implications. In doing so, a close kinship with St. Thomas Aquinas would no doubt be discovered. But we must not be lured into such a byway. We must stick to sociology. The thesis of Sumner and Parsons that action patterns (such as those which underpin the social system—

which *are*, in a sense, the social system) develop from action units, from individual (in the sense of singular) actions, is anticipated by Castiglione: "Our habits are what our actions make them" (ibid., p. 282). He also anticipated the insight of the two great sociologists that the stability of a society depends on the internalization of the folkways or norms of that society in its individual members, even if his formulation may strike us as somewhat primitive: "We ought not to say that the true liberty is to live as we like, but to live according to good laws" (ibid., p. 261).

Castiglione's educational policy is simple. It is entirely in line with the Durkheim tradition handed down by Sumner and Parsons and summed up in the slogan "internalization of norms." "We ought," he writes (ibid., p. 286), "first to teach through habit, which is able to govern the as yet unreasoning appetites and to direct them towards the good by means of that fair use: next we ought to establish them through the understanding, which, although it shows its light more tardily, still furnishes a mode of making the virtues more perfectly fruitful to one whose mind is well trained by practice,—wherein, to my thinking, lies the whole matter."

But to come to the core of the whole book: the educational need of society gives a *raison d'être* to a class which might be thought to have none: the nobility. Their function in the economy of social life is to serve as paragons, as patterns to be emulated (see ibid., esp. p. 22). *Noblesse oblige*, as another age and nation was wont to say. The courtier has to be "an honest and upright man; for in this are included prudence, goodness, strength and temperance of mind, and all the other qualities that are proper to a name so honoured" (ibid., p. 56). In a later context (ibid., p. 107), Castiglione compares the human beings in a society to the instruments in an orchestra. The nobleman, as a model of sociality, must show how they may be brought to harmonize with each other.

> And he will accomplish this if he be courteous, kind, generous, affable and mild with others, zealous and active to serve and guard his friends' welfare and honour both absent and present, enduring such of their natural defects as are endurable, without breaking with them for slight cause, and correcting in himself those that are kindly pointed out; never thrusting himself before others to reach the first and most honoured places; nor acting like some, who seem to despise the world and insist with a kind of tiresome preciseness on laying down the law for everyone, and who, besides being unseasonably contentious in every little thing, censure that which they do not do themselves, and are always seeking occasion for complaint against their friends,—which is a very odious thing.

Castiglione touches only very lightly on the basics of civilization. Thus he says merely in passing that "our Courtier ought not to avow himself a great eater or drinker, or given to excess in any evil habit, or vile and ungoverned in his life," and that "it would little befit a gentleman to make faces, to weep and laugh, and mimic voices" (ibid., pp. 115, 128). He lays much heavier emphasis on self-effacement, and that for two rather obvious reasons: first, because self-effacement is, in all men, the most convincing proof that they have overcome their native self-preference, i.e., their native lack of sociality; and, secondly, because the nobleman is most prone to self-aggrandizement, and if he were to give in to this tendency would completely fail to fulfill his task in life and that of his class. "The Courtier ought . . . to praise the fine achievements of other men with kindness and good will; and although he may feel that he is . . . superior to all, yet he ought to appear not to think so"; "a man ought always to be a little more backward than his rank warrants" (ibid., pp. 116, 96). Passages of this import are scattered throughout the pages of the book. We cannot and need not give them all. Let us merely emphasize that Castiglione is not satisfied with conduct, however good in appearance, which is merely a social technique. The norms must be deeply lodged so that all neighborly actions come, as it were, from the heart. If this depth dimension is missing, we have affectation, and affectation is a scandal and a vice: "The pest of affectation imparts extreme ungracefulness to everything while on the other hand simplicity and nonchalance produce the height of grace," Castiglione asserts (ibid., pp. 54, 35, 38). Therefore it is imperative "to avoid affectation to the uttermost and as it were a very sharp and dangerous rock. . . . Our Courtier then will be esteemed excellent and will attain grace in everything . . . if he avoids affectation."

This rule applies not only to men, but to women. The third book of *The Courtier* deals with the court ladies. A court lady ought "to avoid affectation, to be naturally graceful in her doings, to be mannerly, clever, prudent, not arrogant, not envious, not slanderous, not vain, not quarrelsome, not silly. . . ." She ought to have "genius, wisdom, good sense, ease of bearing, modesty . . ." (ibid., pp. 175, 221). The social relations of the sexes impose strict duties on the men because, in the given circumstances, they are the stronger sex, and the stronger should always take care lest the weaker be hurt.

> There are some who feel bound to speak and assail recklessly whenever they can, let the consequence be what it may. And among these last, some there are who do not scruple to tarnish the honour of a noble lady, for the sake of saying something humorous; which is a very evil thing and worthy of the heaviest punishment, for in this regard ladies are to be numbered among the weak, and so ought not to be assailed, since they have no weapons to defend them [ibid., p. 154].

On sexual morality Castiglione has two important principles to offer: men in love who have to contend with rivals must defeat them by positive means (by merit on their part), and never by negative (denigration); the marriage vows are to be respected, even where marriages turn out badly (ibid., pp. 235, 224, 225).

The protection of the weaker must also be extended to a defeated foe. Even in war, Castiglione writes (ibid., p. 267), "it is fitting . . . to have all the virtues that make for right—like justice, continence, [and] temperance."

While this is merely an incidental remark, the book goes more deeply into the relations which should obtain between a courtier and his prince, and it is in these discussions that his true nobility shows most clearly. Courtiers were then, and still are, commonly regarded as flatterers and toadies who constantly fish for honors, preferment, and money. Castiglione, too, says that his paragon ought to strive for his prince's favor, but for a different reason: he "should try to gain the good will and so charm the mind of his prince that he shall win free and safe indulgence to speak everything without being irksome." This is necessary because it is "his duty, not to allow his prince to be deceived, always to make known the truth about everything, and to set himself against flatterers and slanderers and all those who plot to debase his prince's mind with unworthy pleasures. . . . Just as the physician's aim ought to be men's health, so the Courtier's ought to be his prince's virtue." This is no easy task, for princes, even princelings, have power—too much power—and

> from this it follows that, besides never hearing the truth about anything whatever, rulers are intoxicated by that licence which dominion carries with it, and by the abundance of their enjoyments are drowned in pleasures, and so deceive themselves and have their minds so corrupted—always finding themselves obeyed and almost adored with such reverence and praise, without the least censure or even contradiction—that from this ignorance they pass to boundless self-esteem, so that they then brook no advice or persuasion from others. And since they think that to know how to rule is a very easy thing, and that to succeed therein they need no other art or training than mere force, they bend their mind and all their thoughts to the maintenance of that power which they have, esteeming that true felicity lies in being able to do what one likes. . . . Therefore I think that just as music, festivals, games, and the other pleasant accomplishments are as it were the flower, in like manner to lead or help one's prince towards right, and to frighten him from wrong, are the true fruit of Courtiership.

Castiglione comes very close to saying that the good courtier is a (discreet) teacher of virtue to his prince. If he finds that his master is incorrigibly immoral, he must withdraw from his court (ibid., pp. 250, 283, 248, 264, 285). The difference from Machiavelli's attitudes is so striking that we need not comment on it.

Of course, the ethos of Castiglione also has its limitations. He was a child of his age and his class, and both were warlike. In one revealing passage he discusses the question as to whether higher values are to be found in the pursuit of knowledge or in the mastery of arms and gives no clear answer; yet we may guess that, if pressed, he would have ranked valor above learning (ibid., pp. 61, 62). The true gentleman should not be "too ready" to fight—"except when honour demands it. . . . But when he finds himself so far engaged that he cannot withdraw without reproach, he ought to be most deliberate, both in the preliminaries to the duel and in the duel itself, and always show readiness and daring." However, no one should fight for frivolous reasons. "I greatly like to see a youth, and especially when handling weapons, who has a touch of the grave and taciturn. . . . This quietness of manner has in it a kind of impressive boldness, because it seems the result not of anger but of judgment, and governed more by reason than by passion" (ibid., pp. 30, 90, 91). As we can see, there are limits even to his limitations. The following passage (ibid., p. 58) shows both sides to Castiglione's mind: "Glory is the true stimulus to great and hazardous deeds of war, and whoso is moved thereto by gain or other motive, besides doing nothing good, deserves not to be called a gentleman, but a base trafficker." In these words, low incentives are condemned; yet there is at the same time a tendency to exalt the profession of arms, and that shows that the ethos of his class, which otherwise we see in Castiglione at its best, has to it a definitely nocturnal side.

We get an impressive contrast, not to say a shock, when we turn from Italy in the early-sixteenth to America in the late-nineteenth century which we propose to pick as our second illustration. Martial valor is demoted, hard work and monetary gain are promoted, in the scale of values. Louisa May Alcott and Horatio Alger, Jr., whom we intend to discuss, thought of themselves as novelists. But their books are not really artistic; they are in intention and in effect educational. They present paragons. Alcott is stylistically far more gifted than Alger, which was not difficult, for Alger had no literary grace at all, but the ethos they preach is identical. It is the Protestant ethic so well known to sociologists since Max Weber's pioneering work in this field, the ethos of hard work and of unremitting striving for success.

Louisa May Alcott's bestseller was called *Little Women* and came out in 1868. A superficial reading of the book may well leave one with the impression that the tale is a thoroughly sentimental one, but a closer consideration leads to the insight that the ethical kernel is a hard one, an only slightly softened Puritanism. The first chapter is called "Playing Pilgrims," and this harking back to John Bunyan is highly characteristic. Mrs. March, the mother of the four "little women" with whose development the book deals, reminds them as follows of the beginnings of their education: "Do you remember how you used to play Pilgrim's Progress when you were little things? Nothing delighted you more than to have me tie my piece-bags on your backs for burdens, give you hats and sticks and rolls of paper, and let you travel through the house from the cellar, which was the City of Destruction, up, up, to the house-top, where you had all the lovely things you could collect to make a Celestial City?" There was a deeper sense in this childish game, Mrs. March explains to her girls. Bunyan's pilgrim was and ought forever to be the paragon they have to emulate.

> We are never too old for this [play] . . . because it is a play we are playing all the time in one way or another. Our burdens are here, our road is before us, and the longing for goodness and happiness is the guide that leads us through many troubles and mistakes to the peace which is a true Celestial City. Now, my little pilgrims, suppose you begin again, not in play, but in earnest, and see how far you can get before father comes home [*Little Women, Good Wives* (London & Glasgow, 1962), pp. 26, 27].

The last words indicate the plot around which the various incidents of the story are grouped. The father, Rev. Mr. March, is away as an army chaplain on the northern side during the Civil War and contracts a serious illness while he serves. All that happens is seen in the light of the Protestant ethic which had come down to late–nineteenth-century America from Pilgrim and Puritan days. Louisa May Alcott's little classic is as good an anticipatory documentation of Max Weber's famous thesis as Bunyan's great classic, indeed, as any work which has flowed from that religious tradition. Mr. March presses it on his children. "Remind them," he writes to his wife (ibid., p. 25), "that while we wait [for peace to return] we may all work so that these hard days need not be wasted." In every crisis, work is the answer to the ills of life: "When Mr. March lost his property trying to help an unfortunate friend, the two oldest girls begged to be allowed to do something toward their own support, at least. Believing that they could not begin too early to cultivate energy, industry, and independence, their parents consented, and both fell to work with the hearty goodwill which, in spite of all obstacles, is sure to succeed at last" (ibid., p. 49). Hard work was also the greatest help when a far more grievous misfortune than the loss of money befell the March family, when Mr. March was stricken down by a dangerous disease. The news of it threw the house into confusion, but the faithful and godly servant girl shows which way salvation lay: "Poor Hannah was the first to recover, and with unconscious wisdom she set all the rest a good example; for, with her, work was the panacea for most afflictions." What is unconscious wisdom in the maid is conscious ethos in the mistress. As she leaves to be with her stricken husband, she presses this advice on her daughters: "Don't grieve and fret when I am gone or think that you can comfort yourselves by being idle and trying to forget. Go on with your work as usual, for work is a blessed solace" (ibid., pp. 155, 161).

These lessons were, not new ones, but ones which had already become deeply rooted in the girls' minds. One of them, Jo, modeled, as we are told, on Louisa May herself (see Marjory Swinton's Introduction, ibid., p. 11), wrote a poem to send after her absent parents in order to cheer them up (ibid., p. 165). Two of its stanzas are a very clear summary of the Protestant ethic as Max Weber was to characterize it some thirty years later.

> Along the path of useful life,
> Will heart's-ease ever bloom;
> The busy mind has no time to think
> Of sorrow or care or gloom;
> And anxious thoughts may be swept away,
> As we bravely wield a broom.
>
> I am glad to me a task is given,
> To labour at day by day;
> For it brings me health and strength and hope
> And I cheerfully learn to say,—
> "Head, you may think, Heart, you may feel,
> But, Hand, you shall work alway!"

As the four female paragons grow up, boys unavoidably enter the picture, but their ethos is the same. When Jo refuses Laurence's offer of marriage, he reacts in the typical Calvinist manner. "Laurie was not one of the weak sort who are conquered by a single failure. . . . Some blind instinct led him to fling hat and coat into his boat, and row away with all his might, making better time up the river than he had done in many a race" (ibid., p. 337).

Louisa Alcott also wrote books specifically for and about boys, notably

Little Men and *Jo's Boys,* but in this field she was less successful, which is not surprising because she is—as we have noted—inclined to be a little sentimental. All the more successful in this market was her contemporary Horatio Alger. Estimates of his total sales range from 300,000,000 copies to 16,000,000 (see John Tebbel, *From Rags to Riches* [New York, 1963], p. 11), and if the former figure is absurdly exaggerated, the latter is as certainly far too small. His novels wandered from hand to hand, and the number of their readers was a multiple of the number of copies sold. His impact on the youth of America was in any case so massive that he has every right to find attention in these pages.

Highly popular among the teenagers of his day and well beyond it, Alger was always very unpopular with literary critics, and when artistic yardsticks are applied to his books, he certainly deserves no more than sarcasm and ridicule. That yardstick simply does not fit the case, and we shall say no more about the poverty and paucity of his inventive power, his style, and similar aspects. But to the other negative traits a further one has recently been added: it has been discovered by contemners that he was a homosexual (see E. P. Hoyt, *Horatio's Boys* [Radnor, Pa., 1974], esp. chap. 1). He held the Unitarian pastorate at Brewster, Massachusetts, for a short time and then was expelled for having committed "the abominable and revolting crime of unnatural familiarity with boys," as the American Unitarian Association was told by the Brewster Parish Committee (ibid., p. 6). This sad fact is not entirely unconnected with his success as a mass educator, and we must not pass it over in silence. Indeed, it is the key to the understanding of his life's work.

Among Alger's poems, most of which are less than inspiring, there is one which is so deeply felt that it must command respect. It tells the story of the fall and the redemption of a medieval monk.

> Friar Anselmo (God's grace may he win!)
> Committed one sad day a deadly sin;
> Which, being done, he drew back, self-abhorred,
> From the rebuking presence of the Lord.

But then a great opportunity comes his way. He can help a wounded and stricken man as the Good Samaritan of Gospel fame did. When the patient, restored to health, departs, depression returns, but Anselmo, according to the legend, is granted a sign from on high. He sees writing on the wall:

> Courage, Anselmo, though thy sin be great,
> God grants thee life that thou may'st expiate.
>
> Thy guilty stains shall be washed white again,
> By noble service done to thy fellow-men.
>
> His soul draws nearest unto God above,
> Who to his brother ministers in love. . . .
>
> Henceforth he strove, obeying God's high will,
> His heaven-appointed mission to fulfil.

(*Alger Street*, ed. G. K. Westgard II [Boston, 1964], pp. 34, 35). Needless to say, Friar Anselmo is Horatio Alger Jr., himself. After the catastrophe at Brewster, he never transgressed again. If the Freudians would need another illustration of what they mean by the "sublimation of the sexual drive"—in this case, the homosexual desire—they could find it in the defrocked minister of the Brewster Unitarians. His "heaven-appointed mission" was to moralize boys by means of his pen; and if this pen was a singularly awkward one, this takes nothing from the good intention which inspired him who wrote with it. He worked with a will. Indeed, he worked under the lash of a passion, an obsession. John Tebbel records, in his Alger biography (*From Rags to Riches*, p. 277), that "there are only [!!] 106 genuine Alger books"!

John Tebbel, whose study *From Rags to Riches* we have just mentioned, was no friend of Horatio Alger. Indeed, his book speaks often very harshly of him. Yet even he is forced by the evidence to admit (pp. 86, 78; see also p. 234): "To his millions of readers he was a superb moral figure, a master storyteller, a success. . . . As his writing fame grew, he was becoming a symbol of morality in people's minds. . . ."

The legend of Friar Anselmo is typically medieval and Catholic in feeling because salvation comes to him through good works. But this was not the ethos which Horatio Jr.'s father, the stern Reverend Horatio Alger Sr., had instilled in him in his hard childhood days, which remind one a little of Søren Kierkegaard's early years. It is much rather the Calvinist gospel which was rammed down his throat and lodged in his heart, and which comes out again in all his books. There is a poem, "A Chant of Life" (see *Alger Street*, ed. Westgard, p. 98), which carries the same message as that ascribed to Jo in *Little Women*:

> While the day lasts, work on:
> For night will come apace,
> Life is but a narrow space,
> A breath—and it is gone!
>
> Gaze not with careless eye,
> Stand not with folded hands:
> Burst Sloth's enervate bands,
> And bid her quickly fly.
>
> Press onward to the fight!
> In Life's embattled field,
> The victory shall yield
> To him who toils aright.

Alger knew no better epitaph for his good man, for his paragon, than this:

> "He worked while it was day:
> In Labor's dusty track
> He toiled, and turned not back,
> But still kept on his way."

Max Weber could have wished for no more convincing illustration of his thesis that it was the Calvinist ethos of hard work, disciplined, systematic conduct of life, and endurance to the end, which in the final analysis created the whole apparatus of modern capitalism.

But it was not capitalism with which Alger was concerned, it was boys: but the boys he influenced were the pioneers of capitalism. His is the saga of the self-made man. His novels all repeat in one form or another, in the guise of fiction, the real-life story of people like Cornelius Vanderbilt who rose from "rags to riches." The very titles of Alger's books show their drift. He fitted a few of them together in a pretty quatrain:

> *Strive and Succeed*, the world's temptations flee—
> Be *Brave and Bold*, and *Strong and Steady* be.
> Go *Slow and Sure*, and prosper then you must—
> With *Fame and Fortune*, while you *Try and Trust*

(Tebbel, *From Rags to Riches*, p. 125; Hoyt, *Horatio's Boys*, p. 219). After this self-summary, it is hardly necessary to retell his stories, or even one of them; they are all alike. Let us merely mention that he also wrote two biographies, one of President Lincoln, the other of President Garfield. The former is called *Abraham Lincoln, the Backwoods Boy*; the latter, *From Canal Boy to President*. These titles, too, show what kind of paragon Horatio Alger had to offer. Inspired by the grown men of his age and country, he strove to inspire the oncoming generation with the wish to become and to be like them. And this is, surely, a signal contribution to the spread of a societal ethos.

If we now compare the paragons, male and female, of Alger and Alcott with those of Castiglione, we seem to be pushed, and that powerfully, in the direction of a conception whose influence we have tried, in these pages, to keep down: relativism. A relativistic element is in fact present in what we have called Castiglione's sociological theory. Custom, he says (*The Book of the Courtier*, trans. Opdycke, pp. 7, 8), "often makes the same thing pleasing and displeasing to us; whence it sometimes follows that customs, habits, ceremonies and fashions that once were prized, become vulgar, and contrariwise the vulgar become prized. Thus it is clearly seen that use rather than reason has power to introduce new things among us, and to do away with the old; and he will often err who seeks to determine which are perfect." The Spaniards are grave rather than vivacious; the French, vivacious rather than grave. Thus it is correct in Spain to appear serious; in France, merry. One piece of advice which Castiglione gives runs: "Let the Courtier . . . have the good sense to adapt himself to the customs of the nations where he finds himself" (ibid., pp. 115, 98).

The case of relativism could be strengthened by a comparison between contemporaries of the nineteenth century belonging to different nations. Hoyt suggests that, around the year 1875, the American youngster pursued fortune; the English, fame (see *Horatio's Boys*, p. 154):

The heroes of that contemporary British author, G. H. Henty, were young men who followed great leaders and made names for themselves by engaging in derring-do. Money, when it was mentioned at all by Henty, was simply necessary so that a man could become a hero in proper fashion. But for Horatio and most Americans in the last three decades of the nineteenth century, money was an end unto itself. The important thing was to get rich.

Thus means and ends may change places, and, in Castiglione's words, it is vain to seek to determine what is perfect in culture and society.

Yet all this does not compel us to consider the principle of relativity as an ultimate truth. Even in *The Courtier* the existence of a higher law is asserted, albeit in a rather oblique manner. The second book records a conversation among some noblemen, and one of them, Ludovico Pio, raises the question "whether a gentleman in the service of a prince is bound to obey him in all things that he commands?" No, answers Federico, "you ought . . . to obey your lord in all things that are advantageous and honourable to him, not in those that bring him injury and disgrace. Therefore if he were to command you to commit an act of treachery, not only would you not be bound to do it, but you would be bound not to do it . . ." (*The Book of the Courtier*, trans. Opdycke, p. 99).

Perhaps this passage is not strong enough to show conclusively that the concept of a more than temporal and local order of values was present in Castiglione's mind, but another aspect of his thought proves, and proves beyond any doubt, that it was. *The Courtier* is a truly religious book (and, so we may and must emphasize here, were, in a more modest fashion, the books of Alcott and Alger). On one of the final pages (ibid., p. 305), the author invites his readers to contemplate the Divine Being, Him in whom supreme beauty and the highest benevolence are united, and he pleads with mankind, one and all, to find in Him the Absolute, the Apex of Existence, the Value of Values. "Let us," he exclaims,

> direct all the thought and forces of our soul to this most sacred light, which shows us the way that leads to heaven; and following after it, let us lay aside the passions wherewith we were clothed at our fall, and by the stairway that bears the shadow of sensual beauty on its lowest step, let us mount to the lofty mansion where dwells the heavenly, lovely and true beauty, which lies hidden in the inmost secret recesses of God, so that profane eyes cannot behold it. Here we shall find a most happy end to our desires, true rest from our toil, certain cure for our miseries, most wholesome medicine for our diseases [and] safest refuge from the boisterous storms of this life's tempestuous sea.

These moving words surely show that there is, to say the least, a direction, in which men can seek and find an ethos which is not dependent on time and place, and which is real in the sociological sense of the term, if, and insofar as, the human race allows it some influence on its changing modes of thought and conduct.

TACT

123. We have now reached a point in our investigation where we must raise a question which forces itself upon us and which we as yet cannot answer, a question both necessary and futile: to what extent do the influences which we have so far considered in this volume elevate human conduct above the level guaranteed by folkways and the law, those social agencies which we analyzed in our third volume? How effective is the ethos communicated to us by fairy tale and fable, saga and legend, symbolism and ceremony, and by literature both artistic and educational? *Non liquet!* The trouble is that these factors do not operate alone, but always in conjunction with ethical and religious ideas, and that we therefore cannot isolate and identify their contribution. As we have just seen, a religious element is present in the educational writings which place the picture of a paragon before our eyes, but not only there; religion is somehow or other in and behind the other ethos-building institutions as well, simply because it pervades our whole life. Perhaps some of our readers may think this statement exaggerated; do we not live in a secularized civilization? Indeed, we do, but certain facts must not be forgotten. The process of secularization is very recent; it can hardly be said to have gathered momentum before the French and Industrial Revolutions. A book like the present which studies society, and not just modern society, must therefore give religion its rightful place. Besides, religious conceptions have been only pressed back, not eliminated; they have also been kept alive by powerful religion substitutes such as the deification of nature and of history. Atheism and even agnosticism are rare in their pure form, and it is surely as yet uncertain whether society and culture could survive without a metaphysical prop of some kind.

We cannot, then, separate the various strands which together go to form a seamless robe. The method recommended by Max Weber fails: to think away one of the cooperating factors and then to ask what difference its exclusion is likely to make. It is all very well to call the scholarly mind a laboratory in which a thought experiment of this kind can be carried out. We cannot see sufficiently clearly what the outcome would be. But perhaps it is not wrong—not overly bold—to suggest that the cultural energies discussed in the last nine sections, considered by themselves, would at least give rise to two desirable and important qualities of civilized and cultural conduct: tact and politeness.

It is hardly necessary to speak at length about the subject of tact. Not only is the matter simple, but its principle is entirely negative. Tact demands and commands that we should avoid everything which is apt to anger our fellow-men. Castiglione suggests that the ideal gentleman should not be without a sense of humor, but there is a difference between humor and such attitudes as sarcasm which we must eschew. Care must be taken "not to be so sharp and biting as to be thought spiteful, assailing causelessly or with evident rancour: either those who are too powerful, which is imprudent; or those who are too weak, which is cruel; or those who are too wicked, which is useless; or saying things to offend those he would not offend, which is ignorance." Jokes are in order, but "in these short sayings, the Courtier must take care not to be malicious and spiteful, and not to utter witticisms . . . solely to annoy and cut to the quick" (*The Book of the Courtier*, trans. Opdycke, pp. 154, 134). We get a cruder, but perhaps still clearer, explanation of what tact is in an old proverb which says that in a hanged man's house one must not speak of the rope.

We can achieve a yet deeper understanding of what tact involves if we consider for a moment the etymology of the word. Tact comes from the Latin *tactus* which describes the sense of feeling—the sense which is located, above all, in our finger tips. It is akin to the scientific *tactile* which, in physiological psychology, means perceivable or perceived by the bodily faculty of touch. In the transferred and metaphorical meaning in which the term has to be used in the context of a study of human interaction, tact signifies a sympathetic searching for the tender spots in the psyche of others, coupled with the resolution not to expose or irritate them. Tact is thus a specific against mutual annoyance and conflict; it is a safeguard of social peace. In his great book *The Idea of a University* (Westminster, Md., 1973; p. 208), John Henry Newman writes: "It is almost a definition of a gentleman to say he is one who never inflicts pain." These words not only contribute to the image of an ideal person or paragon which is applicable to all societies—to the Platonic "idea" of a paragon, as we might also say—they also contain, albeit by implication, an explanation of what tact is and what function it fulfills in the economy of social life.

When the phenomenon of tact is analyzed, it becomes clear that it has two sides: the one, individualistic and private; the other, public and social. Let us, for argument's sake, posit the simplest case, the dyad. There are two persons, one of whom shows tact and the other who is, so to speak, the recipient of it. Around the latter there will be, if we may so express it, a protective belt. Knocking at the door before entering a room is an illustration of what we mean; this rule makes certain that we do not irrupt into the personal sphere of another before we are sure that he will not be incommoded by it. So far, social distance is emphasized, not social closeness. But the very same pattern of behavior also serves social peace and human understanding, social integration. For he who shows tact, be it in this particular way, be it in another, demonstrates that he respects his opposite, that he entertains tender feelings toward him, and this cannot but contribute to the smoothness of social intercourse and bring a note of amity and amiability into it. The age-old habit of looking away when something untoward happens to a man, in order not to witness his embarrassment and to be able to disregard it, as if it had never happened, shows in a nutshell how, by the exercise of tact, social life is furthered while—and because—personal pride is served and preserved.

POLITENESS

124. Whereas tact is essentially passive, i.e., consists in the omission of antisocial acts, politeness is active and consists in the commission of activities which express a positive attitude to other human beings. Differently expressed: tact is proscriptive; politeness, prescriptive. There is, typologically speaking, a difference between knocking at the door before entering, and opening the door so that somebody may enter. In the first case, there is certainly a small activity, but it is merely incidental; the salient fact is that he who knocks does *not* enter. In the second case, there are two activities: opening the door by Ego and crossing the threshold by Alter. The whole pattern of good behavior is concerned with an active step. The point which we are trying to make was classically formulated by Rudolf von Ihering in his famous book *Der Zweck im Recht* (Leipzig, 1886; II 368, 369, 482):

> The norms of decency [or tact] are of a negative, those of politeness of a positive, nature. . . . The contrast of the commands of decency and of politeness corresponds to the contrast between the two *praecepta iuris* of the Roman lawyers: *alterum non laedere* and *suum cuique tribuere*. The quintessence of all the rules of decency is the *alterum non laedere*, i.e., the avoidance of what is indecent; that of the rules of politeness, the *suum cuique tribuere*, i.e., the fulfillment of another person's claim to the observation of courteous forms. . . . Politeness establishes rules whose content is, not a mere omission, but an activity in the interest of a person: the positive acknowledgment of his personality.

A typical piece of politeness which highlights the essence of the whole phenomenon is the rule that the newcomer to a circle must be informed at once of the topic which is being discussed. If he is not so informed, he is "out of it"; he is not really admitted to the group. It is a linguistic habit to say in this case that he is treated "tactlessly." But if he is truly welcomed and drawn into the conversation, it is not tact which is shown him, but courtesy. He is given, as we may express it with slight exaggeration, the privilege of membership, but this is a positive act and not a *negativum*, an omission.

In spite of this clear contrast between tact and politeness, there exists a certain parallelism between the two. Politeness, like tact, has an individualistic and private as well as a public and social aspect. It, too, creates a protective belt around a person; it, too, creates distances. We see this best in the verbal forms of courtesy. The French distinguish two forms of address, the cooler and more respectful *vous* and the warmer and more familiar *tu*; the Germans have *Sie* and *Du*. The English language has gotten rid of this complication: the *you*, originally corresponding to *vous* and *Sie*, has driven out the *thou* originally corresponding to *tu* and *Du*. But we need only think of other forms of address to see that Anglo-Saxon culture carries the same phenomena. "Dear Sir," not to speak of "Honored Sir," is *toto coelo* different from "Dear Jack." We must not think of the barriers thus erected as essentially obstacles in and for social intercourse. On the contrary. Excessive directness, excessive informality, may well have a shock effect; it may inhibit rather than lubricate social interaction because it may be experienced as obtrusion, incommodation, or even arrogance. True, such forms as *tu* express and thereby further friendliness, but it must not be overlooked that such forms as *vous* demonstrate respect for the person so addressed and is therefore bound to please him. This, too, is a pathway toward positive and even pleasant human relationships.

The socially constructive character of even the distance-creating forms of politeness becomes quite obvious when, in a thought experiment, we think them away. When the early Quakers refused their fellow-men "hat-honor" and "word-honor," i.e., declined to uncover their heads even indoors and spoke to their superiors, such as parents, in the same way as to the stable grooms, by using, on principle, only the *thou*, they aroused ill will, and it was not least because of these peculiarities that they were forced, first into inner emigration, and then into foreign emigration as well. Theodor W. Adorno (who, let us not forget it, stood all his life on the left of the political spectrum) has therefore argued, and that forcefully, against what he calls the "pseudo-democratic abandonment [*Abbau*] of old-fashioned courtesy." He describes it as a "symptom for the sickening of contact," and gives it as his opinion that we can see behind it the coming of "naked rudeness" (*Roheit*). "The direct word which is thrust upon another person without preliminary consideration, without hesitation, without reflection, already exhibits the form and the sound of a command such as it is directed, under a fascist régime, by those who do not make many words to those who must remain mute" (*Minima moralia* [Frankfurt am Main, 1969], p. 45).

One social function of polite forms which is often overlooked consists in the protection which it affords a person against himself. Just as in law a prescribed form, e.g., the necessity of concluding a contract in writing rather then merely by word of mouth, ensures that a contracting party will not overly rashly incur serious obligations, so in social intercourse prescribed forms have the purpose of preventing a person from all too quickly revealing his feelings or his intentions. In czarist Russia a young girl was not supposed to write to a young man, let alone to hint at her interest in him. In Peter Ilyitch Tchaikovsky's opera *Eugene Onegin*, Tatiana sets this rule aside and earns nothing but disappointment and pain. Her move was premature; it has at the moment an offputting effect; and when Onegin in the end develops the warmest feelings for her, it is, tragically, too late.

But let us come to the core—the positive function—of the whole phenomenon. Briefly formulated, it consists in the express assertion that social intercourse in general, and with actually present persons in particular, is valuable—a *value in itself*, quite apart from any advantages, for instance economic ones, which it brings or may bring. Demonstrations of good will accompany interaction from beginning to end. We say "Glad to meet you" when we are introduced; we say "See you again" when we part, indicating a wish that the relationship, being enjoyable, may continue. We show interest in and concern for others: "How are you? I hope I see you well!" We express gratitude: "Thank you very much," which elicits, or ought to elicit, another formula of good will: "Don't mention it!" or "You are welcome!" To the chapter of interest and concern belong as well congratulations and condolences. The formulas of apology must not be forgotten either: "I am sorry!" "Excuse me!" "Pardon!" They inhibit the development of aggressivity on the part of a person accidentally annoyed and thus reduce the sum total of friction within the societal sphere.

The term "friction" just used was introduced deliberately. As in the case of tact, so in the case of politeness, the philological analysis of the term leads to an understanding of the essence of the thing described. Politeness derives from polish—to smoothen. A smoothened—polished—surface will not run hot. Where it exists, sparks will not readily fly. The metaphor implied is entirely clear and acceptable to the sociologist. An archetypal scene which teaches a deeper lesson than might be supposed is the meeting of two men at a door through which both wish to enter. If they are not polished, i.e., if they are actuated by unrestricted self-preference, pride, and pugnacity, which is the hallmark of uncivilized man, they will clash. If they are polished and polite, they will urge each other to step over the threshold first; conflict will be avoided, social contact rendered agreeable. Comedy has often placed this situation on the stage and ridiculed the mutual complimenting. But in point of fact a serious issue is involved: friction is obviated, peace preserved, graciousness shown, and that is not a small matter.

Yet more revealing than an interpretation of the words polish and politeness is a consideration of the word "Please," traditionally the first expression we expect an infant to learn. If a human being feels a need or entertains a wish for the services of another, he can set about it in two ways: he can ask or he can command. There is a world of difference between these two possible modes. The one will lead to cooperation; the other, to conflict. The one will arouse a readiness to comply; the other, a tendency to resist. We behold here a core phenomenon of social life as a series and system of mutual services. Of course, many people—above all, laymen—will say that the small word "Please" cannot have such incisive consequences; it cannot shunt the train onto the line leading to social harmony. Of course not, taken by itself. Most services are mutual; the expectation of a return in kind is one of the firm bases of coexistence. But that does not mean that the verbal form of the request is irrelevant. If social life is conceived as an equilibrium system of exchangeable services, it appears at once as a kind of mechanism, and mechanisms, machines, will not function well without lubrication. The comparison between courtesy and lubrication of human interaction has often been drawn, and it is introduced here because it is apt. But the social system is more than a multiplicity of exchange acts. If realism is to be preserved, it can be likened neither to a market nor to a machine. Within it, there occur many one-sided services, services without counter-service, and any attempt to interpret them, too, as exchanges must end in artificial constructions (see below, Section 126). If a child asks his mother for an apple, this is the request of a favor, not the proposal to conclude a mutually advantageous contract.

Why is the word "Please" so important in this context? Because it excludes, *a limine*, the presupposition that the person addressed is *bound* or *constrained* or even *obliged* to do what he is asked to do; because it totally obviates the idea that he is an underling, a servant. Human beings are proud; they resent humiliation. The polite formulas of request express, and that quite clearly, that he to whom the request is made is a free agent who has it in his power, not only to obey, but also, if he sees fit, to refuse. Of course, that freedom attributed to the interlocutor or interactor may be entirely fictitious; a waiter is hardly in a position to say nay to a guest who places an order. Yet it is precisely this case of real obligation, of actual unfreedom, which points up the social function of courtesy. For a human being placed in a service position, more especially if it is permanent, will regularly be rather touchy. The words "Please" and "Thank you" will make a real difference to him, the difference being that between being treated as a tool and being treated as a person. All the rules of politeness imply a certain degree of self-abasement; he who might issue an order in a way demeans himself by merely voicing a petition. They imply *a fortiori* a high measure of self-discipline and effective social control, and therefore politeness as such touches upon the very nerve of social ordering. Can there be a greater contribution, then, to the build-up of a societal ethos than close adherence to the rules of courtesy?

The last paragraph has in effect been rather polemical, even though nobody was openly attacked in it. It argued against the widespread opinion that courteous forms are no more than by-products, than embellishments, which, like any luxury, may as well be omitted. It must certainly be conceded that courteous forms may degenerate into empty formalities, formalities without human content, but this signifies very little; laws, too, may be hollowed out, and yet nobody will suggest that, for this reason, society could do without them. In point of fact, there are at least three features usually conjoined with courteous conduct which prove that the social forces oppose the emasculation of these safeguards of social cooperation and social peace. There are, first of all, gestures accompanying verbal behavior which constitute tests, as it were, of its genuineness: getting up, inclining of the head, holding out of the hand, appropriate facial expressions. All these are outer and visible symbols of inner and invisible attitudes. Indeed, there are also "verbal gestures" (as the psychologists call them) operating inside the spoken words themselves. The timbre of the voice betrays the spirit behind the spoken words: *c'est le ton qui fait la musique*, as the French have always insisted. We see that the rules of politeness demand, to use another French phrase, an *effort de sympathie*. There are, secondly, accompanying actions, often certainly petty, but again important because of their value as symbols: taking an overcoat, bringing a chair, and so on. Thirdly and finally, and most significantly, there dwells in all true politeness a double tendency: an endeavor to prevent its own weakening and to engineer its own strengthening. At the time when it was customary to end a letter with the words "Truly yours," it was observed that many correspondents went over to such fuller forms as "Very truly yours" or even "Most truly yours." This searching for means of stronger emphasis stems from the underlying wish to let the existing good will shine through as clearly as possible, and to that extent polite forms are by no means empty, but laden with meaning.

All this does not do away with the fact that politeness may be the vehicle of an egoistic life-policy, of conscious and systematic deception. But it does prove that Jean-Jacques Rousseau badly overshot the mark when, in his *Discours sur les sciences et les arts*, he spoke of a perfidiousness of *politesse*. Eckart Machwirth, in a recent study of the subject (*Höflichkeit: Geschichte, Inhalt, Bedeutung* [Trier, 1970], p. 221), represents the diametrically opposed point of view: courtesy, he asserts, enriches social life, even though it does not provide a gain in the material sense of the word. He also speaks (on p. 221, and on p. 77n17 at the end of the volume) of an "excess" over and above the merely utilitarian benefits of social intercourse, of a spilling over, as it were, of sociality. Politeness is such a spilling over in two senses of the word (see ibid., pp. 281, 283). The one case might be called micro-, the other macrosociological. When some people, or only two, get together to negotiate a business deal, the interests involved are certain to be contradictory, and yet the meeting may be pleasant, even enjoyable, if good manners are preserved throughout. To an economic relationship is thus added a human one; in other words, the economic relationship has "spilled over" into the human sphere. As far as the inclusive society is concerned, there forms, on top of it, a layer which might (with Georg Simmel) be described as that of pure sociability; it certainly has as its under-structure the totality of the purposive modes of interaction, economic and political interaction and the like, but in its own confines contacts serve only one "purpose": namely, that of enjoying human relationships *per se*. This sphere is the product of all the innumerable demonstrations of mutual respect and regard which pervade everyday life, and it in turn reacts on them in a feedback process, thereby increasing the sum total of politeness in the society concerned.

Using the terminology we found so helpful in the second volume, we might say, in an attempt to sum up what has been said so far, that politeness is a typically "allocentric" phenomenon: we act courteously for the sake of secur-ing a pleasant relationship with another person or other persons. May we shorten the statement just made and assert that, in applying the rules of cour-tesy, we act for the sake of another person or other persons? No, not quite. If we act courteously for the sake of securing a pleasant relationship with some-one, there will be a strong autocentric—even egoistic—element in and behind the allocentric mode of action. It may be that the relationship is only a means to an end, that the value pursued is not a social and human value. The glib phrases of the salesman and the bartender spring to mind at once as illustra-tions of what we mean. But there is, to say the least, a tendency for the semi-autocentric forms of courtesy to prepare, to induce, a more highly or even fully allocentric attitude. If we ask somebody, maybe mechanically, "How are you?" and he tells us in reply that he has just sustained a blow of fate, true sympathy may be evoked in us. We are, so to speak, pushed across a borderline. The three phrases "He *has* good manners," "He *knows* how to behave," "He *is* courteous" indicate three stages in a process of internalization. There is a possible progres-sion from a desire to please through a habit of good behavior to—ultimately—inner refinement and true (even maximal) sociality. Just as constant obedience to the laws of rectitude matures into a sense of justice, so constant obedience to the laws of courtesy matures, or at any rate tends to mature, into benevolence. A distillate or precipitate of "good behavior" will become lodged in the ego. Now, what is true of the individual is true of society as well. We need only think of Ferdinand Tönnies' distinction of association and community in order to grasp what is involved. We might say—remaining entirely within the Tön-nies terminology and analysis—that in the context of associational societies the rules of politeness will be implemented for the sake of a pleasant relationship to others, while in communities they will be implemented, and receive greater warmth, for the sake of others. But, as Tönnies has so well explained, associ-ation has an indwelling tendency to grow into community. New societies are as a rule signally lacking in established forms of mannerly conduct, and this is one of the reasons why their mode of coherence is merely associational. Old societies have had time to develop a style of life of which satisfying habits of mutual intercourse are likely to be an outstanding feature, and this is one of the reasons why their principle of integration deserves to be called communitarian. It is only in mature societies that courtesy comes, so to speak, into its own. Society has created these forms of conduct as conduits along which streams of good will can travel, press upward and outward, and reach the surface. In associational societies these channels are by no means empty, but in communities they are apt to be full. Of course, there is also always the danger of formalization, of the decay of the inner meaning, of the emptying out of the outer form, as we noted in another place (see SOCIAL BOND III 87ff.). But societies in which this occurs are in reality communities no longer; they are much rather caricatures of community. On this page, it is not involution, but evolution, which we are discussing.

If we speak of evolution in the present context, as the observable facts certainly allow us to do, the question at once arises what the end point, the acme, of this upward development is likely to be. The answer cannot be simple because improvement, maturation, perfection occur on several levels. One of them is the level of aesthetics. Mohammed Rassem draws our attention to it when, in his deep-delving paper "Über den Sinn der Höflichkeit," he asserts that courtesy contains and exhibits an artistic element (see *Stiftung und Leistung* [Mittenwald, 1979], p. 134). When we speak of good human relations, we are using ambiguous language, for these relationships may be correct, or they may be beautiful (see, on this aspect, Stark, *Sociology of Religion*, v 182). Correct relationships are certainly good relationships, but they are not all they can be. They rank above tension-ridden and conflict-laden relations, but they do not show the quality of harmony which is one of the chief values pursued in humanity's artistic–aesthetic quest.

Another level which some might rank higher, others lower, but which is high by any and every standard, is that of ethics. Goethe saw in the very falsehood, the very fictitiousness which is apt to cling to polite forms, a possible means of ethical improvement. "If we take our fellow-men as they are, we make them worse than they are," he writes (*Wilhelm Meisters Lehrjahre* 8.4). "If we treat them as if they were what they ought to be, we bring them up to the standard which they ought to attain." The word is profound. Other thinkers have felt similarly. According to Kant, courtesy belongs to the parerga of virtue. He calls it one of virtue's "outworks and flanking bastions" (*Die Metaphysik der Sitten.* II. *Metaphysische Anfangsgründe der Tugendlehre*, § 48). He also shared the conviction developed above that "these initially empty signs of benevolence and respect lead step by step to genuine attitudes of this kind" (*Anthropologie*, § 14). But the deeper reason why this stern moralist attributed so much importance to a phenomenon which his contemporary and close intellectual companion Rousseau condemned as pure hypocrisy and hence valueless lies in his basic philosophical anthropology. He distinguishes phenomenal and noumenal man—that is, translated into everyday language, man in thrall to his body and man endowed with free will—a distinction which comes close to contrasting man as a product of nature and man as a creature of society. Clearly, courtesy belongs to noumenal, not to phenomenal, man. There is no such thing as politeness in nature. True, some zoologists speak of animal rituals, of ritualization, but what is ritualized is always an instinctual pattern, an inbred and inborn mode of behavior. But if courtesy belongs to noumenal man, then it is underlain by free will, and hence a moral phenomenon. The underlying freedom can be seen in two ways. There is, on the one hand, a collective freedom to shape the code of manners, a freedom which explains why different cultures have brought forth different symbolisms, such as the polite uncovering of the head in the Occident and the equally polite covering of the head in the Orient. But more important, at this juncture, is the freedom of the individual to implement or not to implement the norms of courtesy. This feature has been strongly emphasized in the literature. Courtesy is voluntary, Rassem avers ("Über den Sinn der Höflichkeit," p. 134), and he is right. And he explains what this freedom means, and what it leads to. Why is it, he asks (ibid., pp. 126, 130, 132), that warmth radiates from courteous acts, and he answers:

> The correct implementation of rules cannot by itself produce this effect. Other elements must necessarily enter in. . . . Such an element is spontaneity or voluntariness of compliance. . . . A quasi-automatic enactment of given schemata, an enactment which has become second nature, is merely a first stage. At a higher stage, it is necessary to choose freely among the available means; something original has to be invented.

Thus the creative and expressive abilities are mobilized in a man who wishes to be truly courteous. "These forces combine to bring forth a sort of empathetic understanding of the person before us. It is [even] possible to speak of sympathy. . . . Even a genuine and spontaneous feeling needs such stimulants." In this way an ethically more elevated attitude springs from the voluntaristic element within polished and polite forms, from the freedom which is a constituent element of it, once the lowest level is left behind.

Of course, this freedom is not complete. Only legal sanctions are absent; informal social pressures certainly are not. The consistently rude person will be denied the benefits of reciprocity; he may be boycotted and ostracized. But it remains true that the actual shaping of polite actions prescribed in the surrounding society is up to the actor. He, and he alone, decides how much friendliness he puts into a "Good Morning," or how much good will into one of the petty services expected from him by others. In this way, courtesy is and remains connected with ethics, albeit only as a parergon, an "outward and flanking bastion."

A third level to which politeness may come to be elevated—a level well above both aesthetics and ethics—is that of religiosity. Several passages from the New Testament may be quoted in which true courtesy, a courtesy of the heart, is recommended to believers—see, for instance, the Epistle to the Philippians 4:5 or the Epistle to the Galatians 5:22, 23—but this passage or that, or even an entire string of them, would mean little for our analysis. What we have to emphasize is that politeness is not unconnected with that love of our neighbor which, next to the love of God, is the highest commandment given in the Gospel. There may be a long way from courtesy to charity, and yet a road leads from the one to the other. There is indeed a great contrast between offering a chair and offering services such as those which the Good Samaritan, that paragon of paragons, took upon himself: in the one case, the sacrifice involved is almost non-existent; in the other, heavy, perhaps connected with true personal suffering. Yet if there is, from our point of view, a difference in kind, it appears from another point of view as merely one of degree.

ETHNOCENTRISM

125. If it is true that a weak reflection of the light of love lies over the outer forms of politeness where they are enacted in freedom and with grace, it is also true that a darker sentiment often underlies them which is akin to enmity and hate. W. G. Sumner calls it ethnocentrism, a term which describes not only the ranking of one's own nation (or ἔθνος) above all others, but more generally the invidious magnifying of one's own group (tribe, clan, family, or what not) to the detriment of others. We have postponed the consideration of this influence which is half positive, half negative, until now because we wished to present first the constructive influences, those little burdened or unburdened with a tendency toward human estrangements, but the time has come now to face it and discuss it. Ethnocentrism produces an ethos which brings us closer to our nearer neighbors, but which creates at the same time a distance toward those who dwell beyond the city gate, and it is manifestly the root from which the major troubles of history have sprung, rivalry, imperialism, and war.

Sumner's analysis of the phenomenon, right at the beginning of *Folkways* (pp. 12, 13), is classical, and we should hear his comments. "The relation of comradeship and peace in the we-group and that of hostility and war towards others-groups are correlative to each other," he writes.

> The exigencies of war with outsiders are what make peace inside lest internal discord should weaken the we-group. . . . Thus war and peace have reacted on each other and developed each other. . . . Each group nourishes its own pride and vanity, boasts itself superior, exalts its own divinities, and looks with contempt on outsiders. . . . Sentiments are produced to correspond. Loyalty to the group, sacrifice for it, hatred and contempt for outsiders, brotherhood within, warlikeness without, all grow together, common products of the same situation.

It might be objected against the use of this quotation in our analysis that Sumner is thinking of only one type of society, namely, the primitive tribe or clan, and of only one sort of situation, namely, armed conflict. But, in spite of his wording, this is not so. The ideologies of modern nationalism are pure ethnocentrism, and so the phenomenon is contemporary as well as ancient. Animosities exist among cities and neighborhoods and families as well as inclusive societies, and so the phenomenon is observable on all levels of social life. It is everywhere in evidence, simply because man is only half-socialized, and because his fuller socialization is a painful uphill struggle.

That these statements are not unduly pessimistic, but rather soberly realistic, can be seen by a quick look back to the topic of the last section, politeness.

The very words used to describe this salutary mode of conduct let the under-lying self-glorification and contempt for others shine through. Courtesy comes from court; the implication is that those outside the court are churlish. Urbanity comes from *urbs*; the implication is that those who live outside the city bound-aries are boors. The derogatory term "rusticity" spells this implication out. This kind of prejudice is very hard to justify. The tendency to develop polite forms of social intercourse is present in all cultures. Even societies which, by most standards, must be considered un- or underdeveloped, evince at times a high degree of refinement in this respect—the Bavenda of South Africa and the Ocean Islanders of Micronesia, for instance (see H. A. Stayt, *The Bavenda* [London, 1931], pp. 157ff.; Arthur Grimble, *A Pattern of Islands* [London, 1969], pp. 32ff., 74ff.). But, justifiable or not, the prejudice prevails; it is next to ineradicable. A paragon who is supposed to be possessed of impeccable man-ners, the English gentleman, is described by Machwirth (*Höflichkeit*, pp. 262, 263) as follows: "The gentleman does not dream of allowing his own per-sonality to be pushed into the background in the interest of his opposite num-bers. He acts in the full consciousness of his own dignity, and his conduct un-derlines his self-regarding value-judgment, his self-appreciation. . . . Even in his readiness to help he shows who he is and what he can do, without, however, being proud and overbearing." If, in this way, even politeness is permeated by feelings of superiority, what is there, what can there be, which is not?

The true bearing, ethos-building and ethic-inhibiting, of ethnocentrism comes to the surface in its religiously caparisoned, religiously suffused, form, in the concept of a holy nation. We therefore postpone its consideration until such time as we are able to present it in its most glaring colors. Here it is mentioned mainly in order to show that all the influences which we have so far enumerated produce not a pure ethic, but only a limited ethos. How can we rise above this level, break through the barriers which hem us in? This question is the subject matter of a branch of philosophy, and we must now ask to what extent its find-ings are realistic and hold out assured possibilities of ethical advance.

2

The Possibilities of Ethical Advance

126. There are many sociologists—and particularly those who would model their discipline on the physical sciences—who are of the opinion that the only correct relationship between sociology and ethics is mutual avoidance. Sociology, so their argument runs, is a factual science; nothing but confusion can result if the student of that which is becomes entangled in the search for that which ought to be. The thought is primitive, and it is surprising that it persists—surprising, above all, because one of the greatest of all sociologists, Emile Durkheim (of whom nobody can say that he was not a scientist in the fullest sense of the word), came to see, after a lifetime of hard work, that the term "fact" cannot mean the same in the social as in the physical sciences. The facts of nature are independent of human willing; the social facts, however, are dependent on human willing; they are underlain by freedom. Social life can develop and endure only if, and to the extent that, the consociated individuals internalize certain norms—those norms which, since Sumner, we call folkways. Sociology is therefore a science of norms, and so is ethics: a link exists, and it is as undeniable as inescapable. Of course, the contrast between the two branches of learning remains: sociology investigates to what extent the order-creating norms are in fact realized; ethics, what can be done to lead their realization further. Whatever in detail the relationship of the two branches of learning, it cannot be one of mutual avoidance if crippling narrow-mindedness is to be avoided.

One firm link is given at once by the fact that moral philosophers do not start from zero when they begin their system-building. They start from an impression of social reality which they receive, in the course of everyday practice, simply by forming part and parcel of a concrete culture. If the term "sociology" is taken in a somewhat loose and non-technical sense, we can say that they start out from a definite sociological position. That sociology may be, and often will be, naïve; the philosopher's own concept of naïve empiricism will be applicable to it; and in this implied sociology lurk many of the defects and difficulties of the ethical doctrines which have been put forward in the course of the centuries. For there are some basic sociological axioms which do not allow of the development of a sound moral philosophy.

The present writer has shown in an earlier work, *The Fundamental Forms of Social Thought* (London, 1962; New York, 1963), that the history of the social sciences has been dominated by three great tendencies: (*a*) the conviction that society is merely a collection of individuals—in other words, that "society" is only a portmanteau term (nominalism); (b) the opposite conviction that society is an integrated whole comparable to the human body, that the term stands for a reality (philosophical realism); and (c) the mediating opinion according to which society is a system which, if undisturbed, develops from multiplicity to unity—differently expressed: that society is neither a fiction (nominalism) nor a fact (realism), but an entity ever in the making, a process. Only this third theory can serve as the basis of an unassailable moral philosophy; the other two cannot.

The nominalistic doctrine, which might more simply be described as consistent individualism, asserts that the dealings of men with each other are in the final analysis exchange relations. If we follow this intuition to its ultimate roots, we come upon the assumption that the exchange relation is the foundation of all existence. Nature is regarded as a merchant who gives things, especially sustenance, in exchange for toil. Because this is the starting point of the argument, it can build its sociological analysis on two other sciences which are seen as more basic: behavioral psychology and elementary economics. Both an animal foraging for food and a buyer catering on a market will continue with their efforts until an equilibrium between outlay or effort, on the one hand, and acquisition or satisfaction, on the other, is reached. This proposition may well be true for ethology and economics, but the question is whether it covers all human behavior. George C. Homans, whose book *Social Behavior: Its Elementary Forms* (New York, 1961) we may consider as a consistent elaboration of this whole mentality, asserts that it does. "With social behavior nothing unique emerges to be analyzed only in its own terms," he writes. "Rather, from the laws of individual behavior . . . follow the laws of social behavior when the complications of mutual reinforcement are taken into account. . . . We hold that we need no new propositions to describe and explain the social" (p. 30). A strange sociology, surely, which knows nothing about norms, about folkways and laws, which takes social peace as an unproblematic *datum* instead of a problematic *explicandum!* "The principles of elementary economics are perfectly reconcilable with those of elementary social behavior," Homans also writes (p. 68). "Both deal with the exchange of rewarding goods." Social behavior is simply "an exchange of activity . . . between at least two persons" (p. 13).

There are, of course, some phenomena which are difficult to fit into this general scheme. Homans himself mentions mother love and sexual love and admits that both are "surely elementary social behavior, yet," he adds, "I have nothing to say about them whatever" (p. 15). He need not have avoided these topics altogether. Both the primal (animalic) sex acts and child-care acts can be interpreted as exchange, and in relation to them the pattern is not even a Procrustean bed. The matter is obvious with regard to sexual intercourse: the partners give each other pleasure. It is less obvious in the case of breast feeding, but a brief consideration proves that the same concept is applicable to it as well: the mother gives milk and receives relief from glandular pressure. But as soon as we move away from these animalic aspects, as soon as we see marriage and motherhood as human institutions, the ethological–economic, nominalistic theory fails. Marriage and motherhood demand sacrifices, but there is no room for sacrifice in this theoretical framework. And because there is no room for sacrifice in it, the catallactic or exchange doctrine cannot be used as a basis for an ethical system.

The upholders of this type of sociology are not unaware of the difficulty, but they try to argue themselves out of it. If a man gives a coin to a beggar—apparently a purely one-sided act—he receives, so the argument runs, in fact an equivalent for it. This is, first of all, the beggar's gratitude. But the protagonists of catallactics are too realistic to insist on this idea. They know full well that there may be no gratitude at all, and if there is a sentiment of this kind, it is often smaller and sometimes even greater than the value of the gift. For this reason, the scene of the supposed exchange act is shifted from the outer world into the inner world of the donor. In his psyche, so it is said, there takes place an exchange between the sacrifice involved and the sentiment of satisfaction which results. He pays, as it were, himself; he buys an experience. The dependence of this sociology on economics is particularly obvious at this point, for, according to neo-classical economics, "Consumption seems really to be a kind of exchange, with conscience for mart and desires as buyers and sellers" (Charles Gide, "The Hedonists: The Psychological School," in Charles Gide and Charles Rist, *A History of Economic Doctrines: From the Time of the Physiocrats to the Present Day*, trans. R. Richards [Boston, n.d.], p. 527). This construction may look quite sound at first sight, but it will assuredly not stand up to critical examination. For the handing over of the coin is a tangible and hard fact, whereas not only the recipient's gratitude but also the giver's inner satisfaction are no more than a piece of imagination, if not indeed a fiction. Gratitude and inner satisfaction are qualities, not quantities; even where they are real, they cannot be considered as exchange equivalents. Their quantification is quite impossible. But the argument of the exchange theorists tries to overcome even this hurdle. The benefit received as a return for the sacrifice undergone, they assert, *must* be an equivalent, "for otherwise the donor would never have made his move." It is not difficult to see that the supposedly scientific "explanation" degenerates at this point into circular reasoning, into a tautology, into pure logomachy. The donor gets an equivalent for his investment; this equivalent is whatever he gets. It is clear that no moral philosophy can be built on such fiction-mongering. Attempts aiming in this direction have always failed, as we shall soon see.

The most pernicious mistake of the tradition which we have just criticized lies in the idea that men enter into relations with others only if they can expect to reap a profit, material or mental. It is this opinion which kills, as it were, the key concept of ethics, the concept of selflessness, even before its birth. The alternative and opposed social theory, the theory which might be characterized as consistent collectivism, is far from this blunder. The question, however, arises, whether it does not fall into a correspondent trap—whether it does not as absurdly exaggerate the social element in man as nominalism exaggerates the persistence of egoism in the adult who has gone through the process of socialization and internalized the norms and values which make for a pacified and pleasant social life, a social life in which altruism is, to some extent, an observable reality.

We may study this second type of social theorizing in Wilfred Trotter's highly successful little book, *Instincts of the Herd in Peace and War* (London, 1916). As the title of the treatise indicates, sociality is to the author an inborn and inescapable trait like any other natural drive, like nutrition, for instance, or sex, so that "ordinary life [is] by a biological necessity, social life," and "gregariousness [is] a fundamental quality of man" (pp. 12, 23). This is manifestly a modernized version of the old conception of society as a natural unity rather than as a multiplicity, a unity in the same sense in which the physical body, the soma, is also a unity. Individuals appear, then, as cells, and cells do not enter into contractual relations with each other. They are function-bearing constituents in an overarching, inclusive organism, and this cooperation—indeed, mutual sympathy among them—is predetermined and permanently guaranteed by laws of life. Heart and lungs do not trade with each other; they are equal servants of the vital whole to which they belong. There is, to speak with Leibniz, a "pre-established harmony."

According to this way of thinking, there is a measure of active altruism in the world, but it can hardly claim to have any right to the epithet "ethical." It implies no moral merit; it lacks the quality of goodness. It springs, not from any will to aid others, but, like hunger and thirst, from the chemistry of the body. Trotter himself draws out these consequences of his basic biologism. "Human altruism is a natural instinctive product," he writes (p. 46). "Man is altruistic because he must be." Trotter used the term "altruism," as can be seen, but he knows full well that, in his mouth, it is a misnomer. "The individual knows another individual of the same herd as a partaker in an entity of which he himself is a part, so that the second individual is in some way and to a certain extent identical with himself and part of his personality" (pp. 122, 123). These words leave nothing to be desired on the score of clarity. The conclusion? Here it is: "Altruism . . . might equally well perhaps be called expansive egoism." Since this "expansive egoism" appears, in Trotter's theory, quite as natural and as inescapable as the narrower egoism of Homans, it precludes as effectively the development of a sound moral philosophy as Homans' competing individualistic approach.

Very different are the implications of a third basic sociology which, in contradistinction to individualism and collectivism or nominalism and realism, might be called "processual." It condemns neither the individualistic–nominalistic nor the collectivistic–realistic doctrine, but asserts that the images which they present are merely metaphors, abstract models which do not, and cannot, be found in the world of experience. In observable societies, groupings can indeed be seen which rest merely on contract—business firms, for example, and joint stock companies, above all—but these are associations included in the social system, and their principle of integration cannot be transferred to the inclusive social system. For they presuppose the enforceability of agreements, and that can only be guaranteed by a set of institutions which rest on a firmer foundation than the wills of the contracting parties. In observable society, groupings can also be found in which the lives of the members are so fully fused that the bond which unites them looks like a natural and instinctual tie, but, once again, the principle of integration of these communities cannot be transferred to the inclusive society because this is not comparable to a close-knit family, to what the Romans called a *communitas totius vitae.* According to thinkers like St. Augustine in antiquity, and St. Thomas Aquinas in the Middle Ages, and technical sociologists like Georg Simmel and Ferdinand Tönnies (to name but two) in recent times, empirical societies are ever on the way from the minimum of integration (considered as the norm by men like Homans) to the social maximum (envisaged by scientists like Trotter). They are on the way, and therefore the basic concept of a sound sociology should be, neither multiplicity nor unity, but *process.*

It is obvious that this conception of social life as a process which leads either from loose to firm integration or, in disturbed conditions, from firmer to looser coherence can serve as a substructure on which an unassailable system of ethics can be erected. For what is it which brings an association of self-seekers by degrees up to the level of a community which may, with some justice, be described as a brotherhood? It is the restructuring of the value systems of the interconnected individuals. As long as their habitual mode of acting and thinking is consistently autocentric, they will enter into relations with others only if, and to the extent that, they may expect to gain; the social bond will then be merely contractual, and the nominalistic doctrine will correspond with the facts. But when, at the end of a long development both personal and collective, they have learned to act and think in an allocentric manner, the common concerns will reach a commanding position. The social bond will then be more than contractual; it will be quasi-natural, and the realistic doctrine will come into its own. Society will then have ceased to be an association, essentially a multiplicity, and become a community, an essential unity. The two poles of the continuum, minimal and maximal sociality, are of interest only to the theoretician. They are limiting cases or ideal types which actually given social systems may and do approach, but which, in their fullness, they can never reach. What matters in and for practice—and hence in and for practical reason—is the energy which gives power to the movements up and down the scale. If there is a downward movement, a sinking toward the condition of a mere side-by-side existence, with the attendant dangers of conflict of interests or even of social disintegration, it is the strength of the body-borne instincts, all of which are self-preferring, which acts as a gravitational pull. If there is an upward movement, a rising toward a situation under which there is a fusion of lives, an identification, experiential and affectual, between self and society, it is the conquest of those instincts, their replacement as action-and-thought-informing principles, as guide-lines, by communal and cultural values, which works as a loadstone, as an engine of advancement. There operates, as can be seen, in the depth of social life, an educational and ethical effort directed toward the ever-closer coordination and consociation of individual selves, toward the ever-more-secure and ever-more-satisfactory integration of society. It may be called this or that, it may be seen as weak or strong, but it is, in its essence, as much of an *élan vital* as that which Henri Bergson discovered in the biotic realm. It, and it alone, provides a safe starting point for ethical speculations. The mechanicism of men like Homans and the organicism of men like Trotter can never hope to reconcile social theory and moral philosophy. In the voluntarism of the third, or cultural, sociology they possess a common ground from which both can start in the pursuit of the mental tasks which are respectively entrusted to them.

THE ETHICS OF SELF-REGARD

127. When we try to place the sociology of George Homans in the wider contexts of the history of ideas, when we search for the ultimate source of his whole mentality, we soon discover that, in the final analysis, it is derived from Sir Isaac Newton. We have already characterized it as a kind of mechanicism, and this epithet is so correct that one can hardly avoid it when speaking of this doctrine. Such prestige as it enjoys is still the prestige of the great astronomer. It is hardly possible to exaggerate the influence which Newton exerted on the coming centuries. He was regarded, and adulated, as the brightest of all luminaries. There were few who dissented from Alexander Pope (see *Works* IV [London, 1770], 57), who expressed a common conviction when he wrote:

> Nature and nature's laws lay hid in night.
> God said: let Newton be! and all was light.

What wonder that it was the passionate desire of social and moral philosophers to do for their subjects what Newton had done for physics and astronomy! What greater ambition could there be than to become the Newton of the human world? Soberly expressed, the task was to find a pendant to the principle of attraction which had been the key with which Newton had unlocked the mysteries of the universe. Once found, it was easy to derive from it the detailed laws which govern, and ought to govern, the dealings of men with each other.

There was no great difficulty about the search. For thirty-five years before Newton's *Philosophiae naturalis principia mathematica*, in 1651, Thomas Hobbes had published his *Leviathan*, and this book offered what was needed. Hobbes was a Newtonian before Newton. His whole philosophy was from beginning to end materialistic and mechanistic. This is obvious in the very first chapter, which deals with the mind of man. All thought comes from physically received impressions. We use the term "impression" even today, but we give it as a rule a psychological and not a physicist meaning. Not so Hobbes. To him the term impression means pressure—pressure of the kind exerted when an electric button is pressed. "The cause of sense," he says (1.1), "is the external body or object which presses the organ proper to each sense either immediately as in taste and touch, or mediately, as in seeing, hearing, and smelling: which pressure, by the mediation of nerves . . . continued inwards to the brain and heart causes there a resistance or counter-pressure." Sense data, such as colors or odors, "are, in the object that causes them, but so many several motions of the matter by which it presses our organs diversely. Neither in us that are pressed are they anything else but diverse motions, for motion produces nothing but motion." The terms pressure and counter-pressure are clearly pendants to the concepts attraction and repulsion which were to be the key words in Newton's vocabulary. Hobbes's psychology (if we may so describe it) was simply a mechanics of the mind.

To this mechanics of the mind there corresponded, in the Hobbist system, a mechanics of society. The social sciences deal with the actions of human beings in their relationships with each other, their actions in the framework of their common life. How are these actions determined? They are determined by certain strivings or endeavors originating within men's bodies. "This endeavor, when it is toward something which causes it, is called appetite or desire. . . . And when the endeavor is fromward something, it is generally called aversion" (1.6). Here again we have pendants to attraction and repulsion, concepts which make it possible to subject yet another department of reality to the laws of mechanics. Objects which attract us are sources of pleasure; objects which repulse us, sources of pain. All human conduct is directed toward the maximization of the former and the minimization of the latter. Man is at all times in quest of the one and in flight from the other. That is his nature. "And therefore the voluntary actions and inclinations of all men tend, not only to the procuring, but also to the assuring of a contented life. . . . So that in the first place I put for a general inclination of all mankind a perpetual and restless desire of power after power that ceases only in death" (1.11). Was it a sociological counterpart to the concept of gravitation which was needed? It is simply men's unceasing pursuit of power and pleasure, his gravitation toward happiness.

Man is therefore, by dint of his physical constitution, unavoidably an egoist. "The highest good of everyone is self-preservation," Hobbes writes in *De cive* (11.6). "For nature has so ordered things that all desire what serves their own well-being." *All*, Hobbes asserts, and thereby hangs the basic problem of social co-existence, of pacification, of security. There is nothing natural about social life. Nature has made us adversaries rather than friends. "If any two men desire the same thing which nevertheless they cannot both enjoy," we read in *Leviathan*, "they become enemies, and in the way to their end (which is principally their own conservation, and sometimes their delectation only) endeavor to destroy or subdue one another." We see that Hobbes is a confirmed and consistent atomist. "It may seem strange to some man that has not well weighed these things that nature should thus dissociate and render men apt to invade and destroy one another," he says, but, he adds, experience proves that this is indeed so. The situation is made even worse by the fact that nature has given to all roughly the same power of self-assertion: "Nature has made men so equal in the faculties of body and mind as that, though there be found one man sometimes manifestly stronger in body or of quicker mind than another, yet, when all is reckoned together, the difference between man and man is not so considerable as that one man can thereupon claim to himself any benefit to which another may not pretend as well as he." This is Hobbes's "state of nature," which is both the starting point of all social developments and an underlying, ever-threatening reality, even after social developments, such as the organization of the state, have taken place. It is a state of permanent contest and conflict. "It is manifest that during the time men live without a common power to keep them all in awe, they are in that condition which is called war, and such a war as is of every man against every man" (1.13).

It is obvious that such a basic philosophy cannot lead to a concept of virtue in the narrower and proper sense of the word. The very terms "good" and "bad" applied to human conduct do not describe, in Hobbes's mouth, actions which help our fellow-men or those which harm or hinder them; they describe moves which benefit or damage the actor's *own* interests. Ethical conceptions are simply inappropriate so far as natural man is concerned. Man acts as he must act; it is as meaningless to call his conduct good or bad as it is to call the fall of a stone toward the center of gravity bad or good. Hobbes himself draws this conclusion from his analysis:

> To this war of every man against every man this also is consequent: that nothing can be unjust. The notions of right and wrong, justice and injustice have there no place. Where there is no common power, there is no law: where no law, no injustice. . . . The desires and other passions of man are in themselves no sin. No more are the actions that proceed from those passions till they know a law that forbids them: which, till laws be made, they cannot know: nor can any law be made till they have agreed upon the person that shall make it [ibid.].

The last words indicate the solution to the problem of social co-existence which Hobbes envisages and which he thinks history has already implemented, and that more than once. It is the submission of all to one. The origin of the state, which sets an end to primal anarchy, arises, of course, from the pristine war of all against all, but not from the fighting itself: much rather from the *frustration* to which this fighting leads. If the contestants, the combatants, are of equal power of self-assertion, as Hobbes maintains, an equilibrium of forces must in the end come about on the battlefield known as society. Another, and a more important, concept of Hobbes's sociological mechanicism is revealed at this point: the balance of egoisms which establishes itself is comparable to the balance of the pushes and pulls in the game known as tug of war and to the balance of a pair of scales where both sides are weighted in the same way. The social equilibrium is, to begin with, unstable. Those who partake in it are always perilously poised between the hope of victory and the danger of defeat—indeed, of death. In order to replace this unbearable state of things with a state of things under which there is no open battle, but only a "disposition thereunto," people agree to accept the yoke of government and law.

> The only way to erect such a common power as may be able to defend them from the invasion of foreigners and the injuries of one another, and thereby to secure them in such sort as that . . . they may . . . live contentedly, is, to confer all their power and strength upon one man, or upon one assembly of men, that may reduce all their wills . . . unto one will. . . . This is the generation of that great Leviathan, or rather—to speak more reverently—of that mortal god, to which we owe, under the Immortal God, our peace and defence.

This done, a difference between right and wrong, virtue and vice, will arise, Qualities like "justice, equity, modesty, mercy and (in sum) doing to others as we would be done to, of themselves, without the terror of some power, to cause them to be observed, are contrary to our natural passions that carry us to partiality, pride, revenge, and the like" (2.17). But once a sovereign exists, everything is changed, and, to the extent that the fear of his iron fist prevails, men put a "restraint upon themselves," and that means that they will no longer lightheartedly attempt to ride roughshod over their neighbors; it means that they become, within certain limits, and in a certain sense, moral.

Even those who reject Hobbes's reduction of man to the status of a mere body and a mere beast will have to acknowledge that his system is impressive: it is characterized by boldness and consistency. But no less obvious are its limitations—limitations which must be particularly clear to anyone who has read the present book up to this point. The humanizing and moralizing influences which we discussed in the first eleven sections (114–24) are nothing to Hobbes. His deep-rooted materialism makes him blind to the very existence of culture and of cultural influences. Yet our main question has to be whether his analysis has revealed an agency capable of improving the tone of social life beyond the level which it reaches through the operation of the basic social controls, and to this query a decisively negative answer has to be returned. The great Leviathan—in other words, organized government—merely makes men less unsociable, less beastly, than they naturally are; it does not make them more sociable and more humane. Hobbes relies exclusively on force—in his parlance, on "pressure" from above—and force cannot evoke neighborliness, let alone love. It can only ensure discipline.

But even though Hobbes is an extreme and consistent mechanicist, his social theory is not the best that mechanicism can provide. Indeed, it would be justifiable to say that, out-and-out Newtonian that he was, he was only half a Newtonian. For the great breakthrough brought by Newton's *Principia* initiated two developments, not one: on the one hand, the elaboration of a mechanicistic theory, and of this Hobbes is certainly a prime example; and on the other, the coming of a thrust toward mechanization in practice, the mechanization, for instance, of production, and this aspect is missing in Thomas Hobbes. He was the creator of a philosophical mechanicism, but remained blind to the possibilities of applied mechanics. The term "social engineering" is of more recent date, but the eighteenth century already recognized—or hoped—that something like that was possible, that society was not only a mechanism of a kind, but, because of that, also improvable through mechanistic means. The main representative of this conviction was Jeremy Bentham. His grand aim was nothing less than a total reconstruction of social life to be engineered by the scientific refashioning of the laws on which it rested. The historical filiation does not run from Hobbes directly to Bentham; there was a detour through France. Thinkers like Helvétius stand as a link between the two Englishmen. But we need not speak of him and his associates for we are not interested in the history of ideas *per se*. Our task is typological, and in this optic Hobbes and Bentham appear as two subvarieties of sociological and moral mechanicism.

Even from a more narrowly theoretical point of view, Benthamism appears as a step beyond Hobbism. "If the physical universe is subject to the laws of motion, the moral world is no less subject to the laws of interest," Helvétius had written in *De l'Esprit* (2.2), and this was still simple Hobbism. But when, in the preface to the same work, he gave it as his opinion that it was necessary to "treat morals like another [exact] science and to develop a new type of ethical doctrine after the model of experimental physics," he enunciated a program which was to be seriously pursued only by Jeremy Bentham. Elie Halévy, whose admirable work *The Growth of Philosophical Radicalism* (trans. Mary Morris; London, 1928) is still by far the best study of this thinker, writes of him as follows: "In laying down the rules of his moral arithmetic, he is trying to construct a kind of mathematical morality analogous to mathematical physics" (p. 29), and in another passage (pp. 52–53) he brings out very clearly the practical, one might almost say, the engineering, aim of this would-be world improver by saying: "Just as science guarantees to men the power to transform physical nature at will and without limits, so also, if it be true to its word, it should guarantee him the possibility of transforming human nature. ..." Here, then, an agency is placed before us which is credited with the power of raising human co-existence well above the level attained in the past, when only the blind forces of life gave it shape and direction. The promise is that the intellect will do better, even in the field of social ordering, than life itself.

Needless to say, Bentham's starting point is orthodox Newtonianism. He is a determinist, and he reckons with two realities which control the human world as attraction and repulsion rule the motion of the heavenly bodies. "Nature has placed mankind under the governance of two sovereign masters, *pain* and *pleasure*," so runs the first sentence of Chapter I of his work *An Introduction to the Principles of Morals and Legislation*. "It is for them alone to point out what we ought to do, as well as to determine what we shall do. On the one hand the standard of right and wrong, on the other the chain of causes and effects, are fastened to their throne." This is Bentham's scientific starting point, and it is in his opinion the only sound basis for a reconstruction and improvement of social life. He calls his doctrine Utilitarianism and writes: "The principle of utility recognises this subjection and assumes it for the foundation of that system, the object of which is to rear the fabric of felicity by the hands of reason and of law." The difficulty of this undertaking is obvious at once. Man and society are in the grip of natural, that is to say, unchangeable and iron, laws; and yet they are to be changed! How can this possibly be done? Bentham thought that the task was not beyond the ingenuity of the social scientist, the social engineer.

Felicity, the great aim of utilitarian politics, presupposes and includes, as a matter of course, a happy and harmonious relationship with one's fellow-men. But how is this to be achieved if every individual, as Bentham consistently maintains, is an out-and-out egoist? "Self-preference has place everywhere," he avers in one place, and in another he writes: "My notion of man is that, successfully or unsuccessfully, he aims at happiness and so will continue to aim as long as he continues to be man, in every thing he does." "What is the language of simple truth?" he asks in a third connection. "That in spite of everything which is *said*, the general predominance of self-regard over every other sort of regard is demonstrated by everything that is *done*: that in the ordinary tenor of life, in the breasts of human beings of ordinary mould, self is everything, to which all other persons, added to all other things put together, are as nothing" (see *Jeremy Bentham's Economic Writings*, ed. Werner Stark, 3 vols. [London, 1952–1954], III 421, 432). These statements are even stronger than they appear at first sight for it must be remembered that Bentham was a member, not only of the wider materialist, but of the narrower sensualist, school: the pleasure which is to be maximized, the pain which is to be minimized, is to him always a physical sensation, a sensation experienced within one's own organism, and therefore exclusively one's own and, at least directly, incommunicable to others. Bentham's atomism, for which there is more evidence than we could adduce here, also determined his basic sociological conviction. The public good is merely the arithmetical sum of the pleasures experienced by the associated individuals, or, rather, organisms. If this general philosophy is taken into account, the integration of society appears as a near-impossibility. It seems a task comparable to the quadrature of the circle or the attempt to jump over one's own shadow.

In Bentham's voluminous works we can identify three separate attempts to solve the problem of social integration. The first is so to define self-regard as to include regard for others as well; differently expressed: to say that man's self-preferring nature also includes an element of native sympathy. Halévy (*Growth of Philosophical Radicalism*, p. 13) calls this "the principle of the fusion of interests" according to which an "identification of personal and general interest is spontaneously performed within each individual conscience by means of the feeling of sympathy which interests us directly in the happiness of our neighbour." This way out of the quandary into which a hyper-individualistic, radically atomistic philosophy must inevitably drift had already been tried by such writers as Richard Cumberland, but though the concept may well fit into the world view of the Cambridge Platonists, it will never blend into that of the Utilitarians. There are several reasons why not. Halévy reveals two. The first is Bentham's overall rationalism: "he mistrusted sensibility and opposed reason to sentiment: he . . . so coloured the philosophy of reform in England as to distinguish it for all time from the humanitarian philosophy which prevailed in the country of Rousseau," the apostle of emotionalism. The second springs from the same root, but is more specific.

> The aim of Bentham, as of all Utilitarian philosophers, was to establish morals as an exact science. He therefore sought to isolate in the human soul that feeling which seems to be the most easily measurable. Now the feeling of sympathy seems to fulfil this condition less than any other. How can it be said without absurdity that the feeling of sympathy varies with the number of its objects according to a law? Egoistic feelings, on the other hand, are better qualified than any others to admit an objective equivalent [ibid., pp. 74, 15].

The pleasure yielded by the consumption of two apples is not quite equal to double the pleasure yielded by the consumption of one, but the "law of decreasing marginal utility" which became the mainstay of modern economics is really a law and a mathematical one to boot. Can it be said that the sympathy felt for more people, for a group, is invariably greater (by whatever margin) than the sympathy felt for one?

Halévy's explanation of Bentham's reluctance wholeheartedly to embrace the principle of the sympathetic fusion of interests is certainly correct, but only partial. Indeed, he failed to unearth the truly decisive reason. A man's felicity may be increased by seeing a fellow-creature happy—though this would seem to apply only to educated and cultured and not to "natural" man—but his gratification is in this case essentially and radically different from any enjoyment derived from a physical cause. "The pleasure of seeing others happy," wrote one of Bentham's disciples, William Thompson (see Werner Stark, *The Ideal Foundations of Economic Thought* [London, 1943], p. 147), "is as much an individual pleasure as the pleasure of eating a pineapple." Maybe. But it is not, and cannot be, a physical sensation, and in a system which knows nothing but physical sensations it cannot possibly find a place. One of the deepest weaknesses of all sensationalism is revealed at this point. The thinkers who belong to this tradition fail to distinguish between pleasure and joy; the two terms are handled by them as if they were synonyms. But they are not. When Christ hung upon the cross, so theologians tell us, He felt joy for He knew that He had redeemed mankind. But He certainly did not feel pleasure.

Halévy, in a passage which we shall presently quote more fully (*Growth of Philosophical Radicalism*, p. 17), maintains that Bentham applied the principle of the sympathetic fusion of interests only "occasionally" and, as it were, "by accident," and this is indeed so. His table of the simple pleasures and pains (see *An Introduction to the Principles of Morals and Legislation*, edd. J. H. Burns and H. L. A. Hart [London, 1970], pp. 42ff.) enumerates fourteen such pleasures and twelve such pains. Of these twenty-six emotions, only four are "extra-regarding," i.e., inspired by the observation of something which has befallen somebody else: the pleasures and pains of benevolence, and the pleasures and pains of malevolence. The latter two are for the most part expressions of envy, and envy is in the final analysis also a self-regarding sentiment, the envy of another man's rich food or of his sexual opportunities, for instance. Thus only two of the twenty-six basic sensations are truly social, and so they constitute no more than marginal phenomena. Bentham included them because he knew that he could use them in his defense against the critics of his conception of man as a pleasure-maximizing and pain-minimizing organism; but this was no more than a debater's trick. Given his basic convictions, any reference on his part to native sympathy was totally illegitimate. Hobbes was more consistent and more honest when he derived the pity felt by a man beholding, for instance, a cripple, "from the imagination that the like calamity may befall himself" (*Leviathan*, 1.6).

Much more in line with his own starting point, and with the whole tradition to which he belonged, was Bentham's attempt to derive sociality and morality from a process of mutual compromising. His guiding idea, as far as this second possibility was concerned, was almost certainly taken from Adam Smith. In a market, so Smith had lucidly explained, buyers and sellers arrive with the determination to make the best bargain and the highest profit they can. It is self-interest, and self-interest only, which inspires them. There is a tug of war: the buyer tries to pull the price down; the seller, to push it up. It all happens in a very mechanistic manner. But the end result is an equilibrium of forces. In the case of two contractants it leads to an agreement, a contract; in the case of the market as a whole, to the emergence of regularity and order. No wonder that Bentham jumped at this opportunity. In one of the great works of his old age, surprisingly enough not yet published, in his "Political Deontology" papers, he writes as follows:

> Whatever . . . be the aggregate mass of the matter of good existing in the community in question, it is the interest . . . of each member of the community . . . to have the whole of it. But . . . no one of them will ever find it in his power to give effect to this his abstract self-regarding interest. Each man's abstract interest finds in . . . the abstract interests of all the others so many counteracting interests. . . . Thus it is that in urging him to the use, enjoyment and preservation with relation to what he has been accustomed to use, or to expect to have it in his power to use, as his own, the interest of each man performs the function of the mainspring of a watch: while in his endeavours to extend his occupation beyond the limits of his own property, he finds himself counteracted by as many conflicting interests as there are [men] in the community, performing, each of them, within his own field or sphere, the office of a regulator in that ingenious piece of mechanism [cited in Stark, *Fundamental Forms of Social Thought*, p. 141].

Elie Halévy has called this the "principle of the natural identity of interests," but this label is not well chosen. It is not asserted that men's interests are identical. Bentham did not think, like Leibniz or Paley, in terms of a pre-established harmony. Men's interests are merely regarded as reconcilable. It would therefore be better to speak of a principle of the spontaneous identification of interests, a description which would also have the advantage of showing up its contrast to the third theory yet to be discussed. Have we here a credible explanation of the origin of order amid a world of conflicting strivings? Certainly, it cannot be urged against the principle of the spontaneous identification of interests, as it could against the principle of fusion, that it is impossible to reconcile it with Bentham's basic atomism. But another argument against it weighs very heavy. Even on the market, the tussle between the contrary wills comes to a pacific conclusion only because it takes place within a pre-existent framework of order, and the origin of that framework is the central *explicandum*, not the dealings which take place under its aegis. But that origination of legality, the principle of the spontaneous identification of interests does not elucidate. Hobbes had written, in one of his bitterest passages (*Leviathan*, 2.17), that "covenants without the sword are but words and of no strength to secure a man at all." More mildly expressed: contracts must be enforceable if a market is to function. But Bentham, unlike Hobbes, does not concentrate his attention on the ultimate problem of co-existence and pacification. What is there to guarantee that buyers and sellers will trade peacefully with each other, will not do violence to each other, will not rob and extort, if society is no more than a battleground of contending interests? Adam Smith, for one, knew very well that the principle of the spontaneous identification of interests could not legitimately be transferred from the analysis of the market mechanism to the analysis of social coherence, for he used it only in his economic treatise on the *Wealth of Nations*, but not in his sociological and ethical study *The Theory of Moral Sentiments.* "The thesis which asserts a direct harmonisation of the various egoisms," Halévy rightly remarks (*Growth of Philosophical Radicalism*, p. 16), "may reasonably be held to be paradoxical."

Halévy describes the third of Bentham's basic theses as the "principle of the artificial identification of interests" and asserts that it constitutes the real core of Bentham's philosophy and program. The following sentence (ibid., p. 36) is so clear and correct that we do well to quote it:

> The very fact that crimes are committed proves that neither the principle of the fusion of interests nor that of the natural identity of interests holds good in these matters; the first, because every time a crime is committed hostile feelings prevail over feelings of sympathy, the second, because the individual finds that his interest, or at least what seems to be his interest, lies in betraying the interest of his neighbour. The problem for the statesman is to define obligations and punishments in such a way that private interest shall be brought by artificial means to coincide with the public interest.

Bentham himself accepts, by implication, this conclusion, for he writes: "Law alone has accomplished what all the natural feelings were not able to do" (*The Works of Jeremy Bentham*, ed. John Bowring [London, 1838ff.], I 307).

If we follow this line of argument to its logical conclusion, we are led back to Thomas Hobbes. Law, order, and security must come from a superordinated authority, from the statesman or legislator. From the point of view of political theory, the contrast between the two thinkers appears sharp: Bentham sees the supreme functionary, not as a threatening beast, a leviathan, but as a benign world-improver: he offered himself to various kings of his time as the willing and able author of a felicity-producing code. But from the point of view of social and moral theory, the difference is small. Or rather: it lies somewhere else. It lies, as we have already indicated, in the engineering aspect of Bentham's thought. Men are selfish; sympathetic feelings achieve little; the equilibration of contrary interests does not achieve much more; but it is possible so to contrive the legal system, so to structure the technique of punishment and reward, that a pacified society will result.

A scheme of this kind will carry conviction only if it is strictly scientific, and that means, mathematical. There is no need to enter more deeply into the arcana of Bentham's moral arithmetic; an indication of its basic idea will be sufficient. As every man tends toward the maximization of his happiness, in the same way as every heavy object tends toward the center of gravity, action will invariably be preceded by a calculation of the pleasures and pains in prospect. "Who is there who does not calculate?" Bentham asks (*Introduction to the Principles of Morals and Legislation*, pp. 173, 174). "Men calculate, some with less exactness, indeed, some with more: but all men calculate." A contemplated action will be carried out if the balance is on the side of personal enjoyment. As far as the individual is concerned, there is no problem. The problem—a very painful one—arises only from the co-existence of individuals. A may, and usually will, try to augment the sum total of his well-being at the expense of B. This must not be allowed, for, apart from the loss of well-being inflicted on the victim, every such act generates a universal alarm: unavoidably, every crime brings with it a shock to the feeling of security, and this is a widespread and ever more widely spreading evil. But the sciences of psychology and law know how to obviate all antisocial conduct. Say, A is a thief who wishes to steal from B. If he hopes to gain one thousand dollars by his exploit, it is only necessary to annex to his delinquency a fine of more than one thousand dollars. By how much the pain of punishment must exceed the pleasure arising from ill-gotten gain is a point of some nicety. If the theft were discovered and avenged at once, it would not have to be much larger; if discovery were uncertain and execution of the sentence distant, it would have to be increased in proportion to that uncertainty and distance. But these are secondary considerations. The principle is surely clear. What Bentham wished to bring about was, simply expressed, an organization of society under which crime would not pay and therefore die out.

It is not quite fair on Halévy's part to assert of Bentham "that he confuses the notions of morals and legislation." He comes much closer to the truth when he writes: "Bentham appealed to the legislator to solve, by means of a well-regulated application of punishments, the great problem of morals, to identify the interest of the individual with the interest of the community" (*Growth of Philosophical Radicalism*, pp. 27, 17, 18). There is no confusion; there is, rather, much consistency. If all human actions are determined by self-preference, morality, however defined, cannot arise, unless it is artificially introduced by one who sees the chaos of human strivings from outside and from above and imposes order and organization on them. The knowledge of the springs of human action enables the legislator to achieve this: his *savoir* gives him *pouvoir*. And this is the purpose and the consummation of all scientific endeavor, whether in nature or in society.

The foundations of this utilitarian doctrine are very shaky. They show three serious flaws, each one of which is sufficient to undermine the entire structure. The first is political. How is the great legislator to come into power? In the seventies of the eighteenth century, when Bentham drafted letters to various potentates, such as Frederick of Prussia and Catherine of Russia, offering his services as a law reformer, his mind was attuned to the idea and ideal of enlightened despotism, but later in life he moved farther and farther away from it. Those in power, he increasingly felt, pursue only their own interests, and not those of their peoples; their own interests, however, are "sinister interests": they aim at exploitation and oppression. Given his basic conception of man, this discovery should not have surprised him! The older he became, the more he drifted to the left. But would an institution like universal suffrage have made it easier to give a chance to a legislator as Bentham envisaged him? Hardly. Democracy works on the principle of the spontaneous identification of interests.

It leads to a mutual adjustment of volitions. But it is not easy to imagine that it would lay its fate in the hands of one individual, however scientific and well-meaning.

The second flaw is more serious. Even assuming that the act of preferring or decision-making is a kind of reckoning (a concession not lightheartedly to be made), how could this vague calculation be made precise? Precision presupposes the possibility of measurement, but it seems impossible to measure the magnitude of pleasures and pains. Quite apart from the obvious differences between different persons, there is no yardstick which could be used. It is possible—indeed, easy—to measure phenomena occurring in the outer world; we can, without trouble, define what we mean by one candle power or one horse power. But how are we to define a unit of pleasure or of pain? In the brains of some modern economists, such as Irving Fisher, pleasure units have led an ephemeral existence. There was talk of one *ut*, and later of one *wantab*, but these imaginings, these spooks, disappeared as quickly as they made their appearance. Bentham was not unaware of the difficulty. "The quantity of the sort of pain which is called grief is . . . hardly to be measured by any external indication," he admits (*Introduction to the Principles of Morals and Legislation*, p. 63). Perhaps taking the pulse would help, but this too would be very uncertain. In spite of this, Bentham sticks to his guns. "A very tolerable judgment . . . may commonly be formed by a discerning mind upon laying all the external indications exhibited by a man together and at the same time comparing them with his actions." This surely would be, not scientific measurement, but merely shrewd guessing! Bentham does not face the truly crucial question: namely, whether sensations are quantifiable at all, whether intensity and extension are identical, whether it be permissible to say of a sorrow that it is greater, if we mean that it is deeper, and so on—thorny problems later lucidly discussed by Henri Bergson. Even John Stuart Mill, though to some extent a disciple of Jeremy Bentham, admitted that there are qualitative differences between experiences of pleasure and pain which cannot be reduced to quantitative terms.

But even this flaw is not so fatal as the third. It interests us particularly because it concerns ethics in the narrower sense of the term. Bentham is totally unable to define virtue in the sense of selflessness, indeed, even to envisage its existence. The fact stares us in the face in the eleventh paragraph of the tenth chapter of the *Introduction to the Principles of Morals and Legislation* (p. 100): "There is no such thing as any sort of motive that is in itself a bad one," he writes, and he italicizes these words. An action is triggered by the last internal consideration—the last internal motive in prospect. "This motive in prospect . . . is always some pleasure or some pain. . . . Now pleasure is in itself good: nay, even setting aside immunity from pain, the only good; pain is in itself an evil; and, indeed, without exception, the only evil; or else the words good and evil have no meaning." This can only mean: no meaning to him, to Bentham. But this fact reveals that he is a prisoner of his own philosophy. It does not allow him to define a good deed as one in which a personal enjoyment is sacrificed for the benefit of a fellow-human. But can a doctrine be called ethical in any sense which, *a limine*, excludes basic goodness?

The total absence of the social and moral point of view leads Bentham into some strange byways. Here are two glaring examples: respect for truth is no absolute duty; corruption on the part of a public servant, no absolute disgrace. "Veracity," he writes (*Works*, ed. Bowring, VI 19), "not less than mendacity, is the result of interest: and, in so far as depends upon the will, it depends, in each instance, upon the effect of the conflict between two opposite groups of contending interests, which of them shall be the result." Elsewhere he says (ibid., IX 66): "In itself corruption is no evil, for neither is the receipt nor the conferring of a benefit in any shape an evil; in so far as it is an evil, corruption is so only in respect of the evil effects produced by it: abstraction made of these effects, it is even a good." We have, in these last words, a textbook example of what Max Weber called *Erfolgsethik*—an ethic, not of principle, but of consequences. But precisely the consideration of, and concentration on, consequences can lead to conclusions which must be pronounced unethical, however ethics is defined. Let us use a simple example in order to make this clear. A schoolmaster enters the classroom, slips on a banana peel, and sits down on the floor. There is pain: physical pain, which may be small; anger and humiliation, which may be more weighty. But there will also be pleasure: the twenty-five youngsters present will in all probability greatly enjoy the joke. If we follow the principle of the felicific calculus, these twenty-five pleasure quantities must be added up and compared to the one pain. If the balance is on the side of pleasure, the event should have taken place and is to be welcomed. A strange consummation indeed!

In view of all this, it is surely impossible to avoid a totally negative judgment on Benthamism considered as an effort in the field of ethics. However man's selfishness is manipulated, it will never yield a true morality: morality can spring only from self-conquest, never from self-regard. Utilitarianism, for all its fancied scientific basis, has nothing to offer which would or could lead society to a higher level of mutual respect and amity than that reached under the guidance of the anonymous forces operative in it.

THE ETHICS OF SENTIMENT

128. Strong as the thrust was which, coming from Sir Isaac Newton, drove the sciences of man in a certain direction, it could not maintain its commanding influence for very long. Pressure produces counter-pressure; for once, a physical law holds good as it stands, even in the social field. From atomism thought turned to holism, from rationalism to emotionality, from calculation to experience. Man was no longer considered as exclusively selfish; a social tendency was discovered in him and asserted to be as innate as self-preference. We must see whether this new school revealed a factor which might, if developed, lead the spontaneously grown ethos of observable societies closer to an ideal ethic.

A *locus classicus* of the new theory is David Hume's *Enquiry Concerning the Principles of Morals*. The second appendix to it, entitled "Of Self-Love," severely criticizes Epicureanism (and hence, by anticipation, Benthamism) and Hobbism; it contains the following revealing sentences: "the nature of the subject furnishes the strongest presumption, that no better system [than these two] will ever, for the future, be invented, in order to account for the origin of the benevolent from the selfish affections . . ." (*An Enquiry Concerning the Human Understanding, and an Enquiry Concerning the Principles*, ed. L. A. Selby-Bigge [Oxford, 1894], pp. 298–99). The fact is, so Hume maintains, that the benevolent and selfish affections are equally constituent elements of and in human nature. Benevolence is there from the very beginning; it does not have to be derived from anything. Characteristically, Hume bases his own theory not on the laws of dead matter, but on the qualities of living creatures, not on mechanics and astronomy, but on biology and zoology:

> Animals are found susceptible of kindness, both to their own species and to ours; nor is there, in this case, the last suspicion of disguise or artifice. Shall we account for all *their* sentiments, too, from refined deductions of self-interest? Or if we admit a disinterested benevolence in the inferior species, by what rule of analogy can we refuse it in the superior? Love between the sexes begets a complacency and good-will very distinct from the gratification of an appetite. Tenderness to their offspring, in all sensible beings, is commonly able alone to counter-balance the strongest motives of self-love, and has no manner of dependance on that affection. . . . Is gratitude no affection of the human breast, or is that a word merely, without any meaning or reality? Have we no satisfaction in one man's company above another's, and no desire of the welfare of our friend, even though absence or death should prevent us from all participation in it? Or what is it commonly, that gives us any participation in it, even while alive and present, but our affection and regard to him? These and a thousand other instances are marks of a general benevolence in human nature where no *real* [i.e., self-regarding, bodily] interest binds us to the object [ibid., 300].

This theory gained the widest possible circulation when it was taken up and developed by Jean-Jacques Rousseau. Instead of speaking of benevolent affections in general, he concentrated on one and saw in it the fountainhead of all the others: the sentiment of pity. An early essay, the *Essai sur l'origine des langues*, speaks of pity as natural to the human heart, but there it still appears as a principle which will remain inactive unless it is activated by reflection and the unfolding of the imaginative faculty (see *Oeuvres complètes*, edd. Bernard Gagnebin and Marcel Raymond [Paris, 1964], III 1130, 1331). Soon, however, it is raised to a higher status and put on a par with the instinct of self-preservation. Thus we read in the preface to the *Discours sur l'origine et les fondements de l'inégalité*: "Speculating about the first and simplest operations of the human soul, I believe I can discern there two principles which antedate [the awakening of the] intellect: the one creates a passionate concern for our well-being and our self-preservation; the other inspires us with a natural aversion to seeing any creature endowed with feeling, and, above all, our fellowmen, perish or suffer" (*Oeuvres complètes*, III 125, 126). In the first part of this treatise, he then goes into specifics, and criticizes Thomas Hobbes in a very energetic manner. Natural man is not vicious, and that for two reasons. The one is that he is innocent. He does not know what good and bad means; as he has no acquaintance with norms, he cannot be said to break them.

> There is besides a second principle which Hobbes has not discovered and which has been given to man in order to temper, in certain circumstances, the intensity of his self-love. . . . It moderates the passionate addiction which he has for his own welfare by an innate repugnance to seeing his equals suffer. . . . I am speaking of pity, a disposition becoming a creature so weak and exposed to so many evils as we are; a virtue all the more universal and all the more useful to man as it precedes in him the coming of all reflection, and so natural that the very beasts give at times evidence of it. Without speaking of the tenderness of mothers for their little ones . . . one can daily observe the reluctance which horses show to trample on living bodies. No animal passes without distress by the corpse of one of its co-specifics; there are even some who give them a sort of burial; and the sad lowing of cattle entering a slaughterhouse expresses their reaction to the horrible scene which they behold [p. 154].

The last sentences are so absurd as to be almost ridiculous. Horses and bovines know no pain of sympathy because they know no pain which is not physical. But we must not allow these absurdities to detain us. We must look at the core of the social philosophy common to Hume and Rousseau and show up the mortal weakness which roots there. Both these thinkers combine two different phenomena: sexual and parental love, on the one hand; human sentiments like kindness and gratitude, on the other. Their thesis clearly is that the benevolent feelings experienced in the mind are akin to motions and emotions which are body-based and body-borne. This, however, is a fatal error. We can best expose it by bringing in a writer of the twentieth century—the same Wilfred Trotter whom we considered in Section 126. He distinguishes four basic instincts: self-preservation, nutrition, sex, and gregariousness (*Instincts of the Herd*, pp. 16, 17). Having asserted that they are of the same nature (in doing this he followed in the footsteps of Hume and Rousseau), he is soon forced to contrast the first three, which are self-regarding and somatic, with the fourth, which is social:

> If we look in a broad, general way at the four instincts which bulk largely in man's life . . . we shall see at once that there is a striking difference between the mode of action of the first three and that of the last. The first three . . . have in common the characteristic . . . of being fundamentally pleasant to yield to. They do not remain in action concurrently, but when the circumstances are appropriate for the yielding to one, the others automatically fall into the background and the governing impulse is absolute master. . . . The appearance of the fourth instinct, however, introduces a profound change, for this instinct has the characteristic that it exercises a controlling power upon the individual from without. . . . The deed, being ordained from without, may actually be unpleasant [ibid., pp. 47, 48].

So great is the conflict between the selfish instincts and the (supposed) social one that Trotter can write (ibid., p. 50): "The primitive instincts are . . . finding themselves baulked at every turn by herd suggestion." At every turn! The words are strong, but not entirely unjustified.

If Trotter had not been totally besotted by his materialistic–biologistic prejudice, he would have seen that his analysis can mean only one thing: namely, that sociality and, *a fortiori*, altruism are not instinctual. And the same goes, *mutatis mutandis*, for Hume and Rousseau as well. They might have seen, and they should have seen, that it is illegitimate to place sexual love and love of one's neighbor in the same category, for to sexual satisfactions nature has annnexed pleasure, to benevolent actions, sacrifice, and that means, pain. The former are pursued with eagerness; the latter, with reluctance. The former, indeed, are natural; the latter, cultural—prescribed by the norms which culture, and not nature, anchors in the individual. Lest it be said that it is unfair to belabor authors of the eighteenth century with a cudgel provided by the nineteenth—Hume and Rousseau could hardly have known that animal behavior is totally controlled by hormones— let us show that they could have avoided their blunder even with the knowledge of their own time. William Paley's *Principles of Moral and Political Philosophy* appeared very briefly after Hume's and Rousseau's deaths (in 1785), and yet he sees quite clearly where they go wrong, though he was in many ways a less brilliant mind than they. If a sentiment of pity were innate and instinctual, he argues (London, 1824; p. 8), it would have to be present everywhere, but it is not: "If an inhabitant of the polished nations of Europe be delighted with the appearance, wherever he meets with it, of happiness, tranquillity, and comfort, a wild American is no less diverted with the writhings and contortions of a victim at the stake." To call benevolence natural is to err in identifying its source: "The laws of custom are very apt to be mistaken for the order of nature." If they are not so mistaken, their true origin is soon discovered:

> Moral approbation follows the fashions and institutions of the country we live in; which fashions also and institutions themselves have grown out of the exigencies, the climate, situation, or local circumstances of the country. . . . The greatest part of those who approve of virtue approve of it from authority, by imitation, and from a habit of approving such and such actions, inculcated in early youth, and receiving, as men grow up, continual accessions of strength and vigour, from censure and encouragement, from the books they read, the conversations they hear, the current application of epithets, the general turn of language, and the various other causes by which it universally comes to pass, that a society of men, touched in the feeblest degree with the same passion, soon communicate to one another a great degree of it. . . . Upon the whole, it seems to me, either that there exist no such instincts as compose what is called the moral sense, or that they are not now to be distinguished from prejudices and habits; on which account they cannot be depended upon in moral reasoning [pp. 12, 8, 9, 11].

But Paley sees yet another and, if possible, even more telling reason why the concept of moral sense cannot be depended upon in moral reasoning. Suppose, he says (p. 12), that we admit for argument's sake the existence of an instinct of benevolence, or of pity, or others of this kind, what, it may be asked, is their authority? No man, you say, can act in deliberate opposition to them, without a secret remorse of conscience. But this remorse may be borne with: and if the sinner choose to bear with it, for the sake of the pleasure or the profit which he expects from his wickedness; or finds the pleasure of the sin to exceed the remorse of conscience, of which he alone is the judge, and concerning which, when he feels them both together, he can hardly be mistaken, the moral instinct man, so far as I can understand, has nothing more to offer.

This possible objection to any and every ethic of sentiment was by no means absent from Hume's and Rousseau's thought and it explains the great complications which the latter saw himself compelled to introduce into his system.

In the more superficial accounts of the history of ethical speculation, Rousseau certainly appears invariably as a representative of the ethics of sentiment. Many passages (like those we ourselves have quoted) seem to justify this characterization, and yet it is fundamentally wrong. If his works are carefully read, it becomes clear that, at the deepest layer of his mind, he entertained serious doubts as to the possibility of deriving sociality, and developing it more fully, from an inborn sentiment like that of pity. The least that can be said is that there are two Rousseaus, one a sentimentalist, the other not. This is the opinion of one of the best experts in the field, Albert Schinz. He sees in the Genevan "two moral tendencies which aim in diametrically opposed directions: one which urges us to follow the inclinations of one's self; it constitutes what might be called the romantic Rousseau; another which demands that one should resist these inclinations; it constitutes what might be called the Roman or Calvinistic Rousseau" (*La Pensée de Jean-Jacques Rousseau* [Paris, 1929], p. 52). Schinz is right; there is ample evidence in support of his thesis. Particularly convincing in this respect is the philosophical novel called *La Nouvelle Héloise*. Its earlier parts belong to the sentimental and permissive Rousseau; its later parts, to the rigoristic. The latter demand self-conquest, not self-fulfillment. And even if it be argued that self-conquest is a kind of self-fulfillment, this argument can but paper over the crack in the structure which remains.

An exposition of all Rousseau's self-contradictions would demand a whole book with many pages. It would show, for instance, that he zigzagged between sociological atomism and sociological organicism, even if it is true that he never identified wholeheartedly with the latter theory. We must willy-nilly concentrate here on the question as to whether his ethical theory is really based on a concept of inborn sociality, a natural sociality capable of further development, or whether he had no trust in this concept, even though he wrote many flamboyant passages in which he makes himself—or appears to make himself—the champion of a naturalistic sociology and ethic.

Even his imaginings concerning pre- and protohistory show that he did not, in the final analysis, believe that social life grows from a natural root. Primal man, though allegedly endowed with a native sentiment of pity, is a solitary creature—like the lion or the eagle, not like the bee or the ant. Nature has willed that this be so. "Men are not made to be crowded together in ant-hills, but to be scattered over the earth," we read in *Emile* (*Oeuvres complètes*, IV 276). He confesses that he cannot explain the origin of social life. He surmises that some natural catastrophe, perhaps a change in the climate, forced men to draw together: it was not in obedience to a nature-given indwelling bent that they did so. But if nature did not create inclusive societies as we know them, did she not at least create those narrower societies which we call families? If Rousseau had had any belief in the power of inborn sentiments to call forth and underpin social forms of life, he would have had to cite—and that consistently—the relations between males and females and between parents and children as his supreme proof of the naturalness of the social bond, or of some social bonds, as so many others have done. But he did not always do so. On the contrary. He more than once denied that there is, in nature, such a thing as an enduring tie between sexual partners, or, for that matter, between mothers and offspring. To speak of the former first: as long as the human race remained in the cadres of nature, "the males and the females got together by accident, as their paths crossed, as occasion served, as desire steered them. Language was unnecessary to explain what they had to convey to each other. They separated with the same ease."

> Once the appetite is satisfied, the man concerned no longer needs this particular woman, nor the woman this particular man. . . . The one goes in one direction, the other in the other. . . . Another woman may then as easily assuage the new desires of the man as the one whom he had known before, and another man in the same way content the woman, assuming that the same drive is still active in her while she is pregnant. . . . There is therefore no reason why the man should look for the same woman nor why the woman should look for the same man.

This is "a fact of the state of nature, that is to say, of a state under which men lived in isolation, and nobody [no individual] had any motive to dwell side by side with anyone else, or men [collectively] perhaps to dwell side by side with each other." Will it be said that there is, after all, such a thing as the sentiment of love, that husbands and wives find each other and stay together because they are naturally attracted to each other? Rousseau has his answer ready. That attraction is observable today, but only because culture has changed us inside out. It is not a primal experience, it is not natural; it is cultural: "In the sentiment of love," Rousseau pleads,

> we must distinguish a moral and a physical element. The physical element is the general desire which induces one sex to unite with the other; the moral element gives this desire a concrete shape and fixes it on one individual object to the exclusion of others, or . . . at least gives it a higher degree of intensity with regard to this preferred object. Now, it is easy to see that the moral aspect of love is an artificial sentiment [*un sentiment factice*]; it is born of social life . . . [ibid., III 147, 217, 218, 157, 158].

Is this the language of a theoretician who can logically maintain that all social life rests in the last resort on a natural feeling?

The passages quoted prove that Rousseau believed neither in the existence of a general instinct of sociality nor in the possibility of broadening the sexual instinct and transmuting it into a kind of social cement. It is in the same spirit that he deals with the philoprogenitive instinct, the attachment of a father and mother to those whom they have brought into the world. He cannot and need not deny that this sentiment is natural; indeed, where he discusses it, he even allows that the family is a natural formation: "The oldest of all societies," he writes, "and the only one that is natural, is the family." But, this said, he immediately reduces even the family to a merely temporary association. "Still," he writes, and this word alone is revealing,

> the children remain tied to their father only as long as they need him for their survival. As soon as this need comes to an end, the natural tie dissolves. The children, freed from the obedience which they owed their father, and the father, freed from the obligations which he owed his children, gain both in the same way their independence. If they continue to live together, this is no longer a natural but a conventional arrangement, and the family itself continues in existence merely through the strength of convention.

In another passage, Rousseau expresses himself even more brutally:

> The mother at first suckles the children for her own benefit; when habit has developed a fondness for them, she nourishes them for their own sake. As soon [however] as they have the strength to look for their own nourishment, they will not hesitate to break away from their mother. And since there is as little chance of their getting together again as there is of their avoiding losing sight of one another, they soon come to the point of not even recognizing one another [ibid., III 352, 147].

All this is said *des premières sociétés*—of original society. But the main implication—namely, that society rests, not on nature, but on convention—applies to all ages, and to modern conditions no less than to the "state of nature." In the first chapter of *Du Contrat social* (ibid., IV 352), Rousseau gives this quite openly as his opinion. He thereby ranges himself on the side of the mechanicists rather than on the side of those who look for a vital, biological root of our common life.

Lest it be said that the evidence so far presented is not wholly convincing because it is taken from Rousseau's political writings which are marred by the conjectural history on which they rest, let us have a look at the educational treatises which, if they cannot be said to be derived from systematic observation, are at any rate based on common experience. What we find in *Emile* and *La Nouvelle Héloise* fully confirms our analysis. In the first pages of *Emile*, the child is depicted as body without soul, and that is to say, without tenderness for others, without love. Even the relation to the mother is painted as loveless. "If the voice of the blood is not strengthened by habituation and child-care acts [*les soins*], it is extinguished in the very first years and the heart dies, so to speak, before it is ever born" (ibid., V 259). In *La Nouvelle Héloise* Rousseau tries to present us, in the heroine, Julie, with the image of a model mother, but her relationship to the little ones is cool and distant. The child is seen and shown throughout to be an autocentric creature. This opinion is entirely in line with modern, scientifically sound conceptions. It is impossible to charge Rousseau with a lack of realism in this regard. But how could he reconcile this child psychology with his assertion that each human being brings so eminent a social emotion as pity with him from the mother's womb? How could he yoke it together with an ethic of sentiment?

That the social emotions are secondary in the sense that they arise only in the course of life is emphasized by Rousseau himself in the parts of *Emile* in which he discusses the transition from childhood to adolescence. The great change which takes place then is the conquest of autocentricity and the parallel blossoming of the emotional life. One of the reasons for this almost magic metamorphosis is the fact that the child is free from sexuality; the youngster, dominated by it. With sexuality the capacity to feel awakens; and since feeling is a salient characteristic of man—i.e., of humanity and humaneness—the onset of physical maturity is the true entry into the human race. Rousseau speaks of a *seconde naissance* (ibid., 490): the birth of the social being in contradistinction to that of the body, which took place fourteen or so years before. The mind totally alters, and with it the entire personality. "What man must give his attention to are his relationships. As long as he knows himself only as a physical being, he must see himself in his relation to the world of things. This is the preoccupation of childhood. When he begins to feel that he is a moral being, he must see himself in his relation to his fellow-men. This is the task of his whole life, but it begins at the point which we have now reached," i.e., at adolescence (ibid., 493).

As can be seen, in *Emile*, Rousseau shifts his ground somewhat. The emotions which underpin and preserve social life are depicted as a product of the process of physical maturation, not as a native endowment already present when the umbilical cord is cut. They are still seen as natural, but, so to speak, in an attenuated sense of that word. In the passages which we have adduced, Rousseau comes close to linking the origin of sociality with the origin of sexuality. But he does not further develop the idea, which makes its appearance in the context of his discussion of adolescence, and that for a very good reason. The sexual drive is not inherently social. Everywhere in nature it leads to fierce competition between the males for the possession of the females, as Rousseau himself acknowledges (ibid., III 159), and in some species it even temporarily dissolves the social bond. The days of the annual rut are not the days of tranquillity and peace! Rousseau himself speaks of sexuality as a "burning and impetuous passion," a "terrible passion . . . which in its fury seems apt to destroy the human race, which it is its function to preserve." "It must be admitted," Rousseau even writes (ibid., 157), and writes specifically with an eye on sexuality, "that the more violent the passions are, the greater the need for laws to restrain them." At this point, however, he turns around and plunges into his conjectural history at its worst. Primal man was not jealous. He had no need to be. There were enough women to go round. Everyone had his chance and his opportunity. Only the corruption of man brought about by culture created evils like sexual competition, possessiveness, vanity, and envy. It is hardly possible to assume that Rousseau himself believed all this: believed in any possible positive influence of awakening sexuality on awakening sociality; he can hardly have regarded so natural a feature as the fight for the female as absent from the early forms of human existence, as absent from hominid and emerging *Homo sapiens*. However that may be, Rousseau, while determined to base the social bond on a natural emotion, does not base it on the emotions arising from the drive to mate.

What has gone before enables us to compare Rousseau's position with that of Hume, and a very instructive comparison it is. Whereas Hume used the good will obtaining between the marriage partners and their tenderness for their common offspring somewhat naïvely as proofs for the existence of an inborn benevolence (allegedly) observable in the inferior species, Rousseau does not and cannot see them consistently in this light. They are, in nature, at best transitory phenomena, and no reliance is to be placed on them so far as social life in general is concerned. From the point of view of modern knowledge, Rousseau's stance is doubly superior to that of Hume. It is superior not only because it operates with more sharply defined concepts, but also because it is more sober, i.e., closer to the facts. But Rousseau's superiority is at the same time also his weakness. The basis of his theory is much narrower than that of Hume. Excluding sexual attraction and parental love, what remains that can be used as a prop for an ethic of inborn, natural, moral sense? Nothing, really. But Rousseau tries, as we have seen, to fill the void with his concept of inborn, natural commiseration, with the sentiment of pity. He must make much of very little, but he asserts (at least in some passages) that he has enough to account for the social bond.

The basic thesis is most clearly and most succinctly stated on a page of the *Discours sur l'origine . . . de l'inégalité* (ibid., III 156): "It is quite certain that pity is a natural sentiment which, moderating in each individual the power of self-love, tends to the mutual preservation of the whole species. . . . It is pity which, in the state of nature, takes the place of laws, mores, and virtue, and with that advantage that nobody is tempted to disobey its sweet voice." This is Rousseau's "here I stand, I cannot do otherwise!" But the pretended conviction is very weak. The fact becomes obvious in the *Essai sur l'origine des langues* where Rousseau expresses himself as follows:

> The social sentiments develop only with our understanding. Pity, although natural to the human heart, would never become active without [the unfolding of] our imaginative faculty which activates it. How is it that we are moved to pity? by stepping out of ourselves and identifying with the sufferer. We suffer with him only insofar as we *judge* that he suffers. . . . It is necessary to realise how much acquired *knowledge* is presupposed by this identification. How could I experience a kind of suffering of which I have no conception? . . . He who has never *thought* about this matter cannot be benevolent or just or sympathetic; nor can he be angry or vengeful. He who has no imagination feels only for himself; he is alone in the midst of the human race.

What are these words, if not an implied, but entirely clear, admission that even pity is not an inborn sentiment but one which develops in life, in *social* life? In addition, Rousseau concedes in the same context that pity was, in prehistoric—"natural"—men, even if it existed, a limited and weak affection: "A stranger, an animal, a monster were for them one and the same thing. Outside of themselves and their family the whole world meant nothing to them" (ed. Charles Porset [Paris, 1970], pp. 93, 95). The very last lines are curious. For had Rousseau not asserted, and that repeatedly, that natural man did not know the institution of the family? But if we take the words "and their family" out of the sentence, it shrinks to the proposition that natural man felt only self-pity and no other.

In this way Rousseau destroys the whole basis of his own theory. In the *Essai sur l'origine des langues* he speaks in phylogenetic terms, in *Emile* in ontogenetic ones, but the upshot is the same:

> At sixteen, the adolescent knows what it is to suffer, for he himself has suffered; but he hardly knows that others also suffer. . . . As I have said a hundred times, the child, because he cannot realize what others feel, knows no pains but his own. . . . In fact, how could we be moved to pity, if it were not by leaving ourselves and identifying with the suffering creature? by abandoning, so to speak, our own being and assuming his? We suffer only insofar as we judge that he suffers [*Oeuvres complètes*, IV 504, 505].

But judgment is beyond the small child as it is beyond the hominid. If pity is indeed what Rousseau calls it (ibid.), the *premier sentiment rélatif*—the first feeling which relates us to others—then it is of tardy growth, in both the history of the individual and that of the race. It is not the root from which sociality springs. Rather it is a fruit which social life is able to bring forth.

Before moving on, we must notice an important passage which shows with all desirable clarity that Rousseau had, when the truth is told, no confidence in an ethic of sentiment. In the first version of *Du Contrat social* (ibid., III 287) he raises the question as to how a man in the midst of moral conflict could resolve his doubts and overcome his scruples, and asserts that it will not be possible for him to fall back on any indwelling light.

> Will he listen to an inner voice? But this voice, so it is said, is formed only in society and in agreement with its laws by the habitual manner of judging and feeling. . . . Furthermore it would be necessary that none of the passions should have risen up in his heart which speak more loudly than conscience and blot out its timid voice, and which have induced philosophers to maintain that such a voice does not even exist.

Rousseau does not hold with these philosophers (he may well think mainly of Hobbes here); but the passage, interpret it how you will, admits that the inner light, the light of conscience, even if it exists, is but a glimmer, not a beacon which helps us to find our way.

All this must induce us to raise the question why Rousseau ever introduced the concept of pity, that feeble conceit, into his theory if he had so little confidence in its efficacy. The answer is not far to seek. Like so many before and after him, Rousseau assumed that it was next to impossible to account for the continued existence of society if it had no sort of backing in the forces of nature, and be it only as weak an influence as he himself assumed the sentiment of pity to be. In taking this view he greatly underestimated the strength of the cultural forces, their creativity, and the will of man himself. It is by no means necessary to assert that nature has *created* society; it is amply sufficient to show that nature has *permitted* its development (see SOCIAL BOND I 20–22, Section 14). It is surprising that Rousseau did not discover this solution, for once or twice he is very close to it. One of his key concepts is the concept of perfectibility, and this he considers a quality which nature has indeed laid on, but which she did not actualize, and which is actualized only in and through social life. "Perfectibility," he writes, as well as "the social virtues and the other faculties which natural man had received as potentialities [*en puissance*], would never have evolved of themselves, and required for their unfolding the accidental appearance of several outside causes which might never have appeared . . ." (*Oeuvres complètes*, III 162). The key concept used here (*facultés qu'il avoit en puissance*) also occurs elsewhere (ibid., 152). There is no reason why sociability should not have been seen as akin to perfectibility, as in fact it is. And there is no reason either why the development of both should not have been assumed to have been triggered by the first fear-induced herdlike aggregation of prehistoric men which, by creating a social environment, allowed so brainy a creature as *Homo sapiens* to raise himself above animality and to convert natural potentialities into cultural realities.

One basic conviction of Rousseau's, however, was entirely correct: the conviction that it is incumbent on the social theorist to point to a factor which (as he himself expresses it) "moderates in each individual the power of self-love." Unfortunately, we cannot stay to discuss his concept of self-love. It is highly problematical. He assumes that two variants of it have succeeded each other in history: the innocent and natural self-love of primitive man which he calls *amour de soi-même*, and the sophisticated egotism of modern man which he calls *amour propre*, a self-love which engenders a clever life-policy and which, as Veblen would have said, contaminated the natural sentiment. He is inclined to argue that our modern *amour propre* is the opposite of the pristine *amour de soi-même* (see ibid., 219), but it is only too clear that this is special pleading, and that the condemned *amour propre* is, in fact, the natural development of nature-given *amour de soi-même*. No matter. The fact remains, and Rousseau acknowledges it, at least by implication, that self-love in all its forms has to be "moderated" by some counterbalancing factor. What is it if it is not the natural sentiment of pity? Rousseau himself gives us an entirely satisfactory answer: it is the power of the laws. He abandons the theory of an inborn emotion-based sociality and substitutes for it an entirely different sociology and ethic.

Whatever the nature of human relationships in the imagined days of the dawn, in recorded history and in observable societies they are characterized by a pervading diversity of interests, and therefore also by a tendency to conflict, open or disguised. This is the starting point of Rousseau's second socio-ethical doctrine, the doctrine, not of the romantic, but of the Roman and Calvinistic Rousseau.

Men are wicked; depressing and uninterrupted experience makes it unnecessary to prove it. . . . Admire human society as much as you like, it remains true nonetheless that it induces people to hate each other in the measure in which their interests clash, to offer each other apparent services, and, in fact, to inflict on each other every imaginable evil. . . . It is not true that, given a condition of freedom, reason motivates us to contribute to the common good by the regard which we have for our own interest; it is far from correct that private interest is linked to public; in the natural order of things, they exclude each other, and the laws of society are a yoke which everyone wishes to impose on all others, but not to assume himself [ibid., 202, 284].

These sentences are very far from the optimistic mood which the belief in an inborn moral sense or tendency must logically engender; they are closer to Thomas Hobbes than to the "romantic" Jean-Jacques himself. This may sound exaggerated and indeed absurd, but it is true nonetheless. The kinship between the Calvinistic Rousseau and the Calvinistic Hobbes has been recognized by several competent observers (see, for example, the excellent discussion in Martin Rang, *Rousseaus Lehre vom Menschen* [Göttingen, 1959], pp. 145, 146). With Rousseau, as with Hobbes, man is led out of the misery of a war of all against all by the organization of the state. The difference between the two thinkers lies merely in their contrasting *political* conceptions: Hobbes wished for an authoritarian government; Rousseau, for a radical democracy. But this does not prevent the two *social* theories from being close to each other, if not indeed identical. Both demanded that the laws should be respected, indeed, venerated, and implicitly obeyed; and both averred that social peace—the very existence and preservation of the social bond—depended on this respect and on this obedience. "By what inconceivable art has it been possible to find the means of disciplining men so that they can be given their freedom? . . . This miracle is the work of the law," says Rousseau in his "Discours sur l'économie politique" (*Oeuvres complètes*, III 248). And in the first version of *Du Contrat social* he writes in the second chapter of the second book, under the title "Du Législateur":

He who thinks himself capable of forming a people [i.e., of establishing a framework of peace and order] must feel that he is able to change, as it were, human nature. Every individual who, by himself, is a perfect and solitary entity, has to be transformed into part of a greater whole of which this individual receives in some way his life and his being. . . . A moral existence, existence as a part, must be substituted for the physical existence in independence which we have received from the hands of nature. In a word, it is imperative to take from man all his proper and innate qualities in order to give him others which are [initially] alien to him. . . . The more these natural forces are suppressed and annihilated, and the stronger and more durable are the acquired ones, the more solid and perfect is the effect of this education [ibid., 313].

Society, an outgrowth of human nature? That idea has completely disappeared! Its place is taken by the conviction that human nature (in the strict, scientific sense of the word) has to be put under control if a life in common is to become possible.

The very same conviction also dominates the closing pages of Rousseau's great educational novel. The disciple has traveled; he is deeply disappointed; he has found perfection nowhere, painful weaknesses everywhere. Jean-Jacques urges him not to think and feel like that:

> O Emile! Where is the man of good will who owes nothing to his country? Whoever he may be, he owes it what is most precious for man, the morality of his conduct and the love of virtue. Born in the depths of a forest, he would have lived in greater happiness and freedom; but, as he would have had nothing to fight against in the pursuit of his inclinations, he would have been good without merit, he would not have been virtuous, and now he knows how to be virtuous in spite of his passions. . . . The public good which for others is only a pretence is for him a real incentive. He learns to fight against himself, to gain the victory over himself, to sacrifice his interest to that of the community. It is not true that the laws are not of advantage to him. They give him the courage to be just, and that even among the wicked. It is not true that they have failed to give him freedom; they have taught him to rule over himself [ibid., IV 858].

We can now, in conclusion, raise again the question which concerns us most— the question as to whether the philosophy of Jean-Jacques Rousseau points to any agency able to lift the societal ethos onto a higher level. It does not seem so. Certainly, he sets no store whatever by the development of pity, assuming even it were possible to develop it. He admits that love will always be confined to narrow circles such as that of the family—but there it exists anyhow, there it is spontaneously developed by the social forces. "It seems that the sentiment of humanity evaporates and weakens when it is extended over the whole earth. . . . It is necessary to limit and to concentrate interest and fellow-feeling in some way in order to give it efficacy. . . . This inclination within us can be of benefit only to those with whom we have to live," we read in the "Discours sur l'économie politique" (ibid., III 254), and in *Emile* (ibid., IV 248, 249): "Every partial society, if it is close and united, alienates us from the more inclusive society. Every patriot is harsh to foreigners. . . . This inconvenience is inevitable. . . . The essential thing is to be good to the people with whom we live." This is simply the ethos of the folkways. It is surely significant that the last advice which Jean-Jacques gives to Emile is to the effect that he should stay in his native country and try to be its loyal citizen: "What matters for you is to live where you can fulfill your duties" (ibid., 858).

Rousseau's final conclusion—namely, that social life can best be improved by the loyal and conscientious fulfillment of society's grown and established laws—can also be found in Hume's *Treatise of Human Nature*, especially in the second part of the third book. Sentiment and sympathy are and remain his key concepts; yet they are not in evidence in the following passages which, between them, present the outlines of a social and ethical theory which has no need of anything like the concept of a moral sense:

> It is certain that self-love, when it acts at its liberty, instead of engaging us to honest actions, is the source of all injustice and violence. . . . We must allow that the sense of justice and injustice is not derived from nature, but arises

artificially, though necessarily, from education and human conventions. . . .
Custom and habit, operating on the tender minds of the children, makes them
sensible of the advantages which they may reap from society, as well as fashion
them by degrees for it. . . . By this means the sentiments of honour may take
root in their tender minds and acquire such firmness and solidity that they may
fall little short of those principles which are the most essential to our natures
and the most deeply radicated in our internal constitution [ed. L. A. Selby-Bigge
(London & New York, 1966), pp. 187, 189, 192, 205].

Particularly significant in this context are Hume's remarks about acquisitive-
ness: "It is certain that no affection of the human mind has both a sufficient
force and a proper direction to counterbalance the love of gain and render men
fit members of society by making them abstain from the possessions of others.
Benevolence to strangers is too weak for this purpose. . . . It was therefore a
concern for our own and the public interest which made us establish the laws
of justice," including the law of property. For the sake of social peace, "property must be stable and must be fixed by general rules," and "our property is
nothing but those goods whose constant possession is established by the laws
of society" (pp. 197, 201, 202, 196). Thus it is the law and not benevolence
which is the basis of the social bond—of "coalition," as Hume expresses it in
his quaint eighteenth-century English or, rather, Scottish (p. 192).

A third ethical theorist who claims our attention is Adam Smith, with his
Theory of Moral Sentiments. He, too, has two doctrines: the one based on the
concept of "pity or compassion," which he counts to the "original passions of
human nature" (New York, 1966; p. 3), the other pointing in an entirely different direction. The former is of relatively little interest for it conforms to the
general pattern which we studied through Rousseau and Hume. The latter, on
the other hand, is of high significance for it anticipates some of the intuitions
on which a good deal of modern sociology rests, including even the present
treatise.

Smith's theory appears at first sight as still more radical than those of his
great contemporaries Hume and Rousseau. He describes a "sense of what is
due to [our] fellow creatures" as "the basis of justice and of society" and calls,
in another context, "our sensibility to the feelings of others" an "instinct" (pp.
149, 213, 214). Even if we make allowances for the comparative looseness of
eighteenth-century speech, the implication of "sense" is that it is something like
seeing and hearing, and of "instinct" that it is something like sexuality. Smith's
extremism is also noticeable in his assertion that "nature . . . has endowed [man]
not only with a desire of being approved of, but with a desire of being what
ought to be approved of. . . . The first could only have prompted him to the
affectation of virtue and to the concealment of vice. The second was necessary
in order to inspire him with the real love of virtue and with the real abhorrence of vice" (p. 170). What these sentences assert is not only an instinctual
desire for virtue, but also an instinctual aversion from hypocrisy! Where, oh
where, is the slightest sense of realism? Smith also ventures far too far forward
when he says of the "emotion which we feel for the misery of others" that "the
greatest ruffian, the most hardened violator of the laws of society is not alto-

gether without it." These words appear on an early page (p. 3); but some two dozen pages later (p. 28) we read the very opposite: "The amiable virtue of humanity requires . . . a sensibility much beyond what is possessed by the rude vulgar of mankind."

Faced with this self-contradiction, all the critic can do is to try to find out on which side the balance lies. In the case of Adam Smith, it lies on the side of pessimism. Indwelling sympathy is a weak sentiment. Here is just one illustration in lieu of many:

> A stranger passes by us in the street with all the marks of the deepest affliction; and we are immediately told that he has just received the news of the death of his father. It is impossible that, in this case, we should not approve of his grief. Yet it may often happen, without any defect of humanity on our part, that, so far from entering into the violence of his sorrow, we should scarce conceive the first movements of concern upon his account [p. 16; see also pp. 7, 22, 23, 33, 35, 65, 66].

Later in the work, Smith admits that general rules of conduct are necessary, besides the spontaneous social feelings, if society is to be secure, and he sets greater store by the former than by the latter: "Without this sacred regard to general rules, there is no man whose conduct can be much depended upon" (pp. 230, 231).

Still more fatal to Smith's own starting point is the repeated admission that the moral sentiment is not native, but acquired—acquired in social life. "Were it possible that a human creature could grow up to manhood in some solitary place, without any communication with his own species, he could no more think . . . of the propriety or demerit of his own sentiments and conduct . . . than of the beauty or deformity of his own face." Sociality is learned:

> A very young child has no self-command. . . . When it is old enough to go to school, or to mix with its equals, it soon finds that they have no such indulgent partiality [as its parents]. It naturally wishes to gain their favour and to avoid their hatred or contempt. Regard even to its own safety teaches it to do so; and it soon finds that it can do so in no other way than by moderating, not only its anger, but all the other passions, to the degree which its playfellows are likely to be pleased with. It thus enters into the great school of self-command.

Fellow-feeling, Smith quite openly admits, is created, not by nature, but by habit. "What is called affection is in reality nothing but habitual sympathy." Even "family affection" is but "habitual sympathy." This applies to the parent–child relationship as to all others: "I consider what is called natural affection as more the effect of the moral than of the supposed physical connection between the parent and the child." Smith goes so far as to ridicule the opposite idea, the idea that a physical bond implies a bond of sympathy as well.

> In some tragedies and romances we meet with many beautiful and interesting scenes founded upon . . . the wonderful affection which near relations are supposed to conceive for one another even before they know that they have any such connection. This force of blood, however, I am afraid, exists nowhere but

in tragedies and romances. Even in tragedies and romances it is never supposed
to take place between any relations but those who are naturally bred up in the
same house [pp. 162, 203, 204, 323, 324, 328, 326].

Smith does not seem to realize that, in such passages, he pours scorn even on
his own thesis, the thesis that "*nature* . . . formed men for that mutual kindness
[which is] so necessary for their happiness" (p. 331; emphasis added).

If there were no more to Adam Smith, we should not even have mentioned
him in these pages. But, like Hume and Rousseau, he realized the necessity of
developing a second—more realistic—social and ethical theory, and that is,
as we have hinted already, remarkable. He clearly anticipates Cooley's concept of the looking-glass self. Speaking of the "human creature" supposed to
have grown up "in some solitary place," he continues: "Bring him into society,
and he is immediately provided with the mirror which he wanted before. It is
placed in the countenance and behaviour of those he lives with. . . . It is here
that he first views the propriety and impropriety of his own passions, the beauty
and deformity of his own mind." Even in a point of detail, Smith agrees be-
forehand with Cooley's analysis when he writes: "We become anxious to know
how far our appearance deserves either [our neighbors'] blame or approbation."
Immediately after this sentence, we encounter another seminal idea which we
usually connect with George Herbert Mead rather than with Charles Horton
Cooley: we endeavor, Smith says, "to view ourselves . . . with the eyes of other
people." "We suppose ourselves the spectators of our own behavior" (pp. 162–
64). But we not only look back on ourselves with the eyes of this individual or
that; we also survey ourselves with the eyes of an abstract "impartial spectator,"
of a person conceived as "reasonable," i.e., with the eyes of an observer who
is really an assumed and imagined incarnation of society. This idea, which
plays the greatest possible part in Smith's text, comes close to Mead's concept
of the "generalised other" (see, e.g., p. 97). Whether or no Smith develops the
Meadean distinction of "I" and "me" as well is a question of some difficulty
which cannot be adequately discussed in a few words; but one passage (on pp.
164, 165) seems to point in that direction. What matters from the point of
view of our investigation is the fact that the ideas which we have described and
shown to be so surprisingly modern lead up to yet another modern sociological
key-conception—Durkheim's and Parsons' "internalization of norms and
values." "We either approve or disapprove of our own conduct," Smith writes
in a particularly crucial passage (p. 161), "according as we feel that, when
we place ourselves in the situation of another man, and view it, as it were,
with his eyes and from his station, we either can or cannot entirely enter into
and sympathize with the sentiments and motives which influenced it." This
means: by habitually looking at ourselves and our style of conduct with the
eyes of the generalized other, we take that generalized other up into ourselves;
he becomes "the man within," the "monitor in our own breast"—terms which
Smith constantly uses. What is this but a theory of socialization and sociality
which bases it, not on native endowment, but on education, including self-
education, not on natural influences, but on the effects of habitual interaction?

That we are not dealing unfairly with our author, that he in fact abandons his own initial stance, become quite clear from the following lines:

> When our passive feelings are almost always so sordid and so selfish, how comes it that our active principles should often be so generous and so noble? . . . It is not the soft power of humanity, it is not that feeble spark of benevolence which Nature has lighted up in the human heart that is thus capable of counteracting the strongest impulses of self-love. It is a stronger power, a more forcible motive, which exerts itself upon such occasions. It is . . . the man within [pp. 193, 194].

But there is no complete reliance even on the man within, simply because he is within. We find it not difficult to falsify his voice: "The violence and injustice of our own selfish passions are sometimes sufficient to induce the man within the breast to make a report very different from what the real circumstances of the case are capable of authorizing" (p. 221). What then? Well, if the *inner* voice is unreliable, we must fall back on an *outer* voice; if *subjective* sentiments fail, we must place our trust in *objective* principles—general rules, as Smith calls them. But these general rules are simply the existing norms of society, and so Smith arrives in the end at the same point as Rousseau. Realism has brought him there, as it did Jean-Jacques. "The coarse clay of which the bulk of mankind are formed cannot be wrought up to [moral] perfection. There is scarce any man, however, who by discipline, education and example [!] may not be so impressed with a regard to general rules as to act upon almost every occasion with tolerable decency and through the whole of his life to avoid any considerable degree of blame" (p. 230). "Scarce any man"; "upon almost every occasion"; "tolerable decency"—considerable doubts are quite obviously still present in the mind of him who was at first prepared to rely on inborn benevolence! He sees himself constrained to call in, because everything else is of no avail, even the strong arm of the law: "The very existence of society requires that unmerited and unprovoked malice should be restrained by proper punishments" (p. 109). Men have *duties* toward each other, and, "upon the tolerable observance of these duties depends the very existence of human society which would crumble into nothing if mankind were not generally impressed with a reverence for these important rules of conduct" (pp. 231, 232).

One of the deepest reasons why Adam Smith in this way virtually abandons the attempt to develop a truly consistent theory of moral sentiments is his realization that the voice of feeling is often, if not always, indistinct. Our moral judgments, he admits (p. 470), "would be extremely uncertain and precarious if they depended altogether upon what is liable to so many variations as immediate sentiment and feeling." To remedy this weakness, he recommends the use of the inductive method—the derivation of general and abstract rules from specific and concrete experiences. But this suggested way out of the difficulty is obviously problematical. If the premises are uncertain and precarious, how can the conclusions based on them be otherwise? One great mind who felt this very vividly was Immanuel Kant, and he resolved therefore to push into a radically different direction.

THE ETHICS OF REASON

129. The two ethical systems which we have surveyed so far are sharply contrasting—as contrasting as their sociological pendants, individualism–atomism–mechanicism, on the one hand, and collectivism–holism–organicism, on the other. It is one thing to say, with Bentham, that men cannot stir out of their native egotism and that human relations can be improved only by a clever manipulation of that very egotism; it is quite another thing to say, with Adam Smith, that nature has endowed them with a spirit of benevolence, and salvation can come from a development of that natural bent. But though constrasting, these two doctrines are also akin. They both root in the same basic philosophy of monism: according to them, there is *one* law which controls nature and humanity at the same time. The great thinker to whom we are now turning, Immanuel Kant, was a consistent and convinced *dualist*. There is a passage, right at the end of his *Critique of Practical Reason*, which makes this abundantly clear. It has been quoted more often than any other in his voluminous works, and must be quoted here as well: "Two things fill the mind with ever new and increasing admiration and awe, the oftener and the more steadily we reflect on them: *the starry heavens above and the moral law within.*" There are two realms, then, two kinds of reality, which we must distinguish, even though they in fact interpenetrate. Their difference becomes quite obvious in the case of man: astronomy, "the . . . view of a countless multitude of worlds, annihilates as it were my importance as an *animal créature*, which, after it has been for a short time provided with vital power, one knows not how, must again give back the matter of which it was formed to the planet it inhabits." Contemplation of ourselves, "on the contrary, infinitely elevates my worth as an *intelligence* by my personality, in which the moral law reveals to me a life independent of animality and even of the whole sensible world."

We must, Kant urges, separate the area of necessity from the area of freedom: animals are in the throes of determination; man is not, insofar as he is, not body, but reason and will. He strives to convince his readers that there is a "distinction between the laws of a natural system to which the *will is subject* and of a natural system which is *subject to a will* (as far as its relation to its free actions is concerned)" (*Critique of Practical Reason*, trans. T. K. Abbott [London, 1879], pp. 376, 377, 188). An earlier treatise, entitled *Grundlegung zur Metaphysik der Sitten*, makes this very clear: "Everything in nature works in accordance with laws. Only a rational being has the power to act in *accordance with his idea* of laws—that is, in accordance with principles—and only so has he a will. . . . Because of this, a rational being must regard himself *qua intelligence* (and accordingly not on the side of his lower faculties) as belonging to the intelligible world, not to the sensible one"—the world of mind, not that of the body. "He has therefore two points of view from which he can regard himself, and from which he can know laws governing the employment of his powers and consequently governing all his actions. He can consider himself *first*—so far as he belongs to the sensible world—to be under laws of nature (heteronomy); and *secondly*—so far as he belongs to the intelligible world—to be under laws which, being independent of nature, . . . have their ground in reason alone" (trans. H. J. Paton under the title *The Moral Law* [London, 1948], pp. 70, 120; all italics Kant's). Kant sums all this up in his characteristic terminology by saying that man is both *noumenon* (or mind) and *phenomenon* (or body) (see *Critique*, p. 130). How those two halves get along with each other is precisely the problem of ethics. Man is eternally caught in a dilemma: He

> is a being who, as belonging to the world of sense, has wants, and so far his reason has an office which it cannot refuse, namely, to attend to the interest of his sensible nature . . . with a view to the happiness of this life [the life of the body, the life of the flesh]. . . . He requires reason in order to take into consideration his weal and woe, but besides this he possesses it for a higher purpose also, namely, . . . to take into consideration what is good or evil in itself, about which only pure reason, uninfluenced by any sensible interest, can judge [*Critique*, pp. 215, 216; see also *Moral Law*, pp. 121, 125].

These quotations have already led us fairly deeply into Kant's system of ethics. As a natural phenomenon, as an animal body, man is dominated by the pursuit of happiness, by the pleasure principle, as all other living creatures are; as a noumenal being, as a mind, he is faced with a choice: either to follow his bodily urges, or to pursue moral purposes. Only in the latter case is he acting morally. In order to make the right decision in every case which arises, he needs a rule to guide himself by: an imperative to which he can and should submit, even against the cravings of his flesh; indeed, a *categorical* imperative which clearly and cogently indicates his moral duties. This call for an objective criterion of good and bad reveals to us yet another salient characteristic of Kantianism and distinguishes it from the two doctrines considered before. According to Bentham and to Smith, that is right and meet which has good *consequences*; according to Kant, that which is good *in itself*. Max Weber, as sociologists well know, contrasted *Erfolgsethik* (the ethic of successful endeavor) and *Gesinnungsethik* (the ethic of principle) (see Werner Stark, "The Agony of Righteousness: Max Weber's Moral Philosophy," *Thought*, 43, No. 170 [Autumn 1968], 380–92). The former follows the Latin proverb *Respice finem* (consider what will come of your action); the latter, the maxim *Fiat iustitia, pereat mundus* (do what is right, even if it means that, as a result, the world should perish). At this crossroad, Kant chose the latter alternative; Bentham and Smith, the former. If a shopkeeper gives us good measure because he does not wish to lose our business, he is, Kant says, acting lawfully, but not yet morally; he acts morally only if he gives us value for our money because this is right. The same applies to other lines of conduct—the avoidance of lying, for instance: "To tell the truth for the sake of duty is something entirely different from doing so out of concern for inconvenient results." These convictions lead Kant to some of his most powerful formulations:

> It is impossible to conceive anything at all in the world, or even out of it, which can be taken as good without qualification, except a *good will*. . . . A good will is not good because of what it effects or accomplishes—because of its fitness

for attaining some proposed end: it is good through its willing alone—that is, good in itself. Considered in itself it is to be esteemed beyond comparison as far higher than anything it could ever bring about merely in order to favour some inclination or, if you like, the sum total of inclinations [*Moral Law*, pp. 65, 70, 61, 62].

The last sentence throws the contrast between Kantianism and Benthamism into high relief. Bentham appears to offer a moral guideline—"maximize happiness"—but, Kant argues, this is absurd. What point is there in urging people to do what they are doing anyway? Besides, the great aim of Utilitarianism is not attainable. Does felicity consist in riches? The rich man is wretched because he worries about his investments. Does it consist in wisdom? The wise man is more concerned about the nocturnal side of existence than any other. "Man . . . has no principle by which he is able to decide with complete certainty what will make him truly happy, since for this he would require omniscience" (ibid., p. 86). Kant echoes in this matter the sentiments of Samuel Johnson, so convincingly expressed in Johnson's grand poem "The Vanity of Human Wishes" and in his moral tale *Rasselas* (see *Selected Writings*, ed. R. T. Davies [London, 1965], pp. 28, 48ff., 203ff., esp. 222, 223, 226, 236–38, 255):

> Wealth heaped on wealth nor truth nor safety buys—
> The dangers gather as the treasures rise.

Like Johnson, Kant believed that happiness, if it is attainable at all, lies, not, as Bentham thought, in an Epicurean life policy, but, on the contrary, in

> obedient passions and a will resigned

(ibid., pp. 49, 59; see also Kant, *Critique*, pp. 160, 161, 172, 173, 175–78; *Moral Law*, pp. 62, 63, 67). Needless to say, Kant also saw that the happiness–maximation principle, far from leading to moral conduct, would not lead even to social peace. For "maximize happiness" means in the first place, and must mean for a being constituted as man is, "maximize your own happiness," and this will unavoidably set neighbor against neighbor (see esp. *Critique*, p. 161).

Smith, too, offers a moral guideline—"be kind"—and this is far from absurd. Yet it is unavailing. We cannot base morality on sentiment (let alone on sentimentality), for the voice of the feelings is ever uncertain. The emotions are shifting and discontinuous: "all feelings, especially those that are to produce unwonted exertion, must accomplish their effect at the moment they are at their height, and before they calm down; otherwise they effect nothing. . . . *Principles* must be built on conceptions; on any other basis there can only be paroxysms, which can give the person no moral worth." Thus the ethic of sentiment appears to Kant as no better than the ethic of self-regard. He was inclined to consider the latter as nearly identical with the former because it links doing good with a certain pleasure, the pleasure of sympathy, and doing evil with a certain pain, the pain of antipathy. After discussing the tradition represented by Jeremy Bentham, Kant writes:

> More refined, though equally false, is the opinion of those who suppose a certain special moral sense, which sense and not reason determines the moral law,

and in consequence of which the consciousness of virtue is supposed to be directly connected with contentment and pleasure; that of vice, with mental dissatisfaction and pain. They thus reduce the whole to the desire of happiness [*Critique*, pp. 369, 178; see also *Moral Law*, pp. 92, 93].

In any case, a man can only feel glad when he has done his duty, or suffer from pangs of conscience when he has not, if he knows what his duty is. But this a theory à la Smith can never tell him. It is a shot in the dark.

Where self-regard and sentiment fail, reason can succeed. Kant calls the moral law "a purely intellectual determining principle" (*Critique*, p. 305), and asserts that it has been attached to our will "as its governor." "Reason," he also writes, "recognises as its highest practical function the establishment of a good will"; and again: "All moral concepts have their seat and origin in reason completely *a priori*, and indeed in the most ordinary reason just as much as in the most highly speculative." *A priori* means: independent of experience, education, observation. The moral concepts are inherent in reason *as such* and "cannot be abstracted from any empirical . . . knowledge" (*Moral Law*, pp. 62, 64, 79). He urges us to consider reason, not as an inherited capacity, for that would mean that it is part and parcel of the system of nature, but rather as something independent of nature and, above all, as independent of the body; the laws of mathematics are true in themselves, not merely habits of thought or functions of the brain, and even God's reason, though He is an immaterial being, is identical with our own.

This belief that it lies in the power of reason to instill ethical principles into individual conduct and to fill society with deep morality is the starting point of Kant's ethics. We can most quickly penetrate to its innermost core if we first cast a glance at his theory of knowledge. This brief detour will prove very helpful. The *Critique of Pure Reason* suggests that the experience of reality is at the lowest level and at its inception no more than a chaos or confusion of sense impressions, and yet we achieve in the end a clear and structured picture of the world. This is possible because we possess understanding. We *impose order* on the manifold. The concepts of time and space, for instance, which are given us, or rather our intelligence, *a priori*—before we ever open our eyes, so to speak— and which inhere in our reason as such, provide an anticipatory scheme in which we can accommodate everything which we discover *a posteriori*, i.e., in and by experience. Time and space are forms of cognition. We receive them, not from observation, but the other way around: observation, and above all orderly and purposive observation, is possible only because we can start out with them and bring them to the task. We shall see that Kant's ethic of practical, i.e., action-controlling, reason runs parallel to his epistemology of pure reason, the reasoning faculty which creates an *imago mundi*.

Man, however, has not only understanding (*Verstand*) but also reason in the narrower or higher sense of the word (*Vernunft*). He is able not only to organize his sense impressions into a coherent whole, but also to determine the outer perimeter of his possible knowledge—to walk around the circumference of his knowledge, so to speak. He can take up a position at the line where the knowable and the unknowable meet and formulate certain conceptions suggested by this stance. One such concept is the "thing-in-itself." Things appear to us as connections of qualities: they are high or low, white or black, hot or cold, and so on. More we cannot possibly know of them. But reason tells us that there must also be an x of which these qualities are the attributes, and this precisely is the thing-in-itself. The thing-in-itself is a marginal concept which lies at or beyond the limits of experience—in the intelligible world, as Kant would say, not in the world of sense. We should not have introduced this idea into our disquisition, concerned as it is with the possible influence of moral doctrines on the tone of human relationships, if it were not the root of his moral philosophizing. For there is one thing-in-itself (and only one) which we do know, and that is man. Man is not only an object (a phenomenon) but also a subject, a citizen of the intelligible realm, an intellect standing over against the sensible sector of reality, technically speaking, a *noumenon*. And it is as *Homo noumenon*, which means also as a free will, that he can give himself a moral law and live up to it, in spite of the fact that, as a body, as *Homo phenomenon*, he is in thrall to his physical urges, to natural inclinations.

Lest this summary be not found sufficiently clear, let us transcribe a few lines from the *Grundlegung zur Metaphysik der Sitten*: "All ideas coming to us apart from our own violition (as do those of the senses) enable us to know objects only as they affect ourselves: what they may be in themselves remains unknown. Consequently, ideas of this kind, even with the greatest effort of attention and clarification brought to bear by understanding, serve only for knowledge of *appearances*, never of *things-in-themselves*." But "man . . . finds in himself a power which distinguishes him from all other things—and even from himself so far as he is affected by objects. This power is *reason*" (*Moral Law*, pp. 118, 119). This possession of reason has incisive and decisive consequences, above all, two: it makes man (at least potentially) free from the determinations to which animals are subject, and it gives him a dignity which nothing else in the universe may claim.

So far as freedom of the will is concerned, Kant admits that it can never be formally proved. It is one of the intuitions which arise at the borderline between the knowable and the unknowable, and such intuitions Kant calls "ideas"; they are not therefore assured truths. But though the existence of free will can never be proved, it cannot be disproved either, and therefore it need not be denied. The sociologist would be inclined to argue at this point that its denial—determinism—would destroy social control, and above all the criminal law, because it would destroy the concept of responsibility, and thus annihilate social life. But this would be arguing from consequences which Kant cannot admit. He remains within his intellectual style by arguing instead that we cannot *think* of our own willing otherwise than in terms of self-determination:

> As a rational being, and consequently as belonging to the intelligible world, man can never conceive the causality of his own will [i.e., his influence on things and events] except under the Idea of freedom; for to be independent of determination by causes in the sensible world (and this is what reason must always attribute to itself) is to be free. To the Idea of freedom there is inseparably attached the concept of *autonomy* [ibid., p. 120].

Kant has, however, yet a second argument, and it is much more homely (*Critique*, pp. 164, 165):

> Suppose some one asserts of his lustful appetite that when the desired object and the opportunity are present, it is quite irresistible. [Ask him:] If a gallows were erected before the house where he finds this opportunity, in order that he should be hanged thereon immediately after the gratification of his lust, whether he could then control his passion; we need not be long in doubt what he would reply. Ask him however: if his sovereign ordered him on pain of the same immediate execution to bear false witness against an honourable man, whom the prince might wish to destroy under a plausible pretext, would he consider it possible in that case to overcome his love of life, however great it may be. He would perhaps not venture to affirm whether he would do so or not, but he must unhesitatingly admit that it is possible to do so. He judges, therefore, that he can do a certain thing because he is conscious that he ought, and he recognizes that he is free.

This freedom—its objective existence and the subjective consciousness of it—raises *Homo sapiens*, or rather *Homo noumenon*, high above the rest of creation: "Autonomy is . . . the ground of the dignity of human nature and of every rational nature. . . . In the kingdom of ends everything has either a *price* or a *dignity*. If it has a price, something else can be put in its place as an *equivalent*; if it is exalted above all price and so admits of no equivalent, then it has a dignity." Ethical theorizing must start from this fact: "Man is not a thing—not something to be used *merely* as a means: he must always in all his actions be regarded as an end in himself"—in all *his* actions, Kant says in this passage, but it is of course even more important that he be regarded as an end in himself by others. This is brought out very clearly in yet another passage: "I say that man, and in general every rational being, *exists* as an end in himself, *not merely as a means* for arbitrary use by this or that will: he must in all his actions, whether they are directed to himself or to other rational beings, always be viewed *at the same time as an end*" (*Moral Law*, pp. 103, 102, 97, 95). On these speculations Kant bases one of his two formulations of that "Categorical Imperative" which he offers to all and sundry as a guide and as a test of their conduct: "Act in such a way that you always treat humanity, whether in your own person or in the person of any other, never simply as a means, but always at the same time as an end" (ibid., p. 96; this whole sentence is italicized in the original).

One operative word in this famous formula is the word "humanity." It can help us to make the jump from the first wording of the Categorical Imperative to the second. The first is more individualistic: treat *any* man as an end in himself, not only as a means; the second is more sociological: treat *all* men as ends in themselves and not only as means. The bridge between the two versions is obvious: if reason is the cause of man's dignity which should ensure him ethical treatment on the part of others, then the whole race must be considered as a community of equals, for reason is present in all of them, and an ethical attitude is owed by all to all. Rationality and humanity are to Kant almost identical expressions. Man, he writes in the *Critique of Practical Reason*, man as we meet him in everyday life, man who all too often obeys the urges of his body rather than the commands of the moral law, "is indeed unholy enough, but he must regard *humanity* . . . as holy." Hence this is the "fundamental law of the pure practical reason": "Act so that the maxim of thy will can always at the same time hold good as a principle of universal legislation" (*Critique*, pp. 257, 165). A similar formulation is of course present in the *Grundlegung* as well (*Moral Law*, p. 88); but even clearer and more instructive, as far as Kant's moral philosophy is concerned, is the following simple sentence of this smaller work (p. 91): "We must *be able to will* that a maxim of our action should become a universal law: this is the general canon for all moral judgement of action."

We shall presently go over to a sociological critique of the *Critique of Practical Reason*, but before doing so, let us briefly illustrate the bearing of this moral system. An example which Kant himself takes up (see *Moral Law*, p. 70) and to which he even devoted a small special investigation, is the wickedness of lying. Our self-interest, and even a (real or supposed) virtue like prudence, may well, on occasions, prompt us to deviate from the truth. But if I ask myself: could the maxim of my action be made a universal law—differently expressed: could everybody be allowed to lie to others—I see fairly quickly that this would not do. For then I should not so much deceive others as be deceived myself, and this I would never accept and approve of.

One way of summing up the Kantian ethic is to say that he insists on *mutuality* in human relations. The Categorical Imperative broadly agrees with the behest of the Gospel: "As you would that men should do to you, do you also to them in like manner" (Lk 6:31; see also Mt 7:12 and, in the Old Testament, Tb 4:16). This alone goes to show that Kant's is a noble ethic. But it is also basically a realistic ethic, and this is even more important for the sociologist. The essential submission of the *Critique of Practical Reason* has been summed up, and that more than once, by saying that good is whatever goes against the grain with us. This is an unbearable oversimplification, but it remains true that the salient demand and command are to the effect that our higher self (*Homo noumenon*, reason) should control our lower self (*Homo phenomenon*, the flesh). A work like the present which rests, from beginning to end, on the conviction that social life is impossible if social control is absent or even insufficiently effective cannot but acknowledge its kinship with the thinker from Königsberg. In our second volume (Section 72, p. 65), we argued along Kantian lines, but it was a modified rather than a pure Kantianism which we made our own there. This modification was unavoidable because the orthodox doctrine as it came from the sage's pen is far too abstract to be easily reconcilable with the insights of a down-to-earth science like sociology.

This brings us to Kant's weaknesses. They must be pointed out without trying to diminish his stature. The first of them is his formalism. This roots very deeply in his whole mental structure. We have already pointed out that there is a striking parallel between Kant's epistemology as set forth in his *Critique of Pure Reason* and his ethic set forth in his *Critique of Practical Reason*. In the former work he asserts that the impressions with which our senses provide us are chaotic and fall into an orderly and coherent pattern only when our understanding imposes a scheme on them, a scheme of which time and space are the most important ordinates. In the latter work he similarly suggests that the inclinations which stem from our bodily senses are chaotic (a conviction later revived by Emile Durkheim) and fall into an orderly and coherent pattern only when our reason imposes a scheme on them, the ideal principle of which is the Categorical Imperative. Now, time and space are *forms* of cognition, and the plenitude of life unfolds *within* them. In the same manner, the Categorical Imperative is a formal rule, and very different contents may be subjected to it. "The moral law is the sole determining principle of a pure will," Kant writes (*Critique*, pp. 296, 297; see also pp. 159, 163). "But since this is merely formal (viz.: as prescribing only the form of the maxim as universally legislative) it abstracts as a determining principle from all matter, that is to say, from every [concrete] object of volition." More simply expressed: it does not tell us in so many words what we should do and what we should avoid. This formalism appeared to Kant as a strength of his position for it made (so he assumed) his formula absolute and universal, as absolute and universal as, for instance, the proposition that twice two is four.

When we come to practice, however, what appears as strength turns out to be a weakness. An example will quickly show that this is the case. Is it ethically permissible to kill in war? At least two lines of argument are possible. Some will say, no. Life is holy, and must not be destroyed under any condition. If I refuse to kill, the maxim of my action could well be, indeed, should be, a law for every man. Others will say, yes. The culture of one's country, the safety of one's people, justify the taking of life. If I defend my house and home, my kith and kin, I am doing what is right. Everyone should spring to arms when his nation is threatened. Fighting for the restoration of peace is a duty incumbent on every one. The Kantian Categorical Imperative does not help us to solve this problem. It is like the fisherman's net which contains fish both sweet and poisonous. The difficulty stems from the fact that Kant offers no *ordo amoris*, no hierarchy of values. What ranks higher, the safety and sanctity of life or the safety and sanctity of the fatherland? Within a formal scheme like that of Kant, this terrible question cannot even be raised. Apart from the trivial, if important, assertion that a creature endowed with reason stands higher in the scale of being than one without it, Kant has no theory of value at all, and this lack robs his scheme of much of its importance.

A second weakness stems from Kant's mechanicism. We described his ethic earlier as a system of mutuality, but we might also have described it as a form of egalitarianism. But an egalitarian ethic is blind to whole sectors of moral life. Here again an example will quickly show up what is involved. Under the feudal system certain virtues were cultivated which have no place—at least no obvious place—in an egalitarian society, for instance, the virtue of loyalty to a superior and, as its counterpart, the obligation to protect, and care for, an inferior, in the sense of the French adage *noblesse oblige*. This kind of devotion —surely a highly moral one—is absent from Kantian thought. If it be argued that he was justified in excluding it from his purview because a democratic society knows no vassalage, it must be answered that there are at least parallel relationships—for what else is the relation between a guardian and a ward, or even between a father and a son under age?

Another (a third) painful limitation of the Kantian ethic is the fact that the highest form of ethical attitude which it knows is mutual respect—more sharply expressed: that it knows nothing of the possibility of a loving attitude. Unavoidably, Kant had to discuss the Biblical injunction to love thy neighbor as thyself, and the following sentence shows how he fits it into his moral doctrine: "To love one's neighbour means to like to practise all duties towards him" (*Critique*, p. 251). The words "to like to . . ." seem to indicate that simply to *do* one's duty is, in Kant's opinion, not enough, but they hardly move in the direction in which the Bible, and especially the Gospel, strive to lead us. The German original (see *Kants Werke* [Berlin, 1968], v 83) has: "gerne thun"; and that means merely: do willingly. This aspect of Kantianism was hotly debated after Kant's death. The good man—or, as the Romantics used to say, somewhat emotionally, "the beautiful soul"—so it was argued, is he or she who does good from inclination and not simply from a sense of duty. It is difficult to deny that this argument has its point. Kant, clever as he was, anticipated it and tried to ward it off. A system of ethics should issue commands, he pleads, and "love out of inclination cannot be commanded; but kindness done from duty—although no inclination impels us, and even although natural and unconquerable disinclination stands in our way—is practical . . . love, residing in the will and not in the propensions of feeling, . . . and it is this practical love alone which can be an object of command" (*Moral Law*, p. 67). This is true, as far as it goes, but the matter cannot be put to rest in this way. The *Critique* has, of course, the same kind of argument, or rather counter-argument, and yet there is a slight, but significant, difference from the text of the *Grundlegung*. Referring to the injunction to love thy neighbor as thyself, Kant writes (p. 251): "The command that makes this a rule cannot command us to *have* this disposition . . . but only *to endeavour* after it." This desirable endeavor is discussed no further by our philosopher, and this is anything but surprising. For Kant's whole philosophy is after all a kind of rationalism, and of this rationalism Kant was a prisoner. Love lies beyond reason, and it remained *terra incognita* as long as an extreme intellectualism, however exalted, held sway.

All these weaknesses of the Kantian ethic are insignificant, however, compared to the one which we discuss last, but which in the order of importance must rank first. Kant's reliance is on the power of reason to direct and inform human action and interaction, but how powerful is reason in this respect if the truth be told? There can be few with any experience of life who would not echo Samuel Johnson's *cri de coeur* (see *Selected Writings*, ed. Davies, p. 49):

> How rarely reason guides the stubborn choice,
> Rules the bold hand, or prompts the suppliant voice!

Kant himself knew that therein lay a problem—from the point of view of social control, *the* problem—of his moral teaching, and in his honesty he freely admitted its existence. Thus he writes at the end of his *Grundlegung* (*Moral Law*, p. 129):

How pure reason can be practical in itself [i.e., determine human action] without further motives drawn from some other source; that is, how the bare *principle of the universal validity of all its maxims as laws* . . . can by itself—without any matter (or object) of the will in which we could take some antecedent interest—supply a motive and create an interest which could be called purely *moral*; or, in other words, *how pure reason can be practical*—all human reason is totally incapable of explaining this, and all the effort and labour to seek such an explanation is wasted.

We must not, however, misunderstand this passage. It means merely that we can never *fully* understand *how* an agency which is outside the framework of the natural world can act as a cause inside it. This is just another way of saying that freedom is a concept located at the borderline between the knowable and the unknowable. But the sentences just quoted do *not* mean *that* the reason-directed will of man (of *Homo noumenon*) cannot act as a determinate influence in the world. We all know that it can. We experience our freedom every time we are confronted with a choice. We are simply confronted with a cleavage between two levels—the theoretical where we are facing a task beyond our powers, and the practical where we are challenged to make decisions well within our power. In the language of Giambattista Vico, Kant might have said that the freedom of man's will is, not formally provable (provable *modo mathematico*), but certain.

Yet at the practical level there are difficulties, though difficulties of quite another kind. We are up against them every time we are called upon to choose. Should we follow the selfish demands of our bodies or rather the moral demands of our reason—that is the dilemma. Man always could turn to the right side, but often he does not. "Man, affected as he is by so many inclinations, is capable of the Idea of a pure practical reason, but he has not so easily the power to realize the Idea *in concreto* in his conduct of life," Kant writes, meaning by "power" the power over oneself (*Moral Law*, pp. 57, 73). "Man feels in himself a powerful counterweight to all the commands of duty presented to him by reason as so worthy of esteem—the counterweight of his needs and inclinations, whose total satisfaction he grasps under the name of 'happiness.' " Still, Kant is optimistic: "Unmixed with the alien element of added empirical inducements, the pure thought of duty, and in general of the moral law, has by way of reason alone . . . an influence on the human heart so much more powerful than all the further impulsions capable of being called up from the field of experience that, in the consciousness of its own dignity, reason despises these impulsions and is able gradually to become their master" (ibid., pp. 78, 79). In the *Critique of Practical Reason* (pp. 259, 265, 245), Kant expresses himself even more confidently:

The true motive of pure practical reason . . . is no other than the pure moral law itself. . . . [There is a] respect [for the voice of morality] such as no man has for inclinations of whatever kind but for the [moral] law only. . . . There is something so singular in the unbounded esteem for the pure moral law, apart from all advantages, as it is presented for our obedience by practical reason, [that] the voice of [it] makes even the boldest sinner tremble. . . .

Who would not wish that Kant were right? But he was totally wrong. All experience proves that the voice of reason is not invariably—indeed, not often—loud enough to overcome the insinuations of self-regard. We can see at this point quite clearly that Kant has no more to offer, so far as the strengthening of the social bond, the improvement of the tone of social life, is concerned, than the other moral philosophers.

The slightest touch of realism must surely lead to the conviction that, in spite of the possession of an intellect, moral education is indispensable if the commands of reason are to get the better of the calls of the flesh. Needless to say, Kant is aware of this, but he makes light of the matter. In one context of the *Grundlegung* (*Moral Law*, pp. 79, 80), he admits that a "pure moral disposition" has to be "ingrafted" on men's minds, but in another (ibid., p. 64) he writes concerning "the concept of a will estimable in itself and good apart from any further end": "This concept . . . is already present in a naturally sound understanding and requires not so much to be taught as merely to be clarified." This is the same lack of realism as before! Kant must have known as little about children as he did about criminals! In the *Critique of Practical Reason* (pp. 247, 179) he follows another track. He admits that it is hard to live in accordance with the Categorical Imperative, but adds that in the course of time, the bitter cup turns sweet:

> As *submission* to the law . . . that is, as a command (announcing constraint for the sensibly affected subject), it [the moral norm] contains in it no pleasure, but on the contrary . . . pain. . . . On the other hand, however, as this constraint is exercised merely by the legislation of our *own* reason, it also contains something *elevating*, and this subjective effect on feeling, inasmuch as pure practical reason is the sole cause of it, may be called . . . self-approbation.

Well and good! But this mechanism can only reinforce the habit of acting rightly once it exists; it cannot explain how it comes into existence. Kant acknowledges this by implication in another passage in which he speaks of the same pleasurable feeling of self-approval. "As the human will is, by virtue of liberty, capable of being immediately determined by the moral law, so frequent practice in accordance with this principle of determination can, at least ["zuletzt"—better: "in the end"; see *Werke*, v 38], produce subjectively a feeling of satisfaction . . . but the notion of duty cannot be derived from it." Precisely. It may be a "duty to establish and to cultivate" this morality-borne feeling of satisfaction, this pride in duty conscientiously done, but it cannot introduce the moral law into the mind. Kant's deduction clearly presupposes that it is there already. He says so himself: "A man must be at least half honest in order even to be able to form a conception of these feelings." But how does a man become half honest? This, surely, is the decisive question. Kant should have taken it more seriously than he did.

It is only in the very last pages of the *Critique of Practical Reason* that Kant turns to the problem of moral education, but even there he discusses this ethically all-important matter in all too desultory a fashion. He begins again by conceding that "it cannot . . . be denied that in order to bring an uncultivated or degraded mind into the track of moral goodness, some preparatory guidance is necessary." At this stage even the promise of advantage and the threat of punishment may be used as strategic devices, "but as soon as this mechanical work, these leading-strings, have produced some effect, then we must bring before the mind the pure moral motive." On this motive, and on it alone, Kant wishes to rely. Children are indeed "backward in the observance of the commonest duty and even in the correct estimation of it," but we can help them in a double way: first, by instilling in them the habit of judging all actions, those of others as well as their own, from an ethical point of view; and, secondly, by holding up to them shining examples of the unselfish fulfillment of duty, by demonstrating to them that the conquest of self-regard leads to the precious possession of self-respect. Besides these two positive recommendations, set forth in a few rapid sentences, Kant gives a negative one, and it is thoroughly characteristic: all appeals to the emotions are to be avoided. "I wish," he writes, they would spare the young "the examples of so-called *noble* (super-meritorious) actions in which our sentimental books so much abound, and would refer all to duty merely, and to the worth that a man can and must give himself in his own eyes by the consciousness of not having transgressed it" (pp. 361, 368, 371–75, 365). Kant is, as ever, consistent: reason is the spring of ethical conduct; reason must also develop it in the individual's mind. But reason cannot really achieve this, as Hume had seen before Kant. The weakness of the Kantian ethic stares us in the face in one half-sentence of his pen. The moral law, he writes (*Critique*, p. 246), demands respect and inspires it. The first half of this statement is certainly correct; the latter, far less so. It is true that a person acting immorally should lose his self-respect and to some extent in fact he does so, but a thief or a rapist or a tax-dodger and countless others consider this a small price to pay for a greater material advantage, for pleasure or gain.

In the context of this rudimentary discussion of ethical education, there occurs a curious sentence with the consideration of which we can fitly close our discussion of this great thinker. "If it is asked," he writes (*Critique*, p. 366), "what then is *really* pure morality, by which as a touchstone we must test the significance of every action, then I must admit that it is only philosophers that can make the decision doubtful, for to common sense it has been decided long ago, not indeed by abstract general formulae, but by habitual use, like the distinction between the right and left hand." Kant does not tell us what speculations lie behind this remarkable statement, but we can easily guess, if we remember that in his opinion all men possess reason—the same reason—and use it in the same manner. Reason then informs all social life, and if it does so, it must also dominate and determine "habitual use"—use and wont, as it is popularly expressed, the folkways, as we, the disciples of William Graham Sumner, should rather say. Thus Kant comes in the end to the conviction that men can test the rectitude of their conduct, not only by applying to it the Categorical Imperative, but also, more simply, by comparing it to the norms of the established ethos, the traditional morality. In this way Immanuel Kant arrives at the same point to which Bentham and Rousseau and Smith, too, were led:

the insight that the consciously formulated ethic of the philosophers is not radically different from the unconsciously developed ethos of the surrounding society.

THE ETHICS OF VALUE

130. The tremendous importance of Immanuel Kant for the history of ideas rests not only on the fact that his was a matchless intellectual achievement, and on the associated fact that through him the century-old conflict between empiricism and rationalism was laid to rest and overcome, but also on the further fact that in him the great inspiration of the religious Reform reached its final phase and ran itself, so to speak, to death. A comparison between Calvin's theology and Kant's philosophy is very instructive. The close kinship between the two world views is fairly obvious. According to Calvin, the world has fallen into sin, and whatever is good within it comes from the outside, from divine grace; according to Kant, the world is permeated by body-borne inclinations and strivings, and whatever is good in it comes from the outside, from the operation of reason. Calvin's world of sensuality becomes Kant's "sensible" world, his *mundus sensibilis*—the step from the former to the latter conceptualization is not wide. True, the philosopher's reason is not the theologian's grace, but even their conceptions of the deity are, to say the very least, not irreconcilable. Kant's "idea" of God is the adumbration of a body-less Person in whom willing and goodness coincide. Calvin, too, thought of Him as the sum and substance of righteousness, and both saw Him as hard and stern. Bringing the comparison down to a simpler level, we can say that Kant's ethic rests—like Calvin's—on a pessimistic estimate of the world of experience; the world has to be overcome by subjecting it to the moral norm of the Categorical Imperative, the historical successor to the Old Testament's Ten Commandments.

As we now turn to Max Scheler, whose ethical doctrine is as close to the findings of the science of sociology as any before or after, we enter into an entirely different intellectual tradition. His roots were Catholic, not Protestant, and therefore optimistic rather than pessimistic. With him the emphasis lies, not on the conviction that man has, in Adam and ever since, betrayed God, but on the opposite persuasion that the world is good and must be so because it has come from the hands of an all-loving Creator. If we try to discover the ultimate root of Scheler's world view we come upon some such conception as the Renaissance conceit of *Plato Christianus*: everything that is has its beginning in some divine idea; this idea is never fully realized (there is room for the Fall even in this philosophy), but it is also always realized to some extent, and therefore the world and all it contains is an assemblage of values. To act ethically means to climb up from the lower to the higher values and to realize the latter. In this manner we work our way back to the Fountain of Being who is also the Value of Values—the personal God of the theistic creed. (For a general assessment of Scheler's lifework, see Werner Stark, "Editor's Introduction" to *The Nature of Sympathy*, one of Scheler's most important writings, translated by Peter Heath [London & New Haven, 1954].)

The difference between Kant and Scheler is perhaps most obvious in their contrasting concepts of conscience. For Kant, conscience is above all a monitor. It warns us not to act in a manner which is contrary to the moral law. For Scheler, it is a repository of insights into the value structure of the world. It shows us in which direction we should aim: it is positive rather than negative, an adviser rather than a critic (see Max Scheler, *Der Formalismus in der Ethik und die materiale Wertethik* [Bern & Munich, 1966], pp. 325, 327; see also p. 86). Characteristic as well is Scheler's polemic against Freud. When we act, we act not only, and not mainly, to relieve tensions, but to achieve positive results, to "build ethical values into our lives" (ibid., p. 30; see also pp. 349–51). Scheler's attitude to the world is one of confidence and trust, not, like that of Kant or Freud, one of suspicion and distrust. It is, in the final analysis, a loving attitude.

There are a number of points on which Scheler entirely agrees with Kant. Like Kant, he decidedly rejects all materialistic systems of ethic, be it of the more Benthamic, be it of the more Rousseauan, kind. He calls it Kant's prime merit to have shown up the weaknesses of these traditions—weaknesses also shared by certain newer moral doctrines, those which start in their moral speculations from concepts like "well-being" or "life," for instance. Experience as commonly understood, and induction as practiced in science, cannot lead to sound ethical insights. The fact, for instance, that murder is rejected in observable societies does not yet suffice as a proof of the proposition that murder is evil. Murder would be evil, even if it were nowhere rejected. The moral philosopher must search for a sounder basis than that (see ibid., pp. 29, 65, 66). This argument on Scheler's part amounts to saying that we need an aprioric and not an aposterioric ethic, one independent of the vagaries and hazards of the facts and features, the blindnesses and blunders, of historical reality—precisely the Königsberger's demand.

Another deep agreement—already implied in the common rejection of materialism—consists in the shared conviction that an ethic of consequences (Weber's *Erfolgsethik*) is in truth no ethic at all, and that only an ethic of principle like that of Kant, or that of the Gospels (Weber's *Gesinnungsethik*), is worthy of the name. Conduct is ethical if it aims at the realization of a higher value than is found in reality; whether this higher value is in fact secured or not is immaterial. The value of an action resides in itself, and is recognizable in itself, and cannot be inferred from the train of events which follow it (see ibid., pp. 127, 130, 133). This is once again Kant's thesis that nothing "in the world or even out of it" is good "except good will."

Scheler, then, is, like Kant, a thoroughgoing anti-materialist, a philosophical idealist. Man is able to act in a way which is independent of his biological organization; indeed, Scheler suggests, the essential aspect of man, the aspect which defines him, so to speak, is the fact that he is a creature, or the creature, who can transcend himself, transcend his life and all life. The great dividing line is usually drawn between animal and man—wrongly, according to Scheler;

it lies much rather between organism and person. There is merely a gradual difference between animal and man, but there is an essential contrast between organism and person—between *Homo phenomenon* and *Homo noumenon,* as Kant had expressed it. For Scheler, as for Kant, man is both contained in the world and at the same time standing over against it; he is active *in* the world, but he is also acting *into* the world, as Scheler has it—a wording which is unusual, but by no means unclear (see ibid., pp. 293, 294, 385).

But it is time that we should go over to a discussion of the convictions which separate the two philosophers. It will surprise nobody to hear that Scheler totally rejects Kant's formalism; it is a poor philosophy, he feels, which offers no more than an abstract test of what is good and what is bad, agreement with, or contrast to, a purely formal principle like the Categorical Imperative. What we need is a material ethic in the sense of a concrete catalogue of desirable actions, an ethic which tells us *in terminis* what we should turn away from and what we should turn toward and strive for. Such a "material" ethic cannot be gained through ratiocination: it is a mistake to think that that which is given *a priori* (independent of observation) is necessarily and exclusively a content of the mind (see ibid., p. 82). There are *a priori* facts; there are moral *facts*—not only ideas or judgments or imaginings. Scheler, in his search for a bedrock on which a convincing ethical doctrine can be built, turns back to experience, but not to naïve experience; we have already seen that he rejects the latter. He places his trust in an analytical experience, an experience which knows how to separate the value aspect of that which we see and grasp from the welter of sense impressions which impinge on us at the same time. It was the inspiration of the phenomenological school in philosophy, the school of Edmund Husserl, which helped him in his quest.

Husserl felt that we are hampered rather than aided when we allow ourselves to be preoccupied exclusively with the natural organization of man and/ or the traditional root problem of epistemology, the "real" existence of objects. A different and perhaps more enlightening vision of reality is possible. When we see three roses or three rabbits or three Russians, we see not only them, we see—we intuit—as well the concept of three. In the concrete, we grasp the abstract; in the sensual, the more than sensual, the essential. Scheler followed this lead (see ibid., pp. 84, 380, 381). When we take a piece of sugar into our mouth, we have an agreeable experience, and for most people—even for most philosophers of the past—the matter stops there. But the phenomenological approach teaches us to analyze this phenomenon. We have in fact a double experience, not a single and simple one: we have a pleasurable *sensation,* and at the same time we feel the presence of a *value,* a pleasure value, and it is really—in the sense of primarily—the latter which we pursue when we desire sweet things, not the former (ibid., p. 56). The former, the sensual gratification, is essentially a secondary or accompanying trait (ibid., p. 79). Sunk in sensuality as we are, dependent on our bodies as we are, we do not normally make this distinction, but in this respect the philosophical attitude must be different from the popular. That the philosophical attitude is more realistic than the popular conception becomes obvious at once when we turn from the consideration of a physical good, like sugar, to a more intellectual or spiritual value.

When we love our home or hometown, for instance, we experience no assignable physical sensation, we pass through no bodily state, we are face to face with a "pure" value. But "the agreeable" is a "pure value" too. The sugar is only its carrier. Similarly, when we admire a landscape, we admire (primarily) its beauty and not the things which constitute it (ibid., p. 182). This simple explanation, it is hoped, conveys to the reader the starting point of Scheler's moral philosophizing. It is his firm belief that there exists a realm of values (or value facts) which, though it is given to us in experience, is in fact independent of experience. Experience merely opens our eyes to its existence; but it exists "in itself," and would exist even if there were no creature to experience it. The basic intuition here recalls, of course, Kant's "thing in itself," but there is this vast difference between the two doctrines that Scheler regards values, not as unknowable, but as knowable, and from this idea—we might almost say, from this insight—an entirely dissimilar system of ethics results.

One of the great thinkers of the past who had a decisive influence on Max Scheler was Blaise Pascal. Pascal, though himself one of the sharpest intellects of all time, knew the limitations of the human intellect very well, and this certainly links him with Immanuel Kant. But unlike Kant, he thought that there are other endowments of the mind which can help us when we have exhausted the possibilities offered by the *ratio*: "We know the truth," he writes, "not only by the reason, but also by the heart, and it is from this last that we know first principles"; and, in another context, even more pointedly: "The heart has its reasons which reason does not know" (*The Thoughts of Blaise Pascal*, trans. C. Kegan Paul [London, 1905], pp. 102, 306). Scheler too was convinced that "the heart"—more soberly expressed: the emotions, love and hate, for instance —are sources of insight, and more particularly of ethical insights. If, on beholding a despicable action, I break into the cry "Fie!" or "For shame," I do so, not because I have *judged* that it is mean and low—judgment presupposes a cool and distant consideration of the facts and introduces an additional intermediary link between observation and reaction—but because I *know*, and know directly and immediately, that it is so (*Der Formalismus in der Ethik und die materiale Wertethik*, pp. 182, 207). "A penetrating phenomenology of the so-called 'stirrings of conscience' shows us that the sensitive, tender and quick-acting 'conscience' is something essentially different from a cold and distant 'judge' who, because of his whole nature, is always far too late" (ibid., p. 210). In beholding a despicable action, I not only apprehend its accidental factual side (I not only have an aposterioric experience), I also grasp its essential value component (its aprioric aspect)—its negative value, its unvalue. I see not only, for instance, that a murderous shot has been fired, but also that evil (evil in itself) has manifested itself. Through the centuries, indeed, ever since the Greeks, *a priori* conceptions were considered as exclusively and unavoidably products of thought—cool, rational thought. Scheler, like Pascal, disagreed. "Even the emotional part of the mind, feeling, preferring, loving, hating and willing, has a primal aprioric content which is not borrowed from speculation and which the science of ethics must demonstrate in total independence from logic" (ibid., p. 82). The traditional link between apriorism and rationalism, he demands, must be broken, and an apriorism of emotionality worked out (ibid., p. 84). If it is evident to the *ratio* that twice two is four, it is equally evident to "the heart" that life is better than death, even though, from a rational point of view, this may be or become doubtful—if it were proved, for instance, that the sum total of pains is higher than the sum total of pleasures. It is in the latter kind of evidence that a scientific doctrine of morality must find its foundation. It has a firm factual basis—the objectively existent and given values which we "see" as surely as we see material objects, though we do not see them through sensual inlets or channels. "Values [are] irreducible basic phenomena of emotive perception" (ibid., p. 270). Scheler's clearest summing-up occurs in the following terse passage: "There is a mode of perception the objects of which are totally beyond the grasp of the intellect, and for which the intellect is as blind as the ear and the sense of hearing are for color—a mode of perception nonetheless which presents to us real objects and an eternal order among them—namely, the values and their hierarchy. This order and the laws governing this mode of perception are as definite, precise, and evident as those of logic and mathematics" (ibid., p. 261).

Jeremy Bentham, too, elaborated a theory of value (see *Jeremy Bentham's Economic Writings* III, ed. Stark, esp. pp. 435ff.), but it was a comparatively flat and naïve one. He knew, in fact, only one *kind* of value, namely, pleasure, and pleasure was defined, in the spirit of materialistic hedonism, as bodily enjoyment. Some of these enjoyments, he argued, are greater than others—if the agreeable sensation involved is more intense or more prolonged, for instance—but it is always the *same* pleasure which is experienced, whatever the source from which it comes. If a man goes to a dinner, the profits of which are to be used for some charitable purpose, he secures two pleasures, the pleasures of the palate and the pleasure of benevolence. These have to be added —so Bentham—if the value of the action or experience is to be assessed. Scheler felt that this kind of calculation was no more realistic than the attempt to add apples and pears, for in his conviction bodily enjoyment was totally different from a mental or spiritual satisfaction. Values, he taught, are not quantities, but qualities, and as such not quantifiable. The contrast with Bentham could not possibly be greater! In this respect, too, Scheler is a faithful disciple of Blaise Pascal, a scion of the whole Catholic tradition, less that of St. Thomas Aquinas whose rationalism he thought excessive than that of St. Augustine: a representative of the Platonic rather than of the Aristotelian tendency within Catholicism. Scheler's world view was, like that of Pascal, consistently hierarchical. "The infinite distance between body and mind is a figure of the infinitely more infinite distance between mind and charity, for this is supernatural," Pascal had written in his characteristically passionate manner.

All bodies, the firmament, the stars, the earth and the kingdoms thereof, are not comparable to the lowest mind, for mind knows all these and itself; the body nothing. All bodies together and all minds together and all they can effect are not worth the least motion of charity. This is of an order infinitely more exalted. From all bodies together we cannot extract one little thought: this is impossible and in another order. From all bodies and minds it is impossible to produce a single motion of true charity: it is impossible, it is in another and supernatural order.

This conception of being as a system of gradations, a pyramid, which had dominated, for instance, Dante Alighieri's *visio mundi*, appeared to Pascal as the only possible background to both ethical theory and practical ethics: "Jesus Christ and Saint Paul use the order of charity, not of the intellect, for they wish to warm, not to teach. . . . The heart has its own order; the mind too has its own which is by premisses and demonstrations; that of the heart is wholly different. It were absurd to prove that we are worthy of love by putting forth . . . the causes of love" (*Thoughts*, trans. Kegan Paul, pp. 226, 227, 228, 127). Scheler took this grand intuition up and tried to elaborate it. St. Augustine's term *ordo amoris* seemed to him the key concept of ethics, the problem in the solution of which the moral philosopher had to prove his worth. "What we have to demand of a system of ethics above all else is a description of the order of values in accordance with the notions of 'higher' and 'lower.' This order rests on the very essence of values"—values considered as objective data, existential realities, value facts (*Der Formalismus in der Ethik und die materiale Wertethik*, p. 117; see also p. 104).

What Scheler himself had to offer in this respect is not easily compressed into a few lines; we can present only two facets of his thought, and even those but briefly, facets which, as we shall see, show how ethics and sociology can be brought into harmony. His analysis of the scale of values enumerates four characteristics which distinguish them as higher and lower, a distinction which is brought home to us in a specific mental act: namely, preferring (or its opposite). We arrange them here in a sequence different from that followed by Scheler himself (see ibid., pp. 107ff.): (*a*) lasting goods are to be preferred to those which are perishable and changing; (*b*) if a certain value *x* must already exist before another value *y* can come into existence, then *x* will be higher up in the scale than *y*—the value which forms the foundation must be higher than the value which is founded on it; (*c*) certain goods give us a deeper satisfaction than others, and the depth of that satisfaction (which we directly experience) also influences the height of the value which yields it; (*d*) those goods are relatively higher which can be enjoyed by a greater number of men without the necessity of dividing them up. We have placed this item last because it is of deep significance for social theory, a significance which is surely obvious, but which will become even more obvious as we proceed.

Of one piece with this analysis of the scale of values is Scheler's distinction of the modalities of value (ibid., pp. 122ff.). Here, too, he elaborates a fourfold schema, but the fact that he again has four items is purely accidental. There are (1) the pleasure values and unvalues, the agreeable and the disagreeable. Since they are mediated by bodily sensations (though they do not consist in them!), they are to be seen mainly from the point of view of the individual. A second group of values can best be described, in English, as (2) welfare values. (Scheler's own terms of *edel*, literally, "noble," and *gemein*, literally, "common," simply will not do in English; they would be totally inappropriate and misleading.) Scheler speaks of life values and thinks of all the goods which subserve and promote health, vitality, and social well-being. The point of view here is essentially that of the community and/or the state. Above them rank (3) the culture values, comprising, above all, truth and beauty. At the apex of the pyramid—for it is a pyramid—are (4) the sacred values, the values of holiness. God is the Value of Values in this scheme, as He must be in any theistic philosophy.

We see the whole message, not to say the whole splendor, of these speculations when we combine the two analyses, or rather point (*d*) of the first with the hierarchical structure (1–4) of the second. In the second, those values appear clearly as the higher ones which can be enjoyed by a greater number of men without the necessity of dividing them up; in other words, those which do not set men against each other, but rather bring them together and unite them. But before we turn to this, in our investigation supremely important, matter, we must briefly explain wherein, according to Scheler, ethical conduct exists. This should really be quite clear already. Ethical conduct is given wherever and whenever a man's intention is directed toward the realization of a relatively high value. It comes to the surface in the act of *preferring*, or rather correct preferring, in the right decisions of the *will*. But the will is not the ultimate element. It depends on a sound *perception* of the objective values, the values-in-themselves, the value facts, and their order of subordination and superordination, on a *knowledge* of the hierarchy of values. This dependence of human decisions on an ontic scheme does not in any way diminish the freedom with which man is endowed. He is able to prefer the lesser values to the greater, and he often does so in accordance with the words which Ovid puts into the mouth of Medea (*Metamorphoses* 7.20–21): *Video meliora proboque, deteriora sequor*—"I see what is good and approve of it, yet I do what is evil." Perhaps we can sum up the central conceptions of our philosopher by saying that the (positive) values which a man sees direct an appeal to him, utter a call—and to that call he can open his ears and his heart and act accordingly, or play deaf and refuse to accept and to comply with it (see *Der Formalismus in der Ethik und die materiale Wertethik*, esp. pp. 47, 49, 214, 482). Scheler's doctrine, far from throwing doubt on the freedom of the will, in fact highlights it, but it also shows it in its fateful connection with inescapable responsibility. This amounts to saying that it is a genuine ethic.

But we must come to the more problematic aspects of Scheler's stance. One of them is his determined rejection of ethical relativity. The order of values, he stoutly maintains, is unchanging; the insights we gain when we act in accordance with it are absolutely valid, as valid as any mathematical truth. But is not relativity a fact? Modern man considers infanticide a heinous crime, but even so civilized a nation as the Greeks practiced it without inhibition, without compunction—to say nothing about the Romans, the Chinese, and many, many others. How then can anyone assert that what is right is always right, what is wrong always wrong? "Three degrees of latitude reverse all jurisprudence," Pascal writes (*Thoughts*, trans. Kegan Paul, p. 61); "right has its epochs. . . . A meridian decides what is truth. . . . Truth on this side of the Pyrenees, error on that! It is droll justice which is bounded by a stream!" Pascal, then, Scheler's inspirer, does not deny the existence of ethical relativity, but he does deny that it is inescapable. The remarkable passage which we have quoted occurs in the chapter entitled "The Misery of Man Without God" (see ibid., p. 15). Men, if they would or could turn from sin, would soon recognize what is (absolutely) right and (absolutely) wrong. It is not the *ordo amoris* which is uncertain; it is only men's knowledge and implementation of it. Scheler's solution is somewhat parallel, but less religious, of course. He has, all told, three answers to the relativists, of which the last is the most telling. First of all, collectivities can refuse to accept and comply with the objective and eternal order of values, just as easily and just as much as individuals can. They can institutionalize a temporal or local "ethos" which is not really ethical. Secondly, there may be error (see *Der Formalismus in der Ethik und die materiale Wertethik*, p. 234). Scheler has argued all along that, before we act rightly, we must realize what is right in the given situation; more precisely expressed: what concrete (more highly ranking) values should be striven for. But, as in all pursuit of the truth, so in this, we may be laboring under deceptions and delusions. Here there is no guilt involved, only an objective misapprehension and misdirection of effort. But Scheler's ultimate argument against relativism, which faced him in and through the school known as historicism, is his doctrine of perspectivism. (The present writer has already discussed it in *The Sociology of Knowledge*, esp. chaps. 4 and 8). The values, he asserts, form an objective structure which is real in the ontological sense of the word, but different societies see only selected aspects of it and never the whole. The pyramid is exactly like any other pyramid; it looks different from east and west, and from every particular point in east and west, yet it is the very same pyramid all the time. What is called relativity is merely a multiplicity of viewpoints or approaches, not a multiplicity of equipollent moralities. In ethics there can be nothing doubtful. Every error-free insight must be eternal and absolute. If it is argued that modern man condemns infanticide while the Greeks condoned it, and that therefore even the commandment "Thou shalt not kill" is not of supra-historical and worldwide validity, it must be answered that this formulation of the problem is entirely wrong. In *every* society it is forbidden to take the life of a full *socius*, of a person acknowledged as a full personality. The Greeks had a definition of man or fellow-citizen different from that of the modern West (see *Der Formalismus in der Ethik und die materiale Wertethik*, pp. 316–19). The slave was not a *socius*; nor as yet was a neonate; nor is the enemy in case of war; nor, where the death penalty is still in force, is the criminal who has loaded himself with a crime defined as death-worthy. But all this takes nothing from the fact, and a fact it is to Max Scheler, that the commandment "Thou shalt not kill"—kill a full-fledged fellow-human—is part and parcel of a universally binding code. There is an absolute order of values, Scheler says in a particularly clear passage (ibid., p. 45), and there is, in every historical and local society, a "dominant" one made of selected elements of the former. "In the sphere of the aesthetic values we call such systems 'style'; in the sphere of the practical [i.e., action-steering] values, 'morality' "—in our own terminology, ethos. (On the polemic against relativism and the specifics of the theory of perspectivism, see ibid., esp. pp. 106, 148, 149, 222, 223, 277, 296–98, 300, 307, 308, 313, 484, 485.)

A second serious objection against Scheler's ethics of value may be that he expects far too much self-sacrifice on the part of the individual. To look only at the two lowest layers of his pyramid: social values are ranked higher than pleasure values, i.e., than bread and butter, the enjoyments of everyday life; the former should always be preferred to the latter. Does this not mean, at the level of practice, that the citizen should cheerfully submit to any demand of the tax-gatherer and forgo the material things which constitute his personal well-being? Is this not the old puritanical ethos which raised abnegation to the pinnacle, as a virtue beyond compare? The suspicion that some such kill-joy attitude lies behind Scheler's moral philosophizing may be, perhaps must be, strengthened by the fact that he places the "values of holiness" above all others, even above the values of culture. This objection, though understandable, is very superficial, and can easily be rebutted. There are two essential arguments against it, both rather telling. Scheler does not say that material enjoyments are without value; he merely ranks them as comparatively minor in importance. They should be pursued, but not to the exclusion of higher values. Indeed, when we call bread and butter, or other foodstuffs yielding a Benthamic "pleasure of the palate," *low* values, we mean not only that they are less exalted, but also that they are *more basic*. We cannot pursue the specifically social values unless we can keep ourselves alive, indeed, adequately nourished; we cannot pursue the specifically cultural values unless we live in a well-ordered, pacified world (*inter arma silent musae*); we cannot raise ourselves to the level of holiness and to a vision of God unless we have first become cultured personalities. The simile of the pyramid holds good even here: it needs a firm basis, and this basis is an adequate supply of material things. To strive for them, even to fight for them, is not, according to Max Scheler, unethical. Only a refusal to aim higher, to climb up toward the apex, would be unethical, for that climbing upward is the very essence of ethical conduct.

Scheler himself places even more reliance on a second counter-argument, and that rightly, because it has greater depth. He denies that persons who pursue the values which, he claims, are evidently higher are thereby impoverished. On the contrary, he asserts, they become richer, though not in terms of material gratification. A simile will help us to sum up and to present his argument. If a man looks at Caravaggio's *Basket of Fruit* in the Ambrosiana in Milan or at Zurburán's *Oranges and Lemons* in the Norton Simon Collection in Los Angeles, he may behold no more than a grouping of luscious fruit which make his mouth water. If that is all he sees, he is undoubtedly a poor man. He is, as a person, greatly enriched if he discovers that these paintings also convey something of the glory of life, the glory of health, the essence of vitality. His enrichment is further increased if he realizes that he stands before a manifestation of beauty —beauty in itself, before an expression of that which is not expressible in mere words (unless they be words of a consummate poet). But the pictures will give him most—they will go to his heart, as it is sometimes expressed—if he grasps the intention of these two profoundly religious artists to show, not humdrum objects, but ideas of the Creator become flesh, if he has an inkling of the Platonic theory of artistic creation by which both Caravaggio and Zurburan lived, the theory which taught that the artist must strive to see things, not as men do, but as God does. "The more valuable a person is and the higher the values at which he aims," Scheler writes (ibid., p. 275), "the more the world of values opens itself to him. The pious soul is ever grateful for space, light, air, . . . and everything becomes peopled with values and unvalues which others experience as 'value indifferent.' The Franciscan word *omnia habemus nil possidentes* [we possess everything if we possess nothing] expresses the direction toward such a liberation of value experience from subjective limitations." St. Francis' "Canticle of the Creatures" is indeed a splendid illustration of Scheler's essential intuition. He also writes (ibid., p. 273): "The more we live in the belly—as the Apostle expresses it—the emptier of value the world becomes."

It is to be assumed that this kind of argument developed by Max Scheler will carry little conviction with many people today. They will be inclined to stick to their first impression, to the opinion that he foolishly advises us to sacrifice the tangible values of bed and board for the intangible, illusive, airy values of the "higher" regions. Yet their resistance to his doctrine would not have moved him; nor will it move those of us who know how to appreciate his philosophy. Every society, so we have seen, articulates only some elements of the objective order of values, accepts and magnifies some, rejects or disregards others. Modern man has made for himself an *ordo amoris* in which, to say the least, the material values, the pleasure values, predominate. What he goes for, to the detriment of other desiderata, is a high level of consumption, a rich standard of living. Other values receive more lip service than real respect; they are but dimly apprehended and halfheartedly pursued. The happiness of the Poverello is not for him! He sees it as an amiable folly. What is wrong, on Scheler's premises, is not his ethical doctrine, but modern, materialistic man's mode of living, acting, and above all preferring. We discover at this point a valuable, indeed, invaluable implication of Scheler's philosophy: a basis, offered and prepared by him, for an incisive critique of culture. We must criticize a culture (like the Indian?) which fails to put forward an effort great enough to provide sufficient food for all mouths. But we must also criticize a culture (like that of the West) which fails to rise above economic and technological endeavor and thinks the domination of the material world a more important goal than the refinement of life and the beatific vision. What Scheler develops, at least by implication, is nothing less than a comprehensive critique of capitalism, very different from, but no less damaging than, that of Karl Marx. The hard fact that the twentieth century has not even been able to produce a profiled, assignable style in painting or music comparable to Gothic or Baroque is alone a convincing proof of the justification of Scheler's strictures.

While it is entirely possible to ward off the two attacks on Scheler's position of which we have spoken, it is not so easy to defeat a third assault. The problem concerned is Scheler's "ontologism." This technical term describes his assertion that values have an existence of their own, independent of those who carry and uphold them, that they are "clear, sensible [*fühlbare*] phenomena" and "real objects" (ibid., pp. 39–41). The opposite of ontologism is psychologism. According to the latter theory, values exist only in the mind and are essentially mind contents; according to the former they exist outside the mind and belong to the realm of reality—the ontic realm. Not only the man in the street, but even the technical philosopher may feel that Scheler has ventured too far in the direction of mysticism, or even that he confronts us with a mystification.

Scheler was a distant disciple of Franz Brentano, the thinker from whom a great deal of modern philosophizing (even in the Anglo-Saxon countries) derives. Brentano, too, had developed an ethical doctrine centered on the concept of value, but he had kept clear of ontologism. "X is good" meant for him only "x is worthy to be loved; x ought to be preferred and pursued; nobody who rightly feels and judges can deny that x is worthy to be loved, and that it is to be preferred and pursued." To the question "How can we know with any certainty that x is worthy to be loved?" Brentano answered that the ethical command is a proposition parallel in convincingness, in binding power, to the logical rule. Nobody doubts that twice two makes four; the truth of this logical conclusion is evident; the sentence "Thou shalt not kill" was to him equally evident in its content. Its acceptance by all rational beings seemed to him assured —as assured as the acceptance of the multiplication table. As can be seen, his idea of morality was built on the operation of the human mind, on the mind's judgments; Scheler's, on the other hand, on the exploration of objective being, on *perception*—and that is where the quarrel lay, and with it the deep problematic of Scheler's contribution. Brentano's little book *Vom Ursprung sittlicher Erkenntnis* (*The Origin of the Knowledge of Right and Wrong*) in no way matches Scheler's massive achievement, perhaps not even his acumen and depth of understanding, but it presents a clear and more sober alternative version of the ethics of value.

It is not possible for a sociologist to set himself up as an arbiter between Brentano and Scheler, between psychologism and ontologism in value theory. The issue is even more momentous than might be assumed at a first glance. Nothing less is involved here than the difference between Aristotelianism and Platonism. When the subschool of Edmund Husserl split from the main stem, from Brentano, this meant a swinging back from the Stagirite to the earlier intuitions of Plato, to a more religious conception of reality. Platonism has never died. It traveled through St. Augustine and Blaise Pascal to such modern philosophers as Husserl and Scheler and found there a new home—or even more: a new center of radiation. It has proved itself as much of a *philosophia perennis* as Aristotelianism, which reincarnated itself in St. Thomas Aquinas and then, in the nineteenth century, in Franz Brentano. The sociologist, tied as he is to empiricism, to descriptivism, may at first, almost instinctively, prefer Aristotle and Brentano to Plato and Scheler. And, indeed, it is easy to build a bridge between Brentano and mainstream sociology. We need only think of that key concept of Durkheim and Parsons, "the internalization of values," in order to see that Brentano's thought comes very close to fundamental aspects of twentieth-century social theorizing.

Nevertheless, it is a simple fact that Scheler is closer to sociological analysis than his adversaries. It is, admittedly, not easy to prescind from his ontologism, but what is a main question to the philosopher is only a side issue for the sociologist. If we decide to avert our eyes from the metaphysical problem which may, after all, be beyond the possibility of solution, we soon see that the order of values, the system of preferences, the chain of ethical imperatives, built up by Scheler corresponds closely to the ethic implied in any and every societal ethos. For every societal ethos demands, and must demand, that the members of society minimize, in their strivings, the pursuit of ends which lead to strife and the threat of dissolution, and follow by preference the values which are sharable and thus strengthen the social bond. Scheler's value pyramid reflects this structure built deeply into every socialized man. It is inspired by a knowledge of reality—perhaps not the suprasensual reality with which he operates, but certainly the tangible reality of social existence which must ever attempt to mute the physical, unavoidably self-preferring greeds and promote the unity-preserving and unity-enhancing tendencies at work in life, culture, and religion.

Why does Scheler place the "welfare values," i.e., the values of *social* welfare, above the "pleasure values," i.e., the values of *individual* enjoyment? Clearly because the latter are an ever-present threat to social integration. It is of the essence of pleasure-providing objects that they can be enjoyed only if they are appropriated and consumed by one individual to the exclusion of others. The piece of bread which I eat you cannot eat, and vice versa. Hence, there must be competition for physical gratifications, and from competition comes tension, conflict, prolonged strife, and war. If the piece of bread is broken and the pieces distributed, this is essentially the sacrifice of a pleasure value (or part of it) to the realization of a social or social-welfare value—in Scheler's terminology, a correct act of preferring, preferring in accordance with a scale forming part and parcel of reality. The pleasure values are, all of them, extensive, quantitative, and localized in the body. How strongly egocentric they are can be seen from the fact that they cannot immediately inspire sympathy—they can at best evoke something resembling it, and that merely mediately and indirectly. The unvalue of pain is perhaps a better example here than the positive value of pleasure. If I see somebody in the throes of a toothache, I cannot share his toothache for it is localized in *his* body; I can only remember what *I* felt when *I* was in the same condition, and recall what I had to go through then. Thus I feel sorry for the victim only to the extent that I am, or was, sorry for myself. In this case we are, so to speak, enclosed, imprisoned in our self-regard. How different are, for instance, the cultural values! I can look at and enjoy Caravaggio's *Basket of Fruit* or listen to and be enthusiastic about Haydn's *Toy Symphony* along with others, without my or their enjoyment's being diminished by the participation of several people in the experience. For cultural values bind, while material values divide. But even cultural values still have a (slight) material side. Painters need canvases and colors; musicians, instruments. Galleries and concerts require an entrance fee. Even these last obstacles fall when we ascend to the sacred values. The love of God can be freely shared by all (*Der Formalismus in der Ethik und die materiale Wertethik*, pp. 110, 247). "Nothing *unites* the creatures [*die Wesen*] so immediately and so closely as the common adoration and veneration of 'the holy' which excludes, because of its whole character, the idea of a 'material' being who would carry it (though not a symbol of this kind)," Scheler writes (ibid., p. 111).

And here we encounter in the first place the "absolutely" or "infinitely holy," the infinitely holy person—the "divine." This value is in principle attainable by everyone because it is the *most indivisible* of all values. Whatever has in fact, in the course of history, been played up as holy and has divided men (e.g., in the wars of religion and confessional strife), it is of the *essence* of the *intention* directed toward the [genuinely] holy that it unifies and links. A possible cause of division lies only in the *symbols* and the *techniques*, not in the holy itself.

What Scheler asserts here is entirely true of the phenomenon which, in the closing sections of the volume, we shall, following Henri Bergson, denominate "dynamic religion"; it is certainly not true of "static religion," i.e., religion which has become involved in and identified with lower values such as those of nation or state or class. But of this kind of religion—which Scheler certainly would not have accepted as an abode of the "genuinely holy"—he is neither speaking nor thinking. He is speaking and thinking of the Father whom all men have in heaven and whose name they hallow.

But we need not climb quite so high on the upward-leading ladder of values in order to see the sociological relevance and convincingness of Scheler's ethic. We may keep close to the bottom and perhaps should do so. On the very dividing line between the pleasure values and the vital values lie certain experiences such as the feeling of comfortableness as a positive item and its corresponding opposite, the unvalue or disvalue of discomfort. Though still akin to pleasure and pain, they are yet different, not to say contrasting, because they are neither localized nor localizable in any assignable spot in the organism. There is no more natural question than the physician's to the patient: "Where does it hurt?" But there could also be no more senseless inquiry that the inquiry of a man who feels buoyant: "Where does your buoyancy sit?" Pleasure and pain are sensations *in* the organism; buoyancy and listlessness, conditions *of* the organism—and this is a great difference. But the difference does not stop there. Vital feelings have a time and space dimension which purely somatic sensations lack. Included in the complex of vital feelings are, *inter alia*, feelings of hope and fear. These, however, concern the future; they are forward-looking, not, like a toothache, confined to a present, however prolonged. Vital feelings are also outward-looking; they concern the organism's relation to the environment, not only its own state. Scheler's example (ibid., pp. 342–44) is the exhilaration which we experience when, on a sunny morning, we walk through a dew-fresh forest. But our environment is not only physical; it is also social; and the social environment contributes much to our vital tone. It gives us, for instance, a sentiment of security. We all know how important this sentiment is for the young child, so easily the victim of unfocused, pervasive fears; it is no less important for everyone else, as Auguste Comte so convincingly argued: society is the mother who shields us all against the dangers threatening from our brutal and niggardly environment. "What is of very special significance, however," writes Scheler in a similar spirit (ibid., p. 342), "is the fact that even the vital feelings, and not only the mental feelings, partake of the power to induce fellow-feeling. For this reason the vital feelings are able to contribute to the laying of the foundations of a consciousness of community—a fact which is totally beyond the possibilities of the physical sensations." Perhaps we may speak here of a vital feeling of belonging, of integratedness, a complex within which the feeling of personal security is a prime ingredient. Culture and religion (the latter understood, not as ecclesiasticism, but as faith) add a great deal to this society-sustaining state of feeling, but it has its deepest basis at the level of vital sentiment.

Scheler's ethic—that much must surely have become obvious in the course of this analysis—is no bloodless speculation about what might be and what should be; it elucidates that which is, or rather that which happens. Society coheres if, and to the extent that, its members prefer the values of social welfare, of culture, and of holiness to the values of pleasure and pain, the hedonic values. Scheler's moral philosophy fully coincides with the findings elaborated in the present work. The only difference between ethos and ethic, or between the sociologist's field of observation and the ethicist's endeavor, is this: the ethos incorporates and secures the society-building preferences which are in fact accepted and adhered to, while an ethic is a guide to further advances which might be possible of achievement. Some such ethic as Max Scheler's is binding on the sociologist. There has been a long and rather useless discussion of the question as to whether the science of sociology should be or could be value free. If by this is meant that the sociologist should not subserve private interests, that he should not propagate political prejudice, that he should not preach, well and good. All reasonable men will agree. But the sociologist cannot possibly be as value free as the natural scientist, for he must know that social coherence, and that means the continued existence of social life, is ever in jeopardy. Every step in the direction of disintegration must give him pause. He, surely, cannot deny that the social condition is a supreme value. To determine the value of a thing, an old tradition advises us to think it away. Think society away, and *Homo sapiens* disappears; what is left is a speechless, mindless beast. If this is not to happen, the higher values identified by Max Scheler must, to a sufficient extent, be preferred to the lower; otherwise, a brutal fight for the trough will replace the framework of order within which, and within which alone, a humane society can exist and progress.

If we now ask, in conclusion, what ethical teaching as a whole can contribute to the improvement, in the sense of strengthening, of the social bond, the answer must be that, considered from a practical point of view, its contribution is rather limited. It is certainly a good thing that the moral problems of human conduct should be made conscious and discussed, but the upshot of these discussions is regularly the insistence that, first of all, the traditional and established norms should be respected. We saw this in the case of Bentham, of Rousseau and Smith, and even of Kant. An important philosopher to whom we shall presently have to pay close attention was fully aware of this: Henri Bergson. He comes near to saying that ethical speculation is a kind of circular reasoning. "The moral theorists take society for granted and consequently also the . . . forces to which society owes its stability and its mobility," he writes (*The Two Sources of Morality and Religion* [Garden City, N.Y., 1935], pp. 91, 89). "Society, with all that holds it together and drives it forward is already there. . . . Real obligation is already there," when they set out to build their systems of ethics. In this way, "reason will more or less rediscover morality, such as common sense conceives it, such as humanity in general practises, or claims to practise it," and that is all. Scheler makes no exception. He says expressly in one context (*Der Formalismus in der Ethik und die materiale Wertethik,* p. 97) that *a priori* ethical insights can come to the individual by way of tradition, which must mean by way of education (see also ibid., pp. 330–31). He would never have denied that further ethical advances on the part of a person must start from the ethical level incorporated and implemented in the social system around and behind him. Ethical teaching is thus a helpmate of the society-building forces, but it brings no additional power into play. Such a power, however, is the concept of a deity, if and insofar as it is part and parcel of an established philosophy of life, of the submerged metaphysics of an age— if and insofar as it is believed to describe the ultimate, all-seeing, all-knowing, all-avenging, and all-loving personal center of being, a concept which, until comparatively recent times, has dominated all cultures and continues to pervade even the largely agnostic or atheistic civilization of today.

3

Static Religion

131. One of the most impressive legacies which the so-called ages of faith have bequeathed to the succeeding centuries is the cathedral of Roskilde south of Copenhagen. Two series of woodcarvings run along its nave, the one on the right side, the other on the left; one depicts scenes from the Old Testament, the other from the New. The panels are so arranged that those which face each other correspond. Thus the Crucifixion has as its opposite the Setting up of the Brazen Serpent as recorded in the Book of Numbers (21:8): "And the Lord said to Moses: Make a brazen serpent and set it up for a sign. Whosoever . . . shall look on it shall live." Christ referred to this incident when He spoke to Nicodemus (Jn 3:14–15): "As Moses lifted up the serpent in the desert, so must the son of man be lifted up: that whosoever believeth in him may not perish, but may have life everlasting." As can be seen, deep theological thought is embedded in these works of art. They illustrate a saying of St. Augustine's which was particularly dear to the Middle Ages: "In Veteri Testamento Novum latet; in Novo Testamento Vetus patet": "In the Old Testament the New is concealed; in the New Testament the Old is revealed"— revealed in its message, revealed in its meaning. The Roskilde carvings are a kind of *Biblia pauperum*, a pictorial presentation of Holy Writ for the use of those unable to read (see Poul Kürstein, *Korstolene i Roskilde Domkirke* [Copenhagen, 1966], passim, but esp. pp. 56, 18).

But this document in stone and wood not only shows the correspondences between the Old Testament and the New, it also brings to mind—and that very clearly—the contrasts between them. At a particularly prominent place—the end of the choir stalls—we see on the left side Moses with the Ten Commandments in his hand, on the right St. John with the Gospel before him. These figures sum up and symbolize, in addition to the two parts of the Sacred Scriptures, the two dispensations which they respectively represent: Moses is the messenger of divine *law*; John, the apostle of divine *love*. Law and love are not entirely irreconcilable, but even where they are reconciled, as far as that is possible, they remain alternatives; indeed, something like black and white. We are hardly going too far when we say that they stand for two different, if connected, types of religion.

When we speak, as we often do, and that justifiably, of a common Judaeo-Christian tradition, the very term we use indicates that we are confronted with a duality, with thesis and antithesis, even if they have come to form a unity and a synthesis. And this is not only a matter of words; it is assuredly also a matter of substance. In the Old Testament, God is the stern ruler of Israel; in the New, the loving father of all men. The conception, the definition, of the Godhead is not the same. And this distinction of two religions, or at least of two aspects of religion, is not confined to the Judaeo-Christian world. Even the Greeks were aware of it, though their ideas in this respect were far less sharply focused than those of the later civilizations.

In what follows, we are not trying to Christianize Plato. This has been attempted, but with at best partial success. Both the Greek vision of God and the Greek estimate of man are different from basic Christian conceptions. When Plato and Aristotle speak of god, they mean either God or the gods or the divine, without, as a rule, making a distinction. When they speak of creation, they do not mean creation *ex nihilo*, but merely forming—ordering—pre-existing, eternal matter. When they speak of sin, they do not think of the lusts of the flesh; their idea is rather that the soul itself is divided into a good, godward part, and an evil one akin to the primal chaos, the darkness which was before the first day. But, this said, we must add immediately that a typological comparison between Greek and Christian religiosity is not entirely without its point. For the Greeks, as for the Christians, religion has two centers: the act of creation, and the fact that the creation is ever tending to return to the creator-god from whose hands it came. The term "redemption" cannot without inexactitude be applied to this striving back toward the origin, but the word "salvation" would already be nearer the mark. The doctrine certainly was that He who has made us does not allow us to founder; but calls us back into fellowship with Him, into that order which He has imposed on matter and within which we, too, can find peace and sanctification.

Among the sources, Plato's *Timaeus* occupies a foremost place. In this dialogue the great philosopher raises the question: "for what cause the author of the universe constructed it?" (trans. Paul Elmer More in *The Religion of Plato* [Princeton, N.J., 1921], pp. 170, 171), and he answers that it was one of the desires of the demiurge that all things should be made as like to himself as possible. God, being himself good, he says, was anxious "that all things should be good." To lay a basis for this universal goodness, he took the universe, as yet "moving without harmony or measure," and out of this disorder "brought it into order, thinking such a state altogether better than the other." The *Timaeus* thus depicts God first of all as the great Efficient Cause, the source of ordered being; but it contains also, by implication, yet quite clearly, a second conception: that of a saving God—the acknowledgment of the Godhead as the great Final Cause, the power which draws everything which had come *from* him back *to* him. We get closest to Plato's meaning when we say that the Creator God carried in him from the very beginning an "Idea" of what man ought to be—of what he ideally is. This Idea is never fully realized, for man is embedded in matter which is recalcitrant and resistant; it is never fully realized because the eternal Idea has descended into time. Yet out of time it struggles back toward eternity; real man has it in him to become ideal man, to conform to the archetype laid down in the divine mind. The following sentences reflect this basic vision:

when the Father who begot the world beheld it in [regular] motion . . . he was
delighted, and in his pleasure formed the design of making it still more like
its [ideal] pattern. . . . he undertook to perfect the universe as far as possible.
. . . the nature [the Idea] of the creature happened to be eternal, [yet] it was
not possible to accord this character in its completeness to what was begotten;
but he took thought to make a certain moving image of eternity, and so ordered
the heaven-bounded world as to make it an . . . image [a reflection], moving in
number, of the eternity abiding in unity; and this we have named time. . . .
Time, then, was created . . . after the pattern of the eternal nature, to the end
that it might resemble this to the utmost degree possible; for the pattern exists
through all eternity, in pure being, and the image [the reflection] exists through
all time on and on, yet as generated and being and about to be [ibid., pp.
176–78].

We must read this passage together with one from the tenth book of *The
Laws* which asserts "that all things have been ordered by God, who has the
world in care, to the salvation and virtue of the whole, each member passively
and actively contributing its part according to its ability" (trans. More, in
ibid., p. 98). As for man's contribution, it lies in self-conquest, in achieving
for and in himself the ascendancy of reason (which is order) over lust (which
is chaos). This self-conquest—this self-salvation—is necessary. "The greatest
evil to men, generally," Plato writes in the fifth book of *The Laws* (trans.
More, in ibid., pp. 276–77),

is one which is innate in their souls, and which a man is always excusing in
himself and so has no way of escaping. I mean what is expressed in the saying
that every man is and ought to be dear to himself. Whereas the truth is that
this absorbing self-love is continually and in all men the cause of all their
faults; for the lover is blinded in regard to the object of his passion, so that he
is a bad judge of the just and the good and the beautiful. . . .

In these words which, to some extent at any rate, justify the concept of a *Plato
Christianus*, a Christian before Christ, Plato comes close to the conviction that
the human race stands in need of salvation, and that its god-willed self-salvation
is a duty laid on it by the powers above. It is often said that the message of
Greek philosophy to posterity is summed up in the words: Know thyself. But
"know thyself" also means: know the darkness within thyself; overcome thyself. The taming of the Old Adam is Platonism's behest, as it is that of Christianity: "that is the first and greatest victory when a man is victor over himself,
as that is the basest and most evil condition when a man is defeated by himself"
(*Laws* I) (ibid., p. 198). All men are invited, as it were, to make their own
reason a replica of God's. That is God's desire; that is God's hope. As we can
see, it is, in Plato's opinion, God's plan to lift empirical, incarnate man to the
level of the divinely conceived ideal pattern of man; there is a call to men to
strive in this direction. For the Christian this call comes through Jesus Christ,
the Second Person of the Holy Trinity, the Word made flesh. Plato does not,
and cannot, personify the call; but the call itself is there, in his theology, as it
is in Christian dogma. He knows therefore two aspects of the Godhead: God
as the Father, and God as the guide, of humanity. Indeed, he even realizes that

the two are one, that the Godhead is both the beginning and the end, efficient cause and final, and these undividedly self-identical in One Spirit.

In Aristotle we encounter a far less religious vision of the world; his thought is closer to science than to mysticism. But he is a theist all the same. God is to him in the first place a transcendent Unmoved Mover, a figure without which he considers it impossible to grasp the laws of the universe. To that extent he agrees with Plato, even Plato's theology. But there is still another parallel between the two. The position occupied in Plato's system by the concept of the Idea is occupied in Aristotle's philosophy by the concept of form. All that is within the observed and observable world, everything and especially every thing, is composed of matter and form. There is an upward struggle from matter (raw material) to form (perfection); a tendency from the former to the latter is deeply embedded in being. Now the Unmoved Mover is pure form, without admixture of matter, and so all upward movement is in a manner bound to be toward him. In spite of this conception, Aristotle is not so close to the idea of a (possibly personifiable) call as Plato is, but he thinks in terms of an attraction of form for matter, or an aspiration of matter toward form, and this is a similar inspiration. Besides the Unmoved Mover, the Creator God, there is thus a second focus in his system which is at least potentially religious and points in the direction of a redemptive principle operative in reality, a principle of finality which is part and parcel of a kind of faith. In any case, however we interpret the Stagirite, he sees not only an act of creation, he sees also a process of ascent toward perfection, and without both these intentions, without this duality, he could never have become the *philosophus* of the deeply believing Middle Ages, the mentor of the philosopher–saint, St. Thomas Aquinas.

This brief side glance at Greek thought at the peak of its development must suffice to prove that the Christian distinction between the God who worked on the first day and the God who worketh still—the God of power and the God of love—is foreshadowed in heathen speculation. In the Gospels, the contrast between a law-giving and a merciful God is far more clearly drawn. It is most dramatically presented in the Sermon on the Mount (Mt 5–8). After the Beatitudes, there comes a string of antitheses which show that law-abidingness is good, but love of God and neighbor better:

You have heard that it was said to them of old: Thou shalt not kill. And whosoever shall kill shall be in danger of the judgment. But I say to you that whosoever is angry with his brother shall be in danger of the judgment. . . . You have heard that it was said to them of old: Thou shalt not commit adultery. But I say to you that whosoever shall look on a woman to lust after her hath already committed adultery with her in his heart. . . . You have heard that it has been said: An eye for an eye, a tooth for a tooth. But I say to you not to resist evil: but if one strike thee on thy right cheek, turn to him also the other. . . . You have heard that it hath been said: Thou shalt love thy neighbour and hate thy enemy. But I say to you: Love your enemies: do good to them that hate you: and pray for them that persecute and calumniate you. . . . For if you love them that love you, what reward shall you have? Do not even the publicans do this? And if you salute your brethren only, what do you more? . . . I tell you, that unless your justice abound more than that of the scribes and Pharisees, you shall not enter into the kingdom of heaven [Mt 5:21, 22, 27, 28, 38, 39, 43, 44, 46, 47, 20].

It would be wrong to assume that these sentences mean to devalue the law, and Christ expressly says (Mt 5:17): "Do not think that I am come to destroy the law. . . . I am not come to destroy, but to fulfill." The law is a step toward a well-integrated society, but only a first step, a preliminary; beyond it lies a further and final step which is imaginable if hardly possible: the introduction of brotherliness into human relationships. The law, supported by legalistic religion (the word legalistic used in a sense which is not pejorative), i.e., religion which roots in the concept of the Creator God as the supreme law-giver and law-enforcer, aims only at total conformity of *outer conduct* with societal norms. Religion in the charismatic meaning of the term—religion as it arises from the belief in a Redeemer God come to call men into a love-informed community with Himself and each other—is more ambitious; it envisages, and strives for, a sanctification of *inner attitudes* which would, if it were achieved, make societal norms, and indeed the very concept of duty, unnecessary because nobody would ever wish to harm his neighbor. This is the perfection which Christ preached to His flock: "Be you therefore perfect, as also your heavenly Father is perfect." When asked to sum up the law, He replied: "Thou shalt love the Lord thy God with thy whole heart and with thy whole soul and with thy whole mind. This is the greatest and the first commandment. And the second is like to this: Thou shalt love thy neighbour as thyself. On these two commandments dependeth the whole law and the prophets" (Mt 5:48, 22:37–40).

The contrast between the law and love was particularly crass in the society which formed the background to the Sermon on the Mount because the traditional code had, on the one hand, ossified, and, on the other, proliferated. The Pharisees, from whose ranks most of the scribes, or doctors of the law, came, though they appear in the Gospels in a very bad light, were anything but enemies of society. On the contrary, they were only too anxious to defend society against any threat of disintegration. They were fanatical upholders of the law but—and this is the point—their law-abidingness was restricted to outer observance, to a cold formalism, and did not lead onward toward inner fulfillment, toward warm charity. Christ's main attacks seem to have been directed against the school of Shammai rather than against the milder and more humane Hillel and Gamaliel. Shammai's understanding of the law—and to some extent even that of Gamaliel and Hillel—was that it had to insist above all on two precepts: ritual cleanliness (not to be confused with physical cleanliness) and sanctification of the Sabbath. Thus, to speak only of the latter aspect, Shammai and his school would not allow a Jew to carry even a needle or a dry fig in his pocket on the Sabbath; indeed, they went so far as to forbid a cripple to use his wooden leg (see Giuseppe Ricciotti, *Der Apostel Paulus* [Basel, 1950], pp. 74, 76). As the Sabbath rest extended to animals and things as well as persons, it was enjoined that colors put into liquids in order to dissolve should be totally dissolved before the arrival of dusk on Friday night so that they would not "work" on the day of rest (ibid., p. 74). Sometimes Hillel was still stricter than Shammai: an egg laid on a feast day after a Sabbath could not, according to him, lawfully be eaten, for the hen had "worked" in maturing it (ibid., p. 71). But what repelled Jesus more than anything else was the fact that the Pharisaic do's and don't's inhibited acts of charity. A beggar stretching his hand into a householder's house or garden in order to collect a gift was considered guilty of a breach of the law; a householder stretching his hand out of his house or over the garden fence in order to give alms was equally considered guilty; thus almsgiving was made totally impossible on one day of the seven (ibid.). No wonder that Jesus openly challenged these norms, defied, and condemned them:

> And it came to pass . . . as the Lord walked through the corn fields on the sabbath, that his disciples began to go forward, and to pluck the ears of corn. And the Pharisees said to him: Behold, why do they on the sabbath day that which is not lawful? . . . And he said to them: The sabbath was made for man, and not man for the sabbath. . . . And he entered again into the synagogue, and there was a man there who had a withered hand. And they watched him whether he would heal on the sabbath days, that they might accuse him. And he said to the man who had the withered hand: Stand up in the midst. And he saith to them: Is it lawful to do good on the sabbath days . . . ? But they held their peace. And looking round about on them with anger, being grieved for the blindness of their hearts, he saith to the man: Stretch forth thy hand. And he stretched it forth: and his hand was restored unto him. And the Pharisees going out, immediately made a consultation with the Herodians against him, how they might destroy him [Mk 2:23, 24, 27; 3:1–7; re ritual cleanliness, see Ricciotti, *Der Apostel Paulus*, pp. 73, 74, and Mk 7:1–15].

Needless to say, the examples of Pharisaic formalism and legalism which we have given are grotesque exaggerations of legality, and the possible abuse of law is no argument against its use, effectiveness, and necessity as an element in the system of social control. Yet one lesson can be learned from the study of it, and it is a supremely important one: namely, that a society which is based only on custom and law is not so good as it could and should be. A society permeated by a spirit of love is assuredly no more than a vision in the sky. But if it is the function of religion to lead men to heaven, then it is also its task to keep that vision alive and to set it up as a great goal to be aimed at and striven for, even if its practical attainment is less than likely, given man's self-preferring physical nature.

The contrast between the two types of society, law-informed and love-informed, imperfect and perfect, is further developed in St. Paul's Epistle to the Galatians, and to some extent also in his Epistle to the Romans. With supreme skill, he symbolizes the opposed dispensations by pitting against each other two figures of the Old Testament: Ismael, the son of a bondwoman, and Isaac, the son of a free woman. Both were Abraham's sons, Abraham's "seed," "but he who was of the bondwoman was born according to the flesh" while "he of the free woman was by promise," i.e., by grace (Ga 4:21, 22). Through

Ismael and Isaac, Abraham became the founder-father of two descent lines, two clans, that is to say, two societies: the one in thrall to legalism; the other enjoying the freedom of the children of God who need no law because they know themselves as brethren, because they are tied together in *one* spirit of mutual love. These things, St. Paul continues (verses 24–26), "are said by an allegory. For these are the two testaments. The one from Mount Sinai, engendering unto bondage. . . . But that Jerusalem which is above is free: which is our mother." Jerusalem, it should be remembered, means "the vision of peace."

The meaning of the Pauline parable becomes quite clear the moment we place it within its concrete historical context. Abraham's children according to the flesh are the contemporary Jews under the Mosaic law, that law which had broadened into the Pharisaic code which Paul, in harsh language, condemns (see esp. Ph 3:3–9). Abraham's children according to the spirit, on the other hand, are all those—whatever their nationality, their descent, their blood —who have opened their hearts to the divine principle of love manifested in Jesus Christ, who, when they cry to God, call Him, not King of Israel, but "Abba, Father" (Ga 4:6). "Not they that are the children of the flesh are the children of God," St. Paul says in his Epistle to the Romans, but "whoever are led by the Spirit of God, they are the sons of God" (9:8, 8:14). And in the Epistle to the Galatians (5:18, 14): "If you are led by the spirit, you are not under the law. . . . For all the law is fulfilled in one word: Thou shalt love thy neighbour as thyself."

The two Pauline epistles which we have reviewed throw a flood of light back on to the Gospels. They help us to understand a few passages which have appeared to many overly harsh. Thus, in one incident recorded by St. Matthew (12:46–50), Christ appears to repulse those nearest to him, those of his own family.

> As he was yet speaking to the multitudes, . . . his mother and his brethren stood without, seeking to speak to him. And one said unto him: Behold thy mother and thy brethren stand without, seeking thee. But he answering . . . said: Who is my mother and who are my brethren? And stretching forth his hand towards his disciples, he said: Behold my mother and my brethren. For whosoever shall do the will of my Father, that is in heaven, he is my brother, and sister, and mother.

This passage must have been among those which inspired St. Paul and induced him to contrast the "children of the flesh" and "the sons of God." The relatives from whom Christ turns away are the members of His clan: the "brothers" to whom the report refers were clan brothers, close to Him merely by the accident of birth and descent. Those whom He calls His true kindred are tied to Him by the bonds of love, by ties not accidental but essential, not physical but spiritual, not legal but charismatic. Christ's words in the scene described by the evangelist reveal His social ideal, His concept of community. A community deserves its name only if it is of one mind and of one heart. The Christianity of Christ Himself is not meant to be a sanctification of imperfect structures such as the world has always produced them, though these are not condemned, indeed, though they are to some extent even upheld; it is a plea to create a kingdom of brotherliness and warmth, a kingdom of love.

The essential duality of the phenomenon of religion, which we have now sufficiently illustrated, was most lucidly analyzed by Henri Bergson, one of the greatest minds of the twentieth century. The very title of the book of which we are thinking is revealing: *Les Deux Sources de la morale et de la religion* (1932). (Because of its unique qualities, we have already mentioned it at the beginning of this volume, in Section 113.) We must strive to make Bergson's insights our own. But before we relate what is acceptable and convincing in his work, we must unfortunately indicate what is merely time-bound and therefore unacceptable. Bergson, born in 1859, was still the child of an age in which biology was thought to be the key to all problems, even those of culture. Admittedly, his biologism is a very attenuated one, attenuated almost to vanishing point. Yet, vestigial as it is, it is still in evidence. His whole philosophy rested on one decisive concept, the concept known as *élan vital*. There is a mighty current of life, he taught, which rushes through dead matter and wrests from it ever higher forms of being: there is a never-ending process of creation. The question which unavoidably arises against the background of such an intuition is this: Does the *élan vital* come from God, or is it god? In 1932, Bergson left the answer open. In the remaining nine years of his life, he is said to have drawn much closer to the former, the theistic, position. We can do no more than study his analysis in the pages which are before us in print.

In its onward and upward rush, life creates *inter alia* societies, but these are of two kinds: Bergson was a great upholder of the theory of *divergent* evolution. Among the Hymenoptera, bees and ants, it tried one experiment; with the species man, quite another. The communities of the Hymenoptera, hives and hills, possess a nature-given order, while the associations of men are endowed with a no less natural freedom which the others lack. Or rather, to be quite exact: freedom among the bees and ants is merely vestigial, a near nothing, while order in the case of man is merely a design which has yet to be realized, and which, in history, is realized by the human race in freedom and responsibility. The realization of this grand design is, however, fraught with difficulties. Man is equipped with reason, while the Hymenoptera are not. Reason is necessary if man is to survive, but it supports individual survival, above all, and is therefore not a mainstay of sociality. On the contrary, if human societies are to endure, there must arise an agency capable of counterbalancing self-regard—inspiring rationality. That agency is religion. Bergson maintains that it springs from a certain innate tendency which he calls, showing his all-too-close association with the philosophy of vitalism, the "myth-making function." He writes (*Two Sources of Morality*, pp. 266, 101):

> if nature, and for the very reason that she has made us intelligent, has left us to some extent with freedom of choice in our type of social organization, she has at all events ordained that we should live in society. A force of unvarying direction, which is to the soul what . . . gravity is to the body, ensures the cohesion of the group by bending all individual wills to the same end. That force

is moral obligation. . . . Let us then give to the word biology the very wide meaning it should have, . . . and let us say . . . that all morality . . . is in essence biological.

This is the error which we combated in Section 128, where we discussed the ethics of sentiment. We need not criticize it once again. In Bergson, however, it appears in connection with a true insight—the realization that religion, as one of the institutions carrying, and watching over, moral obligation, is two-fold: that it appears in two sharply contrasting forms which mix and merge, but are and remain essentially different, in spite of their mixture and merger. There is a *static* religion which tends to defend and preserve established institutions; and there is a *dynamic* faith which liquefies the forms which have become settled and set. Its protagonists lift society up toward ever higher levels of being; their ultimate aim is the attainment of the highest level of being, which is a common life built on mutual love. Such men are generally called saints. Saints are souls who are in contact with the *élan vital* which underlies all evolution and is ceaselessly engendering new forms of existence. They make themselves the servants of that *élan vital*—which means, in a more sociological view, that they are the missionaries of an ideal, charismatic community, of universal brotherhood.

It is possible to welcome the results of Bergson's studies without falling for the special blend of biologism with which it is interwoven. That biologism is today no longer attractive. The saint is not to be seen as a man who is in contact with an *élan vital*, an objective life-force; he is much rather to be regarded as a man who is in contact with *God*, a man who has opened his heart to the call of love which came to humanity in and through Jesus Christ. Only such an opinion is truly religious and at the same time truly realistic, and there are good indications that Bergson understood this before he closed his eyes. It is in any case impossible not to agree with him when he says that the saint makes himself a mold through which the divine spirit can flow into the world and become active within it.

Having disposed of the problematic aspects of Bergson's analysis, we can with confidence turn to its valuable and abiding results. When we look at the norms which keep society together, Bergson explains, we see at first *one* system of obligations, and we get the impression that it is an unbroken unity. But when we look more closely, we discern two different elements: "There is a static morality, which exists, as a fact, at a given moment in a given society; it has become ingrained in customs, ideas, and institutions. . . . There is, on the other hand, a dynamic morality which is impetus." Differently expressed: there are "two things, a system of *orders* dictated by *impersonal* social requirements, and a series of *appeals* made to the conscience of each of us by *persons* who represent the best there is in humanity." The two have one thing in common: namely, that they are both counterweights to reason which is almost always pleading for self-regarding, and but rarely for self-sacrificing, conduct. But they remain distinct, if not indeed contrasting: "The obligation relating to orders is, in its original and fundamental elements, sub-rational. The potency of the appeal lies in the strength of the emotion it has aroused in times gone by, which it arouses still, or can arouse: this emotion . . . is supra-rational" (ibid., pp. 269, 84). We might also formulate Bergson's essential insight by saying that there is a morality which *holds us down* and another which *lifts us up*. The former is "pressure," while the latter is an "inspiration" and an aspiration (see ibid., pp. 34, 64). "Between the first morality and the second," Bergson explains (ibid., p. 58), "lies the whole distance between repose and movement. The first is supposed to be immutable. . . . The shape it assumes at any given time claims to be the final shape. But the second is a forward thrust, a demand for movement; it is the very essence of mobility. Thus would it prove, thus alone, indeed, would it be able at first to define, its superiority."

The realism of this analysis is easy to demonstrate because for proof we can appeal to common experience. We have, all of us, felt the force of social pressure; indeed, we feel it all the time: we know that we are surrounded on every side by informal and formal restrictions. But there can also be few who have not now and then undergone the influence of the other—higher—morality, of the call to righteousness and even love.

> Only those who have come into touch with a great moral personality have fully realized the nature of this appeal. But we all, at those momentous hours when our usual maxims of conduct strike us as inadequate, have wondered what such or such a one would have expected of us under the circumstances. It might have been a relation or a friend whom we thus evoked in thought. But it might quite as well have been a man we had never met, whose life-story had merely been told us, and to whose judgment we in imagination submitted our conduct, fearful of his censure, proud of his approval [ibid., pp. 34, 35].

In 1931, when these words were in all probability written, Bergson was not yet as close to Christianity as he was in 1941 when he died. Had he been, he would have pointed out that for the Christian that "relation and friend" is none other than Jesus Christ, his brother and redeemer, and also, let us not forget it, his eternal judge.

In the confines of the Western culture area, it is indeed Jesus Christ, together with His saints, from whom the call of which Bergson is speaking has come, is now coming, and will be coming to the end of time. This brings us back to the beginning of this section—to the choir stalls of Roskilde. Moses and St. John, Decalogue and Gospel, religious law and divine love—these are two separate, if conjoined, influences on social life which we shall have to consider in the remaining pages of this book. We shall see, what is perhaps sufficiently clear already now, that in and through the latter the society-building forces reach their acme.

But before we turn to the detail, we have still one important point to make. An earlier work by the present writer, *The Sociology of Religion*, has shown that there are, in the final analysis, three types of religious society: namely, established religion (see vol. I), sectarian religion (see vol. II), and the universal church (see vol. III, but also vol. V). Established religion, characterized by a tendency to sanctify or even to divinize the ruler, supports the given order in society: it is conservative. Sectarian religion, on the other hand, is a nodus of negative feelings toward things as they are: it is revolutionary. The universal church comprises, and to some extent reconciles, these two attitudes; hence, its name. It might be thought that the dichotomy of established religion/sectarian grouping is identical with, or at least akin to, the Bergsonian distinction of static and dynamic morality. This is by no means so, however, and we must underline this fact as strongly as we can. It would be a particularly flagrant error to identify the sect with moral dynamism. The aim of this dynamism is always universal brotherhood, for it is this that Christ Jesus propagated when He was on earth: "Go ye into the whole world and preach the gospel to every creature"—these were His last words to His disciples (Mk 16:15). Inside the sect, there is indeed quite often a warm brotherly feeling, but this is as a rule underlaid by, and derived from, contempt for or even hatred of the outsider. In a state church, on the other hand, though it is more often than not strongly nationalistic, there may be currents which deserve to be called charismatic, and that in a universalist sense of the word. Indeed, the whole Bergsonian distinction applies more to persons than to organizations; the hub and center of his analysis is the commanding figure of the saint. It is he who shows his fellow-man what social life might be like if all the impediments to sociality were overcome and removed, if law were replaced with love.

THE SOCIAL FUNCTION OF RELIGION: RELIGION AND SOCIAL CONTROL

132. One way of defining static religion would be to say that it is part and parcel of the system of social control. This formulation at once raises the question as to what precisely the contribution is which it can make to the integration and preservation of ongoing society. Anticipating the results of the sections which are to follow, we can say that, generally speaking, it fills the gap which the two other agencies, custom and law, have left open. Custom and law are supported by certain mental modes of social control, and we considered them in the earlier parts of this volume. They achieved much, but not everything. A yet stronger mode of mental control is needed, That stronger mode is static religion. (Our exposition demands that we return here to a topic already touched on in Section 111 (SOCIAL BOND III 225–29). There we stated the problem involved; here we have to show how life has solved it.)

In order to appreciate the effectiveness of static religion as an agency of control, we must realize that modern society, as it has emerged from the great revolutions of the eighteenth century, is an exceptional and not a normal phenomenon, an experiment of a novel kind. The spread of skepticism, agnosticism, and atheism has robbed religion of much of its power, but in most—indeed, all—other cultures known to history the fear of the gods was an order-supporting influence of considerable strength. There can be no doubt of that; the evidence is massive and convincing.

Even where custom and law are fully developed and effective, even where rich folklore flanks, and cooperates with, the folkways, there remain three weaknesses of social ordering which have to be compensated. The first might be called technical. The pressures making for law-abidingness are not unfailing. Only the crude and open offender is detected and corrected; he who works in the dark all too often escapes. Criminal statistics show only too clearly that merely a fraction of even the most flagrant antisocial actions is brought to the notice of the courts, or, for that matter, to the knowledge of the public. According to an old joke, there is an eleventh commandment besides the ten of Moses, and it runs: "Thou shalt not allow thyself to be caught." It is in all probability better attended to than the others. In the contest between robbers and police, the latter win far less frequently than they should.

This is, surely, a matter of common experience. But common experience teaches much more: it shows that the forms of social intercourse allowed and even recommended by the social codes can be perverted and abused. It is good form to inquire after a man's well-being and health. But if he is a hypochondriac, this inquiry can be so worded as to throw him into depression and despair: How are you? You look very pale this morning! Are you sure you are not sick? There is no defense against such wickedness for it parades in the garb of courtesy and concern. The backhanded compliment, the seemingly kind book review with a nasty sting to its tail, and many, many other phenomena fall into the same class.

Formal law is even more clumsy in this respect than informal social pressures. Judges are but men, and safeguards against errors or partiality on their part are necessary. These, however, offer many opportunities to law-benders and lawbreakers. In polite language, the techniques used are known as lawyers' tricks; in American slang, as "finagling." Even the very best intentions of the lawgiver may be perverted and used for immoral purposes. Thus—to give but one example—in some countries the costs of a legal contest must be borne by the richer contestant. An entirely well-meant, even enlightened regulation! But what happens? A poor person may bring an entirely unjustified action against a rich one, in the hope that the latter will give him a certain sum if he withdraws his case, rather than face a possibly large bill of legal expenses. Pregnant girls have been known to bring paternity suits against millionaires whom they have never seen, in the assumption, often justified, that the latter will prefer paying up to being exposed to a costly, time-consuming, and unavoidably embarrassing comedy in court. The law has indeed safeguards against what is known as "abuse of rights," but it is difficult to apply them in practice. Extortion by means of legal techniques, not to say, by means of the law, is not unknown, and not even rare.

A second serious shortcoming of the basic social controls—we have already briefly referred to it—is connected with the fact that they can only enforce certain modes of *outer* conduct, but leave the inner disposition largely untouched. The Ten Commandments proclaim "Thou shalt not steal," and custom and the law have the means, however imperfect, of ensuring that this injunction is obeyed. But the Ten Commandments also demand that "Thou shalt not covet thy neighbor's goods," and the two agencies of social control so far considered, are powerless when it comes to the implementation of this norm. It is true that a man's habitual modes of behavior have a tendency to generate corresponding forms of thought and feeling: he who always acts politely may, and often will, develop a friendly attitude to his fellow-beings, indeed, become considerate and kind. His whole character may fall in line with his external conduct. But this is merely a tendency, and we have chosen this term advisedly in order to describe it. A tendency may be inhibited and prevented from reaching the end to which it is ordered. Polite actions may be, and often are, instruments—tricks—of a hypocritical life-policy. Far from demonstrating a kindly attitude, they may mask a deep-seated indifference to the welfare of others, or even contempt for and hatred of them. The shopman is not so friendly to his customers as he pretends to be; nor is the fashionable doctor's bedside manner more than a clever technique of deception. Hypocrisy is to some extent useful. It has even been called a compliment paid to virtue by vice. But it is a vice nonetheless, and society must strive to develop the virtue itself and to get rid of its counterfeit. Custom and the law cannot achieve this, but religion can. To use a colloquial expression: it gets under the skin, whereas custom and the law do not.

Here again, the situation within the area of law is even more unsatisfactory than the situation within the field of custom. The worst criminal is allowed to plead not guilty, and this plea—in most cases a deliberate lie—is not held against him. It is for the prosecutor to bring the truth to light: self-incrimination is not demanded. The reason in the background is once again protection of the possibly innocently accused, and the realization that it would be hard to force a man to become his own enemy, to undo himself. But if the law condones this lie, how can lying not be part and parcel of everyday societal techniques?

No less serious than the two weaknesses just exposed is the third: the predominantly negative character of social control. Custom and the law endeavor to prevent evil, but they do not insist on the performance of good deeds. Of course, a statement of this kind must be taken with a grain of salt. The law knows several relationships within which one party must selflessly look after the interests of another. A father, for instance, has to protect, nourish, and educate his children; a guardian, his wards. But it is and remains true that these are exceptions to the rule. There is no legal duty to do good. The folkways are more fertile in this respect. To get up and to offer one's seat to an aged person in a bus or train is a demand of custom, and it prescribes an act which has to be characterized as selfless. In primitive societies not a few actions of this sort are expected; and the expectations, supported by social pressures. An Eskimo who has hunted down a caribou has to distribute some of its meat to others before he tastes the first morsel himself. But such conduct is far less generous than it appears. The giver knows full well that one day the roles will be reversed and he will be the receiver of a "gift" similar to the one which he has made; a principle of insurance is at work. Charity, properly so called, is the result always of inspiration, never of duty. Indeed, charitable behavior is by definition different from obligatory behavior. Though the social codes prepare it, and that even psychologically, it is not evoked by them. It springs from religious motivations. Within the Christian tradition it is an *imitatio Christi*, an outgrowth of the Gospel spirit.

What is it which enables religion where it is fully alive to close the gaps left open by the other agencies of social control? In an investigation like the present the answer has to be that it brings a new type of social pressure to bear. Bentham realized this when he added the concept of a religious sanction to the sanctions which he called moral or social and legal. Moral or social pressure is diffuse and, though not ineffective, too unorganized to achieve much. Legal pressure is more highly organized and therefore in one sense achieves a good deal more. But, as we have just seen, it also has painful limitations: it is in the hands of fallible men, and their lack of information alone is sufficient to hamstring them in their activities. But if there is a ruler of the universe who is all-knowing and all-powerful, then there exists an agency of social control which can perform what the others cannot. It is impossible to deceive Him; He knows men's thoughts as well as their outer conduct; and He demands kindness, indeed, mutual love, and is not satisfied with cold law-abidingness. In this way, religion puts the finishing touches on the system of social control, or, to change the metaphor, provides it with a coping stone without which it would be and remain a mere collection of fragments and not an integrated structure.

Even on the lowest level of cultural development, where fetishism is still in full force, the religious sanction can be seen at work. The anthropologist Hans Himmelheber tells two stories from his personal experience which illustrate this fact (*Der gute Ton bei den Negern* [Heidelberg, 1957], pp. 89, 90). On the way to the African Baule, he and his interpreter approached a settlement, and the interpreter assured him that they were quite safe in the neighborhood. "The village is inhabited by good people," he told Himmelheber. When asked whether he had friends there, he said no, but added that he could see in the distance a small house, a kind of temple, built across the road. "Do you know Surobua, the magician?" he asks Himmelheber. "He has built such huts in all parts of the area. Since then the people round about have become much more law-abiding. . . . A man who approaches the village with evil intentions in his mind will drop dead when he passes through it. Therefore only good people can live here." On closer inspection the sacred structure revealed two small chambers. The one contained the figure of a leopard made from red clay; the other, a giant snake fashioned in earthenware. Both were covered with the feathers of chickens which had been sacrificed to them. A low superstition? No doubt! But one which made for decency and kindliness. A similar experience awaited the anthropologist among the Senuffo. Walking along the road with his interpreter (not the same as among the Baule), he sees a banknote on the ground. "Can't you use it?" he asks the young man. But he gets a surprising answer. "I never touch the property of others. Just look, how dirty the bill is! It has been lying around for a long time already, and nobody but the owner will pick it up. We all in this area believe in Massa." Massa is a fetish made from iron rings and certain animal horns built a few years before by an old man who had dreamed one night that such an idol would turn his fellow-tribesmen toward righteousness. The experiment was made and was to all appearances successful.

So powerful is the influence of even pre- and protoreligious conceptions on social life that one of the greatest pioneers of modern sociology, Emile Durkheim, could come to the conclusion that the Massa of the Senuffo, or the deities of antiquity, or, for that matter, the God of Christianity, are merely personifications—phantasmagoric representations—of society. This, however, is not much more than sociologism, i.e., an undue overemphasis on the social aspect of the phenomenon. Reductionism is rarely a sound theory. Without attempting to fathom the whole mystery of faith, let us merely recall that religion has *inter alia* psychological roots, and suggest that its social effects stem very largely from them. There is, for instance, the fear of death. The "vital impulse knows nothing of death," writes Bergson (*Two Sources of Morality*, p. 138). "But let intelligence spring to life under pressure from this impulse, and up comes the idea of the inevitability of death: to restore to life its impetus, an opposing representation will start up, and from it will emerge the primitive beliefs . . ."—such as the belief in immortality. But there is not only the fear of death, there is also a fear of life. Bergson recognizes this second taproot as he does the first. "*Primus in orbe deos fecit timor*," he writes in another place (ibid., p. 153). "Science has gone too far in rejecting that [assertion] entirely; the emotion felt by a man in the presence of nature certainly counts for something in the origin of religions," though "religion is less a fear than a reaction against fear." This does not mean that there is not some truth in Durkheim's speculations. If, as we have maintained, the system of social control remains incomplete without a religious coping stone, then there is a social need for some form of socializing and moralizing faith, as well as a psychological need or needs, and the Massa of the Senuffo is one answer to it, as were the parallel beliefs of the Australian brownmen on whose culture Durkheim based his analysis. Bergson sees both sides. "Man cannot exert his faculty of thought without imagining an uncertain future, which rouses his fears," he says (ibid., pp. 204, 205), and in this passage he exposes one function of religion: namely, to take the sting out of natural worry. But he also writes (ibid., pp. 204, 210): "Of all the creatures that live in society, man alone can swerve from the social line by giving way to selfish preoccupations when the common good is at stake. . . . Reflexion cannot be relied upon to keep up [a minimum of] selflessness. . . . That then is the office, that is the significance of the religion we have called static. . . ."

In recent sociological discussions, the concept of "functional imperative" has played a major role. Is religion—the belief in an ultimate guarantor of the social order, an all-seeing avenger of lawlessness—a functional imperative of this kind? General opinion today would certainly be disinclined to grant this, but the idea of a perfect judge in heaven behind the imperfect judges on earth has at least one characteristic which is—as both historical observation and logical analysis prove—common to all functional imperatives: ubiquity, presence in all cultures which have existed and endured. This fact has been convincingly demonstrated in a rich and most instructive book: Raffaele Pettazzoni's *The All-Knowing God* (trans. H. J. Rose [London, 1956]). We cannot possibly hope to use all the material which this great scholar has collected, but we can and will do two things: pick out an illustration here and there from his store in order to support our analysis; and correct one error which has crept into his analysis and which, if unremoved, would weaken the case which we are endeavoring to make.

One of the most precious historical documents which Pettazzoni used (see his p. 424), and which we can use as well, is Robert Fitzroy's *Narrative of the Surveying Voyages of H.M.S. Adventure and Beagle Between the Years 1826 and 1836*. Published (in London) as early as 1839, it puts us in contact with a truly primitive people, the inhabitants of Tierra del Fuego, and that at a period when they were not yet greatly altered by influences from outside. These Yagan or Yamana were convinced that misdeeds, even if undetected by human eyes, will not in the end escape due punishment. Fitzroy indeed writes: "I have never witnessed or heard of any act of a decidedly religious nature," and adds: "I am inclined to think that they have no thought of a future retribution." But if they have no thought of a future retribution, retribution in hell, they do have a very vivid apprehension of retribution in the immediate present, retribution on earth. Fitzroy refers to "their believing that the evil spirit torments them in this world, if they do wrong, by storms, hails, snow" and the like, and calls the existence of this conviction, very salutary from the point of view of social control, a "fact" (p. 179). On the next page we get a further pertinent statement and enlightening illustration:

> The natives whom I carried to England often amused us by their superstitious ideas, which showed, nevertheless, that their ideas were not limited by the visible world. If any thing was said or done that was wrong, in their opinion it was certain to cause bad weather. . . . A great black man is supposed to be always wandering about the woods and mountains, who is certain of knowing every word and every action; who cannot be escaped, and who influences the weather according to men's conduct.

One of these Fuegians, York,

> related a curious story of his own brother, who had committed a murder. . . . York said, in telling the story, "rain come down—snow come down—hail come down—wind blow—blow—very much. Very bad to kill man. Big man in woods no like it, he very angry." At the word "blow," York imitated the sound of a strong wind; and he told the whole story in a very low tone of voice, and with a mysterious manner, considering it an extremely serious affair.

From the religious point of view, this may appear a rather primitive belief, but as a safeguard of law-abiding conduct it can hardly have been entirely ineffective. "Afterwards York's brother was very sorry for what he had done, particularly when it began to blow very hard." Let us not forget either, in this context, that the oldest parts of our own Old Testament, too, think in terms of punishment in this life rather than of punishment beyond.

Other primitive inhabitants of the southern tip of South America have already concretized these vague beliefs and personified the law-enforcing agency in a manner more reminiscent of later creeds.

> Among the Ona of Selk'nam, who occupy practically the whole of the Isla Grande in Tierra del Fuego and are the extreme advanced post of the Patagonian hunters, the Supreme Being, who does not create, is known as Temáukel and thought of as a spirit. He is generally spoken of as "the One there above" or "the One in heaven," and indeed has his dwelling "beyond the stars." He can see everything and knows everything, never sleeps and perceives and knows all that happens. He watches to make sure that all his commands are implicitly obeyed and punishes those who transgress them with illness and early death, or with some epidemic which smites whole communities. To prevent a child doing something wrong, he is told that Temáukel sees everything, and to dis-

suade a young man from misbehaving himself with another's wife, the elders will tell him that "the One there above hears what you whisper to a woman." For Temáukel, besides seeing everyone and everything, hears what everyone says, and knows even his most hidden thoughts and intentions [Pettazzoni, *All-Knowing God*, p. 422].

In presenting the case of the Ona, we have in fact presented most, if not indeed all, primitive peoples, for parallel beliefs are traceable the wide world over. The details are, of course, different, but if we take a typological view, that is, if we concentrate on what is essential, they pale and vanish. The god Temáukel has a pendant in the Boyma and Daramulun of the Australian aborigines (ibid., pp. 350ff.), the Gawang of the Konyak Nagas of Assam (ibid., pp. 289ff.), the Peluga of the Andaman Islanders (ibid., p. 301), the Karei of the Semang of Malacca (ibid., p. 310), the Petara of the Iban or Sea Dyaks of Sarawak (Borneo) (ibid., p. 331), the Aluelap, with his son, Lugeleng, of Micronesia (ibid., p. 342), the Io or Iho of the Maori of New Zealand (ibid., p. 344), the Manitu of the Algonquin such as the Cree, the Oke of the Iroquois (ibid., pp. 373, 382), the Papachunati of the Cuna Indians of Panama beneath the North American continent and the Hila of the Caribou Eskimos above it (ibid., pp. 416, 355). What gives color to the pages of Pettazzoni's work is the frequent change of the divine names (of which we have adduced a few but by no means all). The substance of the beliefs clustering around the various divinities is very much the same.

In the above survey, we have given examples from all continents except Europe (of which we shall speak presently) and Africa. But Africa is in no way different from the other culture areas. "The idea of a Supreme Being who sees and knows everything is common to the generality of the miscellaneous populations of Negro Africa, be they hunters, tillers of the soil or herdsmen, patrilineal or matrilineal, totemists or animists, Bantu, Sudanese, Nilotics or Kushites," Pettazzoni writes (ibid., p. 34). "Omniscience is usually attributed to a celestial Being who is the author of weather phenomena and uses them to exercise a punitive sanction over men and their doings." This scholarly summary might well suffice, but let us still hear the authentic voice of one of the African peoples which is also a summary of a kind, a poetic summary (see ibid., p. 37): "In a hymn of the Akan (Ashanti) the omniscience of God, Onyame, is elaborated in the following terms:

> The sun shines and burns brightly down upon us,
> The moon rises in her splendour.
> The rain falls and the sun shines again,
> But the eye of God excels all these things,
> Nothing is hidden from it.
> You may be in the house, you may be in the water,
> Or in the thick shade of the trees,
> It is over you in every place.
> You think you are more cunning than an orphan child,
> You plot to take his goods and you cheat him,
> And you think 'No one can see me.'
> Consider, you are before the eye of God."

Coming now for a moment to Europe, or, to be precise, to the earlier cultures of Europe, we find that the Zeus of the ancient Greeks is none too different from the Temáukel of the Ona and the other heavenly avengers we have enumerated. "Among the Olympians," Pettazzoni writes (ibid., p. 145),

> omniscience is attributed especially to Zeus . . . and this is an omniscience . . . which has regard particularly to the destiny of men and to their deeds, and is associated with a punitive sanction. So in the *Iliad* (XVI, 385–388), Zeus punishes men who "in their assembly . . . thrust out justice, caring not for the watchful gaze of the gods." His punishment consists of a violent tempest, thus showing his nature as a god of the sky and especially the weather sky. His omniscience likewise is of one nature with his celestial character, by virtue of which he sees everything which men do.

Besides Homer, Pettazzoni parades further witnesses, such as Theognis and Pindar, but perhaps his best source is Hesiod, whose *Works and Days* (265–268, 238–242) we quote in a more pleasing translation than he uses (*Hesiod*, trans. A. S. Way [London, 1934], p. 8):

> That man doeth hurt to himself who causeth his neighbour to fall,
> And the plotting of mischief harmeth the plotter most of all.
> All-seeing and all-comprehending, the eye of Zeus oversees
> All this . . .
> . . . for them who of wanton outrage and brutal deeds are fain
> Doth far-seeing Zeus Kronion stern retribution ordain.

It might be thought that the development of higher intellectual sophistication would have tended to weaken these primitive imaginings, but the contrary is in fact the case. The advent of more rationalistic forms of philosophizing did nothing to undermine them; if anything, it strengthened them.

> Socrates, according to Xenophon's *Memorabilia* [I, 1, 19 and 4, 17–19], credited "the gods" or "deity" with omniscience. He departed from the conception of the gods contained in the traditional popular religion especially in this, that he would not suppose them cognisant of [only] some things but not of others, believing instead that they know everything, i.e. all that men say, do or secretly contrive, so that the divine omniscience is made up of universal hearing and vision (with omnipresence and universal oversight added), and nothing can escape it. Plato again speaks [in *The Laws* 901D, 905A] of the omniscience and universal vision of the gods and the impossibility of the sinner escaping their chastisement, even if he should hide in the bowels of the earth or fly up to the sky [Pettazzoni, *All-Knowing God*, p. 149].

With Socrates and Plato we leave the level of the simpler civilizations behind and ascend to that of the comparatively evolved cultures. We find among them more complicated, yet essentially identical, convictions. In Egypt,

> in a poem addressed to the king, dating from the New Kingdom, we read: "When thou restest in thy palace, thou art told how it is in every land; thou hearest the words of all lands, thou hast millions of ears. Thine eye shines brighter than the stars of the sky, and thou canst see better than the sun; though one speak with his mouth in a hole of the earth, yet it comes to thine ear. If one do what is hidden, yet will thine eye perceive it" [ibid., p. 50].

These words, taken from the document known as the Anastasi papyrus, can only be interpreted correctly if we remember that, according to Egyptian mysticism, the pharaoh or king is not so much a mortal person as an incarnation of the immortal Re, the high god and sky god. "This all-seeing and all-knowing capacity of the king," Pettazzoni explains (ibid.), "has for its prototype that of Re, the Sun." In the Vedic religion of India, the god Varuna plays the same role as Re (and, for that matter, as Temáukel). The Atharva-Veda (4.16.4), quoted by Pettazzoni (ibid., pp. 118–19), asserts:

> The great guardian among these [gods] sees as from anear. He that thinketh he is moving stealthily—all this the gods know. If a man stands, walks or sneaks about, if he goes slinking away, if he goes into his hiding-place; if two persons sit together and scheme, king Varuna is there as a third and knows it. He that should flee beyond the heaven far away would not be free from king Varuna. His spies come hither from heaven, with a thousand eyes do they watch over the earth. King Varuna sees through all that is between heaven and earth, and all that is beyond. He has counted the winkings of men's eyes. . . .

No less omniscient than Varuna is T'ien in classical China. "He too looks at what happens here below, especially at the conduct of men." A passage of the *Shu-King* (4.9.1.3) runs as follows: "In his inspection of men below, T'ien's first consideration is of their righteousness." In the course of time, "T'ien, owing to his patently celestial nature and the idea which is connected with him of a cosmic law governing the whole universe (Yih-king), takes on a less and less personal character, especially in the speculative developments of traditional thought. Nevertheless, T'ien, even in this philosophical phase, does not lose his attribute of knowing (and seeing) all" (ibid., pp. 273, 275). Thus, in this detail, we might compare Kung-tse and Meng-tse with Socrates and Plato. Among the Neo-Confucians, the great Chu-hsi still thinks like his forebears: "T'ien knows all our good [actions] and all our crimes. It is as if T'ien noted them down and numbered them up. Your good deeds are all before God, and my evil deeds will also be before Him" (ibid., p. 276).

We might easily prolong the list of our illustrations, speaking, for instance, of the Aztecs and Mayans, the Babylonians and the Phoenicians, the Iranians and the Hittites, but there is little point in constant reiteration. Let us rather come to the roots of Western culture, which means, in the first place, to Biblical Judaism. Those who know the Old Testament will surely, on reading the foregoing pages, have been reminded of Psalm 138 (according to the count of the Vulgate):

> Lord, thou hast proved me, and known me:
> thou hast known my sitting down, and my rising up.
> Thou hast understood my thoughts afar off. . . .
> Behold, O Lord, thou hast known all things. . . .
> My [very] bone is not hidden from thee. . . .
> Whither shall I go from thy spirit?
> Or whither shall I fly from thy face?
> If I ascend into heaven, thou art there:
> if I descend into hell, thou art present.

Other psalms have similar passages. Or take the book called Ecclesiasticus. It deals more particularly with a sin which is always committed under the cover of the night—adultery:

> Every man that passeth beyond his own bed, despising his own soul, and saying: Who seeth me? Darkness compasseth me about, and the walls cover me and no man seeth me: whom do I fear? the Most High will not remember my sins. And he understandeth not that his eye seeth all things. . . . And he knoweth not that the eyes of the Lord are far brighter than the sun, beholding round about all the ways of men . . . and looking into the hearts of men, into the most hidden parts [23:25–28].

We might continue here with quotations from the Book of Job (e.g., 34:22) or the Book of Wisdom (e.g., 1:6), but this would hardly serve any useful purpose. We have surely said enough.

A short side glance at Islam is in order at this point. For the sociologist, it is natural that he should cite as a star witness the great pioneer of his own science, Abdul Rahman Ibn Khaldun. In the invocation which precedes his Muqaddimah, we read: "Praised be God! . . . His knowledge is such that nothing, be it revealed in secret whispering or [even] left unsaid, remains strange to Him. His power is such that nothing in heaven and upon earth is too much for Him or escapes Him." Several suras of the Koran make this belief in the omniscience of God an integral part of the Moslem creed (for instance, 6:59–60, 24:35, 57:4, 59:22, 67:13–14). Let us hear the passage from the sixth chapter:

> With Him are the keys of the Unseen. . . .
> He knows what is in land and sea;
> not a leaf falls, but He knows it.
> Not a grain in the earth's shadows,
> not a thing, fresh or withered,
> but it is in a Book Manifest.
> . . . unto Him shall you return,
> then He will tell you of what
> you have been doing. . . .
> He sends recorders over you till,
> when any one of you is visited
> by death, Our messengers take him. . . .
> Then they are restored to God. . . .
> His is the judgment . . .

(Arthur J. Arberry, *The Koran Interpreted*, 2 vols. [London & New York, 1955], I 156).

From all that has gone before, it must surely have become obvious that belief in an all-seeing, all-hearing deity is part and parcel of practically all theological systems, the word taken in its widest connotation. If there are exceptions, they cannot possibly be significant. Yet here we meet with a curious attempt on Pettazzoni's part to limit the universality of the phenomenon. He asserts that omniscience belongs predominantly, if not exclusively, to sky gods, i.e., personifications of the sun, and such as have historically developed from this type of religious conceptualization. Earth gods, on the other hand, are not considered to be all-knowing. "The attribute of omniscience is . . . not inherent in the monotheistic idea of God, nor in that of a Supreme Being, nor in that of deity in general," he writes (*All-Knowing God*, p. 5). "The plain fact is that according to the evidence it is mostly sky-gods and astral gods, or gods somehow connected with the heavenly realms of light, to whom omniscience is ascribed. This is not to be wondered at, if we remember that . . . divine omniscience is a visual omniscience which naturally depends on light." One cannot help being amazed when one finds that Pettazzoni forgets an essential fact again and again coming to the surface in his own survey of the material—the fact that the gods are for the most part considered as all-hearing as well as all-seeing. But let us allow him to have his say. He tries to support his argument by a reference to the Greek pantheon. The earth-goddess "Demeter, who is one of the greater deities, is not omniscient, for she does not know where to find her ravished daughter." On the other hand, "Helios is omniscient, and he certainly is not one of the chief gods." What is this supposed to prove? At most this: that where, in a polytheistic system, one god or goddess is not credited with the power of omniscience, others must be. In Greece, these others included not only the modest Helios, but also the mighty Zeus, father of the Olympian family, a sky god, certainly, but more still the high god, the highest of the gods.

It is impossible to know whether Pettazzoni's own material contains evidence which tells against his assertion that chthonic deities are not usually regarded as omniscient. But it is certain that sources which have escaped him show that the primitive religious consciousness finds it not difficult to credit the earth or earth goddess—sisters, as it were, of Demeter—with the same power as the sun or a sun god. As we shall see in the next section, deities are regularly invoked when oaths are sworn or promises are made; since they know everything, they see the truth or falsehood of an asseveration and can judge the purity of the promessor's intentions; they are both invaluable witnesses and reliable guarantors. Now, according to Jacob Grimm's *Deutsche Rechtsaltertümer* (edd. A. Heusler and R. Hübner, 2 vols. [Leipzig, 1899], I 154ff., esp. 163ff.; II 547), the Germanic tribes knew an oath invoking the earth or earth mother, and the ritual concerned is very revealing: two parallel incisions were made into a grass-grown piece of land and the sward loosened in this way slightly lifted. The person taking the oath thereupon pushed his feet under the loosened sward and then made his statement or gave his promise. Certainly, a widespread formula was "by the southern sun" and "by the holy light," but swearing "on the greensward" existed side by side with it and maintained itself, at least in northern Germany, well into modern times (see Friedrich Thudichum, *Geschichte des Eides* [Tübingen, 1911], pp. 16, 17). Passages in the Gospel according to St. Matthew (5:35) and the *Iliad* (3.279–82, 14.270–72) lead us to suppose that Jews and Greeks , too, knew a habit of swearing "by the earth."

As can be seen, a wider and perhaps less slanted study of the sources would have led even Pettazzoni to recognize that a belief in divine omniscience is by no means restricted to religious cultures clustering around sun worship. In the same way, a deeper logical analysis would have shown him that the quality of omniscience *is* inherent in the very concept of a Supreme Being, and especially in monotheism, for how can an omnipotent God not be also omniscient? But our disagreement with the great scholar stems neither from a different use of the sources nor from a contrast in conceptualization; it springs much rather from an unlikeness of fundamental attitudes. The sociologist will unavoidably see the root of the credal element which we are discussing in a social need—a "functional imperative"—the need for an ultimate guarantor of peace and order who is not imperfect, like the human judge, but perfect, all-knowing as well as all-powerful. Pettazzoni, with his own particular background, was too one-sidedly interested in the relation of man and nature; the sociological aspect did not find due attention on his part. Whenever and wherever a society strives for maximal integration and harmony, the concept of an eternal judge will tend to appear.

A strong and sustained upsurge of rationalism will, of course, ultimately erode this belief and with it one of the great historical safeguards of societal peace, but it is important and instructive to note that even the far-advanced eighteenth century still firmly held to it. Let us hear two voices from that time, one British, the other French, one individual and the other collective—Adam Smith and the representatives of the revolutionary *Commune de Paris*. Smith, in his *Theory of Moral Sentiments*, published in 1759, anticipates the results of Pettazzoni's researches when he writes: "In every religion and in every superstition that the world has ever beheld . . . there has been a Tartarus as well as an Elysium; a place provided for the punishment of the wicked as well as one for the reward of the just." In these very last words, Smith goes beyond Pettazzoni's insights for he reveals not only the *what*, but also the *wherefore*, of the phenomenon. Even clearer in this respect is a passage later in the book:

> When the general rules which determine the merit and demerit of actions come thus to be regarded as the laws of an all-powerful being, who watches over our conduct, and who, in a life to come, will reward the observance and punish the breach of them, they necessarily acquire a new sacredness from this consideration. . . . The idea that however we may escape the observation of man or be placed above the reach of human punishment, yet we are always acting under the eye and exposed to the punishment of God, the great avenger of injustice, is a motive capable of restraining the most headstrong passions, with those at least who, by constant reflection, have rendered it familiar to them [pp. 132, 241].

The French Revolution, as is well known, instituted a Cult of Reason, in an attempt to provide a modern substitute for traditional religion, and when The Convention passed its decree, the *Commune de Paris* sent a letter of approval and congratulation. In it occur the following lines:

> Yes, indeed, the Supreme Being, who keeps all nature in motion, deigns to direct his benevolent regards toward the men of good will. This thought, without a doubt, leads the citizen in the direction of virtue; it is the reward of the goodness which it has induced him to love. . . . If the idea of the existence of a deity is [thus] precious for the man of good will, it is hateful to the evildoer, and in this way it is useful to society. The perverted person, alarmed by this doctrine, believes himself incessantly accompanied by a powerful and awe-inspiring witness whom he cannot escape and who sees him and watches him

even while his neighbors are asleep [F. A. Aulard, *Le Culte de la raison et le culte de l'être suprème, 1793–1794* (Paris, 1892), pp. 281, 285, 286].

The foregoing pages have already revealed the salient fact: the fact that in history the belief in divine omniscience has never been merely a theoretical tenet, but always also a conviction of incisive consequences—beneficent consequences, we might say, if the coherence of society is indeed a value to be cherished and to be pursued. Let us now, in conclusion, adduce some evidence which goes to show how conscious society has always been of this support which religion provides for the survival and the smooth functioning of social life. We quote first, without apology and out of historical order, the words which Shakespeare in *Hamlet* (III.iii.57–64) puts into the mouth of the conscience-plagued king, Claudius. They show, with incomparable clarity, how and why God, as the eternal, omniscient judge, is, soberly speaking, the highest instance in the system of social control:

> In the corrupted currents of this world
> Offence's gilded hand may shove by justice,
> And oft 'tis seen the wicked prize itself
> Buys out the law; but 'tis not so above;
> There is no shuffling, there the action lies
> In his [sic] true nature, and we ourselves compell'd
> Even to the teeth and forehead of our faults
> To give in evidence.

In the Old Testament, the hardest sayings come from the prophet Amos, the great hater of social injustice. He inveighs against those who sin out of covetousness (9:1–4):

> there shall be no flight for them: they shall flee, and he that shall flee of them shall not be delivered. Though they go down even to hell, thence shall my hand [God's hand] bring them out: and though they climb up to heaven, thence will I bring them down. And though they be hid in the top of Carmel, I will search and take them away from thence: and though they hide themselves from my eyes in the depth of the sea, there will I command the serpent; and he shall bite them. And if they go into captivity . . . , there will I command the sword. . . . And I will set my eyes upon them for evil, and not for good.

There is a widespread opinion according to which Greek religiosity was a rather smiling one, in contrast to Judaism and Christianity with their stern conceptions. A closer look must dispel this impression. The evildoer was no more leniently handled in Athens than at Jerusalem. The *Frogs* by Aristophanes gives us some idea of the more popular beliefs. In order to get to the other world, the departed has to cross a large lake. He must pass through stretches filled with snakes and monsters, through moor and bog and filth, before the myrtle grove of the blessed is reached. The pathway is as narrow as a sword, and no one who is loaded with guilt can successfully traverse it: he must fall into the waters underneath. If Plato's *Gorgias* 81 (525cff.) is to be trusted, Socrates was very close indeed to the Christian tradition because he, too, made a distinction like that between purgatory and hell. In Hades, those guilty of forgivable faults suffer pains which ultimately free them from their relatively minor injustices. But those who arrive laden with major injustices, with unforgivable sins, have to endure eternal torments of the worst kind. They serve as warnings to all who are tempted to follow in their footsteps. The firm belief that justice is ultimately done and that the powers above guarantee that this shall be so sustained Socrates in his darkest hour. The one thing about which he had no doubt, so Plato's *Phaedo* (63c) reports (see More, *Religion of Plato*, p. 72), was that his soul is about to pass into the presence of gods who shall judge, not as men do, but justly and righteously.

As for Plato's own philosophy, it rested on two strong pillars: his conviction that men are apt to fall into sin and that they are justly punished by the gods; and his belief that the punishment, always merited, is meted out in the course of a transmigration of souls. To speak of the second aspect first—metempsychosis. It was his view that "He that lived well the appointed time should pass again to the home of his kindred star, there to enjoy a happy and congenial life. But failing this, he should be changed in his second incarnation to the nature of a woman; and if still in this case he ceased not from wickedness, according to the manner of his evil-doing he should change always to some such bestial nature as resembled the character born within him." If these conceptions resembled Indian rather than Christian ideas, the other chief element in Plato's creed is near-Christian. The Christian estimate of man—the doctrine of the Fall—suggests that he is prone to evil. The great Greek philosopher entertained a similar opinion. A shadow lies over every human being. "In the terms of Plato's philosophy it might be defined as an inherent reluctance of the soul to face honestly the dualism of man's nature and . . . to acknowledge its own darker member and turn from that to what is akin in itself to the gods." The gods gave to humanity laws by the observance of which they might ennoble themselves, and these laws were "established and pronounced to the souls, to the end that [the powers of heaven] might be guiltless of the evil hereafter incurred by any of them" (ibid., pp. 184, 251, 185).

A quotation from the fourth book of *The Laws* will show the exactitude of this summary. The wise Athenian speaks in the following terms to his young interlocutor:

> "This," as Homer says, "is the justice of the gods who inhabit Olympus"—that he who grows in vice shall make his journey to the more vicious souls, and that he who grows in virtue shall journey to the more virtuous souls, receiving in life and in all his deaths such treatment as it behooves like to receive from like. Think not that you or any other shall ever escape this justice or shall ever boast to have outwitted the gods; above all other laws of justice this law has been ordained by those who have ordained, and it were well to heed it with all care. For never shall you be unheeded by it; neither in your littleness shall you sink into the bowels of the earth, nor in your exaltation shall you mount in flight to the heavens, but you shall pay the fitting vengeance of the gods, either while abiding here, or when you have made your journey to Hades, or have been conveyed to some place more savage than these [in ibid., pp. 101–102; see also pp. 262, 263].

In yet another context of *The Laws* (see ibid., p. 250) Plato calls "the storied vengeance of the nether world" "the ancient and universal belief of mankind." He sums up his convictions in a terse but impressive sentence (ibid., p. 75): "No one who believes in the gods as law and custom ordain has ever voluntarily done an impious deed or uttered a lawless word." In all this the later Platonists followed their master with great faithfulness.

Judaism and Hellenism—the piety of Amos and the reasoning of Plato—formed the twin root from which Catholic Christianity was to grow. But something entirely different and incomparably superior entered into it as well: the concept of a loving and therefore forgiving God, preached and lived by Jesus Christ. In Bergson's terminology which we have made our own: dynamic religiosity broke into the static religions of antiquity and created a new spiritual condition, a condition characterized by its complexity. With the problem which this development brought with it, we shall have to grapple later on. Here let us conclude by pointing out that the support given by the older creeds to social integration, the belief in an all-seeing and all-just Eternal Judge, was unavoidably preserved under the new dispensation. Indeed, it was in a way still more highly profiled. There arose the vision of a Last Judgment at which the goats and the sheep, the wicked and the good, would finally be separated, the former to suffer eternal damnation, the latter to receive the reward of never-ending bliss. Many a sculptor and many a painter placed it impressively—physically —before men's eyes. It also met them in the words of the great hymn—the *Dies irae*—traditionally ascribed to Thomas of Celano, which might be freely translated as follows:

> Day of judgment, day of doom!
> Fire shall the world consume
> As foretold by prophets gloom.
>
> Oh, what trembling there will be,
> When the judge shall take his see
> To assay iniquity!
>
> Of each deed is record made.
> When the book is open laid,
> No guilt's price remains unpaid.
>
> What shall I, a wretch, then say?
> Who for me can plead and pray,
> If the just must dread that day?
>
> King of awesome majesty,
> Whose best gift is granted free,
> Fount of mercy, save thou me.

These terrifying words were, for centuries, sung or recited during every Mass for the dead, that is, precisely at the time when every member of the congregation was fully aware of the transitoriness of human life, and when the ethical doctrine of the responsibility of the individual for that life, the necessity of giving an account of his doings, was sure to make the deepest impression. The *Dies irae* has doubtlessly contributed powerfully to the socialization and moralization of generations of men.

One final word before we leave this subject. Not only is God the judge of all men, but he is more particularly the judge of judges. Judges are as fallible as all other humans, but their injustices must necessarily have far more serious consequences than those of the common run of men. The Old Testament (2 Chr. 19:1, 5–7) reflects the fear, ever present in every society, that those called to be defenders of right may turn into promoters of wrong: "And Josaphat king of Juda returned to his house in peace to Jerusalem. . . . And he set judges of the land in all the fenced cities of Juda, in every place. And charging the judges, he said: Take heed what you do: for you exercise not the judgment of man, but of the Lord. And whatsoever you judge, it shall redound to you. Let the fear of the Lord be with you. . . ." These last words certainly contain an admonition, perhaps even a threat, but, if so, it is only mild. Not so the words of the prophet Isaiah (5:22–24): "Woe to you . . . that justify the wicked for gifts, and take away the justice of the just from him! Therefore as the tongue of the fire devoureth the stubble, and the heat of the flame consumeth it: so shall their root be as ashes, and their bud shall go up as dust. For they have cast away the law of the Lord of hosts, and have blasphemed . . . the Holy One of Israel." God is not only behind the judge on the bench but also above him, and these associated facts should guarantee that right remains right and that wrong disappears from the life of society.

RELIGION AS A SUPPLEMENT OF CUSTOM AND LAW. THE SACRED OATH

133. We have just heard King Josaphat urging his judges to remember that they were exercising not only the judgment of man, but also that of the Lord. This formulation brings to the surface the general support which religious ideas give to the social order: they sanctify tradition and add to the weaker arms of the law the stronger arm of heaven. This is a point which Bergson's book *The Two Sources of Morality and Religion* throws into high relief. "Originally the whole of morality is custom," he writes (p. 123), "and as religion forbids any departure from custom, morality is coextensive with religion." On the next page he continues:

> The myth . . . will never clearly distinguish between the physical order and the moral or social order, between intentional orderliness due to obedience of all to a law and the orderliness manifested in the course of nature. . . . Even to-day we have hardly rid ourselves of this confusion; traces of it linger in our language. Mores and morality, regularity and regulation, uniformity *de facto* and uniformity *de jure* are in each case both expressed in much the same way. Does not the word "order" signify both systems and command?

He who has created the system of nature has also issued the commands that keep the mill of society grinding, and that without undue friction.

Still, there is and remains a contrast between an objective necessity on the one hand and a subjective and voluntary submission on the other, and no very high development of rationality is needed to reveal it. Yet—and this is Bergson's salient point, which bears all the marks of a true insight on its face—the gap between the two is closed by religiousness. "The first effect of religion is to sustain and reinforce the claims of society," Bergson argues (pp. 12, 13). Certainly,

> the law which enunciates facts is one thing, the law which commands, another. It is possible to evade the latter; here we have obligation, not necessity. The former is, on the contrary, unescapable. . . . True enough; but to the majority of people the distinction is far from being so clear. A law, be it physical, social or moral—every law—is in their eyes a command. There is a certain order of nature which finds expression in laws: the facts are presumed to "obey" these laws so as to conform with that order. The scientist himself can hardly help believing that the law "governs" facts. . . . But if physical law tends to assume in our imagination the form of a command when it attains to a certain degree of generality, in its turn an imperative which applies to everybody appears to us somewhat like a law of nature. The two ideas, coming against each other in our minds, effect an exchange. The law borrows from the command its prerogative of compulsion; the command receives from the law its inevitability.

It is clear where the great force comes from which ties the two variants of law together: it is the crowning concept of religion, the belief in a godhead who is supreme lawgiver of both nature and humanity. "Religion therefore, in our eyes, succeeds in filling the gap, already narrowed by our habitual way of looking at things, between a command of society and a law of nature."

There is little which needs to be added to the clear analysis which Bergson has elaborated. Let us merely recall that religion, through its imagery, manages to make the assumed identity of earthly and heavenly law visible and impressive. On the top of the stele on which the famous Laws of Hammurabi are inscribed, we see the sun-god Shamash, father of Kettu (Justice) and Mešaru (Righteousness), handing the code to his representative in the subastral world. We may safely consider this representation as a universal symbol. Even the Old Testament, so disinclined to be pictorial, asserts that Moses received God's commandments directly from him on Mount Sinai (Ex 19ff.; Dt 5).

But the influence of religion on social life, its integration and continued coherence, is not restricted to a general strengthening of social control and hence of the social bond; it also shows itself in the closing of certain specific gaps, or, say, the healing of certain concrete weaknesses, from which the institutions of society, being the work of imperfect creatures, unavoidably suffer. There are, for instance, a number of crimes which it is next to impossible to discover; incest springs to mind at once, for its only witnesses are, almost invariably, the perpetrators themselves. How can their dark deed be brought to light? The Code of Hammurabi just mentioned knows how to get at the truth: it demands that a person under suspicion be made to swear a solemn oath. The Babylonians obviously believed that a reliable asseveration of innocence (or even admission of guilt) would not be made unless the gods are invoked and asked to be its witnesses and, in case of falsity, avengers. Adultery is a similar case. The following verses from the Fourth Book of Moses (Nb 5:11ff.) are not quite clear, so far as the ritual involved is concerned, but they are very clear when they are taken as a piece of legal procedure, and at the same time as a call upon God to help where human efforts in the pursuit of truth fail:

> And the Lord spoke to Moses saying: Speak to the children of Israel and thou shalt say to them: The man whose wife shall have gone astray and, contemning her husband, shall have slept with another man, and her husband cannot discover it, but the adultery is secret and cannot be proved by witnesses . . . he shall bring her to the priest. . . . And when the woman shall stand before the Lord, he [the priest] shall uncover her head, and shall put on her hands the sacrifice of remembrance and the oblation of jealousy. And he himself shall hold the most bitter waters wheron he has heaped curses with execration. And he shall adjure her and shall say: If another man hath not slept with thee, and if thou be not defiled by forsaking thy husband's bed, these most bitter waters, on which I have heaped curses, shall not hurt thee. But if thou hast gone aside from thy husband, and art defiled, and hast lain with another man, these curses shall light upon thee. The Lord make thee . . . an example for all among his people. May he make thy thigh to rot, and may thy belly swell and burst asunder. . . . And the woman shall answer: Amen, amen. And the priest shall write these curses in a book, and shall wash them out with the most bitter waters, upon which he hath heaped the curses, and he shall give them her to drink. . . . And when she hath drunk them, if she be defiled and, having despised her husband, be guilty of adultery, the malediction shall go through her, and her belly swelling, her thigh shall rot. . . . But if she be not defiled, she shall not be hurt, and shall bear children.

The last three words show that "thigh" is a delicate cover term for "genitals" and was surely so understood. The threat held over the head of the accused woman was thereby made more impressive, one might almost say: more poetic. For if she had indeed sinned and denied the fact, the punishment for the misdeed and the lie which followed it was to fall where the sin had been committed.

Hegel has spoken of a "cunning of reason" (*List der Vernunft*), meaning in this context *objective* reason, i.e., that striving for purposive solutions to social problems which permeates the processes of collective life, and which sometimes seems to use tricks such as subjective reason, the conscious strategy of the individual in the pursuit of his own ends, also invents. Here we have a case in point. The oath mobilizes, so to speak, the culprit's fear of sickness or other evil and presses it into the service of truth and social control. For the oath is essentially a conditional self-condemnation: if I lie, may Heaven strike me with disaster! The truncated formula which has survived into our rationalistic age—"so help me God"—ran originally:"so help me God unto eternal life," which meant, of course, at the same time, "so preserve me God from everlasting torment in hell." In history, the malediction pronounced upon oneself was often much more concrete and therefore still more frightening. We have just encountered one example, but there are numerous others. The Romans swore on their eyes; so, somewhat surprisingly, yet understandably, did the Samoans (see A. E. Crawley, "Oath (Introductory and Primitive)," *Encyclopaedia of Religion and Ethics*, ed. James Hastings 13 vols. [Edinburgh & New York,

1955], IX 431). Among the Greeks, the Erinyes, never resting, never sleeping pursuers and tormentors, were "personified oaths and curses" (ibid., 433)—to use a colloquialism, perhaps a little too frivolous in this context, chickens coming home to roost. But easily the most alarming formula, and also one of the most widespread, was to the effect that lightning should strike the taker of the oath if his oath was false. Both the Greeks and the Romans, besides many primitive peoples, used this device. "In the Homeric formulae of oaths," Pettazzoni informs us (*All-Knowing God*, p. 145), "Zeus is the first of the deities called upon to witness and guarantee what is sworn to and punish any violation of it which may occur. . . . So at Olympia a statue of Zeus Horkios, Zeus of the Oath, . . . had in either hand a thunderbolt with which to punish false swearers." In Rome, Jupiter, the highest of the gods, ensured the sanctity of the oath and the condign punishment of perjury.

> Juppiter was a sky-god, and therefore his sanction was exerted by means of the thunderbolt (Iuppiter Fulgur). The oldest and holiest oath was taken in the name of Iuppiter Lapis, and the *lapis* in question was a thunderstone, that is to say a pointed flint supposed to be the vehicle and remnant of the thunderbolt. To swear *per Jovem Lapidem* meant that the swearer, if he broke his oath, exposed himself to being smitten by Juppiter's thunderbolt by way of punishment [ibid., p. 163].

In his *Titus Andronicus* (V.i.77–80), Shakespeare puts some words into the mouth of one of his characters which fit well into the context of the present section. Aaron says:

> . . . that I know:
> An idiot holds his bauble for a god,
> And keeps the oath which by that god he swears. . . .

This is quite true! But no society has entrusted the holiness of the oath and the suppression of perjury to a god who may be likened to a bauble. On the contrary. It is invariably the supreme divinity, like Zeus and Jupiter, who is called upon to aid society in this respect.

As far as this detail is concerned, there is once again complete unanimity across the continents. We might at this point restart our journey from one end of the globe to the other, but this is hardly necessary. What we said of divine omniscience in the last section applies here as well, since the concept of omniscience is quite obviously the root and the mainstay of the whole institution of the oath. We adduce only one or two instances in order to prove beyond the shadow of a doubt that the supervision of oath-taking is everywhere placed into the most capable hands. Let us begin with those proto-Chinese who are known as Miao-tse or "Children of the Land." "It is a fact," Pettazzoni writes (*All-Knowing God*, p. 282), "that the Miao of to-day possess the idea of a supreme celestial Being or principle called Ndo. The word *ndo* means the physical sky, the firmament, also weather, seasons, but it also means the Supreme Being, God. . . . 'Ndo sees' and 'Ndo knows' are expressions in current use, particularly in oaths. . . . All this finds an exact parallel among the Tungus." In Africa corresponding traditions abound. "Among the Bantu of Ruanda and

Urundi . . . Imana is all-knowing and all-seeing, and nothing is hidden from him. This is plain from numerous proverbs, turns of speech and . . . swearing, as 'Imana sees me,' 'Imana watches over me,' 'May Imana see and punish you.' " Similarly, "among the Galla or Oromo . . . one of the most usual forms of asseveration, in oaths and elsewhere, is 'Waqa knows,' or 'Waqa sees me' " (ibid., pp. 35, 40). One of the most primitive tribes of North America is the Athabascan. "Their usual oath-formula was 'That-which-is-on-high-heareth-me' or 'I am in the presence of That-which-is-on-high' " (ibid., p. 371). The situation is the same among the Iroquois, Dakota, Crow, Kiowa, Tarahumare, and Tarasco (ibid., pp. 383ff., 405, 20). It makes little difference that later civilizations substituted oaths on their sacred books. Thus Moslems swear on the Koran, Jews on the Hebrew Bible, and Christians on the Gospels. These three religious communities have always remembered King Solomon's prayer to God (2 K 8:31–32; see also 2 Chr 6:22–23): "If any man trespass against his neighbour and have an oath upon him wherewith he is bound, and come because of the oath before the altar of thy house, then hear thou in heaven. And do and judge thy servants, condemning the wicked and bringing his way upon his own head; and justifying the just and rewarding him according to his justice."

We must and can leave the further detail to the science of religion. For the core area of sociology, two other uses of the device we are studying are interesting and important: the promissory oath and the oath of office. Both are effective safeguards of law and order. When a contract of any kind is concluded, there is the danger that one party or the other, or indeed both, may intend not to fulfill the obligations which they have taken upon themselves; when a man is placed in a position of authority and power, there is the parallel danger that he may use it, not for the benefit of the public, but for his own enrichment. Both dangers are diminished, and in favorable cases even removed, when the contracting parties and the appointed power holders swear that they will act as they should. Speaking more especially of early Anglo-Saxon society, but by no means only of it, Pollock and Maitland write: "There is no evidence of any regular process of enforcing contracts, but no doubt promises of any special importance were commonly made on oath, with the purpose and result of putting them under the sanction of the church. There is great reason to believe that everywhere or almost everywhere a religious sanction of promises has preceded the secular one" (Sir Frederick Pollock and Frederic Maitland, *The History of English Law* [Cambridge, 1898], I 57, 58). The Hebrews, Greeks, and Romans certainly strengthened the binding power of the treaties which they concluded by solemnly inviting divine punishment if they were untrue to their word.

How fruitful the intervention of religious conceptions was in the development and stabilization of human interaction can be seen by a side glance at the history of commerce, and especially international trade. The Romans had a somewhat minor deity, Mercury, who, like Jupiter, was omniscient. His proper function was to watch over the safety of the roads and the sanctity of contracts, both equally essential to the exchange of commodities between south and north. As we know from Caesar's *De bello Gallico* (7.17.1), the Romans discovered in Gaul an apparently parallel deity whose name appears as Visucius, perhaps

from the Celtic *visu* or *vissu* which means "to know." When business trans-
actions between Roman and Gaulish traders were arranged, it was reassuring
to call upon Mercury-Visucius to witness the pact and to act as guarantor of
good faith (see Pettazzoni, *All-Knowing God*, pp. 198, 199). The Romans
might not have feared the wrath of Visucius nor the Gauls that of Mercury; but
both of them would have been decidedly reluctant to fall foul of the god of
commerce, and of the commerce-supporting oath, in their pantheon.

The oath of office—the "swearing-in"—is still so much part and parcel of
political practice that it is hardly necessary to say much about it. Has it de-
teriorated and declined into an empty formality? Who knows? Only one thing
is certain: namely, that in a believing age it is of considerable power. The
temptation to act against it—"power corrupts"—is, however, great in every
society and therefore these oaths are often rather dramatic and severe. Thus
the Byzantine Empire introduced in the year 535 the following formula:

> I swear by Almighty God and His only begotten Son, our Lord Jesus Christ,
> and by the Holy Spirit, and by Mary, the holy and glorious Mother of God
> ever virgin, and by the four Gospels which I hold in my hands, and by the holy
> archangels Michael and Gabriel, . . . that . . . in my administrative work I shall
> keep my conscience clean and shall serve in all honesty and take upon me all
> necessary labors and cares, and that with devotion and without craftiness and
> deception. . . .

Then follows an enumeration of the duties one by one, and the oath concludes
with these dreadful words:

> If I shall fail to act in anything as I have now solemnly promised, may I, not
> only here, but also in the world to come, receive and accept, at the terrible
> judgment of God, our supreme Lord, and Jesus Christ, our Redeemer, what
> is justly coming to me, together with Judas and the leprosy of Giezi and the
> trembling of Cain; and in addition, may I be visited by the punishments which
> are laid down in the laws of their imperial majesties [cited in Thudichum,
> *Geschichte des Eides*, p. 14].

If these words sound harsh, what shall we say of the following oath, demanded,
as late as 1896, of the higher court officials in the kingdom of Siam? (ibid.,
pp. 123, 124):

> May the blood drain from every vein of my body; may lightning split me into
> two parts; may crocodiles devour me; may I be condemned to carry water in
> bottomless baskets through the fires of hell; may I, after my death, wander
> into the body of a slave who has to endure, through as many years as there are
> grains of sand in the desert and drops of water in the sea, the hardest possible
> treatment; may I be reborn as a blind, deaf, and dumb beggar covered with the
> most repulsive sores; may I be thrust immediately into hell if I ever break my
> oath.

Such a formula sounds shocking and even absurd, yet, no less than milder
forms, it clearly shows what the essence of the oath is: a conditional self-
imprecation, a conditional curse upon one's own head.

Because of the specifically religious nature of the oath, we must, before we
leave this subject, bring up the unambiguous prohibition of oath-taking which

is contained in Christ's Sermon on the Mount (Mt 5:33–34)—a surprising injunction since the oath looms so very large in the Old Testament (see Lv 27, Nb 30, Dt 23:21–24, and Jg 11:30ff.): "You have heard that it was said to them of old, thou shalt not forswear thyself . . . but I say to you not to swear at all." This admonition is repeated in the Epistle of St. James (5:12), but otherwise it is not to be found in the New Testament. Mark, Luke, and John do not record it. More interestingly still, St. Paul freely used oath-resembling terms of speech, for instance, "God is my witness" (Rm 1:9 and Ph 1:8; see also 2 Co 1:23 and 11:11, 31; Ga 1:20; 1 Th 2:5, 10; 1 Tm 5:21; see further Heb 6:13ff.). Later on, no Catholic or Orthodox, and no Protestants like Luther and Calvin, forbade the oath. Do we not have here before us a falling away from Christ's behest and from His high standards? Do we not have before us a proof of that "routinization of charisma," of which Max Weber has made so much in his sociology of religion? This may seem a very difficult problem to handle, especially for those who, like the present writer, believe that Weber exaggerated the legalization of Christianity because he saw only the church of the bishops, the administrative officers, and not that of the saints, the perpetuators of the Founder's charisma (see Stark, *Sociology of Religion* IV, passim, but esp. 136ff.).

In fact, however, this apparent difficulty is easy enough to remove. There are two contrasting reasons why Jesus should have spoken out against oath-taking. The first is that the oath had become meaningless in the world in which He moved. W. Ernest Beet, an outstanding expert (see "Oath (NT and Christian)," *Encyclopaedia of Religion and Ethics*, IX 434, 435), has explained how deep this particular device of social ordering and judicial procedure had sunk in the course of time. "[T]he Jews held," he writes,

> that only oaths so distinguished from the mere promise, and only some of these, need be kept. An elaborate system of distinctions between oaths, which would have moved the admiration of a mediaeval casuist, had been gradually evolved; a lie was not held to be sinful unless sworn to, and even perjury itself was at worst venial, unless the broken oath had been taken in a particular form. Such a system necessarily cut at the root of that good faith apart from which a well-ordered social organism becomes impossible. . . .

If this characterization of the contemporary condition is correct—and there is no reason to doubt that it is, even though later Jewish ethics, as reflected in the rabbinic literature, took a far sterner view, a view closely akin to that of Jesus—then Jesus objected to the abuse of the oath-taking ceremony which had crept in rather than to the proper use of it. Beet also draws our attention to another salient point: namely that verses 34 through 36 expressly condemn, not the formula "by God," but only such less solemn and more colloquial phrases as "by heaven" and "by my head." He writes:

> The fact that the oaths mentioned in this prohibition, in which there is no specific citation of the Divine Name, are typical examples of just the kind of oath that many Jews of that day lightly took, and broke without scruple, renders it not improbable that what our Lord had in mind was not so much the oath seriously taken and honourably observed as the light swearing . . . that all too frequently degraded the oath into a form as useless as it was profane.

It was particularly the more conservative Protestant reformers, and in the first place John Calvin, who removed the prohibition of oath-taking from the Christian code of ethics by saying that in Matthew 5:34, Christ had spoken, not as universal lawgiver, but merely as a local preacher. (Their removal of the ban on interest, on usury, was along parallel lines.) But there is a second consideration, and it weighs more heavily in the scales. Very close attention to the wording of verse 37, in conjunction with verse 48 of the same chapter, will help us to discover what is involved. Verse 37 runs: "Let your speech be: Yea, yea, No, no. And that which is over and above these is of evil." This surely means that the formulas of asseveration which constitute the core of oath-taking, and indeed the whole institution of the oath, are the products of a wicked world, are "of evil"—products of a world in which the naked assurance is not to be trusted, in which lying is endemic. If the hearers of the Sermon on the Mount were to be true disciples of Christ, i.e., godly men—and Christ admonished them in verse 48 to be "perfect, as also your heavenly Father is perfect"—then the oath could have no place in their circle. Honest in all things, their mere word would be as good as any other declaration, however decked out and dramatized. To invoke God was, to say the least, unnecessary, a work of supererogation, and would as such fall under the injunction of the Second Commandment: "Thou shalt not take the name of the Lord thy God in vain" (Ex 20:7). Those revolutionary sects who thought of themselves as saints—the Essenes in antiquity, for instance, and in modern times especially the Quakers—therefore quite logically refused to swear, even in court. As for the Catholics and Orthodox, they accepted the solemnization of important asseverations and the traditional self-imprecations connected with them as regrettable but helpful devices needed in an imperfect, crime-ridden world. With this attitude toward the oath, with this conception of its function in society as it was and is, the student of social control must certainly agree.

SACRED THINGS

134. In the context of our research effort, the institution of the oath is no more than a narrow illustration of a very broad tendency—the tendency of religion to supplement the operation of the society-building and society-sustaining forces where these prove unequal to their task. Logically we must expect the same phenomenon on a particularly large scale when and where the state, as the order-creating agency *par excellence*, is particularly weak. A study of history proves that this is indeed so. When feudalism splintered political power into minute fragments, when the petty nobles to all intents and purposes became uncontrolled masters in their territories and the influence of emperor and king was reduced to the lowest level, it was the Church, backed by a strong popular movement, which promoted the cause of public order and safety by fathering and fostering, first the so-called *pax Dei*, and later its successor, the *treuga Dei*, two peace-promoting efforts in a world lacerated by internecine petty warfare and bleeding from a thousand wounds.

Our concrete illustration must necessarily be the case of France for nowhere else in the West did feudal anarchy develop to the same extent. England would not serve our purpose at all. In his native Normandy, William the Conqueror was an energetic supporter of the peace movement. When he crossed the Channel and made himself lord of the island, he was resolved to defend and preserve with a strong hand public order and safety in his newly won kingdom, and he succeeded fairly well. As early as under Edward the Confessor, the Domesday Book had spoken of a *treuva regis*, but the expression *treuga Dei* did not occur. William was much more powerful than Edward, however, and under him "the king's peace" became the mainstay of England's social life. Where he had led, his able sons, William II Rufus and Henry I, followed. It was only after the latter's death in the year 1135 that the country drifted into a condition of rising lawlessness which made the intervention of the Church desirable. A council at London, convened in 1143, passed several canons one of which ordained "that the ploughs in the fields, with their ploughmen, should enjoy the same peace as if they were on consecrated ground," and threatened breakers of this law with excommunication. With the accession of Henry II in 1154, the brief interlude of royal debility was over, and it was once again the king's peace, and not the "peace of God," which was in command. Of course, we must not overlook the fact that the king's peace was also a "peace of God"; or, perhaps we should say, was also a priest's peace, a sacred peace, for the king of England was considered as God's representative on earth (see Stark, *Sociology of Religion*, I, esp. 56ff.; Hartmut Hoffman, *Gottesfriede und Treuga Dei* [Stuttgart, 1964], pp. 244, 254ff.).

The canons of the Council of London in 1143 remind the experts of the canons of the Council of Rouen held in 1096 (Hoffmann, *Gottesfriede und Treuga Dei*, p. 255; see also p. 176): both contain, as a central concern, the defense—we might even say, the sanctification—of the plowman and the plow. But the Council of Rouen was no isolated event; it was one of a large number of Church assemblies with the same purpose in view: the pacification of the land. The chain begins with the Synods of Le Puy (975/994) and Charroux (ca. 989) and ends in the thirteenth century only after the central power or the major regional powers had developed enough muscle to hold down the lawlessness of the petty nobles. We are not concerned here with the historical detail; nor need we try to assess the effectivity of the whole movement: while not totally successful, it was not totally without success either. We would only consider two aspects: the close articulation of the movement with the nature and the needs arising from the contemporary social situation and its religious basis or bases.

As far as the first point is concerned, we can best achieve a proper understanding if we try to familiarize ourselves with the historical facts and then endeavor to see them in their relationship to the socio-legal background. "The older of the arrangements is the *pax Dei* (*paix de Dieu*), the peace of God," writes Robert Holtzmann in his well-known work *Französische Verfassungsgeschichte* (Munich & Berlin, 1910; pp. 164, 165).

The peace of God took a number of persons and objects under its permanent protection. For instance: priests, peasants "and the other poor," churches and things connected with the cult, and at a later date women, merchants, mills, domestic animals, and the like. . . . The peace of God applied to only a limited number of objects, but its duration was not restricted. . . . The *treuga Dei* (*trêve de Dieu*, i.e., "God's armistice") was different. It covered everybody and everything, but only for a limited period, for some days of the week. . . . It created a general condition of peaceableness from Saturday night to Monday morning. . . . This *treuga Dei*, which was usually imposed in connection with a *pax Dei*, was widened in the following years . . . and extended to the time span from Wednesday night to Monday morning.

Certain other seasons of the year, for instance, Lent, were also included in a diocese here and there. During such time feuding was prohibited, even if the secular law considered it as allowable self-help.

The transition from the *pax Dei* to the *treuga Dei*, or rather the addition of the latter to the former, reflects a great change which, around the year 1000 or so, came over legal thinking and ordering in general, and is explained by it. The Frankish and Germanic tribes were at first organized in descent groups, sibs or clans, and a man's legal status depended on his family affiliation. A Salic Frank lived—wherever he happened to be—by the Salic law; a Ripuarian Frank, by the Ripuarian law; and so on. The lawyers speak in this connection of a *lex sanguinis*: the blood was decisive—which meant, negatively, that the dwelling place, the territorial affiliation, was not decisive. It became decisive, however, when the nomadic past was finally forgotten and attachment to a permanent homestead turned into the normal and necessary thing. Then the *lex sanguinis* faded out, and the *lex soli*—the law of the soil—took its place. Now, clearly, the *pax Dei* was part and parcel of the still-surviving *lex sanguinis*, for it protected persons, but did not pacify areas. The *treuga Dei*, on the other hand, links with the *lex soli* for, though it did not last the entire year, it always spread over an entire diocese or dukedom and admitted of no local exceptions. The peace movements of the tenth, eleventh, and twelfth centuries were thus institutions of the inclusive societies, born of their underlying principles of social organization, and not merely efforts of preachers and prelates, pious wishes promoted from the pulpit.

Nevertheless, the *pax Dei* and *treuga Dei* were essentially religious phenomena, and that not only because charismatic leaders, like Abbot Odo of Cluny, and popes, like Nicholas II, inspired them. The division of the week into a period when feuding was (reluctantly) allowed (Monday morning through Wednesday night) and a period when it was banned (Wednesday night through Monday morning) rested on the Gospels, for the days which were forbidden were the days of Christ's passion, crucifixion, and resurrection. The medieval habit of thinking of time, not in the modern manner as an empty medium *in* which events take place, but as filled with meaning—not as colorless, so to speak, but as colored by specific hues—helped to bring quiet to the long weekends because they were hallowed hours, hours when respect and love for the Savior demanded that His spirit should reign for a while and sin cease. But the deeply religious character of *pax* and *treuga Dei* also becomes obvious, and perhaps still more clearly, in another historical detail. When Wido, Bishop of Le Puy, in 975, called the synod which, as we have seen, in-

stituted the first *pax Dei*, he had the relics of St. Vivien brought in and demanded that the oath to obey the canons which had just been passed be taken
on these relics. At Charroux, in 989, the same thing happened, only this time
it was not St. Vivien but St. Junien. At Limoges, in 994, it was St. Martial; at
Poitiers, in 1010, St. Maxentius; at Mende, some time before 1036, St. Enimie;
and so on. Why was this pattern established, and why was it repeated every
time? It was assumed that the local saints who were invoked would watch,
from their heavenly abode, over the implementation of the agreed canons and,
in case of need, act as accusers of those who had broken their promise to keep
the peace before the dread tribunal of Almighty God, the judge of all who, for
whatever reason, escape on earth the consequences of their earthly misdeeds
(Hoffman, *Gottesfriede und Treuga Dei*, pp. 17, 19, 27, 28, 32, 33, 40). *Pax*
and *treuga* rested on a *lex domini*, a divine behest; it was the divinity, therefore, who was their enforcer, at least in the final resort. The Council of Nar-
bonne, convened in the year 1051, emphasized the sacrilegious nature of any
breach of the sworn peace order most dramatically. *"Qui Christianum oc-
cidit,"* it declared (ibid., p. 39), *"Christi sanguinem fundit"*—he who kills a
Christian, sheds the blood of Christ.

Of special interest is a synod which was held at Poitiers some time in the
very first years of the eleventh century (the exact date is unknown). Characteristically, it was called, not by the metropolitan, Siguin of Bordeaux,
though he was present, but by Duke William V of Aquitaine. It ordained not
only that lawbreakers should be admonished to do what was expected of them,
but that, in case of need, they should be coerced (ibid., p. 32; see also p.
250). A penal expedition was to be organized, and the combined force of all
brought to bear on the one who resisted order and law—an example of the
zajazd which we discussed in Section 110 (see SOCIAL BOND III 225). Here we
see how the religious peace movement prepared the coming of the public order
which we know today. It died only when stronger hands took over the hard,
high task which it had pursued in darker days.

In societies in which order and safety are in the keeping of relatively
strong secular authorities, such as our police and our courts, the religious
forces will not have to concern themselves with the pacification of normal,
everyday life, but there will still be plenty of work for them to do. For there
remain areas of darkness, so to speak, into which the light of day does not
penetrate and into which the arm of the law does not reach. If a man has
planted a tree somewhere in his fields, at a distance from his homestead, who
will protect it—protect it, for instance, during the night? Neither can he himself watch it twenty-four hours every day, nor can we imagine a system of
organized public supervision intense enough to guarantee its safety. Where all
other means fail, societies have regularly developed the conception that trees
are sacred and that he who harms them commits not only a crime, but, what is
more, a sin, which will, sooner or later, bring divine vengeance down upon his
guilty head. The Melanesians and the Polynesians have evolved the concept of
mana; the Plains Indians—the Omahas, for instance—the concept of *wakan*;
the Malays, that of *pantang*; and other primitives, similar conceptions. The
basic idea everywhere is the same—a protoreligious or at least metaphysical

imagination. If we slightly rationalize it, we can sum it up very simply by saying that, according to these systems of belief, every man carries in himself a
portion of the universal life-force whose power is evident in nature, especially
in the fact of fertility, and that he communicates something of this mysterious
indwelling force to the things which he creates. These are his not only according to law, but also by dint of a deep and abiding mysterious connection. They
are, so we may perhaps express it, *loaded* with his *mana*, they are "taboo"; and
anyone else who appropriates them against the will of their maker and pro-
prietor does so at his peril. Property marks on trees and other things are not
merely sober signs of secular import; they are also warnings to those who
covet them that their willful appropriation exposes them to a magical threat.
Where such convictions prevail, it is easy to develop and safeguard a form of
property which has, for a very long time, remained unprotected in the rationalistic parts of the world—incorporeal property (see Robert H. Lowie, "Incorporeal Property in Primitive Society," *Yale Law Journal*, 37 [1928], 551ff.;
see also his *Primitive Society* [London, 1960], pp. 225, 226, 228, 230, 232).
While Kant had to go out of his way to produce a pamphlet against the illicit
reprinting of his books, while many a nineteenth-century songwriter had to
starve because others pirated his works, Lowie does not hesitate to speak, in
connection with several primitive societies, of the existence of a "copyright"
("Incorporeal Property in Primitive Society," 556). The term is apt or at least
permissible, but the "right" concerned is part of a religious, not of a legal, code.

We see the operation of the *mana* concept as a defense of otherwise insufficiently protected property particularly clearly in the case of the Maori nobles,
for here it appears in a magnified—one might almost say, grotesque—form.
" 'Great chiefs were by nature tapu on account of their divine birth, they being
able to trace their genealogies up to the gods of heaven and earth,' " Edward
Treagear writes in *The Maori Race* (Wanganui, 1904; pp. 192ff.; see the extract in W. I. Thomas' sourcebook *Primitive Behavior* [New York & London,
1937], pp. 329, 331, 332): " 'If such chiefs performed certain actions, such
as entering a common house, leaning against a post, eating a portion of food,
etc., the house, the post, or the remaining scraps of victuals were tapu to
others. . . . If the shadow of a great ariki fell across a food store . . . or a food pit
. . . the contents became tapu.' " No wonder that " 'his presence in a village
was watched with great anxiety' "! But, here as everywhere, the abuse of an
institution should not cloud our understanding of its proper use, in this case,
of its property-preserving function and effect. On the whole, " 'The tapu was
a very convenient thing, in spite of its immense drawbacks and constrictions,
in making private [i.e., secure] small personal effects such as ornaments, dress,
etc.' "

This kind of tabooing power among the Maoris is merely a particularly
powerful instance of an entire series of similar prohibitions and defenses. To
give but one example of the rest: " 'A bit of flax tied to a door secured it and
the valuables within' " (ibid., p. 332). To move to another area of the globe:
in West Africa fetishes were used to provide a police guard for the preservation
of property which the real police, if such there were, were unable to watch.
M. H. Kingsley reports in her book *Travels in West Africa* (London, 1897;

pp. 448, 450, 285) that: "Charms are made for every occupation and desire in life. . . . Some kinds of charms, such as those to prevent your getting drowned, shot, seen by elephants, etc., are worn on a bracelet or necklace," but "charms are not all worn upon the body; some go to the plantations and are hung there, ensuring an unhappy and swift end for the thief who comes stealing." True, even the natives know that this protection is not unfailing, but disappointments diminish the belief in the power of these magical precautions only very little. They remain effective as safeguards of property. Miss Kingsley might well have used them as an illustration of her general proposition that "there is always some fragment of sound sense underlying African institutions."

We are suggesting, then, that the beliefs and rituals connected with magical conceptions are, at least sometimes, supports of the social pattern and of the smooth functioning of human interaction, but an anthropologist whom we have already quoted several times—Hans Himmelheber—takes a different view. "We must realize," he writes (*Der gute Ton bei den Negern*, pp. 90, 91),

> that the religion of the Negroes, in contrast to Christianity and Mohammedanism, demands no ethical attitude of its votaries. The suprasensual powers in which the Negroes believe are not concerned about the moral conduct of people in their mutual relations. On the contrary: they promote wicked ways of thinking! The Negro can do good to his fellow-men in full publicity without the help of magic; if he does, he will secure "a good name" for himself. But if he harbors evil designs against his neighbor, he turns, in the privacy of his hut, to his fetishes and asks them with the help of sacrifices to make the enemy sick or to destroy his cattle. . . . The creator of [the fetish] Massa understood quite correctly where the roots of evil lie in the behavior of the Negroes: in his fetishism which fans and feeds the immoral element in man.

Far be it from us to deny the truth content of these words! Magic is only too often black magic, a vehicle of hate, an abreaction of aggressivity. But Himmelheber is blind to its other, its socially helpful, side, its operation as a filler-in of lacunae in the system of social ordering. In fact, he contradicts himself. For the fetish Massa to which he refers, and who has figured in these pages before (see p. 206), is a thoroughly good influence among the Senuffo and has taught them to keep their hands from other people's property, be it even a bank note lying abandoned on the ground.

We might pit against Himmelheber another prestigious anthropologist— F. E. Williams—who writes this in his *Orokaiva Society* (Oxford, 1930; pp. 325ff., 328ff.) concerning a tribe of New Guinea:

> The various tangible protection marks [on things], whatever their sanctions, . . . have no real value as physical barriers to trespass or [thieving] appropriation. The commonest is *papara* or *ese*, the frond of coconut palm tied about the butt, which means that no one is to climb for nuts. The *heri* is a strip of bark or liana tied to uprights and encircling a house or some forbidden ground. . . . These signs are often . . . obeyed automatically and without any reflection or motive; . . . they may be regarded out of pure consideration for the man— neighbor, relative, or friend—who has set them up; but there is an additional sanction, simply that of sorcery. The very name, *inja*, of one of these conventional signs is that of black magic. . . .

So far, so good; or rather, so far, so bad; so far we are still close to Himmel-heber's negative judgment of the bearings of magic. But, Williams goes on to explain, there is another aspect of it as well, a wholesome aspect:

> Sorcery is not merely a protector of property; it operates in all walks of life. A man will hesitate to wrong another in any way, if he thinks of the crippled leg or the crop of boils which vengeance armed with magic may give him in return. In short, . . . sorcery, despite being in itself the most hated of crimes, is undoubtedly, by reason of the superstitious fear it inspires, a stalwart guardian of individual rights.

The fact is that we are confronted, at this point, with an instance of the phenomenon which Wilhelm Wundt has called "the heterogony of purposes," and which Bernard de Mandeville had summed up, long before, in the adage that "private vices" turn into "public benefits." The primitive who has resort to sorcery with the exclusively selfish aim of securing his own property creates, unbeknown to himself, a mentality through which property *in general*, that is to say, a *social* institution, is made safe, and society as a whole strengthened. But this does not mean, as we have freely admitted, that there is not a kernel of truth in Himmelheber's assessment. The heterogony of purposes—that "divine chemistry," as it has also been called—will operate the more effectively, the greater the element of genuine idealism in the religious tradition which pro-vides the background. In heathen religions, this element is smaller than in Christianity. This can be said without falling foul of the canons of scholarly objectivity, and that because of a strictly factual trait of the Christian faith—the fact, about which a good deal will be said before long, that it is not only a static, but also a dynamic religion, in the sense which Henri Bergson has given to these terms.

Karl von Amira, one of the deepest students of the field which we have now to investigate—the penetration of the legal tradition by Christian conceptions —wrote this in a lecture delivered in the year 1876 (*Über Zweck und Mittel der germanischen Rechtsgeschichte* [Munich, 1876], p. 15): "The acceptance of Christianity and the foundation of a Christian world monarchy . . . laid new duties on the law. The law now existed not merely for the protection of one's fellows, but also for the realization of the kingdom of God on earth." This is perhaps somewhat exaggerated, but it was certainly the bounden duty of the converted princes to impregnate society with the Gospel spirit. Illustrations of an endeavor in this direction are not wanting. In a substantial essay of a later date, "Über die germanischen Todesstrafen" (*Abhandlungen der Bayerischen Akademie der Wissenschaften*, Philosophisch-philologische Klasse, 31, No. 3 [1922]), von Amira pointed out that the early Christian kings evinced a definite dislike of the death penalty, whereas in heathen times there had been little hesitation before executing a miscreant. In England, for instance, King Ælfred (Alfred) asserted that Christianity had abolished the death penalty for all crimes (except treason) in the case of a first offender, a signal mitigation of the earlier practice. More important still: the execution of a criminal was no longer considered a cultic act. Among the heathens, the condemned criminal had been seen as a meet sacrifice to the gods. This is particularly clear in the case of the dreadful punishment of "breaking on the wheel." The wheel was a symbol of the sun god; the mangled corpse, tied to the wheel's spikes, was offered to him as an expiation of the deed which had stained the community. The other main mode of dispatch, hanging, was no different. The corpse on the gallows was left to the god of the wind. A gruesome detail can prove that this interpretation is correct: the caitiff had to *swing*. All this was over as soon as the Germanic and Romanic tribes came to embrace the Christian religion. The new God wanted no sacrifices; what He wished was that the sinner should repent and live. The sacrificial theory of punishment was replaced by the theory of deterrence, a very different basic attitude.

How deep the change was can also be shown by another detail. It was, since time immemorial, a widespread custom to place, at the first spring sowing, a loaf of bread on the ground and lead the plow over it. This, clearly, was an offering to the gods of vegetation. After Christianity had taken a firm hold, the "plow bread" remained, but it was given to the poor: the rite now led to an act of charity and was no longer an attempt to buy the good will of a chthonic deity (ibid., 83, 51, 52, 277–30). As von Amira expresses it (ibid., 233), the god-idea had become ethicized.

Still, the difference between pre-Christian and Christian times must not be exaggerated. The main tradition remained unchanged, and this is anything but surprising since it had been born of the needs of society, and these basic needs continued to be the same. If the heathen Anglo-Saxons had regarded the desecration of their cultic implements as a *nidinges dead*, an impious, sacrilegious, disgusting, and horrifying act, their Christianized sons now saw the breaking and entering of a church, the stealing of chalice and paten, the soiling of priestly vestments, and so on, in exactly the same light. One set of hallowed objects was exchanged for another, and that was all that happened. So far as purely mundane things were concerned, not even that much happened. To remain with our earlier example: a tree was thought holy in the days of Horsa and Hengist; it was also thought holy in the days of Alfred and Canute.

If one wanted to find out which things exactly were placed under the personal protection of the gods or God, he would obtain a precious lead in the history of the law, more especially the penal law. Interference with these specially protected objects led in the case of the discovery and identification of the culprit to exceptionally hard punishments, in many cases to the doubling of fines and/ or even to a death sentence. The decortization of a tree, for instance, apparently a fairly frequent act of malicious damage, was fiercely avenged. The stated penalty was evisceration; the intestines of the perpetrator were wound around the mutilated stem. But this did not mean that law officers were able to provide adequate protection. If the bark was stripped off under the cover of darkness, no threat, however dramatic, was of any avail. The tree had to be placed under the care of the all-seeing divinity; only then could it be considered as safe. We cannot undertake to elaborate a comprehensive list of the objects singled out in this way from the mass of ordinary things; nor is this necessary for our purpose. We are concerned only with the underlying principle. The principle was that help from above was prayed for and thought to be forthcoming, wherever the strength of human agencies was inherently insufficient. We shall, and must, restrict ourselves to two examples which are quite obviously of vital importance: the plow and the border stones, both of which figure prominently in religious and proto- or pseudoreligious folklore.

A plow, even a primitive one, is a heavy implement; taking it out to the distant fields in the morning and dragging it back to the homestead in the evening would be very hard and trying work. Much better to leave it in the open! But this, of course, is rather risky. Who is to watch it overnight? Would it not be broken and useless when the farmer returns to it at the beginning of the next day? Here lies a problem for any agricultural community, and it was religion, the word understood in its widest sense, which helped to solve it. We shall now try to show how.

The religious speculations in and of most agricultural societies understandably center in two concepts: the sky father and the earth mother. In Japan Izanagi stands over against, and linked with, Izanami; in India, Indra with Prithivi; in Greece, Zeus with Gaea; in Rome, Jupiter with Ceres. The pairs are husband and wife: the life-giving male and the life-receiving female principle. The rain which Indra sends down, especially in a thundery downpour, is the semen which the womb of Prithivi receives and which renders it fruitful. In the framework of this basic mythology, the plow has a very important part to play, for it is the plow which opens the soil and makes it possible for the waters from heaven to penetrate it. No wonder that in Latin there is an obvious philological connection between the word for plow, *aratrum*—"I plow" is *aro*—and the word for altar, *ara*; no wonder either that in Greek the terms "to plow" and "to beget" or "to fertilize" are nearly identical. Particularly intense has been the preoccupation of the collective imagination with the blade of the plow, the plowshare, for it is this which actually breaks the soil open. It has been likened to lightning; it has also, in a remarkable anticipation of Freudian ideas, been likened to the male organ of generation which sets in motion the latent fertility of the female organism. (On all this, see *Handwörterbuch des deutschen Aberglaubens* VI, ed. Hanns Bächtold-Stäubli [Berlin & Leipzig, 1934–1935], cols. 1718–28; see also Jacob Grimm, "Deutsche Alterthümer," *Kleinere Schriften* II [Berlin, 1865], 56).

We have, then, to begin with, two separate starting points: an economic need and a metaphysical speculation; as the Marxists would say, an element of the substructure and an element of the superstructure. The conception of the plow as an inviolable thing, a thing under the special protection of the gods, is the result of a meeting and merging of these originally independent tendencies. Those who are familiar with the sociology of knowledge will find it easy to understand how and why this synthesis comes about. Both the basic theories which have dominated this science are applicable: the theory of elective affinity and the theory of the organic interrelation between life and thought (see Stark, *Sociology of Knowledge*, pp. 245ff.). According to the former, material needs strive for linkage with appropriate, helpful thought-ways while theoretical thought-ways strive for entry into practical affairs; according to the latter, substructures and their superstructures are always contained in one and the same historical framework and thus from their inception are parts of a comprehensive interrelated whole. Whatever the explanation, the plow is holy, and interference with it a crime and sin which will not remain unavenged, be it avenged in this life, be it in the next.

Just how deep the roots are which this conviction of the plow's sacredness develops in the socio-cultural subsoil can be seen from an Irish legend recorded in Jeremiah Curtin's *Tales of the Fairies and of the Ghost-World* (London, 1895; pp. 127ff.; see also Anatole Le Braz, *La Légende de la mort* II [Paris, 1928], p. 205).

> Once there was a farmer, a widower, Tom Reardon, who lived near Castlemain. He had an only son . . . and the boy's name was John. The farmer married a second time, and the stepmother hated the boy. . . . She was turning the father's mind against the son, till at last the farmer resolved to put the son in a place where a ghost was, and this ghost never let any man go without killing him. One day the father sent the son to the forge with some chains belonging to a plough. . . . It was nearly evening when the father sent him.

On the way back, "when two miles from the forge, a ghost rose up before John, a woman; she attacked him and they fought for two hours, when he put the plough-chain round her. She could do nothing then, because what belongs to a plough is blessed." Twice more John Reardon is attacked in this way, the attackers being sisters of the first revenant. The second was "a deal more determined and stronger" than the first; the third yet more determined and yet stronger, "red lightning flashing from her mouth." No matter; the power dwelling in the plow-chain defeated them all. Modern rationalistic man smiles or even sneers at such stories, but he should not forget that they entered the collective unconscious and created a complex of conceptions there which made it psychologically next to impossible, even for a deviant, to interfere with a plow.

Christianity, when it came, depressed such imaginings to the position of groundless superstitions, but its priesthood was careful not to destroy the moral effects which the traditional folklore had engendered. It found its own way of preserving and propagating the idea that the plow is, in a sense, sacred, by developing the rite known as "blessing of the plough." Within the Anglican communion at any rate, it is still carried out (personal knowledge). In Cambridgeshire, for instance, the parish assembles on "Plough Sunday" (formerly "Plough Monday," the first Monday after the Epiphany) for this purpose. Plows are carried into the church or placed as close to it as possible. A farmer then addresses the officiating clergyman as follows: "At the beginning of another year, we bring these ploughs to our parish church, that you may ask God's blessing on them and us. . . ." Some versicles of Psalms 24 and 124 (Anglican numeration) are then recited, whereupon the celebrant continues: "O God, who dost give each man his work to do for thy sake, prosper, we pray thee, the work and workers of the fields and farms of this parish throughout this new year. Let the ploughman's hopes be fulfilled in a plentiful harvest." It is interesting to note a certain cleavage between the petition and its fulfillment. A blessing is asked on the plow (a thing); the benediction is bestowed on the plowman (a person). The blessing of things went out when the Reformation and rationalism broke in and modified the tradition. In some places, it is true, the words "God speed the plough . . . the share and the coulters," are included, but even they are more the expression of a pious wish than a hallowing in the full meaning of the term. Yet in the eyes of the country-folk of Cambridge-shire, the rite no doubt raises the plow even now above the level of a merely technical tool.

It would be tempting to discuss the folklore hanging around the plow in still greater detail, but we must desist. Only one additional remark is necessary. Once the idea had taken root that the plow is sacred, it tended to broaden out and be transferred to other agricultural tools as well. Thus the harrow, too, began to enjoy the same protection. But even here the process did not come to a stop. In a widening circle, it strove to cover yet other implements, though it must be surmised that the coverage became thinner and thinner as it moved outward from its original core.

From the sanctified nature of the plow derived the idea that the furrow drawn by it is also sacred, and this in turn led to the custom of plowing around a field, especially a newly acquired one, in order to protect it, both from the malignity of demons, and the possible depredations on the part of men. What the chief danger was can be seen from a charming and moving (and—alas!—not unrealistic) story of the great Swiss novelist Gottfried Keller: *Romeo und Julia auf dem Dorfe* ("A Village Romeo and Juliet"). The acres of two farm-ers are divided by a strip of no man's land. They respect it for a while, but then the temptation becomes too great for them. First the one and then the other plows a furrow in the abandoned ground, thus illegally adding to their property. After the first follows a second, and then further ones, until the two depreda-tors meet in the middle. Then an enmity springs up between them, with cata-strophic consequences to their hapless children who are deeply fond of each other. Now, the temptation to which the two foolish men yield is a very wide-spread, indeed, a universal, one. The moving of border stones is one of man-kind's oldest and most persistent crimes. As an antidote, the collective forces developed the conviction that borders and border stones are sacred, and that those who interfere with them will, if they escape human justice, pay a heavy price for their misdeed in the beyond.

In his article "Landmarks and Boundaries," published in the *Encyclo-paedia of Religion and Ethics* (VII 789–95), J. A. MacCulloch has presented a very meritorious survey of the historical material, and though his evolutionist attitude strikes one today as somewhat antiquated, the factual information provided is as sound now as it has ever been. We may safely entrust ourselves to his guidance. Speaking of the "lower culture," he writes (pp. 790, 791):

In New Zealand the *kumara* and *taro* grounds were contiguous and divided into portions, carefully marked by stones over which incantations had been said. This rendered them so sacred that to move one brought death to the remover. . . . Among the village peoples of N.W. India . . . [b]oundaries and cattle paths are religiously preserved, and the curse is uttered: "May the man who destroys a boundary, a cowpath, or a ditch have his lands sown by others, or may they lie waste. . . ." Among the Kandhs boundary-lines . . . are sacred to Sundi Pennu, god of boundaries. . . . A boundary-god also exists among the Gonds.

Little appears to change when "the higher culture" replaces the lower: "The Babylonians called boundary-stones *kudurru*. . . . They were sacred to certain divinities," to the sun-god Shamash, among others. The *kudurru*, too, carry inscriptions which curse anyone who tries to displace them and calls on the protective divinities to visit the perpetrators with a heavy hand. The Jews of Biblical times followed the same pattern. "Cursed be he that removeth his neighbour's landmarks," we read in the Book of Deuteronomy (27:17), and in the Book of Job (24:2, 24): "Some have removed landmarks. . . . They are lifted up for a little while and shall not stand, and shall be brought down . . . and, as the tops of the ears of corn, they shall be broken."

That a simple evolutionary pattern cannot be applied in this field is shown by a side glance at the Greeks and Romans. MacCulloch sees them in the same light as the Babylonians and Hebrews. Gods, he suggests, watched over the border stones:

> In early *Greece* heaps of stones . . . or erect stones . . . , or both together . . . were placed to mark paths, as well as frontier-limits and bounds of private lands. . . . They were under the protection not only of Hermes . . . , but also of Ζεὺς ῾Ορϊος. . . . Plato says [*Laws* 8.842f.] that "one should be more willing to move the largest rock which is not a landmark than the least stone which is the sworn mark of friendship and hatred between neighbours." The consequences will be doubly fatal—a penalty coming from the gods and one coming from the law [p. 792].

Among the Romans, too, stones fixed the borders of fields and woods. "The earliest form of the boundary-mark was a post or stone. . . . This landmark represented Terminus, god of boundaries, and, as Ovid says, possessed divinity" (ibid.; reference to Ovid's *Fasti* 2.640; see also N. D. Fustel de Coulanges' classic *La Cité antique* [Paris, 1890], pp. 70ff.). The quotation from Ovid shows quite clearly that the Romans, and probably the Greeks, carried on a much more archaic, much more primitive, idea than the Semites, even though the culture of the latter took shape a good deal earlier than theirs. The border stones are not so much protégés of the gods as gods themselves. The article "Terminus" in the *Real-Encyclopädie der klassischen Altertumswissenschaft* (edd. A. Pauly, G. Wissowa, and W. Kroll [Stuttgart, 1934], 2.9, cols. 781–84)—a work even more prestigious than the *Encyclopaedia of Religion and Ethics*—begins with the words "The Romans venerated the border stones (*termini*) as divine beings. . . ." This did not, of course, prevent them from having a god by the name of Terminus and even a Jupiter Terminalis as well, but the salient fact is that primeval conceptions akin to fetishism and animism survived in this high culture well into Christian times.

As for Christian times properly so called, and particularly the Middle Ages, we must note first of all that a very cruel form of the death penalty was connected with the shifting of border stones. It is the punishment inflicted in Shakespeare's *Titus Andronicus* (V.iii.179–182; i.e., the play's end) on the thrice-villanous Aaron:

Set him breast-deep in earth and famish him;
There let him stand, and rave, and cry for food:
If any one relieves or pities him,
For the offence he dies.

Sometimes even this digging-in was not thought punishment strong enough to fit the crime, and the plow was led over the hapless man. But Jacob Grimm, the great pioneer of folkloric studies, cannot bring himself to believe that this barbarous technique of execution was ever really inflicted ("Deutsche Grenz-alterthümer," *Kleinere Schriften* II 59ff.). There is, of course, no way of finding out whether his surmise is correct or not. But it does seem that the later centuries were in fact not quite so hard as the earlier. The plowing-over ceased, and it became customary to give the miscreant a modicum of food and sometimes even a knife or similar instrument. If he managed to free himself and to abscond, it was considered that he had paid the price for his evil deed (see Amira, "Todesstrafen," 153).

The reason for this alleviation was not, however, merely tenderness of heart or compassion. It was much rather the fact that other, and worse, punishments were thought to be in store for the perpetrator—punishments in the beyond. The *ignis fatuus*, the will o' the wisp, the phosphorescent lights at times appearing above marshy land—personalized in English folklore as Jack o' Lantern—were thought to be the souls of departed men who had in their lifetime removed border stones to their neighbors' prejudice. They could not, of course, get into heaven, but even hell would not have them. "It is not rare that one encounters, during the night, on rural paths or cart-roads, men bent double under the weight of a heavy stone which they have the greatest difficulty of keeping up on their backs," Anatole Le Braz reports, speaking of the beliefs of the people of Brittany (*La Légende de la mort* II 28, 29). "They drag themselves along in deep pain and forever repeat, in a lamenting tone of voice, the same question . . . 'Where shall I put this?' These are Anaon [souls] of the removers of border stones whom God has condemned to wander in this way through the land. . . ."

Even these are, of course, quite primitive beliefs, but we come fairly close to a core idea of the Christian faith, to the idea of judgment, when we hear that the people of Brittany say: the removed border stone, with all its weight, will be thrown into the scales when the soul's merits and demerits are weighed before the tribunal of the All-High (ibid., p. 28). Rightly does Le Braz suggest that this form of thought has arisen because the damnified neighbors expect justice only at the hands of the all-knowing God.

We discover at this point the very same tendency as in the case of the plow: the tendency to transfer the supposed sanctity to other, similar objects. Thus not only the borderline between field and field is sacrosanct, but also the borderline between land and sea. The dykes are holy (see Amira, "Todesstrafen," 214, 215), and the destroyer of them threatens the same fate as the thief of landed property. This proves that religion is indeed what it has so often been called: a leaven which, if allowed to work, will permeate the whole paste—the whole system of society.

SACRED PLACES

135. Jacob Grimm has pointed out that in the belief system of the Germanic tribes the holiness of the plow is indissolubly connected with the holiness of the plowed field ("Deutsche Grenzalterthümer," 61), and so it would seem appropriate to continue in this section, which is to be devoted to the sacralization of places, with a further consideration of agricultural societies, to show how the special protection thought to be enjoyed by certain implements of agriculture is also thought to be attached to the soil on which they are used. But we have chosen to proceed differently, and that for a good reason. What we have to prove is that religion intervenes whenever and wherever there is a weak spot within a social system, and therefore it has seemed advisable at this point to move a problem into the center of our attention which is not necessarily connected with rural life. We shall speak first, not of the holiness of arable land, but of the holiness of the market place. This brings us to a rather different kind of social setting.

The contrast between threats to peace and order in the village and threats to peace and order in the market consists in this: that the danger comes in the first case from outside the social system, i.e., from criminal elements, whereas in the second case it comes from within the social system itself, from those who operate and implement it. The peasant's main enemy is nature; the trader's, his fellow-man. Buying and selling are adversary relationships: the buyer wishes to pull the price down, the seller to push it up; the seller wishes to deliver goods of as low a quality as he possibly can, the buyer insists on as high a quality as he thinks he is entitled to. This alone makes peace on the market problematic. But there are other causes of tension as well. To mention only one: the fact, and indeed merely the suspicion, that bad weight had been given —a trouble which the standardization of measures has only partially removed. So there is every reason to fear that the dealings on the market may lead to open conflicts, and this fear is obviated, this danger is banned, by developing the idea that the market square is watched by the higher powers and its peaceableness ensured by them.

In the first volume of his well-known work *Die Entstehung der Volkswirtschaft*, Karl Bücher has asserted (Tübingen, 1922; p. 325) that the weekly markets held by the aborigines of Central Africa in the midst of the primeval forest are thought by the local people to stand under special protection. F. I. Schechter has followed this theme further, and his account is especially valuable because he has used not only recent sources but older ones as well. The latter show us phenomena which have evolved out of cultural tendencies as yet uninfluenced by Western civilization and/or Christian missionaries. We give, by way of illustration, two samples from his collection:

> Andrew Battell, in his *Strange Adventures* on the African Gold Coast at the end of the sixteenth century, reported that at Loango "in the banza . . . or chief city, the chief idol is named *Chekoke*." Every day they have there a market, and the *Chekoke* is brought forth by the *Ganga*, or priest, to keep good rule, and is set in the market place. . . . In the twentieth century the

markets of the Birilsa and Kassena tribes of the Northern Gold Coast are likewise described as "being under the direct control of an earth-god." Violation of his wishes were punishable religiously—sometimes a community would be, so to speak, excommunicated from all intercourse in the markets, and all other communities saw to it that the order of the market *tindada* (the high priest of the local earth-god) was obeyed [F. I. Schechter, "Law and Morals in Primitive Trade," *Essays in Tribute to O. K. McMurray*, edd. Max Radin and A. M. Kidd (Berkeley, 1935), pp. 580, 615].

Other parts of the world show similar institutions: "In the Bukana Pig-Market in New Guinea, a bit of root is burned and the ashes are secretly and symbolically sprinkled over the market 'so that they may impart their coolness to the foot of a buyer who should be fired with anger' " (ibid., p. 582).

Among the ancient Greeks, it was Hermes, the god of trade, who looked after the markets and ensured the smoothness of market dealings, but the market peace had an even mightier protector, the High God Zeus himself, who appears in this context under the name of Zeus Agoraios, a pendant to Zeus Horios whom we encountered in the last section. An interesting light on the matter at hand is thrown by a passage in Herodotus' *Histories* (4.23). Herodotus speaks about a nation dwelling in the east, the Argippeans, and makes the following colorful and surprising remarks: "These people are wronged by no man, for they are said to be sacred; nor have they any weapon of war. These are they who judge in the quarrels between their neighbours; moreover, whatever banished man has taken refuge with them is wronged by none" (*Herodotus*, trans. A. D. Godley, 4 vols. [London & Cambridge, Mass., 1971], II 223, 225). One's first reaction to this report would naturally be to consider it as utterly fantastic and to assume that the historian has all too credulously accepted a pure fairy tale for the truth. But one of the greatest social scientists of the nineteenth century, Julius Lippert, has shown that this is not so (see his *Kulturgeschichte der Menschheit* I [Stuttgart, 1886], 456ff.). What Herodotus has given us is indeed a rumor, but behind the rumor there hides a recognizable reality. Lippert identifies the Argippeans with the Permians, the inhabitants of the great trading center of Perm (now Molotov), where the important trade routes along the Volga and the Karma met, a place known as far south as Byzantium where it was called Permia, and as far north as Scandinavia where it was called Bjarma. The physical description given by Herodotus agrees with what we know of the Argippeans or Permians from other sources: they were typical Finns. It is not they who are sacred; sacred, rather, is their market, a pacified area where arms are not carried and where fugitives can find asylum. "There is no doubt," writes Lippert (ibid., p. 459),

> that the merchants who gave Herodotus his information sketched a true picture of a neutral meeting place of the most archaic kind. The "pacification" of the territory into which men otherwise strange and hostile to each other ventured for the sake of trade, the "sacredness" of the tribe under whose aegis the land lay, their lack of arms, their office of arbitration, the law of asylum—all that is most naturally interconnected and proves that the people of northern Asia and of Europe had, even in very early times, entered into peaceable relationships as far as this matter [namely, commerce] was concerned.

The Greeks, too, traveled on occasion as far as Perm, and they must have drawn courage for this venture from their belief that their god of trade, Hermes, was traveling with them.

The fact that Hermes was the protector of markets as well as of mark stones, and the parallel fact that Zeus Agoraios was, of course, identical with Zeus Horios, are also reflected, more pictorially, in the habit of erecting stone steles in the market squares which recall the boundary stones around the fields. The Christian Middle Ages carried on with this tradition by placing crosses on such columns, and this is the origin of the mercat (or merchant) crosses of Scottish towns, Edinburgh and Glasgow, for instance. A Christian should not, and normally would not, quarrel when standing under the cross! But the connection between churches and markets was in fact very much closer than might be expected. It was at the same time a local, a temporal, and a personalized connection. Markets were in most cases held around the church and churchyard; the larger ones were so timed as to coincide with ecclesiastical feasts—the German term for a fair is characteristically *Messe* even today; and this Mass was regularly one in honor of a particular saint who thus became the personal protector of the assembled multitudes and their dealings. Needless to say, the church building and its area, usually a burial ground and therefore holy even according to pre-Christian ideas, was the sacred soil *par excellence*. The market place, associated as it was with the place of worship, participated to some extent in the sacral character of the latter. True, what went on on the market was often far less edifying than what went on under the church roof, but the market profited nonetheless from its closeness to the church's precincts, as far as pacification is concerned.

We do not have to spend much time in proving that the church itself, or rather its inner space, was sacrosanct to the highest degree. To medieval and Catholic ideas, God in a manner is present in person, in the tabernacle, and who would dare to outrage the Lord of Heaven and Earth by committing a crime in His own house? There is only one point to be made in this connection. It was generally assumed that the awe inspired by the sacred precinct would penetrate even the criminal's heart. One of the greatest criminals of world literature is Denmark's King Claudius. He has already murdered his brother and wed his widow (also a serious misdemeanor at the time); he is preparing to murder his brother's son, Hamlet, as well. Cunningly he tries to do the deed through the hands of young Laertes whose father, Polonius, Hamlet has laid low. Claudius eggs Laertes on (IV.vii.124–129):

> Hamlet comes back; what would you undertake
> To show yourself your father's son in deed
> More than in words?

Hotblooded Laertes is ready with an answer:

> To cut his throat i' the church.

But so far Claudius does not dare to go: the church must not be stained.

No place, indeed, should murder sanctuarize;
Revenge should have no bounds. But, good Laertes,
Will you do this, keep close within your chamber.

Shakespeare's text speaks clearly enough of the shedding of blood in the church: "to cut his throat." This was felt to be too outrageous by the Bard's German translator, A. W. Schlegel, and he tones down the line of Laertes: "Ihn in der Kirch' erwürgen"—"to throttle him in the church." Murder remains murder, but this man felt that a bloodless dispatch was less outrageous than a bloody one. The sentiment displayed in this rare deviation from the English original is surely noteworthy.

Some churches, especially older ones, carry on their doors the legend *domus Dei, porta coeli*—the house of God is the gate of heaven. The metaphysical character of the Christian concept of a holy place, a sanctified area, comes to the surface in this formula. It contrasts clearly and sharply with the parallel concept inherent in the primitive cultures which preceded it. The latter was physical, not metaphysical. Just as it was believed that a man communicated his *mana* to the things which he had fashioned or merely touched, so it was believed that a tribe communicated its *mana* to the soil on which it dwelled and worked. A certain linkage with later modes of thinking is to be seen in the fact that for both pre-Christian and Christian religiosity the burial place of the departed was inviolable. But even the living could make a place taboo: among the Maori,

> "of course a chief's house was tapu, and on one occasion the people of a village became tapu from eating the wild cabbage which had grown on the site once occupied by a chief's house. . . . Not only was the chief's house tapu on account of his sacredness . . . but every house was to be avoided in reference to some of its parts. . . . All fruit, roots, etc., growing in sacred places were tapu. In great fishing expeditions all those engaged in making or mending nets were tapu, so also was the ground on which the nets were made, and the river on whose banks [the] work went on. . . . it was not until the regulation ceremonies were finished, the net wetted, and a fish taken and eaten by the owner of the net, that the tapu was lifted . . ." [cited in Thomas, *Primitive Behavior*, pp. 332, 333].

These lines, taken ultimately from Edward Tregear's book *The Maori Race*, show that the market peace and the peace of the netmakers' shore grew ultimately from the same root and lie strictly parallel: they are responses of the proto-religious and religious spirit to the need of society for secure peace and quiet in situations in which tensions are apt to develop and conflicts to erupt.

The sanctity of the Maori's netmaking and netmending grounds is purely temporary and locally restricted. We see the same idea in a much broader application as we turn now to primitive ideas concerning the relationship of a tribe to its ancestral land. We gladly give the word here to R. H. Lowie who was particularly expert in all matters of aboriginal property and property-rights (cf. above, p. 229). "The attitude of the Australian aborigines toward their land is extremely interesting," he writes (*Primitive Society*, p. 203).

A local group, not necessarily the whole tribe . . . occupied a certain tract and was indissolubly connected with it. . . . Information on some of the tribes suggests that the intensity of the attachment . . . may be due to mystical reasons, more especially, to the localization of the individual's totemic ancestors; removal to another region would destroy contact with these mythical beings. . . . Trespass was extremely rare and the white settlers in West Australia found it difficult to make black [or rather brown] shepherds herd sheep anywhere but on their ancestral territories.

These notions protected not only their own lands, but those of others as well. "Wars occurred, but the notion of expropriating the vanquished never even dawned upon the mind of the conquerors." We have already referred to this world-historically important fact in our discussion of the origin of the state in Section 106 (see SOCIAL BOND III 166).

How strong and how persistent these conceptions are can be seen from a news item which, at the end of October 1980, made its appearance in the world press. It reported that a California Indian had nailed his left hand to a cross and had his right hand fixed to it by barbed wire, to protest a plan to erect a skyscraper on the soil of an old burial ground of his tribe.

We can place the pre-Christian Germanic tribes halfway between the primitive and the Christianized cultures. Their holy precincts were areas set apart for cultic purposes, and in this respect they resemble the later churches and churchyards. But they usually centered on some natural feature, on some mighty oak, for instance, such as the one which the Apostle of Germany, St. Boniface, felled at Geismar near Fritzlar. He was never forgiven for this deed, a crime of desecration according to local tradition, and both he and other missionaries paid with their lives for what they had done (see Amira, "Todesstrafen," 41, 77). From the religious point of view, there is, of course, a strong contrast between a tree-centered and an altar-centered, a nature-given and a consecrated, place of worship, but so far as its pacification is concerned, there was or is not much difference.

There is also little difference with regard to the observable tendency we have already discussed and placed in the foreground: the extension of the church's peace to the market or markets. But the process did not stop there; indeed, it is surprising how far it went. Let us note here—we lay emphasis on this detail, because our analysis is basically typological—that the further widening of the market peace resembles at first the *paix de Dieu* with its personalism and later the *trève de Dieu* with its territoriality (see above, p. 227). In the beginning, the religion-based protection creates a special status for those who intend to visit a market; the higher, quasi-sacred peace which arises is the merchants' peace, and it belongs to a group of individuals or a guild as such; in the course of time, however, it becomes attached to the roads, and anyone who travels on them enjoys the advantages of such developments (see Rudolf His, *Das Strafrecht des deutschen Mittelalters*, 2 vols. [Aalen, 1964], I 229, 230; see also I 224). It is remarkable precisely from the typological point of view that a similar religious protection and psychological protectedness came to be attached to other pathways as well: the way to and from the church, and the way to and from the plow (see Karl Weinhold, *Über die deutschen Fried-*

und Freistätten [Kiel, 1864], pp. 5, 12). These later ideas unfolded perhaps rather infrequently to their full extent, but even a tendency in their direction is significant enough.

Anyone who has ever visited any of the older European towns knows that their center is the church with its adjacent churchyard and the nearby market square. These three, so to speak, constitute the heart of the city, and so it is not surprising that the entire city—everything enclosed in its protective walls—is regarded as an area of special, God-protected peace. We have advisedly spoken of the city's heart: the homes around it are its body, and what applies to the chief organ must apply to the other cells as well. Organological thinking was deeply embedded in the pre-capitalist mind: what applied to the part, applied to the whole; Adam's sin was the sin of mankind. Nevertheless, it is impossible to assume that the town's peace was ever so entire as the church's or the market's peace. It obviously did not penetrate into its darker alleyways, its nooks and corners. A tendency toward extension right up to the city walls was certainly there, but the energy behind it was not sufficiently strong. "As a rule only crimes of violence are considered as breaches of the town's peace, not, however [for instance], theft" (His, *Das Strafrecht des deutschen Mittelalters*, I 22). Theft inside the church is seen as a much more serious crime (see ibid., II 197), and it is not unusual to find the death penalty set on it.

The town thus had to rely for peace and safety more on its police and could expect less from the influence of religion. This is a fact, but we must not jump to the conclusion that the religious forces were ineffective outside of *ecclesia* and *forum*. They created another sacred precinct, besides church and market, and it was all-important: the house. The adage "A man's home is his castle" is today understood in a sense which it received in the age of absolutism. It is supposed to mean that it is illegal for an agent of the government, and especially for the secret police, to enter a man's home without express permission from an independent court. But the proverb is much older than the absolutist age. It occurs in the town ordinances of Vienna as early as the year 1221: " 'For every citizen, his home is a castle, and likewise for those who live with him and those who flee to it or simply enter it' " (cited in Weinhold, *Über die deutschen Fried- und Freistätten*, p. 8). Other examples from the thirteenth century are by no means wanting (see Adolf Neeff, *Der Hausfrieden* [Stuttgart, 1900], p. 7). This older usage carried a different connotation. The burgher's house was likened to a nobleman's castle, and the latter was not only a fortified place but also an especially sanctified area: it was built around a chapel and thus comparable to a city built around a church and cemetery. Of course, the burgher's house did not contain a chapel, but it did contain a hallowed kernel nonetheless: the hearth. The sacredness of the hearth is indeed a primeval conception; fire is one of the basic symbols, in the sense of Carl Gustav Jung, i.e., one of the symbols with the help of which mankind has attempted to master, or at least to live with, the mysteries of existence. The law has here and there expressed the people's sense of the holiness of the home in particularly dramatic penalties: he who breaks the peace of the house by an act of manslaughter is to have his own dwelling devastated and destroyed (His, *Das Strafrecht des deutschen Mittelalters*, I 220).

It is a fair guess that in the popular consciousness and the collective un-conscious the sacredness of the house ranked above the sacredness of the city. This conception was so strong that it proved fertile as well. With the peace of the house was sometimes connected a peace of the acre, of the garden, of the barns, and of the byres. Even the bleaching meadows may be included (ibid., I 221, 234; II 198, 199). Furthermore, particular houses may enjoy a particular —particularly sacred—peace, in part simply because they are often isolated and thus more easily in jeopardy: the mill and the smithy (ibid., II 197, 198).

Concluding our brief account of the *pax domus*, let us still mention that the helpful influence of religion is doubly felt in times of acute crisis: during a con-flagration. A crime, and especially theft, during that emergency was adjudged an extraordinarily heinous sin (ibid., I 282, 283, 226, 227; II 194, 195). Night-time is likewise considered as a period when the higher powers watch while their human protégés sleep. The famous lawbook known as the *Schwaben-spiegel* declares in this sense that "the night shall have a better peace than the day" (ibid., II 225; I 194).

The elements of religiously suffused legal lore which we have just considered remind one more of the peace of the plow discussed in the last section than of the market peace moved into the foreground in this: they are attempts to ward off criminality rather than attempts to mitigate conflicts of interest. We must now for a moment return to the social situation characteristic of the market, that is, to a situation in which there is an inherent and inescapable danger of conflict, conflict laid on, conflict so to speak arising, from within. Two institu-tions are in this respect comparable to the market: the consultative and legis-lative assembly, on the one hand; the court of law, on the other. Sometimes these two are not distinguished, as in early times; sometimes they are, especially where the Montesquieuan separation of powers obtains. When public business is discussed, it is to be expected that opinions differ and parties form; there is certain to be a struggle for influence, and this may well lead to open clashes. This is not, however, strictly necessary; it is merely normal. But in the court-room tension is unavoidable. However much centuries of legal development have achieved, a legal contest is and remains a battle, if with unbloody arms. Were it not for certain safeguards, the opposed sides would quite likely come to blows. These safeguards are, of course, in the first place legal, but religious conceptions come to the aid of the law of procedure and help as decisively here as elsewhere, and possibly even more (see ibid., I 227ff.; II 121ff.). Through-out history the village assembly and the courtroom are practically everywhere sacred places where particularly restrained conduct is demanded and depar-tures from it are thought to stand under a supernatural sanction. Both have, down to very recent times, been opened with religious ritual. Even modern parliaments begin their sessions often with a prayer, and even decidedly laicistic states, like France, have not removed the crucifixes from the courtroom walls.

We have now only one kind of sacred area left for consideration, but it is a sociologically very interesting and important one: the place of refuge or asylum. Let us begin once again with the concrete social interest which is one of the roots of this institution. When a major crime is committed, for instance, an assault on a person with the aim of killing him, there is the greatest danger that it will provoke retaliation and thus generate a second crime: the intended victim, if he survives, may make an attempt on his pursuer's life; if he does not survive, his next of kin may remember the adage "an eye for an eye" and act accordingly. This threat is particularly intense in the tribal communities because whole clans will invariably be involved; in more individualistic societies, it will be smaller, but it will be present all the same. The way of legal prosecution will be considered only after the first red-hot fury has evaporated and calmer counsels begin to prevail. Thus it is highly desirable that between the criminal action and the possibly also criminal reaction a period of delay—a period of suspended enmity, as it were—be interposed, and this is achieved by providing places of refuge in which the culprit may find temporary safety from his pursuers, the avengers of his deed. Such sanctuaries are, of course, acknowledged and even defended by the officers of the law, but they are in the last resort religious rather than legal institutions.

That they are indeed religious rather than secular institutions can be seen from the simple fact that, throughout history, it has invariably been the place of worship which has also been the haven of refuge. We can once again provide illustrations from every continent. M. H. Kingsley, whose book *Travels in West Africa* we quoted not long ago, writes in that work (p. 466): "From the penalty . . . of . . . accusations of witchcraft there is but one escape, namely flight to a sanctuary. There are several sanctuaries in Congo Français. The great one in the Calabar district is at Omon. Thither [for instance] thieves . . . fly, and if they reach it, are safe." Edward Westermarck has collected parallels from Australia, America, and Asia:

[A]mong the Aruntas of Central Australia there is in each local totem centre a spot called *ertnatulunga*, in the immediate neighbourhood of which everything is sacred and must on no account be hurt. The plants growing there are never interfered with in any way; animals which come there are safe from the spear of the hunter; and a man who is being pursued by others cannot be touched as long as he remains at this spot. . . . In many North American tribes certain sacred places or whole villages served as asylums. Thus the Arikaras of the Missouri had in the centre of their largest village a sacred lodge called the 'medicine-lodge,' where no blood was to be spilled, not even that of an enemy. . . . In the Caucasus holy groves offer refuge to criminals, as also to animals, which cannot be shot there ["Asylum," *Encyclopaedia of Religion and Ethics*, II 161].

This curious inclusion of the beasts is also recorded from ancient Greece. Deer found a safe place of hiding in the sanctuary of Apollo in Kuridium, and it was believed that dogs would not pursue them there. But, of course, the main purpose was to give men in the throes of flight and fear a breathing space. The temple of Apollo at Delos, that of Athena at Tegea, that of Asclepios on Kos, and many others, were *asyla*. In Rome, the institution of a place of asylum was closely connected with the legend of the city's founding. Romulus was believed to have opened one of the slopes of one of the Capitoline Hills (see Livy 1.7.5ff.), and the whole depression between both these hills was later regarded as sacrosanct. When the republic ended and the empire began, the temple erected in honor of Julius Caesar received the same privileged position (see Günter, *Psychologie der Legende*, pp. 32, 33).

The Old Testament, as is well known, carried the *lex talionis*. Blood cries for blood, it was said: "Whosoever shall shed man's blood, his blood shall be shed" (Gn 9:6). The duties of the avenger are clearly stated and earnestly enjoined: "The kinsman of him that was slain shall kill the murderer; as soon as he apprehendeth him, he shall kill him" (Nb 35:19, 21). To the deliberate murderer asylum is denied: "If a man kill his neighbour on set purpose and by lying in wait for him: thou shalt take him away from my altar that he may die" (Ex 21:14). And again (Dt 19:11, 12): "If any man hating his neighbour lie in wait for his life and rise and strike him and he die; and he flee to one of the cities [of refuge]: the ancients of this city shall . . . take him out of the place of refuge and shall deliver him into the hand of the kinsman of him whose blood was shed. And he shall die." These words, while denying the benefit of asylum to malice aforethought, by implication grant it to less culpable manslaughter, and the principle is clearly spelled out (Ex 21:12, 13): "He that striketh a man with a will to kill him shall be put to death. But he that did not lie in wait for him . . . I will appoint [him] . . . a place to which he must flee." The implementation of this program is reflected in the Book of Deuteronomy (4:41ff., 19:2ff.): "Moses set aside three cities beyond the Jordan at the east side that any one might flee to them who should kill his neighbour unwillingly and was not his enemy a day or two before, and that he might escape to some one of the cities." Three other such cities were to be added later, making six, half the number on each side of the Jordan, "that he who is forced to flee for manslaughter may have near at hand whither to escape." The Moslem religion, too, erected similar places of refuge, the most celebrated being, of course, the Ka'bah. Ibn Khaldun (*The Muqaddimah: An Introduction to History*, trans. Franz Rosenthal, 2 vols. [Princeton, N.J., 1958], II 256) says of it that "God . . . granted asylum and protection against all harm to those who take refuge in it and to the cattle that graze on its pastures. No one has anything to fear there. No wild animal is hunted there. No tree is cut down for firewood."

The Christian and Catholic Church, remembering the word of her Founder that the sinner should not perish but be converted and live, tried to give the right of asylum as wide a definition as possible, as soon as it emerged from the era of persecution. An early council, the Council of Orange, in the year 441 passed a canon which ran: "Those who have taken refuge in the church should not be handed over, but should be defended in view of the holiness [*reverentia*— the term also suggests awesomeness] of the place." No restrictions are appended to this resolution. Care was taken to widen the circle of protection from the church building itself to the adjacent area—e.g., the priest's house or the complex of agricultural structures around a monastery. In the nave the fugitive could not remain for long; it was not even considered quite right that he should sleep there. But in a barn he could hide forever. For this reason restrictions were soon placed on the whole institution. We cannot discuss them all, nor need we do so. Sometimes a few of the more serious crimes were exempted. Thus,

Justinian ordained that murderers, adulterers, abductors of young girls, and debtors of public dues should not be able to enjoy safety in an ecclesiastical district; it was lawful to apprehend them there. In the north, the whole institution was resented and resisted because, before their Christianization, the Germanic, Frankish, and Scandinavian tribes had always practiced blood revenge, resembling in this respect the Jews of antiquity. Besides the systematic exclusion of certain qualified misdeeds, limitations were also placed on the duration of safety. It should last only three days, or a month, or six weeks and three days, the span most frequently mentioned, or possibly a year; conditions varied. In many places, the criminal could simply be starved out of his place of hiding. The rationale of this penal policy is easy to discover. There was no reason why a miscreant should escape due punishment. It was therefore the law in many territories that the fugitive should be surrendered as soon as the proper court proceedings against him began. But this did not militate against the true purpose of the law of asylum. That purpose was, as we have indicated, to shield the perpetrator against private vengeance and especially immediate pursuit in red-hot rage (see His, *Das Strafrecht des deutschen Mittelalters*, I 290, 408). The Church could not well attempt to stay the arm of the law. But she did something else, following in this also her Master's behest. She exacted a promise that the surrendered culprit should not be punished in life and limb, i.e., should not be executed or maimed, in other words, that unbloody penalties should be substituted for bloody ones, and this stipulation appears to have been generally accepted (see, on all this, R. B. Bindschedler, *Kirchliches Asylrecht und Freistätten in der Schweiz* [Amsterdam, 1965], pp. 3–19, passim; see also His, *Das Strafrecht des deutschen Mittelalters*, I 405ff.).

Why did this important and wholesome institution decay and disappear? In answering this question, it is not sufficient to refer vaguely and generally to the pervasive process of rationalization which has diminished the influence of Church and religion, although this certainly had something to do with it. Of greater importance is the fact that a determined adversary arose to the right of asylum: absolutism. It did not suit the absolute monarchs that there should be nooks and crannies into which their *sbirri* could not penetrate, and they were stronger than the princes of the Church. Pope Gregory XIV tried, in his constitution *Cum alias*, issued on May 24, 1591, to regulate, reform, but above all to reassert, the ecclesiastical law of asylum, and in the royal ordinance of Villers-Cotterets of 1539 even France had still acknowledged it, though with considerable modifications. In the seventeenth century, however, the French kings killed it altogether (see Holtzmann, *Französische Verfassungsgeschichte*, pp. 166, 456, 457). In Austria, the deeply religious empress Maria Theresa anchored it, as late as 1775, in her penal legislation, but her son, the rationalistic Joseph II, excluded it from his penal code, and thus it was fated to fade out (see Weinhold, *Über die deutschen Fried- und Freistätten*, p. 15). In England, the merger of church and state, effected by Henry VIII's Law of Supremacy, had deprived the Church long before this of any and every possibility of excluding the beadle carrying an arrest-warrant from its domain; the dissolution of the monasteries and the emptying of the tabernacles did the rest.

The churches were no longer privileged places. In this, England did not stand alone: all the Protestant countries retained at most remnants of the once-powerful institution beyond the first days of the revolution known as the Reform.

The right of asylum arose in response to a social need. It was destroyed in response to a "need," not of society, but of small nodi of irresponsible power-holders, and their interests were largely at variance with the interests of society at large, or at least the bulk of it, the citizens. What is true of the absolutist kings of the seventeenth and eighteenth centuries is true of the dictatorships of the twentieth century as well. It is a futile yet intriguing question how many innocent people would have escaped persecution, arrest, torture, and annihilation if the old ecclesiastical law of refuge in the sacred precinct had still been in force in the days of Hitler and Stalin, Gestapo and Ogpu? Clearly, it could not be. But our query shows, at least by implication, what mankind loses when it turns away from religion and Church. Whatever the latter may be, and it is certainly *inter alia* also a bureaucratic structure, it is in any case a vehicle of mercy and grace as well.

Indeed, is it entirely true to say that the institution of asylum was exclusively, or even predominantly, a response to a simple and sober social need? Can it be asserted that it had no other root? It would not seem that this is possible. There lay in it—in its inception and in its practice—an element of charity, and only a blind person could miss it. Its aim was to soften the blow which would fall on the back of the sinner; it was a plea to remember that an erring brother is a brother still. In this way the whole phenomenon points forward, beyond the confines of static religion, to that dynamic religiosity whose spirit is not of this world, but of a higher dispensation, in which law is subordinated to love and not love to law.

SACRED PERSONS; ESPECIALLY THE STRANGER

136. Opening our discussion of the sacralization of things and the consequent defense of them against depredation and willful destruction, we took the Maori culture as our illustration from the primitive world, and we saw that objects become holy if they belong to, or are touched by, sacred persons. We must now speak of these sacred (and hence heaven-protected) persons more directly, and in doing so we may with profit turn to the same general area. The word *ariki* which we used on page 229 translates "priest-chief" (see Thomas, *Primitive Behavior*, p. 330), and this compound term reveals to us that there are, to begin with, two distinct, if often associated, types: sacredness by dint of descent, and sacredness by dint of consecration. E. S. C. Handy writes as follows in an interesting article entitled "Polynesian Religion" (reproduced in ibid., pp. 325–29):

> "The divine chief was a transmitter: linked by an unbroken chain of first-borns to the primal gods, his was mana directly transmitted and made subject to conduction wherever the potential was needed—in agriculture, industry, war.

On the other hand the mana of the priest . . . , which might be almost though not quite as great as that of the chief, was largely diffused mana, acquired as a result of consecrational ceremonies and his continual association with sacred beings, objects and rites . . ." [p. 325].

In these lines we have before us a picture not only of Polynesia, but also of Europe, and not only of a primitive, but also of a higher, culture: namely, that of the Middle Ages. The kings were sacred because they carried the blood royal in their veins; the priests were sacred because they were ordained and the bishops because they had been anointed with holy chrism. The co-existence and the competition of these two kinds of privileged men filled a thousand years of eventful history. The murder of St. Thomas Becket by the minions of Henry II in Canterbury cathedral on December 29, 1170, was a grand climax of it, but by no means the only one. As the present writer has spoken at some length of holy kings and ordained priests in his *Sociology of Religion* (especially in Volumes I, III, IV, and V), no more need or will be said about them here.

There is only one distinction elaborated in our earlier work which is of material importance at this point: the difference between priestly (and priest–kingly) charisma, on the one hand, and the charisma of the saint, on the other (see ibid., IV, pp. 1ff. and 167ff.). Both are men set apart and in a sense close to the deity; both are therefore ever in God's eye. But kings and priests enjoy such prestige as they possess only because of the social status which they occupy: their privileges are due to their position in the class hierarchy. Their charisma (if the term be allowable in their case) is due to objective causes and not to any individual distinction. A king or a priest may be as unsaintly as the devil himself, and yet it may be said of them, as the old ballad of the Vicar of Brae has it, that they are "by God appointed, and those are damned who dare resist or touch the Lord's anointed." A genuine saint, however, has no splendid or even merely secure place in the social system. He is often a lonely man, an outsider. The love which he arouses, the devotion which he inspires, are results of his personal qualities, of the warmth which radiates from him, the saintliness which he displays. He is far from (legally) inviolable; there is no crime of *lèse-sainteté* as there is of *lèse-majesté*. Indeed, the Saint of Saints, Jesus Christ, became the victim of a judicial murder. This difference between objective and subjective charisma, priest and king, on the one side, and genuine saint, on the other, is part and parcel of the Bergsonian distinction between static and dynamic religion. The sacralization of functionaries in church and state serves the existing social set-up. It is an aspect of society's self-stabilization. The saint, however, is a disturber. He would induce his fellow-men to take a step in the direction of the kingdom of God. For this reason, only king and priest properly belong in this section.

But while these two figures are at present of comparably small importance for our investigation, another and very different one is of considerable interest: the stranger. He enjoys, as we shall see in the sequel, a high religious status. His transformation from an underprivileged into an overprivileged type is one of the most remarkable achievements of the anonymous forces in and of society. A scholar of renown, P. J. Hamilton-Grierson, has suggested that the analysis of this development not only should start from social interest, as we ourselves have done in the case of plow and market, but need not, in search of an explanation, look beyond it. Differently expressed: the religious factor need not necessarily be brought in; it is at best a secondary factor, auxiliary to the first and basic one. "To what cause," he asks ("Strangers," *Encyclopaedia of Religion and Ethics*, XI 895), "are we to attribute these modifications of the early rule—the rule that the stranger must die in the interests of the community?" And he replies:

> The rule is modified because experience has taught the community that its interests are better served by sparing and protecting than by killing him. . . . The trader [for instance] is maintained and protected as soon as those who wish to deal with him find that, in order to secure his presence, they must provide for the safety of his property and person. . . . if experience shows that the practice thus formed is generally advantageous to the members of the community, it will gradually be adopted as a general practice, which, approved by public opinion, will, in its turn, become obligatory upon all, as part and parcel of the common custom.

So far, it is possible to go along with Hamilton-Grierson. But now he takes a big stride, or rather a jump, which appears difficult to share and to approve: "when custom gives free rein to kindly feeling," he writes (ibid., 896), "that kindliness reaches not only the stranger who is, in some sense or to some effect, useful to the community, but also the useless stranger—the beggar, the weakling, and the wanderer." This step from an entirely egoistic attitude, as that to a trader with whom one wishes to do profitable business, to an entirely altruistic attitude, as that to a beggar whom one must give alms, is not so easy! Only a strong new influence which, though it cooperates with custom, is different from custom, can motivate and realize such an advance, and that influence is religion, obedience to the gods or God.

Merely with regard to one figure is Hamilton-Grierson fully in the right— the envoy. But precisely where he mentions him (and that happens outside the analytic passages which we have quoted) he places relatively strong emphasis on the religious factor: "the office and the privilege attached [to the person of an ambassador] originate in the elementary needs of savage societies; and here, as in so many other instances, religion invests with its form and supports with its sanctions the institution which those needs have created" (ibid., 893). This is certainly true, but the ambassador is protected not only by God and the gods, but also by those whom he represents and who sent him. Their armed might stands behind him at all times. But the beggar, the weakling, and the wanderer? They have nobody to shield them from harm but the powers above, real or imagined. Without them, their life would not be worth a single penny. "Holy unto the immortal gods are those who, beset by sufferings, ask for aid," writes Homer (*Odyssey* 5.446), and this voice from early Greece bares the root from which the sacredness of the stranger grows.

Our disagreement with Hamilton-Grierson should not, of course, prevent us from making good use of the materials which he has collected. They help us, first of all, to illustrate the great change, or rather the greatness of the change, which religious influences brought about in the dawn of culture. Philologists tell us that there is an historical connection between the Latin words *hostis*, enemy, and *hospes*, guest—an impressive proof that black has, in the course of development, become white. "[A]s a general rule the savage fears and hates the stranger, and looks upon him, certainly as an enemy, and, it may be, as a being brutish, monstrous, or devilish," Hamilton-Grierson reports ("Strangers," 884). "[T]he Yahgan conception of the world beyond the family group (or little aggregate of family groups) as a hostile world may be taken as representing the 'primitive' conception. . . . It may be noted, as showing the position which the stranger . . . occupied in early times, that a series of words which meant originally . . . 'alien' have come to mean 'miserable. . . .' " A good example is the German term *Elend* which basically signifies "out of the land," i.e., out of one's own land, but describes in current usage wretchedness, unhappiness, and pain.

The Greeks noted with some disapproval that the savage—"barbarian"— tribes whom they knew were harsh to newcomers. Thus Herodotus (4.103; see also 106) writes in the fifth century B.C. that the Tauri make a human sacrifice of those who are shipwrecked on their shore; and Strabo says in the first century B.C. (7.3.7; see also 4.5.4) that the Scythians of the same area not only sacrifice strangers, but even devour their flesh. But Livy turns the tables and asserts (31.29.15) that the Greeks themselves thought of themselves as in perpetual warfare with all born abroad. It would ill become a man of the twentieth century to feel as superior to the Greeks in this respect as they did to the Tauri and the Scythians generally, for xenophobia has remained a live sentiment, as all those came to know who, in the present age, were driven from house and home and had to turn refugee.

We say: xenophobia has remained. Would it be possible to go further and suggest that it has, in recent centuries, been re-invigorated? In the absence of any possibility of quantification, it is impossible to answer this question with any assurance, but one thing is certain: namely, that the safety once enjoyed by strangers has lost a most important prop—the conviction that they are under divine protection. We behold here one of the consequences of the process called by Max Weber the "disenchantment of the world"; more soberly expressed: the disappearance of superstitions and the decay of even rationally defensible religious convictions. The Greeks also had, beside their Zeus Horios and Zeus Agrapaios, Zeus Xenios, and he who raised his hand against a ξένος raised it also against Xenios. The complex of ideas called humanitarianism— assertion of the rights of man, of the sanctity of international law, and the like —has a wide appeal, but it has little power. But powerful was Zeus Xenios among the Greeks, for he was lord of heaven and earth, and his right hand was armed with lightning. When Odysseus, shipwrecked, asks Nausicaa for meat and drink, she feeds him, accompanying her kindly action with the remark that strangers are sent by Zeus (*Odyssey* 6.207ff.). Later on in the poem (17.483ff.) the belief is expressed that the gods, in the guise of aliens and hiding under different appearances, walk abroad in order to find out how the hosts treat their guests—an idea which appears in religious lore of other nations as well.

Let us stay a little longer with the Greeks. The words put into the mouth of the civilized Athenian in Plato's *Laws* (5.729ff.) reveal the attitude of most Hellenes. "We must consider," he says (trans. More, in *Religion of Plato*, pp. 272–73),

> that the most sacred of business dealings are those with foreigners; since these are under a god's care, whose vengeance is quicker upon all sins touching foreigners than upon those touching citizens. This is because the foreigner, being devoid of comrades and kinsmen, is more an object of pity to men and gods. He that is abler to avenge is more zealous to help, and there is none so able and zealous as the peculiar daemon and god of the foreigner who follow in the train of Zeus the Protector. He, then, who has a spark of prudence will be very cautious to make his journey to the end of life without committing any of the sins against foreigners. But of the sins touching either foreigners or citizens that is the greatest which concerns suppliants of any sort; for the god who is witness to an agreement made with a suppliant becomes the suppliant's special guardian, and will not leave him unavenged if any wrong, even the least, befall him.

In the Hebrew Scriptures, no fewer than three passages insist on the inviolability of the stranger: Exodus 22:21, Leviticus 19:33–34, and Deuteronomy 10:19. The passage in Exodus sounds the fundamental note, as it were; Leviticus elaborates it: "If a stranger dwell in your land, and abide among you, do not upbraid him: but let him be among you as one of the same country. And you shall love him as yourselves. . . . I am the Lord your God." The last words remind the believer that here a divine commandment is pronounced, not merely a moral recommendation unbacked by sanctions. And Deuteronomy repeats: "Do you therefore love strangers: because you also were strangers in the land of Egypt."

As for the Germanic nations, the opera lovers in our midst will immediately think of that most dramatic scene in Wagner's *Valkyrie* where Hunding comes home and finds on his own hearth his arch-enemy, Siegmund, whom he has, moreover, every right to suspect of adultery, already committed or at least intended, with his wife, Sieglinde. With an heroic effort at self-control, he fights down the desire to kill the hated intruder on the spot; the temptation to do so is strong, but he desists. While you are in my house, he declares, you are safe. You may stay the night. Tomorrow we meet in deadly combat out in the open where the law of hospitality does not protect you—that law which Hunding well knows has Wotan for its defender. Many would be inclined to argue that such material should not even be mentioned in a scholarly treatise, and that the passage concerned is no more than a proof of Wagner's vivid imagination. But this would not merely be narrow-minded; it would also be downright wrong. Wagner was intimately acquainted with the historical sources, especially the Nordic ones, and he knew what he was saying. We are told about the deeply respectful attitude of the Germans to the strangers who had stumbled into their midst both by insiders and by outsiders, both by Teutons and Romans. Caesar (*De bello Gallico* 6.23) and Tacitus (*Germania* 21) speak about it with one voice. Tacitus writes:

No race indulges more lavishly in hospitality and entertainment: to close the door against any human being is a crime. Every one according to his property receives at a well-spread board: should it fail, he who had been your host points out your place of entertainment and goes with you. You go next door, without an invitation, but it makes no difference; you are received with the same courtesy. Stranger or acquaintance, no one distinguishes them where the right of hospitality is concerned. It is customary to speed the parting guest with anything he fancies [*Dialogus, Agricola, Germania* (London & Cambridge, Mass., 1963), p. 295].

Caesar expresses himself more tersely, but he uses a word which is highly expressive. Strangers, he says, *sanctos habent*—they consider them as inviolable, indeed, as sacred.

If it be said that hot-blooded men like Hunding would have been so incensed by Siegmund's adultery that the religious belief in the holiness of the stranger would have been set aside by him, we must in reply point to two passages in the Hebrew Scriptures which show that, at that level of development, the inviolability of the guest was placed even above the inviolability of a family member. The Book of Genesis reports (in chapter 19) that Lot had invited two strangers into his house and that the rabble outside wanted to assault him. "Lot went out to them and shut the door after him and said: Do not so, I beseech you, my brethren; do not commit this evil. I have two daughters who as yet have not known man. I will bring them out to you, and abuse you them as it shall please you, so that you do not evil to these men, because they are come in under the shadow of my roof" (verses 6–8). The Book of Judges (19:20–24) tells a very similar story—a story in which a daughter's honor is offered in return for the safety of a guest.

Another author who, like Wagner, was also an expert historian, Sir Walter Scott, writes in *The Fair Maid of Perth* (London, n.d.; p. 398): "An appeal to the hospitality of the wildest Gael was never unsuccessful; and the kerne, that in other circumstances would have taken a man's life for the silver button of his cloak, would deprive himself of a meal to relieve the traveller who implored hospitality at the door of his bothy."

Lack of space forbids us to speak about the Arabs and the Chinese (and many smaller societies as well), though both the Chinese and the Arabic peoples are well known for their generous hospitality. But a word should be said about the Japanese because we possess a firsthand account from the pen of a highly qualified observer. Its date is significant. The experience it reports falls into a period when outside influences had not yet had time to inundate even the countryside, and so we get a glimpse of a spontaneously grown and obviously archaic attitude. Michel Revon writes as follows in that excellent repository of reliable information, the *Encyclopaedia of Religion and Ethics* ("Hospitality (Japanese and Korean)," VI 815):

To-day a foreigner travelling in the interior of the country may still find the ancient hospitality, which was never eclipsed except by the fault of those who were the first to profit by it. The present writer can bring his personal experience to witness. One night in 1896, when travelling in Yamato, he found himself lost in the open country. After walking for a long time in the dark and in drenching rain in search of a village where he might find a means of transport, he arrived at a peasant's hut and knocked at the door. Imagine a Japanese travelling in the country in Europe and arriving at midnight at a peasant's house: there would be furious barking from the watch-dog, hostile suspicion of the unknown wanderer on the part of the master of the house, and, to put things at their best, a poor shelter offered at last, with no good grace, in some outhouse. The Japanese cottage, on the other hand, was opened immediately; the father and his family all got up to receive the stranger on their knees; they were very pressing in their offers of a bath and a friendly meal. After this came the classic questions in Homeric style: "Honourable stranger, whence comest thou? Whither goest thou? What is thy country?" and so on. Finally, when the guest was ready to depart, the father sent two of his sons several miles distant to bring a *jinrikisha* and runners to carry him to Kyōto. It is hardly necessary to add that these poor peasants would not take any remuneration, and the only way in which their guest was able to repay them at all was by discreetly making presents to the youngest members of the family.

Let us now in conclusion cast a glance at the Christian tradition. When the Gospels, and all that developed from them, are searched, it is found that the theme of hospitality and its sacredness is very prominent throughout. When Christ sends out his apostles, He tells them to rely on the willingness of the pious Jews to welcome and support a wanderer:

> And he called the twelve and began to send them [out] . . . and he commanded them that they should take nothing for the way, but a staff only: no scrip, no bread, nor money in their purse. . . . And he said to them: wheresoever you shall enter into a house, there abide till you depart from that place. And whosoever shall not receive you, . . . going forth from thence, shake off the dust from your feet for a testimony to them [Mk 6:7–11].

We are surely not going wrong when we suggest that the last words mean: for a testimony against them, for the denial of hospitality was to Jesus a serious sin. *Per contra*, the grant of hospitality was to Him a signal merit. In speaking of the Last Judgment, of the separation of sheep and goats, saints and sinners (Mt 25:34–43), He expresses Himself as follows:

> Then shall the [heavenly] king say to them that shall be on his right hand: Come, ye blessed of my Father, possess you the kingdom prepared for you from the foundation of the world. For I was hungry, and you gave me to eat; I was thirsty, and you gave me to drink; I was a stranger and you took me in. . . . Then shall the just answer him, saying: Lord, when did we see thee hungry and fed thee; thirsty and gave you to drink? And when did we see thee a stranger and took thee in? . . . And the king, answering, shall say to them: Amen I say to you, as long as you did it to one of these my least brethren, you did it to me.

We have no need to follow the theme through the First Epistle of St. Peter (4:9) and through St. Paul (Rm 12:13; Heb 13:2; see also 1 Tm 5:10) to such early writers as St. Jerome and St. John Chrysostom and then down the centuries. Only one especially resplendent link in the chain should be mentioned: St. Benedict's "Holy Rule." In the fifty-third chapter, it says that all visitors who arrive at an abbey's door should be welcomed as if they were Christ Himself. This was not only a pious wish. This was a binding command, and every Benedictine house had its guest master who saw to it that it was carried out. The authority of St. Benedict was supported by various legends which grew from the religious subsoil. So it was said that Oda, daughter of King Childebert of Austrasia, once had a visitor in her hospital when she was told that the larder was empty. She went to look herself, and behold! it was full. The visitor had been the Lord. St. Jodocus and his disciple Vurmar one day had only a single loaf of bread; just then a beggar called. The saint gave half of it to the stranger. Soon a second and a third arrived, and again Jodocus commanded that the shrinking supply be shared. Vurmar demurred, but Jodocus insisted. Finally, a fourth beggar came to the door and received what was left. At that moment four boats laden with victuals were seen to draw near. Vurmar did not have to go hungry for long! The anonymous biographer of ca. 800 stops at this point. But when Florentius retold the story around 1015, the fourth beggar was identified as Jesus Christ (Günter, *Psychologie der Legende*, pp. 129, 130; see also p. 190 *re* Veronica of Mercatello). What is surely remarkable in all this is the continuity of religious development and the unity of religious consciousness: as Zeus stands behind the shipwrecked Odysseus, as Wotan stands behind the fugitive Siegmund, so Christ stands behind every needy person who knocks at the door. Indeed, it is He who knocks.

Whoever entertains a guest incurs costs; he must submit to inconveniences; he brings a sacrifice. If we welcome a stranger with a glad heart, as the Gospel demands, we have risen above creaturely limitations and shown genuine charity. It might therefore be thought that the subject of hospitality should have been treated in the chapter entitled "Dynamic Religion," and not, like here, under the heading "Static Religion." Admittedly, we have a border phenomenon before our eyes, and in many cases a host's attitude will in fact be determined by the higher type of religiosity distinguished by Henri Bergson rather than the lower. Yet, by and large, we are still in the area of static religion. One reason for saying this is that the institution of hospitality has, generally speaking, sprung from fear of the stranger, not love of him. He must be appeased; his curse is to be averted. But where such conceptions as the evil eye are still present, the level of dynamic religiosity is not yet reached. Furthermore, the stranger is not really accepted *as* a stranger; he is much rather transformed, for a time, into a fictitious insider. He belongs to a house; the householder is his housefather. "The stranger is without rights. . . . Hospitality afforded him legal protection. . . . Any insult to the guest involved the host and his sib as well" (Hermann Conrad, *Deutsche Rechtsgeschichte* [Karlsruhe, 1962], I 15). The whole institution of hospitality still had a decidedly legal character. But, as we intimated at the end of the last section, where law is still stronger than love, the highest level is not yet attained. Indeed, the very distinction between "us" and "them" has to be left behind if the spirit of dynamic religion, in the full sense of the word, is to come into its own.

4

Dynamic Religion

137. The sociologist is neither a theologian nor a philosopher. He should think twice before venturing into any of these areas. But he cannot always avoid it. If two different concepts of the deity have two different kinds of influence on social life, it is his duty to concern himself with the basic theologico-philosophical conceptualizations involved and to investigate their bearings. Assuming that he is a man of broad culture, they will assuredly not escape his grasp.

Even a slight acquaintance with the history of religious ideas can teach that there have always been two competing definitions of the divinity. God can be seen, either as the stern judge of His subjects, or as the loving father of His children. So persistent are both these intuitions that neither will yield to the other, and the great dogma of the Trinity, One and Undivided, has been the result. But though there has been this reconciliation of opposites, the contrast has not entirely disappeared. Both the Old Testament and the New are part and parcel of the Christian creed or creeds: in the one, God is the King of Israel; in the other, the Father of Mankind. Catholics and Calvinists alike accept the Apostles' Creed, but the latter are closer to the old Hebraic ideas, while the former cling to the word of St. John the Evangelist that God is Love. In our context, the definition according to which God is essentially the Eternal Judge is more of the spirit of static, the conviction that He is essentially a wellspring of benevolence, mercy and grace, more of the spirit of dynamic, religion. As Bergson so often and so well expresses it, religion can be either a power which holds us down or a power which raises us up, either the imposition of a discipline or a call to brotherhood. It is with the latter belief and its social consequences that these closing sections of our book have to deal.

The assertion that all men are equally the children of one Father in heaven is the core of the message of Jesus Christ, most movingly revealed in the Sermon on the Mount. The prophets of Israel have been called His precursors. Indeed, He has often been described as the last of the prophets of the old dispensation and the first of the saints of the new. In one or two sentences Bergson seems to come close to this opinion: "no current of thought or feeling has contributed so much as the thought and feeling of Jewish prophets to arouse the mysticism which we call complete, that of the Christian mystics," he writes (*Two Sources of Morality*, p. 240). And again: "Christianity, which succeeded Judaism, owed largely to the Jewish prophets its active mysticism, capable of marching on to the conquest of the world" (ibid.). Yet, on the very same page,

Bergson rejects the thesis that there is an unbroken link between, say, Isaiah and Jeremiah, on the one hand, and Jesus of Nazareth on the other. "There is no doubt," he argues,

> that Christianity was a profound transformation of Judaism. It has been said over and over again: a religion which was still essentially national was replaced by a religion that could be made universal. A God Who was doubtless a contrast to all other gods by His justice as well as by His power, but Whose power was used for His people, and Whose justice was applied, above all, to His own subjects, was succeeded by a God of love, a God Who loved all mankind. This is precisely why we hesitate to classify the Jewish prophets among the mystics of antiquity. . . .

In these words Bergson puts his finger on the two great limitations of all static religiosity: its ethnocentrism, which is earlier on a narrow tribalism, and at a later period a deep-rooted nationalism; and its one-sided emphasis on justice, which means, by implication, also on retribution and punishment. "Jehovah was too stern a judge," Bergson writes (ibid.), and if Judaism is seen from the vantage point of the Gospels, this remark appears entirely justified. Thus a gap is opened up between the two dispensations, and the voice of Jesus is seen to be the vehicle of a revolutionary mind. This gap is somewhat narrowed by the fact that the social ideal preached by the prophets is not too far from that of Christ, if the tribalistic–nationalistic exclusivity connected with it is removed. Of this aspect we shall speak in our final section.

Bergson has rightly laid strong emphasis on the henotheistic character of early religion, religion even in the culture areas which, to say the least, prepared the ground for the strict monotheism of Christendom. Henotheism is the belief in a god who is not the only one; he is the private possession, so to speak, of a tribe, a city, or a people, while other tribes, cities, or peoples are allowed to have their own privately owned gods or godlings. "In Egypt, for example," Bergson writes (ibid., p. 193),

> each of the primitive cities had its divine guardian. And these gods were distinguished one from the other precisely by their connexion with this or that community; to call them "He of Edfu," "He of Nekkeb," was clear enough. . . . It was the same in Babylonia, where the city of Ur had as its goddess the moon, the city of Uruk the planet Venus [etc.]. . . . Often protectors and protected stood or fell together; the gods of a city gained by the aggrandisement of that city. War thus became a struggle between rival deities.

The mentality of the Jews was, at least to begin with, no different. They, too, were originally henotheists rather than strict monotheists, however little this fact may suit the book of some religionists. Adolphe Lods has made this very clear in a remarkable passage of his rightly celebrated work *Israel* (trans. S. H. Hooke [London, 1932], pp. 461, 462):

> However much the ancient Israelites may have been impressed with the inscrutability of the divine will, they were, at all events, thoroughly convinced that the will of Jahweh was always directed towards the good of his people. . . . The one certain fact was that Jahweh was bound to Israel. . . . The care of Jahweh for his people appears in all the circumstances in which Israel is in-

volved . . . and always takes the form of a personal intervention. . . . The foremost of such situations was war. The national struggles of Israel were called "the wars of Jahweh." The enemies of the nation were the enemies of its God. . . . In time of war, Jahweh aided his people in counsel as well as in action: he aided them in counsel by revealing through oracles, dreams, or omens, the fortunate or fatal result of the intended campaign, and by pointing out the necessary strategy . . . ; in action he aided them by spreading panic among the enemy, by pouring down hail upon them, by causing the sun and moon to stand still in order to allow his people to dispatch the fugitives, by producing a storm or an earth-quake. . . . In Hebrew poetry, Jahweh is "a man of war"; he overwhelms his enemies with his arrows and smites them with his sword.

It is a long way from desert days when these convictions first sprang up to the days of the efflorescence of the Israelitic and Judaic kingdoms and cultures, from Moses and Joshua to Isaiah and Jeremiah, but Hebrew religion remained substantially nationalistic. It continued to be part and parcel of a tribal and/or national patriotism, and for this reason we must class it, with the other ancient creeds, as a form of static religion, however elevated it became in and through the prophets. A total study of the matter is out of the question here, but a few selected details will suffice to show that our judgment is not unfair. Let us look first at some of the minor prophets and then at the major ones, Isaiah, Jeremiah, and Ezechiel.

In the third chapter of Zephaniah, we read a very hard word which has embarrassed those who would rather tone down the nationalistic element in this prophet's preaching: "My judgment is to assemble the Gentiles and to pour upon them my indignation, all my fierce anger." This threat is, of course, supposed to come from God; Zephaniah regards himself as God's mouth and tongue. One of the most profound students of the prophetic literature, Josef Scharbert, comments on this passage as follows (*Die Propheten Israels um 600 v. Chr.* [Cologne, 1967], p. 27):

> Some interpreters suspect that versicle 8 is a later reworking which made out of an original announcement of a day of judgment over Jerusalem or Juda an announcement of this bearing addressed to the heathen peoples. But if this is their view, they misunderstand Zephaniah's theology of history. For this prophet, Israel, the people of Yahweh, is the center of all the peoples and the true object of the divine government of the world. All events in world politics are seen in relation to the people of Yahweh; in them, Yahweh speaks to His people, either in order to warn and correct them, or in order to comfort and save them.

Other nations are indeed involved, but only in a secondary manner. They are, in the first place, Israel's present adversaries; they are also, in the second place, Israel's potential and, maybe, future friends; but in themselves they have no value of their own. After studying the Biblical text very carefully, Scharbert concludes (ibid., p. 35):

> The main theological conceptions can be summarized quickly: Israel is the proper object of the divine scheme of the world. All nations are in the hands of Yahweh, and through Yahweh they are united with Israel in a common destiny. If Israel proves untrue to Yahweh, he will smash it on "the day of Yahweh" together with the heathen nations; but if it were to use the interval

for penance and reform, Yahweh would annihilate the nations who have induced Israel to defect; Israel itself, however, would be reprieved and then, later, convert the other nations so that the Jews may serve Yahweh in peace and in unity with the rest of the world.

If this is not typical ethnocentrism, nothing is.

The spirit of Habacuc and Nahum is no different. Habacuc prophesies that God will arouse the Chaldeans (i.e., Babylonians), set them against the Assyrians who oppress Israel, and give them the victory. Thus everything is so contrived that it is Israel which will benefit and triumph. "The ancient Israelitic idea of a holy war of Yahweh against Israel's adversaries is revived" (ibid., p. 46). The third chapter of this book carries the title "A Prayer of Habacuc the Prophet," and Scharbert discusses it under the heading "A Hymn to Yahweh." This hymn reveals the fundamental theological conception of all static religion: God is a god of power. Before him goes pestilence—so Scharbert translates verse 5—behind him the burning fever. "Yahweh brings all the misery over Israel's enemies which the heathen attribute to the sickness-bringing demons" (ibid., p. 45). The image of Yahweh which is painted in the sequel is that of a warrior. And why does he go to war? "Thou wentest forth for the salvation of thy people," says the hymn (versicle 13). "God will come from the south and the holy one from Mount Pharan. . . . The curtains of the land of Madian shall be troubled" (vv. 3, 7). Nahum's idea of the deity is similar to Habacuc's. "The Lord is a jealous God and a revenger: the Lord is a revenger and hath wrath: the Lord taketh vengeance on his adversaries and he is angry with his enemies" (1:2). In this prophet, the hatred against Assyria reaches the height of a paroxysm. Speaking of Nineveh, he cries: "Woe to thee, O city of blood. . . . the gates of thy land shall be set wide open to thy enemies. . . . Behold I come against thee, saith the Lord of hosts, and I will burn thy chariots even to smoke: and the sword shall devour thy young lions. . . . There is no end of carcasses" (3:1, 13; 2:13; 3:3).

Whose voice is this? Scharbert (ibid., p. 59) writes of Habacuc and Nahum: "They speak entirely in the spirit of King Josia and his advisers and fill the people with enthusiasm for the hoped-for liberation from the Assyrian yoke." In these two prophets, nationalism reaches its acme. Their deep religiosity should not be doubted, and their trust in the god of their fathers is impressive and admirable. But he is the god of their fathers only. To the others he is merely a step-god, if a term parallel to stepparent may be permitted. Indeed, even from the point of view of the traditional religiosity of their own nation, there is something missing in Habacuc's and Nahum's attitude: "Out of their mouth we hear not one single word about the sins of the people, the failure of the kings and priests, the necessity of penance and conversion. . . . Here precisely lies the great difference from their contemporaries Zephaniah and Jeremiah, but also from their predecessors Isaiah and Micah, Amos and Osee."

What then about the penitential prophets, Isaiah and Jeremiah, and also Ezechiel who, together with them, is counted among the group usually described as the major prophets? We cannot, unfortunately, enter into a discussion of the detail; it would take us far too far afield. Suffice it to say that, generally speaking, they resemble Habacuc and Nahum (see ibid., esp. the summary on pp. 470ff.). To come, however, to some extent, to grips with their ethnocentrism we may, perhaps, for a moment concentrate on a detail within the detail, the relation of Israel to Edom, because this theme appears in all three of them. This is what Isaiah writes in his thirty-fourth chapter (vv. 1, 5–9, 13):

> Come near, ye Gentiles, and hear. . . . My sword is inebriated in heaven: behold it shall come down upon Idumea [i.e., Edom]. . . . There is a victim of the Lord in Bosra and a great slaughter in the land of Edom. . . . Their land shall be soaked with blood. . . . For it is the day of the vengeance of the Lord. . . . And the streams thereof shall be turned into pitch, and the ground thereof into brimstone. . . . And thorns and nettles shall grow up in its houses, and the thistle in the fortresses thereof: and it shall be the habitation of dragons and the pasture of ostriches.

In the Bibles which contain the annotations of that Bishop Richard Challoner who, in the eighteenth century, re-established the Catholic hierarchy in England, we read at this point the following remark from his pen: "Under the name of Idumea, or Edom, a people who were enemies of the Jews, are here understood the wicked in general." The contrast between static and dynamic religion, or at least one facet of it, comes clearly to the surface here.

Jeremiah lived a century or so after Isaiah, but the accents are the same. The seventh verse of the forty-ninth chapter indicates the subject of the next following passages: "Against Edom." We read (vv. 13, 17, 18):

> I have sworn by myself, saith the Lord, that Bosra shall become a desolation, and a reproach, and a desert, and a curse: and all her cities shall be everlasting wastes. . . . And Edom shall be desolate: every one that shall pass by it shall be astonished and shall hiss at all its plagues. As Sodom was overthrown and Gomorrha and the neighbours thereof, saith the Lord: there shall not a man dwell there and there shall no son of man inhabit it.

Finally, Ezechiel (25:12–14):

> Thus saith the Lord God: Because Edom hath taken vengeance to revenge herself of the children of Juda, and hath greatly offended, and hath sought revenge of them: Therefore thus saith the Lord God: I will stretch forth my hand upon Edom and will take away out of it man and beast, and will make it desolate from the south: and they that are in Dedan shall fall by the sword. And I will lay my vengeance upon Edom by the hand of my people Israel, and they shall do in Edom according to my wrath and my fury, and they shall know my vengeance, saith the Lord.

The same spirit has entered even the Psalms. The last three verses of Psalm 136 (7–9) run as follows: "Remember, O Lord, the children of Edom in the day [of the liberation] of Jerusalem. . . . Raze it, raze it, even to the foundation thereof. O daughter of Babylon, miserable: blessed shall he be who shall repay thee thy payment which thou has paid us. Blessed be he that shall take and dash thy little ones against the rock."

These passages are not quoted here in order to show the Psalmist and the three prophets in a bad light. This must be said and strongly emphasized. They are quoted, not in order to criticize, but in order to characterize. From the human point of view, their bitterness is easy to understand. Israel and Juda suffered greatly under the brutality of their neighbors, and above all under the knout of their Assyrian conquerors (see Scharbert, *Die Propheten . . . um 600*, p. 60). Of course, in an investigation of religious conceptions and influences, the human point of view is not decisive. But even from the religious point of view, or rather from the point of view of the science of religion, much may be said in mitigation of the first impression, which cannot but be one of revulsion. Ethnocentrism has dominated most of religious thought from its inception to the present day. The prophets were no different from other spiritual leaders, and even the uncompromising universalism of the Gospels has not driven patriotism from the temple: witness Anglicanism, witness Orthodoxy, whose nationalism has been shown up, in all its facets, in the present author's *Sociology of Religion* (i 77f., 111ff.). In this workaday world, hatred of the outsider is a widespread, not to say ubiquitous, sentiment, but a voice has broken into it which has pleaded *Love your enemies*; and this voice has been the voice of dynamic religiosity, a religiosity which would lead mankind beyond the limits in which it is at present self-enclosed.

The same hard feelings which the prophets entertained toward those of other nations, they sometimes entertained even toward their own. Thus Jeremiah, a native of Anathoth, feels unbridled hostility for his kinsfolk and neighbors there. He imagines that Yahweh says to him: "Even thy brethren and the house of thy father, even they have fought against thee" (12:6). So he prays: "Thou, O Lord of Sabaoth, who judgeth justly and triest the reins and the hearts, let me see thy revenge on them! . . . Gather them together as sheep for a sacrifice, and prepare them for the day of slaughter" (11:20, 12:3). And Yahweh's supposed answer? "I will bring in evil upon the men of Anathoth. . . . Their young men shall die by the sword, their sons and their daughters shall die by famine" (11:23, 22). Scharbert comments on these passages as follows (*Die Propheten . . . um 600*, p. 190):

> Jeremiah's prayer for vengeance on his relatives and fellow-citizens should not inspire us with self-righteous indignation. Jeremiah is a man of his time and does not know yet Jesus' Sermon on the Mount. Like every pious man of his people, he finds it quite in order if god avenges unjust oppression and wicked persecution according to the principle of talion, that is to say, if he lets the adversary experience the same fate which they had prepared for the godly man.

We have now reached the second great shortcoming of all static religion: its conception of the deity as essentially a punishing judge, an avenger of lawless conduct. The principle of justice prevalent in the early phases of Jewish history is formulated in the Book of Leviticus (24:20): "Eye for eye, tooth for tooth." It is not surprising that this *lex talionis* should have been adopted, for, apart from everything else, it promises to be most effective as a means of deterrence; it is likewise not surprising that the same principle should also have been ascribed to the deity, the eternal judge, for was he not essentially a supporter of the human judge, a completor of human justice, a prolongation, as it were, of the human judge and his activity a prolongation of human justice? But if we analyze these conceptions, we soon come upon a curious paradox. The eternal judge is all-knowing and all-powerful and therefore much stronger than the human judge; but the threat of retribution and retaliation issuing from him has always been felt to be much weaker. The explanation of this self-contradiction lies in the fact that God's verdict and its execution are delayed. He judges only after a person's death and punishment cannot begin before then. But what is far off is not seen in its true colors; distance diminishes the intensity of an impression. A delusion is created in this way, but it is a delusion which wayward man all too readily accepts. In studying this matter, one is reminded of E. von Böhm-Bawerk's once famous book *Positive Theorie des Kapitalzinses* (1889). One hundred dollars or pounds a year hence, he explains, are not worth to a man as much as one hundred dollars or pounds now. A man would never put money into a savings bank if he did not get his 5 or 6 or 7 per cent in order to close the gap. The explanation of the phenomenon of interest now follows different lines, but the psychological law enunciated by Böhm-Bawerk stands. It is as old as mankind; it is part and parcel of basic psychology. The order-defending forces in society, too, had a gap to close, and they did it by painting the threatened punishment at the hands of the deity in the most glaring colors. Thereby something entered into religion which has an awful family likeness to sadism. Of course, this trait is characteristic of static religion only. It has nothing to do with Him who said, according to the Gospel of St. Matthew (18:22), that we should forgive our brother seventy times seven times.

One text which throws the contrast between the two forms of faith into high relief is in the twenty-eighth chapter of the Book of Deuteronomy, verses 15 through 68. The large number of versicles is noteworthy: they all contain maledictions, enumerating the blows which will rain down on the sinner. We can only give a few samples:

> The Lord shall send upon thee famine and hunger. . . . May the Lord afflict thee with miserable want, with the fever and with cold, with burning and with heat, and with corrupted air and with blasting: and pursue thee till thou perish. Be the heaven, that is over thee, of brass, and the ground thou treadest on, of iron. The Lord give thee dust for rain upon thy land, and let ashes come down from heaven upon thee, till thou be consumed. . . . May the Lord strike thee with a very sore ulcer in the knees and in the legs, and be thou incurable from the sole of the foot to the top of the head. . . . The Lord strike thee with the ulcer of Egypt, and the part of thy body, by which the dung is cast out, with the scab and with the itch: so that thou canst not be healed. . . . And all these curses shall come upon thee, and shall pursue and overtake thee till thou perish, because thou heardst not the voice of the Lord thy God, and didst not keep his commandments and ceremonies which he command thee [vv. 20, 22–24, 35, 27, 45].

No wonder that Bishop Challoner, in a note appended to the first malediction (v. 15), distances himself from the spirit revealed in it. But the 108th Psalm is not much milder (see esp. vv. 6–15).

The assumption of the author or authors of Deuteronomy is that divine vengeance will come down on the head of the culprit within his life, i.e., on earth, for ideas concerning the hereafter were still vague when these pages were penned. When, in the so-called higher religions (we need not pause to discuss the justification of this term), the conviction established itself that God judges and punishes after death, the Böhm-Bawerkian problem presented itself anew, but with even higher intensity, for the threatened retribution seemed now yet farther off. Not surprisingly, it was solved in the same way as before. Thus there arose the imagination of a hell or hells with torments that many have found unendurable even in the telling. It was not rare for people to faint during hellfire preachings such as they not uncommonly were in the eighteenth century.

The material at our disposal is overwhelming. It comes from all the world religions. Let us look first at Buddhism and later at Islam, interspersing a reference to Plato's *Republic* in order to show that the supposedly carefree Greek religiosity was laden with the same ballast. Let us then end with a Christian text, or rather a text from the Christian centuries.

The Buddhist tradition knows eight hells. A commentary on the book called *Jataka* (verses 270 and 271) describes them as follows: (1) "Beings are here cut to pieces by the keepers . . . and come repeatedly to life to suffer the same punishment." (2) "Beings are struck down with blazing weapons, and, while lying on the ground, are cut into eight or sixteen pieces. . . ." (3) "Beings on burning mountains are crushed like sesamum seeds or sugar-cane. . . ." (4 & 5) called *Roruva*. "There are two hells of this name Jālaroruva, 'Roruva of flame,' and Dhūmaroruva, 'Roruva of smoke,' where beings are correspondingly tortured." These places are denominated in Sanskrit "the place of 'wailing' " and "the place of 'great wailing.' " (6) " 'Heating,' where beings are fixed on spikes the height of a palm-tree and burnt." (7) " 'Great heating,' where beings are cast down from a blazing iron mountain, below which blazing stakes are set up." (8) "Flames arise from each of the four walls, and from the top and bottom, and strike the opposite sides." "Here there is no interval of cessation either of the flames or of the pain of the beings" (see Edward J. Thomas, "State of the Dead (Buddhist)," *Encyclopaedia of Religion and Ethics*, XI 830). The Mahayana tradition particularly carried these ideas into the future and developed them further.

With the Greeks we find nothing equally elaborate. The Tartarus of which Homer speaks holds some quite abnormal sinners like Tantalus and Sisyphus whose sufferings have become proverbial. Otherwise the idea of hell is left rather vague, with one exception which, in our context, is not insignificant: perjurers were consigned to it, for, like Tantalus and Sisyphus, they have sinned grievously. But even in Greece, the collective imagination was at work and produced myths, one of which is told in Plato's *Republic* X, 614B–616A (trans. Paul Shorey [London & Cambridge, Mass., 1963], pp. 491ff.): the Pamphylian warrior Er was

slain in battle, and when the corpses were taken up on the tenth day already decayed, was found intact, and having been brought home, at the moment of his funeral, on the twelfth day as he lay upon the pyre, revived, and after coming to life related what, he said, he had seen in the world beyond. He said that when his soul went forth from his body he journeyed with a great company and that they came to a mysterious region where there were two openings side by side in the earth, and above and over against them in the heaven two others, and that judges were sitting between these, and that after every judgement they bade the righteous journey to the right and upwards through the heaven . . . and the unjust to take the road to the left and downward. . . .

Those directed downward could, after suffering the penalty for their misdeeds, emerge again and go on to heaven. One of the souls appearing from below and traveling upward tells Er the sad story of the eternal fate of one Ardiaeus. This man

> had been tyrant in a certain city of Pamphylia . . . and had put to death his old father and his elder brother, and had done many other unholy deeds, as was the report. . . . When we were near the mouth and about to issue forth and all our other sufferings were ended, we suddenly caught sight of him and of others, the most of them, I may say, tyrants. But there were some of private station, of those who had committed great crimes. And when these supposed that at last they were about to go up and out, the mouth would not receive them, but it bellowed when anyone of the incurably wicked or of those who had not completed their punishment tried to come up. And thereupon, he said, savage men of fiery aspect who stood by and took note of the voice laid hold on them and bore them away. But Ardiaeus and others they bound hand and foot and head and flung down and flayed them and dragged them by the wayside, carding them on thorns and signifying to those who from time to time passed by for what cause they were borne away, and that they were to be hurled into Tartarus.

We now take a long jump from Plato to Mohammed. The Koran asserts in sura 3.9 (Arberry, *Koran Interpreted*, I 74) that "God is terrible in retribution," and if certain passages in this book of prophecy had to be taken as the truth, this would indeed be so. Evildoers will be "dragged on their faces into the Fire" (54.45) (ibid., II 249). There they will taste "boiling water and pus, and other torments of the like kind coupled together" (38.55ff.; see also 78.30) (ibid., II 162, 230). As if boiling water and pus were not bad enough, another sura (18.25) goes further; if the damned "call for succour, they will be succoured with water like molten copper, that shall scald their faces" (ibid., I 320). "Lo, the Tree of Ez-Zakkoum is the food of the guilty, like molten copper, bubbling in the belly as boiling water bubbles" (54.40ff.) (ibid., II 209). Equally bloodcurdling is yet another passage, sura 4.55 (ibid., I 108):

> . . . those who disbelieve in Our signs—We shall certainly roast them at a Fire; as often as their skins are wholly burned, We shall give them in exchange other skins, that they may taste [once more] the chastisement.

It is hardly credible, but it is a fact that later generations still "improved" on the Koran, by suggesting, for instance, that the bodies of the victims will be increased so that they may suffer more, but we shall not stay to investigate these further "embellishments."

Among the Christian Fathers of the first centuries, we find both puritanical and Pelagian tendencies—in other words, both sternness and mildness—and to the former group belongs Hippolytus Portuensis, also known as Hippolytus of Rome, from whose fragment "Against Plato, on the Cause of the Universe" we wish to quote (trans. S. D. F. Selmond, in *The Anti-Nicene Fathers*, edd. Alexander Roberts and James Donaldson, 10 vols. [Buffalo, N.Y., 1885—], v 221, 222, 223). He speaks first of "Hades, in which the souls both of the righteous and the unrighteous are detained" until the Last Judgment; "in this locality there is a certain place set apart by itself, a lake of unquenchable fire, into which we suppose no one has ever yet been cast; for it is prepared against the day determined by God, in which one sentence of righteous judgment shall be justly applied to all. And the unrighteous . . . shall be sentenced to this endless punishment." Hippolytus then goes on to describe how "the righteous [are] being conducted in the light toward the right," while

> the unrighteous are dragged toward the left by angels who are ministers of punishment, and they go of their own accord no longer, but are dragged by force as prisoners. And the angels appointed over them send them along, reproaching them and threatening them with an eye of terror, forcing them down into the lower parts. And when they are brought there, those appointed to that service drag them on to the confines of hell. And those who are so near hear incessantly the agitation, and feel the hot smoke. And when that vision is so near, as they see the terrible and excessively glowing spectacle of the fire, they shudder in horror at the expectation of the future judgment. . . .

Indeed they feel the consequences of their eternal damnation already, for the Last Judgment will simply continue the doom pronounced immediately after death. Those

> who have done well shall be assigned righteously eternal bliss, and to the lovers of iniquity shall be given eternal punishment. And the fire which is unquenchable and without end awaits these latter, and a certain fiery worm which dieth not, and which does not waste the body, but continues bursting forth from the body with unending pain. No sleep will give them rest; no night will soothe them; no death will deliver them from punishment; no voice of interceding friends will profit them.

Later legends are sometimes similar in content (see Günter, *Psychologie der Legende*, pp. 287ff.). One, connected with St. Patrick, describes the horrors of hell in gruesome detail, but—and this shows once again the whole contrast between static and dynamic religion, law and love—whoever calls at the right moment to Jesus Christ for mercy escapes them all (ibid., p. 288).

We are turning now from these imaginings to what we have already called the Christianity of Christ, and shall again call by this name, and first to His attitude toward tribalism and ethnocentrism. He rejected both in the most determined and most dramatic manner. The passage in the Gospels which springs to mind at once is the parable of the Good Samaritan (Lk 10:30ff.). It has a much deeper meaning than is usually assumed and helps to explain the hatred of Jesus on the part of the Jews. The Samaritans were to Christ's contemporaries roughly what the Edomites had been to their forebears 600 or 700 years before: their pet aversion, the neighbors who were the main objects of their enmity. The dislike between the two peoples had a long pre-history (see 2 K

23:19), but with that we are not concerned. We mention it only to indicate the depth of the cleavage. The Jews denied the Samaritans both *connubium* and *commercium*: they would not intermarry with them and would not accept food or drink at their hands. The Gospel according to St. John (4:9) reflects this fact. Jesus asks a Samaritan woman for water and she answers in surprise: "How dost thou, being a Jew, ask of me to drink, who am a Samaritan woman? For the Jews do not communicate with the Samaritans." The Gospel according to St. Luke (9:52ff.) records another incident which is equally revealing. Jesus decides to go to Jerusalem, "and he sent messengers before his face: and going they entered into a city of the Samaritans, to prepare for him. And they received him not. . . ." Those in Jesus' entourage reacted as most, if not all, Jews would have done: "When his disciples, James and John, had seen this, they said: Lord, wilt thou that we command fire to come down from heaven and consume them?" But Christ "rebuked them saying: You know not of what spirit you are. . . . And they went into another town."

If this refusal to participate in a prevailing hatred had been all, it might not have stirred up too much resentment against Jesus. But He did much more: He openly challenged the prejudice of his fellow-citizens. It was not a pious Jew who succoured the stricken man, not a priest and a levite who saw quite well what a predicament their fellow-Jew was in—they passed him by and did nothing to help him—but a Samaritan, one of those despised "filthy" people from across the river, across the hills. He is held up as the good man, indeed more: as the victim's brother, even though the victim was a Jew and the other not. The parable is set in the frame of a searching question put to Jesus by "a certain lawyer": "Who is my neighbour?" (10:25, 29). After telling the story, Christ asks the interlocutor a question on his part: "Which of these three, in thy opinion, was neighbour to him that fell among the robbers?" and he cannot but reply: "He that showed mercy to him. And Jesus said to him: Go and do thou in like manner" (36, 37). The text reads: do in like manner, but it also teaches: feel in like manner! Let *any* man be your brother!

The Parable of the Good Samaritan is not an isolated or stray passage. It must be read together with others which are less well known, but no less significant. On one of them we have already touched: the meeting of Jesus with the Samaritan woman at the well. Originally, Jesus wished to keep his messianic mission secret. This *Messiasgeheimnis*, as German theologians call it, has been one of the great themes especially of German Christology. Here we are concerned with its abandonment. Where did Christ reveal Himself? To whom did He reveal Himself? He revealed Himself in Samaria to a Samaritan woman. After expressing her surprise that a Jew should condescend to ask her for water, "Jesus answered her and said to her: If thou didst know . . . who he is that saith to thee: Give me to drink; perhaps thou wouldst have asked of him, and he would have given thee living water." After the woman's question: "Art thou greater than our father Jacob, who gave us the well [here] . . . Jesus answered . . . Whosoever drinketh of this water shall thirst again: but he that shall drink of the water that I will give him shall not thirst for ever. . . . The water that I will give him shall become in him a fountain . . . springing up into life everlasting" (Jn 4:10, 12–14).

In revealing Himself first, not to a Jew, but to a Samaritan, Jesus undoubtedly meant to set a symbolic action: His messianic mission is to all men. But symbolisms of this kind frame His entire life. The three wise men who come to adore Him shortly after His birth are traditionally interpreted as representatives of the three continents (America and Australia being then unknown). This is the reason why one of them is always painted as a black man, to signify Africa. The entry into Jerusalem shortly before His passion and death carries a similar meaning. He rides on the colt of an ass through the streets. Why did He choose an ass? The answer is that the horse was a beast of war and had always been seen as such; the ass as an animal symbolic of peace (see Mi 5:10; Zc 9:9). Such symbolisms are easy to understand; they are clear; but clearer than any symbols are Christ's parting words emphasizing once again the universality of His mission: "Teach ye all nations!" (Mt 28:19).

The meaning of Christ's sacrificial death on the cross—of the Atonement—is unfortunately a matter of controversy. Did He die for all men, or only for some, for the elect? The sociologist, the student of the science of religion, should not enter the lists, but he should and must point out that the idea of a limited atonement is irreconcilable with the form of religion which Bergson has called dynamic. A God who would not love all would not be Love itself.

But what does this supreme love imply as far as social life, as far, above all, as human failings, crimes, and sins are concerned? Does it mean that He will never punish, that punishment is contrary to His deepest Self? A belief of this kind would greatly weaken social coherence, that unity among neighbors which every word in the Gospels is meant to promote, to deepen, and to sanctify. We are touching here upon an ultimate mystery which it is impossible for the human mind to penetrate: the reconciliation, or rather the possibility of reconciliation, of supreme power and supreme love. Even the root doctrine of the Holy Trinity, One and Undivided, merely states the problem. It appeals to the faith of men, not to their intellect, which is incapable of fathoming the mystery in all its depth.

But if this is so, what then is the difference between static and dynamic religion with regard to eternal punishment, punishment on the part of the Eternal Judge, which is needed to support and to supplement the order-creating action of human justice? While nobody can offer a complete answer to this question, a few arguments may be assembled which will take us some way toward an acceptable solution.

Because the belief that God is the ultimate guarantor of peace and amity in the city of men is a near necessity in this sublunary world, it is anything but surprising that Jesus did nothing to weaken the traditional conceptions. He says expressly that He is not come to destroy the law, and the word "hell fire" occurs in the framework of the chapter which contains the Beatitudes, the most moving cry of the divine mercy (Mt 5:17, 22). There are even a few passages of considerable harshness. One of them is the announcement of the Last Judgment (Mt 24); another, the story of Lazarus and Dives (Lk 16:19–31), for the hardhearted Dives is tormented in a burning fire and not—or at least not at once—released. But our approach to the Gospels should not be that of the philologist or the lawyer: we should not stick to the letter, but try to grasp the pervading spirit. And this will indeed tell us what punishment is and means in the context of a dynamic religiosity.

We are told that we can recognize what a thing is if we consider the fruits which it bears. From the Gospels have sprung two developments which are truly revealing. The one is the doctrine of purgatory. It reconciles, to some extent at least, the idea that God is the avenger of misdeeds and yet at the same time a loving father. For there is suffering in that place, due to the sins which the individual concerned has committed in this life, but it is not vengeance. Its purpose is not retribution, but reformation, a cleansing of the guilty soul of the earthly dross which is still clinging to it, a purification which it should not shun but seek. The question as to whether the seeds of the doctrine of purgatory are to be found in the Scriptures or not has been hotly debated, and has been one of the main bones of contention dividing the confessions. The remarkable passage in the First Epistle of St. Peter (4:6) which declares that the "Gospel [is] preached also to the dead" has been variously interpreted. The sociologist need not become a party to this quarrel, but he should point out that those who have denied the scripturalness and indeed the existence of purgatory were always at the same time those who headed back to the Old Testament, the concept of a limited atonement, and the characterization of God as the great avenger, the ever-angry יהוה (YHWH).

The second development from the Gospel message of God's mercy even to sinners is the institution of confession. True, the confessional is a tribunal, but its purpose is, once again, not retribution, but restoration—the restoration of a disturbed relationship. When an antisocial act has been committed, it can be wiped away by repentance and reparation of the damage done (a duty invariably laid on the penitent), and this alone is the end pursued. We have spoken of restoration; we might as well have spoken of reformation. The God of dynamic religiosity wishes not for the death of the sinner, but that he should change his evil ways and live. There are few parables in the Gospels which show more clearly the authentic message of the New Testament than the Parable of the Prodigal Son.

Rudolph Sohm and Max Weber have asserted that the early history of the Christian Church was one of progressive legalization. Since the present writer has already shown that this assertion is unjustified and untenable (see *Sociology of Religion*, IV, esp. pp. 137ff.), no extended discussion is needed here. One decisive argument was and is that the great jurist and the great sociologist saw only the outer form of the Church and not its inner life, the administrative apparatus and not the heavenward striving of the faithful which this apparatus serves. Differently expressed: they saw only the monsignori and not the saints. But the saints have always upheld the primacy of love over law, the superiority of dynamic over merely static religion. To this day, a story is told in Siena of how St. Catherine was late for Mass one day and, having thus broken a law, decided not to approach the communion rail. But when she looked up, Jesus was standing before her and she could receive the sacrament from Him. A naïve legend? Perhaps, but one of deep significance. Even more charming is an incident from the life of St. Benedict and his sister, St. Scholastica, which St. Gregory the Great relates in his *Dialogues* (2.24) (edd. Adalbert de Vogüé and Paul Antin [Paris, 1979], pp. 230ff.). Scholastica, Gregory reports, was in the habit of visiting Benedict once a year.

> One day she arrived as she was wont to do, and her venerable brother came down with his disciples to see her. . . . It was already getting dark when they took their meal. They were still at table . . . when his saintly sister asked Benedict [a favor], saying: "I beg of you, do not leave me this night; let us talk until morning of the joys of life in heaven." He answered: "What are you suggesting, sister! I cannot possibly remain outside the monastery [during the hours of darkness]."

It was the legislator Benedict who was reacting in this negative way to the kindly suggestion, the author of the Holy Rule, and it is understandable that he did not wish to infringe a norm which he himself had set. But he was taught on this occasion that law has not the last word. The legend continues:

> The sky was at the time perfectly clear and without a cloud. When the saintly woman heard the refusal of her brother, she folded her hands on the table and inclined her head in order to pray to God. The moment she raised it again, there was violent lightning and thunder, and a torrential downpour of such intensity that neither the venerable Benedict nor his companions could take one step beyond the threshold. When the saintly woman had covered her head with her hands, she had shed streams of tears, and these tears had changed the sky from serenity to rain. . . . [Benedict] had not agreed to stay of his own free will; now he was forced to remain where he was.

Gregory comments as follows: "The power of Almighty God worked a miracle which frustrated [Benedict's] wishes, a miracle which had its origin in a woman's heart. It is by no means surprising that a woman was on that occasion stronger than he. . . . According to the word of [St.] John, 'God is love,' and . . . so she was more powerful because her love was greater"—greater and more powerful than the law.

All this, it may be argued, does not take away from the fact that even the New Testament teaches that the law has to be obeyed, and that all men will be judged in accordance with it and, in case of guilt, condemned to punishment, temporal or eternal. This is, of course, true, but precisely here we find one of the clearest distinguishing marks between static and dynamic religion. The lawyers contrast declaratory and constitutive judgment. A constitutive judgment creates a new condition; a declaratory judgment merely states that this condition already exists. In the first case, the judge inflicts a punishment out of the plenitude of his power; in the second, he explains that the guilty man has already incurred the punishment through his own conduct. This may look like hair-splitting, but it is not. The distinction makes it clear that, in the eyes of dynamic religiosity, it is not God who condemns but the sinner who condemns himself. The idea is age-old. Even in fairy-tale and saga, the end of a tale of wickedness is sometimes that the culprit must choose his own penalty. (See the Grimms' no. 89 for an example.) Nearer to the Gospel spirit are the reproaches which Yahweh is supposed to direct through the mouth of Isaiah to the ungrateful Jews: they are a "vineyard"—the Jews are often poetically so described in the Bible—which should have yielded sweet grapes, but bore only sour ones. "And now, O ye inhabitants of Jerusalem, and ye men of Juda, judge between me and my vineyard" (5:3). Scharbert explains the deeper meaning of this passage (*Die Propheten Israels bis 700 v. Chr.* [Cologne, 1965], p. 223): "For those who listened to Isaiah," he writes,

> the comparison assumes a macabre meaning by dint of the fact that they, who are meant where there is talk of a vineyard, are being called upon to pronounce the verdict between the [divine] vinedresser and the accused vineyard. Since the judgment cannot be in doubt [i.e., cannot but be condemnatory], they must sentence themselves. Isaiah here uses the favorite technique, applied since the days of the prophet Nathan, to induce the culprit, with the aid of a parable, to find himself guilty [2 S (or 2K) 12:1–7, and 3 K 20:35–43].

It may, of course, be argued that adding the consciousness of being the cause of one's own suffering subtracts nothing from the physical pains in which the merited punishment consists; does not, for instance, cool the flames which surround a soul found guilty in hell or even in purgatory. This is entirely true, but here we come to a last contrast between dynamic and static religion, and it is perhaps the most important. To dynamic religion, God is not one who lets a person's skin burn off and then restores it, so that it may burn off again. He is a fountain of mercy, a wellspring of love. How, then, can He punish at all?

Christian mystics have always held that the talk about torments in the beyond must be taken to refer, not to physical sufferings, but to spiritual experiences, above all to an unfulfilled desire to see God, and to share, through and with Him, eternal blessedness. The difference between souls in purgatory and souls in hell consists in this: that the former can be sure that they will be granted the beatific vision after they have been prepared for it, while the latter know that they will never enjoy it. Thus Heinrich Seuse, or Suso, pleads in the eleventh and twelfth chapters of his *Little Book of Eternal Wisdom* that words purporting to describe the beyond, be it the prison of the damned or the abode of the blessed, should be taken as metaphors, as "crude comparisons," which reflect and express in a gross, material way realities which belong to a higher spiritual world and are therefore entirely different. "O ye pains of this world and pains of that, how different are ye!" (*Heinrich Susos, genannt Amandus, Leben und Schriften*, ed. Melchior Diepenbrock [Regensburg, 1884], pp. 352, 349). Thus St. Theresa of Avila speaks in the thirty-second chapter of her autobiography of an "inner" fire which consists in a sorrow of the soul akin to hopelessness and despair, and which is more intense than any pain of the body can ever be (*Oeuvres complètes de Sainte Thérèse de Jésus* I [Paris, 1922], 357). Even in the Islamic world, the same idea struggles upward in the religious consciousness. Al-Ghazzali asserts that "nothing of the delights of paradise can be compared to the delight of meeting God" (cf. F. A. Klein, *The Religion of Islam* [London, 1906], p. 96). Of this delight of delights, the sinner deprives himself by his own deeds.

In two related parables—that of the talents (Mt 25:14ff.) and that of the pounds (Lk 19:12ff.)—Jesus appeals to us to develop the endowments which we possess. The highest of them is the ability to love. He who loves will love more and more intensely and will thereby draw nearer, however imperfectly, to that Divine Love which, to the representatives of dynamic religiosity, is the root of both creation and redemption. He who does not love will become less and less capable of loving and thereby cut himself off from God and man. He will drift away and drop out of that great current of grace which has called the universe into being and sustains it, and thus his isolation will be his self-condemnation and his self-inflicted doom.

In a work which is unfortunately burningly nationalistic and yet at the same time deeply Christian, *The Brothers Karamazov*, Fëdor Dostoevski ascribes to one of his characters an intuition which was undoubtedly his own (see 7.4). Alyosha Karamazov is a disciple of the saintly Zossima, and Zossima means everything to him. But he dies, and the young man, distraught, flees from the monastery. In the evening he returns, exhausted. He enters the chapel where Zossima's coffin stands and where, in accordance with the custom of the Eastern Church, the Gospels are read out by the side of the bier. The officiating priest has just reached the second chapter of St. John, and a tremendous insight comes to Alyosha: the kingdom of heaven is like the marriage feast at Cana. The feeling of joy which dominates on such an occasion, raised to the highest intensity, dominates it, and all men are invited to partake in it. Zossima is already there. Alyosha believes that he can hear the voice of his master who asks him not to be afraid of the Lord present among the crowd. "He is awesome in His majesty . . . but He is infinitely merciful. He has become one of us out of sheer love and He rejoices with us. . . . He waits unceasingly for new guests, to the end of all time." Unfortunately some men have not prepared themselves for the marriage feast and know that they would never be able to share its mood. It is they who are lost—they are excluded, not by that Eternal Love which presides over the supper, but by their own otherness.

In this vision—the vision of a community of an unclouded, all-pervading love—we behold the great goal which dynamic religion invites mankind to pursue, even in this present, workaday world. Given man's animal and therefore self-preferring nature, it seems barely a possibility. Yet this social ideal has also a somewhat more factual and realistic aspect with which alone the sociologist as such has to concern himself. It will form the subject matter of the next section, this volume's last.

THE SOCIAL IDEAL OF DYNAMIC RELIGION

138. If we look on the social ideal of Christianity, not from the point of view of its religious inspiration, but from the point of view of its historical origins, we find that it is the reflection, and to some extent, of course, an idealization, of a concrete collective experience—the experience of clan life. The members of the clan thought that they all were descended from a common ancestor, and this alone went some way toward inducing them to treat each other as brothers. There were also several substructural features which underpinned clan solidarity, common ownership of the herd, for instance, or group sovereignty over the soil, and similar institutional arrangements. In the land in which Christianity came to birth, the clan tradition was strong; so it was in the countries to which it spread (see Stark, *Sociology of Religion*, v 27ff.), and the fact that it could spread is to a large extent due to this circumstance.

The clan and its solidarity lived in the memory of the Jewish people as a precious possession. Witness the Prophets, to whom we must now for a moment return. They were not forerunners of Christ insofar as they preached a nationalism which He rejected; but they were His forerunners insofar as they entertained a social ideal which He took over, elevated to greater heights, and hallowed. A precious lead is given us in the thirty-fifth chapter of Jeremiah. The Jews in general are contrasted there with a small group in their midst, the Rechabites. The Rechabites appear in a very good light; the Jews in general, in a bad. And why? Because the Rechabites had preserved, through the centuries, the ways of life of desert days and its morality, whereas the majority had become corrupt. When put to the test, the Rechabites say: "Jonadab, the son of Rechab, our father, commanded us, saying: You shall drink no wine. . . . Neither shall ye build houses, nor sow seed, nor plant vineyards, nor have any: but you shall dwell in tents all your days. . . ." God, through the mouth of Jeremiah, is said to approve of this small clan inside Juda and to hold it up as a model to the Jews: "Thus saith the Lord of hosts, the God of Israel: . . . The words of Jonadab the son of Rechab . . . have prevailed . . . but I have spoken to you . . . and you have not obeyed me" (vv. 6, 7, 13, 14). Why this praise of men who stubbornly cling to a period long past and who, in a dramatic symbolical attitude, in an attitude of eccentricity, continue to proclaim the superiority of the desert way of life?

To understand the matter correctly, we must take up a certain red thread which runs through the writings of the Prophets and allows us to identify their social ideal. Later we shall look at some stations on the way. We shall, however, come much more quickly to our destination if we entrust ourselves to the guidance of a social philosopher who stood, in comparable circumstances, for the same ideal, but realized much more clearly and much more fully why he did —Abd-ar-Rahman Ibn Khaldun. Two millennia lie between this great thinker and Isaiah and Jeremiah, but this need not prevent us from seeing the latter through his eyes. We are concerned, not with the historical detail, which would be very different, but with the direction of the historical drift, which is the same. Giambattista Vico has asserted that history shows *corsi* and *ricorsi*— developments and their (near) repetitions. Here we have a case in point, and it is the *ricorso*, the repetition, which has led to greater insight than the *corso*, the earlier experience. Our detour will prove very much worthwhile.

Ibn Khaldun had firsthand experience of two kinds of social ordering, that of the Berbers in the desert, and that of the Arabs in the cities, of North Africa, e.g., the inhabitants of the Maghrib and of Cairo. He knew the life of the tents and the life of the towns. He found that the difference between them consisted essentially in the dissimilarity of their *asabiyah*. This key term of his analysis is difficult to translate, but it means roughly sociality and solidarity, and in its full signification has the undertone of brotherhood and brotherliness. "Group feeling," so a translator has rendered the word, "means mutual affection and willingness to fight and die for each other" (*Muqaddimah*, trans. Rosenthal, I 313). The *asabiyah* of the tent dwellers, Ibn Khaldun observed, was strong, that of the city people weak, and that was the reason why he preferred the former to the latter, even though he realized that the latter were culturally far more refined.

Ibn Khaldun's whole social theory rests on exactly the same basis as the present work: natural man (Kant's phenomenal man) is not social; cultured man (Kant's noumenal man) is. "The qualities of haughtiness and pride are innate in animal nature," Ibn Khaldun writes (ibid., 337). "Thus, [every one] develops the quality of egotism which is innate in human beings." "Injustice and aggressiveness are in the animal nature" (ibid., 380, 381; see also II 285). How is it then that people co-exist in reasonable peace? "Human beings must by nature cooperate," Rosenthal translates, though Bulaq interprets the original to mean: human beings are by nature hostile to each other, "and that calls for a restraining influence" (ibid., 300). "According to their nature, human beings need someone to act as a restraining influence and mediator in every social organization, in order to keep the members from fighting with each other" (ibid., I 284). Social control, then, is the alpha and omega of *asabiyah*, of sociality. Social control—education and acculturation—creates it. "At the base of it is the fact that man is a child of the customs and the things he has become used to. He is not the product of his natural disposition and temperament. The conditions to which he has become accustomed . . . become for him a quality of character and . . . have replaced his natural disposition" (ibid., I 258). Anticipating a word of Blaise Pascal's (see *Thoughts of Blaise Pascal*, trans. Kegan Paul, p. 65), Ibn Khaldun says tersely: "Customs are like a second nature" (*Muqaddimah*, trans. Rosenthal, II 117).

Judged on the basis of their ability to effect the transformation from animality to manhood, two types of society must be distinguished, Ibn Khaldun asserts. "Civilization may be either desert civilization as found in outlying regions and mountains. . . . Or it may be sedentary civilization as found in cities" (ibid., I 84, 85). The former—the culture of the tents—is highly successful in the area of socialization because in it social control is powerful. Speaking, for instance, of family-destroying adultery, Ibn Khaldun writes (ibid., 47, 48): "In the desert, no such thing could remain a secret. There are no hiding places there where things can be done in secret. The neighbors (if they are women) can always see and (if they are men) always hear what their women are doing, because the houses are low and clustered together without space between them." This mutual supervision produces neighborliness and morality, but also many other characteristic virtues: "The desert attitude requires kindness, reverence, humility, respect for the property of other people, and disinclination to appropriate it, except in rare circumstances." The Bedouin's qualities are, above all, moderation and restraint (ibid., II 89, 90).

As soon as a tribe becomes fixed to a definite locality, it undergoes moral degeneration.

> The second generation changes from the desert attitude to sedentary culture, from privation to luxury and plenty. . . . Thus, the vigor of group feeling is broken to some extent. . . . The third generation, then, has forgotten the period of desert life and toughness, as if it had never existed. Luxury reaches its peak

among them, because they are so much given to a life of prosperity and ease.
. . . Group feeling disappears completely [ibid., I 344, 345].

Social involution sets in.

> Corruption of the individual inhabitants is the result of painful and trying efforts
> to satisfy the [factitious] needs caused by their [luxurious] customs. . . . Im-
> morality, wrongdoing, insincerity, and trickery, for the purpose of making a
> [high standard of] living in a proper or improper manner, increase among
> them. . . . Everybody vies with everybody else. . . . Thus, the affairs of the people
> are in disorder, and if the affairs of individuals one by one deteriorate, the town
> becomes disorganized and falls into ruins.

But even worse befalls. "When the [moral] strength of a man and then his
character and religion are corrupted, his humanity is corrupted, and he becomes, in effect, transformed into an animal." Yet animal existence—survival
—too is threatened. "Among the things that corrupt sedentary culture, there is
the disposition toward pleasures and indulgences in them. . . . It leads to diversification of the desires of the belly, for pleasurable food and drink. This is followed by diversification of the pleasures of sex through various ways of sexual
intercourse, such as adultery and homosexuality. This leads to destruction of
the species" (ibid., II 293, 303, 294, 295, 297; see also the anticipatory summary in I 253–55).

The Prophets of Israel saw things in the same light. So, incidentally, did Ibn
Khaldun Jewish history. He praises Moses for leading his people forty years
through the desert so that they could develop a live *asabiyah* which enabled
them to conquer the promised land; and he states that 1400 years later a typical sedentary civilization had sprung up among them, implying that this was
the reason why they could be subjugated by the Romans (see ibid., I 287ff., II
287, 288). Naturally, what was to the cool and scholarly Moslem observer
merely a welcome confirmation of his theory was to the burning Jewish patriots
a matter of the most passionate concern. We shall try to show that their great
love, too, was the social condition and tradition of desert days, and their great
aversion the luxuriousness and corruption of later times. They were Ibn Khal-
dunians before Ibn Khaldun.

Ibn Khaldun's alternative—moral strictness as found in the tents or moral
laxity as found in the towns, community, or association?—was ever before the
Jewish people (see Lods, *Israel*, trans. Hooke, pp. 418ff.). According to the
Book of Joshua (24:15), that great leader put before them, after their settlement in the promised land, the question whom they would rather serve: the
gods of the Amorrhites in whose country they were now dwelling, or the God
whom they had brought with themselves from the desert? "As for me and my
house, we will serve the Lord." This remarkable passage must be understood
as doubly symbolic: first of all, because it reflects no concrete event, but a
permanent dilemma; and, secondly, because it was not two divinities between
whom the Israelites were invited to choose, but two comprehensive cultures,
within which, in the style of the day, the religious conceptions played, of
course, the leading part, the part of the *pars pro toto* of a comprehensive
morality and ethos. The masses are reported to have expressed a willingness

to do as their leader did: "And the people said to Josue: We will serve the Lord our God: and we will be obedient to his commandments" (verse 24). In fact, however, in later days only a fraction fulfilled this solemn promise: the Rechabites, as we have already seen; the prophets as we shall see now. Soon there was talk of a "faithful remnant," and the call to "return" became the keynote of that remnant's preaching. "And the children of Israel offended the Lord their God with things that were not right. . . . And the Lord testified to them in Israel and in Juda by the hand of all the prophets and seers, saying: Return from your wicked ways, and keep my precepts . . . according to all the law which I commanded your fathers" (2 K 17:9, 13). This is the message of Amos and Osee; this is also the message of Micah (see 7:14, 15); this is, above all, the message of the two greatest prophets, Isaiah and Jeremiah.

Jeremiah begins his prophetic activity with a bitter accusation, the charge of infidelity. He compares Israel to a girl who has thrown over the bridegroom to whom she had pledged her troth and who runs wantonly after other men:

> And the word of the Lord came to me, saying: Go, and cry in the ears of Jerusalem, saying: thus saith the Lord: I have remembered thee, pitying thy youth and the love of thy espousals, when thou followest me in the desert, in a land that is not sown. . . . What iniquity have your fathers found in me, that they are gone far from me and have walked after vanity and have become vain? . . . I brought you into the land of Carmel, to eat the fruit thereof and the best things thereof: and when ye entered in, you . . . made my inheritance an abomination [2:1, 2, 5, 7].

"Go about through the streets of Jerusalem, and see and consider, and seek in the broad places thereof, if you can find a man that executeth judgment [i.e., does what is right]. . . . They have made their faces harder than the rock and they have refused to return" (5:1, 3). It is only a return to the ethos of the desert which will bring salvation—to the ethos and to the whole way of life on which it rested. In the thirty-third chapter we hear for a passing moment the voice of hope, not of doom:

> Thus saith the Lord of hosts: There shall be again in this place . . . an habitation of shepherds causing their flocks to lie down . . . and in the land of Benjamin and round about Jerusalem, and in the cities of Juda, shall the flocks pass again under the hand of him that numbereth them, saith the Lord. . . . There shall be heard again . . . the voice of the bridegroom and the voice of the bride. . . . I will make the bud of justice to spring forth unto David, and he shall do judgment and justice [act righteously] in the earth [33:12, 13, 10, 11, 15].

Osee (12:9) expresses the same wishful dream still more clearly. God, he asserts, promises Israel that he will lead them back to the life of the tents so that the days may return when they were still at one with him (see Scharbert, *Die Propheten . . . bis 700*, p. 171).

Unfortunately, this vision of future righteousness and bliss is merely a daydream. The historical reality is different. Osee complains that the Jews knew God only in the desert, "the land of the wilderness," but since their bellies have become full, they have forgotten him (12:5, 6). Micah decries a tendency toward anarchy (7:2, 4, 5, 6):

The holy man is perished out of the earth, and there is none upright among men: they all lie in wait for blood, every one hunteth his brother to death. . . . He that is best among them is as a brier. . . . Believe not a friend, and . . . keep the doors of thy mouth from her that sleepeth in thy bosom. For the son dishonoreth the father and the daughter rises up against her mother . . . and a man's enemies are they of his own household.

In exactly the same vein, Jeremiah calls his people "an assembly of transgressors": "Let every man take heed of his neighbour, and let him not trust any brother of his: for every brother will utterly supplant [do down] and every friend will walk deceitfully. . . . They have [all of them] laboured to commit iniquity" (9:4, 5). Scharbert summarizes the preaching of the prophets concerning the social condition of Israel as follows (*Die Propheten . . . bis 700*, p. 154; see also *Die Propheten . . . um 600*, esp. pp. 163ff.):

There is no longer any community spirit. The collective life—community—dissolves. Perjury, disregard of property, breakup of the marriage bond and contempt for fellow-men get the upper hand. This moral descent has as its consequence a decay of culture and civilization and finally the return of chaos, even as far as the soil is concerned: it turns into a steppe, and while the useful species of animals dwindle, the noxious ones proliferate.

If we now try to translate the gist of the Prophets' preaching from their passionate language into the dispassionate language of sociology, we can say that what they deplore is the passing of a society in which the communal values ranked above personal interests, and the advent of a society in which the latter were paramount and the individual could freely indulge his animal propensities. We can trace this descent in the utterances of the successive preachers. First pastoral life is replaced by a settled agricultural existence. Soon fertility cults enter the Yahweh religion and falsify it. Licentious rites, such as temple prostitution, appear, as Osee in particular notices (see Scharbert, *Die Propheten . . . bis 700*, pp. 84, 85, 162, 189); then the small peasant loses ground and large agricultural properties develop, as Isaiah states in an impassioned outburst: "Woe to you that join house to house and lay field to field, even to the end of the place: Shall you alone dwell in the midst of the earth?" (5:8). Finally there is commercialization; a proper proto-capitalism springs up (see Scharbert, *Die Propheten . . . bis 700*, p. 212). Isaiah complains of it, but stronger still is the voice of Amos (see ibid., pp. 108, 109, 119, 120). In him we catch already the accents of a coming class conflict, of the final destruction of community through its splitting into rich and poor. Jeremiah shows a century or so later that the profit motive has become dominant: "From the least of them even to the greatest, all are given to covetousness" (6:13; see also 8:10). Man is to man no longer a brother to be loved, but a stranger to be exploited.

Nearly 600 years lie between the death of Jeremiah and the birth of Christ, but the situation when He came was still the same; so was the yearning for a community of human warmth as it had once existed, or was believed to have existed, in the far-off days of Moses and Joshua. The spirit of money-grabbing was still considered the chief obstacle to a truly satisfactory social life. Because He shared this conviction, Jesus chased the dealers from the Temple—the only aggressive act in a life characterized by humility and compassion: "When he had made . . . a scourge of little cords, he drove them all out of the temple . . . and the money of the changers he poured out, and the tables he overthrew" (Jn 2:15). We must not see this incident in isolation, but in connection with the whole Gospel account; we must not one-sidedly look at its negative side, but rather try to grasp its positive aspect as well. It is brought out by the Parable of the Lilies of the Field (Lk 12:21, 22, 27, 29, 31):

> He that layeth up treasure for himself . . . is not rich towards God. . . . Therefore I say to you, be not solicitous for your life, what you shall eat; nor for your body, what you shall put on. . . . Consider the lilies, how they grow; they labour not, neither do they spin. But I say to you, not even Solomon in all his glory was clothed like one of these. . . . And seek not what you shall eat or what you shall drink, and be not lifted up on high. For all these things do the nations of the world seek. . . . But seek ye first the kingdom of God and his justice, and all these things shall be added unto you.

These words are not a commendation of passivity or poverty as such: they are a plea for a sound order of values. We should put first things first, and the sublimest goal we can pursue is a right relationship to our fellow-men.

In a sense, therefore, Jesus still thinks like the Prophets, and yet His ideal is radically different from theirs. His ideal is not a clan of blood brothers, but a society of brothers in the spirit—in the Holy Spirit, as a theologian would express it. To Him, the community to be aimed at is not the family, the off-spring, of Abraham, but the family, the children, of the Father whom all men have in heaven. We enter into it, not by generation, but by regeneration—by throwing off the old Adam and putting on the new. The old Adam was carnal; the new is spiritual. In Him the animality of the human race, and the selfishness which this animality entailed, are finally overcome.

Karl Marx has been called the Last of the Prophets, and it is an intriguing question to ask in what relation his social ideal stands to that revealed in the Gospels. There are undoubtedly striking similarities, as long as we actually speak of Marx himself and not of his distant disciples, many of whom have poured a good deal of water into his wine. What Marx hoped for was that the human race would in the future return to the fraternity of the primitive clan, to original communism conceived as a flawless community. No doubt, this is a modernized version of the grand vision of a communion of saints on earth and, as such, an expression, if an untraditional one, of one of the deepest aspirations of the human race. But there is a cardinal difference between the two visions, that of Christianity and that of communism, which contrasts them sharply—contrasts them like black and white. Communism wishes to achieve its aim by changing a feature of the outer world, by abolishing private property; Christianity, on the other hand, pleads for a change of the heart, of the innermost core of the inner man. Socializing the means of production is easy, but it helps very little. Where the program has been carried out, new forms of human estrangement—indeed, of class contrast—have sprung up, above all that between the commissar—the man in power—and the man in the street, the powerless individual. Marx entertained a monocausal conception of evil: the culprit, the villain of the piece, is private appropriation. Christianity, with an older and deeper knowledge of humanity, realizes that this will not do. You do not kill a hydra by cutting off one of its heads. The real enemy of the brotherhood of man is man's inborn animality and self-preference. A socially ideal condition of the human race cannot be reached unless and until this characteristic is overcome. Christ overcame it when, in an act of supreme selflessness, He laid down His life for His fellows, and therefore the Cross is a guiding post for humanity even in its quest for a good society.

Index

Abraham a Santa Clara, 44, 45

Absolutism, 248; *see also* Dictatorships; Rulers

Adolescence, 156, 158

Adorno, Theodor W., 124

Adultery, 33, 38, 66, 68, 70, 105, 196, 212, 219, 220, 247, 253, 274, 275

Aeschylus, 22, 35, 79–84, 86–88, 90, 91, 93

Aesop, 38–41, 44, 46

Aesthetics and aestheticism, 100, 101, 128, 130, 184–86; *see also* Art and artists; Style

Agnosticism, 121, 192, 203

Alcott, Louisa May, 115–17, 119, 120; *see also* Paragon, The

Alger, Horatio Jr., 115, 117–20; *see also* Paragon, The

Allocentricity, 33, 127, 137

Almsgiving, 198; *see also* Benevolence; Love, Christian and divine

Altruism, 135, 136, 152; *see also* Benevolence

Ambassadors, Sacredness of, 250

America, United States of, 50–52, 60, 62, 115, 117, 119; *see also* Legends

Amira, Karl von, 231, 232, 237, 242

Amos, 215, 217, 277; *see also* Prophets, The

Andersen, Hans Christian, 16

Anglicanism, 62, 234, 235, 262; *see also* England and the English; Religion

Animals, 151, 166, 170, 179

Animism, 236; *see also* Fetishism

Anti-legends, 55–57; *see also* Legends

Appleseed, Johnny, *see* Johnny Appleseed

Apriorism, 181; *see also* Kant, Immanuel; Scheler, Max

Aquinas, St. Thomas, 111, 137, 182, 188, 196

Arberry, Arthur J., 212, 265

Aristocracy, 69, 112, 113, 120, 225, 226; Relation to princes, 113, 114, 120; *see also* Feudalism

Aristophanes, 215

Aristotle, 86, 87, 188, 194, 195

Art and artists, 63, 64, 67, 70, 186, 189; Ethos-building, 67, 71, 72; Political, 65,

66; *see also* Aesthetics and aestheticism; Style

Association (as defined by Tönnies), 35, 77, 78, 80, 85, 88, 90, 91, 101, 127, 128, 137, 275

Astrology, 91, 99

Asylum, Right and places of, 239, 244–48; *see also* Places, Sacredness of

Atheism, 121, 192, 203

Atomism, 143, 145, 149, 153, 166

Atonement, 139, 268, 269; *see also* Redemption

Atreus, The House of, Saga of, 32–35

Augustine, St., 137, 182, 183, 188

Aulard, F. A., 215

Austen, Jane, 110

Autocentricity, *see* Self-preference

Ballads, 50–53, 56, 57, 63

Balzac, Honoré de, 65

Beatific vision, 187, 271

Beatitudes, The, 196, 197, 257; *see also* Gospels, The

Beethoven, Ludwig van, 63

Beggars, 250; *see also* Strangers, Sacredness of

Benedict, St., 255, 269, 270

Benevolence, 127–29, 144, 149–52, 157, 162, 165–69, 182; *see also* Hume, David; Politeness; Rousseau, J.-J.; Smith, Adam; Sympathy

Bentham, Jeremy, 3, 141–50, 166–68, 177, 179, 182, 191, 206, 207; *see also* Utilitarianism

Berdyaev, Nicholas, 73

Bergson, Henri, 3, 31, 45, 137, 138, 148, 190, 191, 200, 202, 207, 217–19, 231, 249, 255, 257, 258, 268; *see also* Biologism; Religion

Bible, The, 87; *see also* New Testament; Old Testament

Biologism, 200, 201; *see also* Bergson, Henri

Bishops, Anointment of, 249; *see also* Persons, Sacred and symbolic

Blood revenge, 88, 90, 245–47; *see also* Vengeance

Racine, Jean, 98, 100
"Railroad Bill," 56, 57
Rassem, Mohammed, 61, 128, 129
Rationality and rationalism, 5, 16, 29–31,
39, 43, 59, 61, 88, 100, 143, 149, 174–78,
181, 182, 214, 219, 234; see also Kant,
Immanuel
Realism, Philosophical, 134, 136
Reason, see Kant, Immanuel; Rationality
and rationalism
Rechabites, The, 273, 276
Redemption, 25, 49, 55, 56, 106, 194, 196,
272; see also Religion, Dynamic
Reductionism, 207
Reformation, The, 44, 56, 91, 178, 225, 234,
248; see also Calvin, John; Luther, Martin
Relativism, 119, 120, 184, 185
Religion, 120, 121, 129, 189–91; see also
Christianity; Islam; Prophets, The; Sanctions, Religious; Saints; Trinity, Doctrine
of
Religion, Dynamic, 3, 4, 190, 198, 200, 205,
217, 257–79; contrasted with static re-
ligion, 193, 194, 196–99, 201, 202, 231,
248, 249, 261, 263, 266, 270, 271; de-
fined, 3; see also Bergson, Henri; Chris-
tianity; Gospels, The; Mysticism; Redemption
Religion, Static, 190, 193–255, 259, 260,
262, 263; defined, 3; see also Ethnocentrism; Nationalism; Patriotism; Religion,
Dynamic
Religiosity, Christian and Greek compared,
194–96; Jewish and Greek compared, 215
Renaissance, The, 91; see also Castiglione,
Baldassare; Shakespeare, William
Repentance, see Penance
Republic, 59, 60, 147, 148, 160, 173; see
also State, The
Responsibility, 170, 218
Retribution, 20, 80, 85, 89, 96, 98, 105, 108,
109, 208, 214–17, 258, 263–66, 268–71;
see also Crime and punishment, Concate-
nation of; Guilt; Nemesis; Punishment;
Vengeance
Reward, 21, 107, 108, 146, 214
Ricciotti, Giuseppe, 197, 198
Richardson, Samuel, 40, 41, 70, 71, 73
Ritual, 60, 62, 78, 230; see also Ceremonies
and ceremonials
Rivalry, see Competition
Rockwell, Joan, 9, 16, 66, 67, 71, 73, 74, 78,
79, 89, 101–103
Röhrich, Lutz, 9, 11, 14, 15, 17–23, 25, 27,
34, 35, 54

Romanticism, 29, 31, 40, 160, 174
Rome and the Romans, 184, 220–23, 233,
236, 245, 246, 252, 253
Roth, Joseph, 59
Rousseau, J.-J., 126, 128, 150–65, 177, 179,
191; compared with Thomas Hobbes,
151, 160; compared with David Hume,
152, 153, 157
Rulers, 114, 141, 202, 225, 226, 247, 248,
249; seen as symbols, 58–60; Sanctity of,
249; see also Aristocracy; Monarchy; Persons, Sacred and symbolic
Russia, 62, 64, 124

Sabbath, Sanctification of, 197, 198
Sagas, 31–36, 49, 75, 121; contrasted with
fairy tale, 15, 31–36, 39; Guilt in, 33–
36, 49; Pessimism of, 32, 33; Realism of,
32, 33
Saints, 52–57, 189, 190, 201–203, 224, 228,
240, 249, 269; see also Legends; Sanctity
Salvation, see Redemption
Samaritans, The, 266–68
Sanctions, 3, 4, 206, 222, 252; see also
Punishment
Sanctity, 49, 54, 72, 184, 186, 189–91; see
also Saints
Sanctuary, see Asylum, Right and places of
Sarcasm, 121
Scharbert, Josef, 259–62, 271, 276, 277
Scheler, Max, 178–92; compared with Im-
manuel Kant, 179
Schiller, Friedrich von, 67, 84, 99–102
Schubert, Franz, 64
Science, 1, 2
Scott, Sir Walter, 63, 74, 103, 107, 108, 253
Sects, 202
Secularization, 121
Self-preference, 95, 96, 100, 126, 127, 135–
37, 139, 140, 142–47, 150, 155–57, 159,
161, 165, 166, 168, 169, 176, 195, 272,
274; see also Egocentricity; Individualism
Seneca, 90, 100
Sensualism, 143, 144, 148
Sex and the sexes, 10, 103, 134, 151, 152,
156, 157, 275; Disciplining of, 15, 113;
Relation of, 113; see also Marriage
Shakespeare, William, 40, 76, 77, 91–98,
215, 221, 236, 237, 240, 241
Shammai, School of, 197, 198
Siblings and sibling rivalry, 12–14, 22, 23;
see also Conflict; Family, The
Simmel, Georg, 127, 137
Sin and sinners, 49, 55, 72, 80, 81, 85, 87,
98, 100, 105, 106, 110, 185, 194, 212,